Administration
of Justice

Administration of Justice

AN INTRODUCTION

J. Norman Swaton

Loren Morgan
Chief of Police
Downey, California

D. VAN NOSTRAND COMPANY
NEW YORK CINCINNATI TORONTO LONDON MELBOURNE

D. Van Nostrand Company Regional Offices:
New York   Cincinnati   Millbrae

D. Van Nostrand Company International Offices:
London   Toronto   Melbourne

Copyright © 1975 by Litton Educational Publishing, Inc.

Library of Congress Catalog Card Number: 74-17619
ISBN: 0-442-28114-5

All rights reserved. No part of this work covered by the copyright hereon may be reproduced or used in any form or by any means— graphic, electronic, or mechanical, including photocopying, recording, taping, or information storage and retrieval systems— without written permission of the publisher. Manufactured in the United States of America.

Published by D. Van Nostrand Company
450 West 33rd Street, New York, N.Y. 10001

Published simultaneously in Canada by
Van Nostrand Reinhold Ltd.

10 9 8 7 6 5 4 3

PREFACE

This book provides a general introduction to the administration of justice in America. It covers the three components of the system, law enforcement, the courts, and corrections, and offers insights into the history and interrelationships of these three branches for both students who are considering careers in the criminal-justice system and in-service readers who may not have acquired such background during their more technical training.

The book is divided into five parts, within which each chapter contains overviews, summaries, and review questions (with answers in the back for self-testing and reinforcement). The interdependence of member agencies of the system is reflected in the organization of this text in that we present the various agencies in their relationships with each other. For students not yet committed to a particular career, we discuss something of the life style in each agency.

Timely, sometimes controversial, excerpts from newspapers and other media supplement the basic text. These descriptions of real-life situations and issues give the student a more concrete view of the problems and rewards of a career in administration of justice.

To give the student a general orientation, Part 1 begins

with man's recognition of the need for laws and traces the development of our criminal-justice system from its English roots to its present form. The causes and scope of the crime problem in America are described in this section from both a historical and theoretical perspective.

Part 2 covers the system itself. Chapter 3 introduces the components of the criminal-justice system and defines the member agencies, while Chapter 4 describes the phases of the process from commission of a crime through apprehension and entry into a corrections segment. These chapters give the reader a working knowledge of the process and the people involved in it.

Part 3 deals with the responsibilities of local, state, and federal law enforcement agencies, describing operations, entry requirements, and life styles. A similar treatment is then given to each of the line and support functions of police agencies.

Part 4 examines the expectations of law enforcement agencies as seen by the courts, the community, and the police themselves. We explore the impact of landmark court cases, the nature of police–community relations, and the personal demands of police service, especially as it is affected by the requirements of professional behavior.

Finally, in Part 5, we identify and evaluate trends in administration of justice that seek to improve the quality of police efforts (selection, education, training), the composition of the force (women and minorities), and the mode of operation (system changes and philosophical and technological changes).

We would like to thank those who have contributed to this book, especially Joanne Swaton, for so many things beyond our ability to express (and for her patience and typing), and Jim Shade, for providing a model of what a law enforcement officer should be and for his thorough, uncompromising review of endless drafts.

An Instructor's Manual providing instructional objectives and test questions is available from the publisher.

J. Norman Swaton
Loren Morgan

TO THE STUDENT

Whether you're contemplating a career in law enforcement or actively pursuing one, this book has something to offer you.

For the student reader we offer a realistic look at the profession—both the opportunities and the facts of living with the choice once you've made it. If you see yourself as starting on a career which offers a constant challenge to both your mental and physical capabilities, you'll find no argument here. On the other hand, if you expect to find your daily life matching the neatly organized flow of events depicted in the mass media, you may be in for a surprise. Somewhere between the super-cop image of television and the "It's a job" attitude of the fifteen-year man who somehow never made sergeant lies the truth; and that's what we hope to give you here.

For the in-service reader we offer a look at the rest of the system within which you operate. A career in law enforcement isn't limited to the patrol unit. Nor are transfer to investigation or promotion to a supervisory position the only opportunities for advancement. To paraphrase the biblical quotation, "In the house of the law there are many rooms." This book will give you a look at all of them, each with its responsibilities, its frustrations, and its unique rewards.

Few other careers carry with them so many varied opportunities to deeply affect the lives of your fellow man. Few impose the degree of demand for excellence of performance. The fact that one can't accept the opportunity without also accepting the responsibility is something that should be considered very seriously by both groups of readers to whom this book is addressed, and dedicated.

CONTENTS

PART 1 THE NEED FOR A SYSTEM OF JUSTICE 1

    1. **History and Philosophy of Law Enforcement and Criminal Justice 3**

    Overview • The Need for Laws • The Formation of Laws • Development of Codes of Law • The English Roots of Our System • Development of Law Enforcement in America • Summary

    2. **The Causes and Scope of Crime 33**

    Overview • The Criminal Rationale • The Needs of Man • Early Theories of Criminal Behavior • Twentieth-century Theories of Criminal Behavior • Categories of Criminal Behavior • Crime Reporting • Summary

PART 2 THE ADMINISTRATION OF JUSTICE 61

    3. **Elements of the Criminal Justice System 63**

    Overview • The Purpose of the System • The Police • The Prosecutor • The Grand Jury • The

x   CONTENTS

Trial Jury • Defense Counsel • The Courts • Correctional Institutions • The Juvenile Justice System • The Need for an Integrated Information System • Summary

4. **The Process of Criminal Justice   91**

Overview • The Basic Process • The Juvenile Justice Process • Summary

PART 3   ORGANIZATION AND OPERATION OF LAW ENFORCEMENT AGENCIES   119

5. **The Agencies   121**

Overview • Municipal Police Departments and Sheriffs' Offices • State Agencies • County Agencies • Federal Agencies • Private Agencies • Summary

6. **Line Operations   157**

Overview • The Line Chain of Command • Specialized Operational Units • Summary

7. **Support Services   180**

Overview • Radio-Telephone Communications • Records • Equipment Maintenance • Property • Prisoner Control • Personnel and Training • Research and Planning • Statistical Analysis • Community Relations • Internal Affairs • Summary

PART 4   ROLE EXPECTATIONS WITHIN THE SYSTEM   199

8. **The Constitution and the Courts   201**

Overview • The Constitution and the Bill of Rights • *Weeks* v. *United States* (1914) • *Silverthorne Lumber Co.* v. *United States* (1920) • *Gitlow* v. *New York* (1925) • *Brown* v. *Mississippi* (1936) • *McNabb* v. *United States* (1940) • *People* v. *Cahan* (1955) • *Mapp* v. *Ohio* (1961) • *Escobedo* v. *Illinois* (1964) • *Miranda* v. *Arizona* (1966) • *Chimel* v. *California* (1969) • Effects of Court Rulings • Summary

9. **Police and Community** 227

    Overview • Why the Marriage is Needed • How the Police See Their Role • How the Community Views the Police • Police in the Ghetto • Community Programs • Summary

10. **Professionalism and Ethics** 247

    Overview • Toward a Practical Definition • Role Conflicts for the Police • The Police Personality • Job-related Problems • Law Enforcement Code of Ethics • Summary

PART 5 TRENDS IN LAW ENFORCEMENT AND CRIMINAL JUSTICE 271

11. **Selection, Education, and Training** 273

    Overview • The Selection Process • Recruitment • Education and Training • Summary

12. **Minorities and Women in Law Enforcement** 302

    Overview • The Role of the Minority Officer • Programs for Increasing Minority Representation • Problems of the Minority Officer • The Need for Female Personnel • New Roles for Policewomen • Problems of the Female Officer • Summary

13. **Operational and Philosophical Developments** 329

    Overview • Citizen Involvement in the Criminal Justice System • Coordination of the Criminal Justice Effort • The Courts • The Prosecutor's Office • Juvenile Programs • Corrections • Changes in the Police Role • Organizational and Deployment Developments • Manpower Utilization • Technological Developments • Summary

GLOSSARY 365

BIBLIOGRAPHY 378

ANSWERS 381

INDEX 389

Administration of Justice

PART 1

The Need for a System of Justice

CHAPTER 1

HISTORY AND PHILOSOPHY OF LAW ENFORCEMENT AND CRIMINAL JUSTICE

OVERVIEW

The roles of every element of our justice system have probably never been in such a state of flux as they have been for the past decade. Social changes barely dreamed of by our parents now occur at such a pace that it seems there is barely time to adjust to each before it's being demeaned as "establishment." Yet, every human being needs some order in his daily life—some thread by which he can relate what is happening to him to something that has happened in the past and some means of anticipating how what is happening is going to affect his future.

If you're considering or are involved in a law enforcement or criminal justice career, this thread of continuity is best provided by a basic understanding of the history and philosophy of the system. Is there really a need for laws? If so, why? How did the need evolve and does it still have any relationship to its original form? Why do we make a distinction between civil and criminal disregard for the needs of society? Why must we pay some members of society to protect us from others?

This chapter explores these questions and others to give you a starting point for the study of contemporary law enforcement and criminal justice presented in this text.

THE NEED FOR LAWS

Philosophical discussions of law and the need for it take place every hour of every day. The settings range from erudite assemblies of learned men to one-on-one debates between drinking companions.

"Man is basically good," cries the latent anarchist, "and, left alone by government, will behave unselfishly and in the best interests of all other men."

"Nonsense," retorts his fascistically inclined opponent, "man is not to be trusted out of sight. There must be order and to have order there must be complete control by the state —benevolently, of course!"

Reasonable people, such as you and I, realize that there is a workable truth somewhere between these two extreme points of view. In order to direct our efforts at finding this truth, let's think about what each of the extremists quoted above has going for him.

Anarchism (literally "no ruler") has never been seriously tried on any large scale. It's conceivable that in that long-sought, best of all possible worlds, it could work just fine. It may even have worked somewhere around the origin of man's involvement with other man. History doesn't record the exact point in time at which this ideal relationship of man to his peers ceased to exist, but it's safe to assume that it was not long after the first group of two or more humans was formed. At that point, although it's doubtful the members of the group realized it, the same basic problems we face today were faced for the first time.

Until man decided to exist in peace at the same time and in the same place with other animals like himself, there was no such thing as "society." Up until that time, the individual members of the human race enjoyed the only real and complete freedom that was to exist on this planet. Other than the occasional true hermit, who lives and dies without human contact, such luxuriant independence and freedom has never since been known. For as soon as societies started to form there began the continuing process that we still face today: deciding what amount of personal independence and freedom we are willing to give up as the price for being allowed to live with and receive help from our fellow humans.

If that seems a little abstract, consider how it may have been for the first society. Let's assume that there were only two members at that time. The first reaction may have been for each to try to avoid the other and to continue on his separate way without even the minor annoyance of having another animal similar to himself around. Since this primitive society was what anthropologists like to refer to as "food gatherers and hunters" who only had as resources that which nature provided without help from man, the thought probably arose that it would be easier to catch meat if they worked together. There are no chronicles of these times so we can only presume that somewhere during this idyllic relationship it became apparent to both members that while it was acceptable behavior to use one's weapon on rabbits, its use on another member of the society was unacceptable. At this point society had begun to develop its *culture*, the behavior typical of the group.

Every society has a collection of *customs* which makes up its culture. These are the standards of behavior which will and will not be accepted and after which all members of that society are obliged to pattern their individual actions. The nature of man is such that the possibilities for individualistic behavior are virtually limitless. Thus it has been obvious since the beginning of society that each group must draw lines as to what it will tolerate. These lines have always been different from one society to another, just as they are different today from one state to another or from one city to the next.

When a society establishes a custom or norm for behavior, it sets up a *sanction*, a reward or penalty for following or not following the custom, to go with it. In the case of the custom described above for our hypothetical original society—the use of weapons—the sanction may well have been the ultimate one of application of physical force to the person of the offender —in other words, the "eye-for-an-eye" concept of justice. If this is true, and there is no reason to think otherwise, the society had actually conceived its first *law*, as distinguished from custom because of the severity of the sanction.

While we can only surmise what may have occurred in a prehistoric society, we can study primitive societies which exist today. In doing so it is interesting to note that the emphasis in their laws is on their personal relationships. Homicide is universally considered unacceptable in such societies, as is adultery (although the latter is sometimes condoned if the husband has loaned his wife to another). Surprisingly, there is little emphasis on crimes against property. The lack of concern over theft in primitive societies probably arises from the fact that food-gathering and hunting social units are so busy with activities essential to survival that their only property, food and tools related to obtaining food, is shared willingly. When such societies discover controlled agriculture and domestication of animals, however, property assumes a new importance and becomes the subject of laws. In other words, once cultural items other than a wife are elevated to a level of importance where they can be borrowed, lent, or misappropriated, they too become sources of litigation.

To return to comparison of behavior control under anarchism and fascism, we can dispose of the latter in fairly short order. Recent history provides enough examples to establish the undesirability of such an approach to government by law. A more realistic comparison would be between anarchy and monarchy (literally, "one ruler"). So many forms of monarchy exist today, ranging in power from nominal to virtually absolute, that it's difficult to form a useful definition. It can be said, however, that under monarchy the need for laws is still recognized, whether they are derived from the mind of one person or from the collective minds of some legislative body. However, in most forms of what we must consider enlightened society, laws are based on the same principle as they were in primitive societies: the behavior exhibited by *most* members of the society becomes the pattern of behavior demanded of *all* members of the society.

In our particular form of government, which is commonly called a *democracy* but in actuality is a *republic,* lies the closest approximation yet of the truth we set out to find in the beginning of this chapter—an effective, median political theory. The same basis for law exists—behavior acceptable to the majority—and a workable approach to defining this behavior has been established. The basic concept of democracy contains the apparent paradox that the ruled are also the rulers. When first conceived in ancient Greece, it was widely held that democracy was in fact anarchy—no government at all. Aristotle at one point rated it the lowest form of legitimate government, claiming that it was most likely to decay into tyranny because it considered, "only the poor, not the common good." In actuality, Athenian democracy finally failed because it extended its essential equality under the law to only "freemen," a term which really meant only Athenians. While Aristotle himself favored monarchy, it was his rediscovered influence which later led to the statement of the essentials of good government as:

1. it must rule for the *common good* (always a subject for argument as to definition);

2. it must be *representative of the community* (again, the principle of majority behavior);
3. it must have its *authority immediately derived from the community* (which, of course, is in direct opposition to monarchistic theory).

The parallels between these ancient objectives and our needs today should be fairly easy to draw.

THE FORMATION OF LAWS

It seems unlikely that much thought was given to the classification of goals in early formulations of law. A need, such as prevention of depopulation through homicide, was recognized and a law with an accompanying sanction was established. To be sure, the principle of deterrence was in effect established, but it was probably not given formal consideration. It is more likely that desire for vengeance was foremost in the minds of society. Supporting this view is the fact that it was the offended party or family which was accorded the responsibility for all aspects of law enforcement, including adjudication and application of sanctions.

Laws in general have two aspects: the *substantive,* which defines behavior as acceptable or unacceptable, and the *adjective,* which defines how and by whom the law is to be enforced. A main difference between primitive and modern societies lies in the nature of the adjective aspect. For example, whereas primitive society delegated enforcement directly to the offended party, civilized society gives this power to clearly defined public agencies. With the passing of this responsibility from the individual or family unit to government, the primary goals of lawmaking, control of behavior of individual members, remained the same, but the objective of maintaining society as a continuing unit was added. Revenge as a goal gave way to consideration of the *common good,* the concept that even though a particular behavior involves little moral blame or little harm to any individual, it may be designated as unlawful if it negatively affects the peace and well-being of the community at large. This principle, of course, is the foundation for most of our current laws, including the so-called "victimless crimes" now facing such a strong challenge from many segments of society.

Another interesting comparison between the adjective aspects of primitive and civilized law is in the forms of punishment used as deterrents. The concept of imprisonment is seemingly too cumbersome for the primitive society. Physical force against the person of the convicted offender, to maim or kill him, is still used in such groups, and restitution in the form of damages paid by the guilty to the offended party is also common. But the only form of isolation from the rest of society seems to be banishment or exile. As with the concept of enforcement of laws against victimless crimes, the value to society of imprisonment is currently facing a challenge. The stated goals of imprisonment are (1) the deterrent effect on potential lawbreakers, (2) the protection afforded society by the isolation of members who exhibit persistent antisocial behavior, and (3) the possibility of rehabilitation. The challenge today seems not to be so much with the goals themselves as with the effectiveness of the way in which we pursue them. The problems and ramifications of this challenge are too many and too involved to be pursued on these pages, and we will confine ourselves to listing the goals of this segment of lawmaking.

The overriding, and most difficult to achieve, goal of law is the establishment of justice. Over 2,000 years ago Plato said that men censured injustice not so much because they feared committing it as because they feared becoming victims of it. Whether this is true or merely cynical is relatively unimportant. The important fact is that, recognizing the possibility of injustice, laws are designed individually and placed collectively within the framework of a system for the purpose of ensuring justice both to the individual and the society to which he belongs.

DEVELOPMENT OF CODES OF LAW

As the earliest societies developed more customs to meet expanding demands brought on by greater organization, administration of justice under law became increasingly complex. Early law on personal relationships became cluttered, first by the emergence of crimes against property and then by the need for laws regulating commerce. Fortunately, the ability of man to write developed at about the same time as the laws, and he began to set them down as formalized statements.

Although Hammurabi probably produced other achievements of which he was equally proud, the Babylonian ruler is best remembered for his codification of some 288 laws of his land. Carved upon a stone eight feet high around 4,000 years ago, this earliest known code of laws may still be seen in the

Louvre Museum in Paris. It's not known if anything unique is represented by the content of the code except the fact that it was compiled with a view to universal application rather than for enforcement within the culture of a single city. While it does contain some comparatively narrow references to family solidarity, it surpasses tribal customs and prohibits blood feuds or marriage by capture, both earlier social weaknesses. The king was established as the sole and ultimate assurance of justice within a system which provided for supervision of judges and appeal from their decisions. A police system and a regular postal system were also established either at the time of, or by, the code. Women were accorded freedom and dignity and apparently might belong to any of the three, not entirely clear, classes recognized by the code: *men* (not a sex distinction), *beggars,* and *slaves.*

In criminal law the code followed the principle of *lex talionis* (literally, "law of retaliation"). For example, the eye-for-an-eye-and-tooth-for-a-tooth approach called for cutting off the hand that struck a father or stole and prying out of the eye that looked into forbidden secrets. False accusation of another person of a capital crime was punished by death as was a wide variety of crime such as certain types of theft, criminal negligence, and avoidance of service to the state. The death penalty was even extended to children whose parents had committed certain crimes resulting in death to the wronged party's children. The most common penalty, however, was monetary fine and there was no provision for imprisonment, although exile was provided for some crimes, notably incest.

Later civilizations developed codes of their own, most retaining the concept of *lex talionis.* The Draconian Code of early Greece contained death as the penalty for most offenses until it was revised by Solon around 600 B.C. About the time of the birth of Christ the Romans had developed a code which was quite advanced but, by the time of the Emperor Justinian (500 A.D.), had become so full of deadwood that it required extensive revision. The revised Justinian Code is still the basis for most European law. In France during the nineteenth century, Napoleon developed a code which is still the basic law of Louisiana, even though the majority of American law is based on the English system.

English Common Law is so called because, unlike the law in codes which derived from proclamations of kings or decisions of legislatures, it grew out of old customs. With the unification of England under one king, judges faced the problem of administering justice according to the customs of many different and separate localities. Eventually the commonalities of these various sets of customs yielded broad principles which the judges felt would be applicable everywhere in the kingdom and these were called "common" law. As new decisions were made by application of the common law to new situations, they were added to the structure of laws creating, in effect, a code.

In America each state has its own set of codes established by the various state legislatures. *Penal codes* cover criminal acts which are considered to be crimes against the state; *civil codes* cover wrongful acts generally considered to be between individuals rather than against the whole state; *business and professional codes* cover commercial and professional transactions; *vehicle codes* obviously cover operation of vehicles; *welfare and institutions codes* deal primarily with the protection of those unable to provide themselves with basic care, and so on. The law in these codes is considered *statute law*, even though it may have its base in English Common Law, because it is enacted by the legislative branch of the government. When a judge tries a case and finds it necessary to include in his decision a clarification of statute law under a particular set of circumstances, the result becomes *case law* which is recorded in the form of a summary of that particular case, rather than as a law unto itself. In trying a case with similar aspects, attorneys often make reference to case law by citing the case, pointing up the similarities between it and the case at hand, and quoting the decision. The actual law which applies, however, is the statute law as written in the code of the state; the case law only serves to establish *precedent* which the attorney hopes will allow the judge to apply the law in the way he feels is necessary for his client. In cases where there is no provision for the situation under any of the codes of the state, the judicial system looks elsewhere for its model of behavior and, as noted already, that model is almost always found in English Common Law.

Civil and Criminal Codes

Except for vehicle code violations, the situations in which a law enforcement officer most frequently finds himself involved in dealing with adults are covered by the civil and criminal codes of his state. Juveniles and others unable to care for themselves are covered by separate codes such as the welfare and institutions code.

The philosophy of civil and criminal codes is similar in that both demand retribution for wrongful acts. Enforcement of civil law, however, is not the responsibility of police. Rather, the courts must resolve the question of blame for the wrongful act, called a *tort,* as opposed to a *crime,* in such cases. In doing so, the court will assess penalties either in the form of money to be paid to the wronged party or the requirement that some specific form of behavior either be performed or refrained from. Some of the most dangerous situations a police officer finds himself in, however, begin as civil matters. For example, the family dispute, which can so easily escalate into commission of criminal acts against persons, usually begins as a private matter between two citizens but can end up in physical harm and often to the person who must become involved to keep the peace.

Criminal violations include acts against the entire body of society and, as such, fines levied as retribution are paid to the state rather than the harmed individual. It's not uncommon, however, for the injured party to seek further retribution in his own behalf through application to the civil court. In other words, a single wrongful act can well result in the offender receiving punishment in both the criminal and civil courts. Only in the criminal court, however, can the punishment include imprisonment.

Classifications of Crimes

Criminal acts fall into one of two categories according to their type of origin. (1) An act is called *malum in se* if it is considered to be *evil in itself;* (2) it is called *malum prohibitum* if the legislative bodies responsible for formulation of law in the state have declared it a *prohibited evil.* Crimes classified as *mala in se* (the plural form) include crimes against the person, such as armed robbery or assault and, in general, are those crimes which threaten the health and well-being of the community. *Mala prohibita* crimes are those declared illegal by various societies and typically include such offenses as gambling. Violations of vehicle code sections normally fall into the *mala prohibita* class unless physical damage or threat of it are involved.

Criminal violations are also classified as either *misdemeanor* or *felony.* Felonies, of course, are the more serious crimes. Under English Common Law they originally called for forfeiture of land, goods, or both and were subject to additional penalties as provided for the individual offense. In modern usage the term means a crime which is punishable by death or imprisonment in a state prison, as opposed to a county or municipal jail. Fines may be levied in addition to the imprisonment, and a person convicted of a felony may lose certain normal rights of citizens such as the right to hold public office or a position of trust, such as certified public accountant or notary public. Typical felonious crimes are homicide, armed robbery, burglary, and so on.

Misdemeanors are the lesser crimes and generally include most offenses in the *mala prohibita* category. Fine and imprisonment in the county jail are the maximum punishment for misdemeanors. A third, and still lesser form of violation of law is the *infraction*. An infraction is not punishable by imprisonment and does not carry with it the right to trial by jury or use of the public defender; otherwise, infractions are treated the same under law as misdemeanors. For example, gambling and prostitution are misdemeanors, but most violations of vehicle or business codes would be infractions. Infractions do not constitute criminal acts as do misdemeanors.

Evolution of the Police

In earliest societies it has been said that enforcement of laws was handled on a family basis with the head of the family unit enforcing law both within and on behalf of it. Technically, this is not entirely accurate in that one of the differences between law and custom is the nature of the sanctions and the people who may apply them. Thus, the family enforcer was dealing primarily with customs rather than laws. When sanctions became specified, and associated with specific behavioral transgressions, the era of law, rather than custom, began. The completion of the transition from custom to law came with the designation of persons in public position, rather than within the family, to enforce the sanctions.

In addition to the requirement that the person designated to enforce the laws be a public officer, it is necessary that he have status recognized as allowing him to do so. As early as the time of Hammurabi this was realized and an official police force was established "so that the strong do not oppress the weak, that the widow and orphan be protected." The motto of the Los Angeles Police Department, "To protect and to serve," might seem to indicate that not much has changed in 4,000 years. We don't know the exact manner in which Hammurabi's police force operated, but it's safe to speculate that, though the concept was the same, the specific mode of daily operation bore little resemblance to that of the modern enforcement agency.

Earliest police were probably the strongest young hunters who were assigned the dual role of enforcing tribal customs. As the need for a military function evolved, law enforcement was most likely assigned as a collateral duty of the war-making unit. The paramilitary nature of today's police organizations probably stems from this origin, though it is generally traced only back to the Romans in the time of Augustus.

THE ENGLISH ROOTS OF OUR SYSTEM

As with so many aspects of our culture, including the Common Law basis for our legal system, law enforcement in America is derived largely from the earlier English system. The comparison is an interesting one because it gives new meaning to terms we all know and accept with, perhaps, less than full understanding.

Early English Law Enforcement

During the Anglo-Saxon period the basic units of society in England were groups of ten families called *tithings*. Each group was headed by an elected leader called, not too surprisingly, a *tithingman*. Following the system used by the military, each group of ten tithingmen, representing 100 families, was headed by another elected official called the *reeve*. These men held the powers of both police and judge. The next larger sociopolitical unit was the county, called a *shire,* and this was headed by an appointee of the crown called the *shire-reeve*. The similarity of our name for the chief law enforcement officer of a county, the sheriff, is neither coincidental nor mysterious. The shire-reeve, however, had powers far exceeding those of our sheriff. He was, in fact, the entire local government, exercising judicial as well as tax-collecting authority. In time this authority was diminished and the shire-reeve finally retained only the power and responsibility for maintenance of law and order and preservation of the peace.

A citizen who was wronged, or who knew of an offense, was obliged to raise a *hue and cry* at which point the rest of the good citizens in the area were compelled to join him in pursuit of the fleeing felon. The shire-reeve accorded the pursuing group the status of *posse comitatus* (literally, "power of the county") and, together with his tithingmen, the posse brought the offender to whatever passed for justice in the area (not as facetious a remark as it may seem, as you will shortly see).

A few centuries later, during the Norman period, mounted full-time law enforcement officers called *comes stabuli* ("officer of the stable") were employed to help the shire-reeve enforce the then military law of the country. From this position ultimately evolved the title of constable, still that of the basic law enforcement officer in England and used, though diminishingly, in America as well.

Around the thirteenth century there was established the position of *bailiff,* charged with the responsibility of maintaining a night watch within the locked gates of the city. Although paid for their service, the night watch was conscripted from the male populace over the age of sixteen and members were untrained for their job. Certain landholders, called *serjeants* because they had acquired their land through their military service, were often called upon to assist the bailiffs as the cities grew in size. In the following century training of police was instituted and 24-hour protection was afforded cities of larger size. The day force was called the *ward* and the night the *watch.* Thus the round-the-clock force was referred to collectively as the "watch and ward," a term and system which was prominent in American law enforcement until the middle of the nineteenth century.

By the sixteenth century crime had reached the point where normal watch and ward police could not handle it adequately and businessmen were compelled to supplement police activities with private *merchant patrols.* In addition to guarding the merchant's property, they served as detectives in attempting to recover stolen goods. Similar private police forces still exist in our country and were once a much more significant percentage of the total law enforcement effort than they are today.

In the period from 1500 to 1800 (called the "watch and ward" period) there were at least three types of police used in England: civilian, military, and church. The first significant progress toward the modern police concept came near the end of the period, largely as the result of the efforts of Henry Fielding, the author of *Tom Jones* and other works, turned magistrate. Under his influence a permanent, trained police force was established, as were the first police courts. He also established a group of mobile police called the *Bow Street Runners.* Named for the location of their headquarters, this group is

THE ENGLISH ROOTS OF OUR SYSTEM 15

variously described in modern literature as either "specially trained detectives who sped to the scene" or "a colorful group of cutthroat bounty hunters." In any event, the seeds were sown and the stage set for the entry of the man who probably had the single greatest influence on police work as we know it: Sir Robert Peel.

Sir Robert Peel. Peel, from whose name the British term *bobby* is derived, instituted great reforms and consolidated the many forces operating at the time into one, the Metropolitan Police. Their headquarters were set up in part of an area called Scotland Yard for its early ownership by Scottish kings. The year 1829 is thus an important one, not only for the passage of the Metropolitan Police Act by Parliament, but for the recognition accorded Peel's statement of twelve basic principles which so drastically changed the nature of the police in his time and

Sir Robert Peel, the man responsible for setting up the Metropolitan police force in London in 1829.

The headquarters of the Metropolitan Police Force, 4 Whitehall Place, London, a large house backing on to Scotland Yard

are still operative today. These principles provided the basis for professional status by insisting on standards of attitude and manner of performance of duty, appearance, training and selection of the force, use of a probationary period, measurement of effectiveness by the absence of crime, and the use of identifying numbers for police officers. They also provided for increased effectiveness through the collection of crime data, distribution and deployment of the force based on experienced need, establishment of a paramilitary force under government control, centrally located headquarters accessible to the public, and the dissemination of crime news.

Peel's dedication matched his perception. He is said to have personally screened some 12,000 applicants to select the 1,000 men who made up the initial force. Acceptance of the new force was almost anything but immediate and enthusiastic. The first patrol was mobbed by a citizenry resentful of the concept, and one member was killed and two severely injured. An apparently good choice had been made for leadership, however, and shortly the esteem of the department began to build. Two men were selected to head the organization: a lawyer named Richard Mayne and army Col. Charles Rowan, who was familiar with the workings of police in Ireland. During their control of the force it became so successful that Parliament passed permissive legislation allowing other municipalities (the Metropolitan Police force was established only for the London area) to form similar forces if they so desired. When this desire did not occur rapidly enough, subsequent obligatory law was passed requiring each county to establish its own tax-supported law enforcement agency. With the passage of this act in 1856 police work is considered to have entered the modern era.

The English Legal System

Having now seen the contributions of English law enforcement to our present society, let's look briefly at the development of their legal system as a whole. The Anglo-Saxons shied away from capital punishment but employed a system of trial that left much to be desired by the accused. Called *trial by ordeal*, it featured such tests of guilt or innocence as the ability to survive immersion in a river while bound hand and foot and weighted with stones or walking over a hot bed of coals. Drowning or burning of the feet were considered proof of guilt. It is not recorded how many were adjudged innocent by this process, but it seems safe to guess that the percentage was fairly low. While the influence of this part of our heritage appears limited to the witch trials in early Massachusetts, there is another aspect of the Anglo-Saxon culture that does survive today. This is the emphasis on restitution, in the form of monetary damages paid to the offended party. The combination of these two concepts in a single system of justice seems strange but, fifty years from now, many things we do today will probably seem almost as difficult to reconcile.

During the Norman era, beginning with the eleventh century, the local-rule form of government favored by the Saxons gave way to a strong national, or central, government. During this period William the Conqueror separated the enforcement and judicial duties of the shire-reeve, creating the position of *vicecomes* to handle the judicial aspects of the law.

In the twelfth century Henry I contributed definitions of felonies (arson, false coinage, murder, and robbery) and misdemeanors (all other crimes). The Norman influence still being in effect in the form of a strong national government, the king was given ultimate enforcement power and the first right of civil suit for all damages. However, the trial by ordeal was eliminated and a panel of *selectmen* was created, the forerunner of our grand jury. Their charge was to investigate crimes and return a *Vere Dictums* (literally, "truly say") which has its modern counterpart in the true bill of the grand jury and, of course, our *verdict*.

In the thirteenth century the rights of freemen were articulated as never before in the Magna Carta which is familiar, in name at least, to every schoolchild. Considered the beginning of British democracy and with an obvious effect on our own Constitution, this document separated the powers of state and local government and prevented gross infringement of individual freedom. The provision that, ". . . no freeman shall be taken, imprisoned, or proceeded against, except by the lawful judgment of his peers or in accordance with the law of the land . . ." established the concept of due process of law which carries over so importantly in the Fifth Amendment to our Constitution.

The Westminster period of English law development lasted from the thirteenth to sixteenth centuries and is noted generally for allowing freemen, on their own behalf, to call upon the power of the courts to protect them from abuses by the land barons. The concepts of the *justice of the peace* and release on *bail* also originated during this era. Both survive today in much the same form although the power of the justice of the peace is widely duplicated in other judicial agencies. The concept of bail today is severely criticized by some as being either discriminatory in favor of the wealthy or ineffective in keeping hardened criminals off the streets.

An English courtroom, 1858.

Also during this period the Star Chamber came into being. Today this term refers to any secret, arbitrary, and unfair proceeding. In early England these courts of the king, who allegedly could do no wrong, were brutal trial boards which extracted confessions by beatings and other tortures until the seventeenth century when Charles I abolished them. Interestingly, Charles was himself murdered and the judge, in sentencing one of those found guilty of taking part in the crime, decreed that the convicted man be drawn, hanged, dismembered, disemboweled, and forced to watch the burning of his removed parts before being beheaded. Whether or not the convicted culprit cooperated by remaining alive long enough for the full sentence to be carried out is not recorded. The event does, however, place an interesting perspective on what might otherwise seem like a relatively enlightened period of justice under law.

In this same century the right of *habeas corpus* (literally, "you should have the body"), which had been guaranteed for centuries, finally was provided with a practical mechanism for enforcement. The Earl of Shaftesbury, Anthony Cooper, was largely responsible for passage of the Habeas Corpus Act in 1679. This act made a reality of the right of an arrested person to be presented before a court or judge within a reasonable period of time, apprised of the exact nature of the charge against him and, if appropriate, released on bail. Such writs, of course, exist today as an important part of our own criminal justice system.

DEVELOPMENT OF LAW ENFORCEMENT IN AMERICA

Considering the ethnic roots of our population in America it's not surprising that the influence of the European, and particularly the British, experience is so plainly visible. Immigrants brought with them preferences and fears based on their lives in the old country, and from the very beginning these attitudes shaped American law enforcement. Large among these attitudes is the insistence upon separation of the apprehensive and judicial aspects of the system. With occasional exception due to temporary local conditions of time and public sentiment (such as vigilante actions in the old west), the role of the police has always been kept distinct from that of the courts.

The Colonial Period

As early as the 1600s New England had a semblance of a police force in the form of a *schout* (literally, *sheriff* and pronounced *skout*) in the early Dutch settlements around New York. Principally a peace officer, this position also carried with it some of the duties of magistrate. In the middle of the century, Peter Stuyvesant established an eight-man *rattle watch* to patrol the city at night. The name for the group derived from the fact that the members carried large rattles, similar to today's party noisemakers, to warn potential offenders of their presence. Apparently this was an early recognition of the value of the repressive function of the patrol effort which has its modern counterpart in the clearly distinguishable markings common to police cars. Boston, at about the same time, had a night watch responsible for repression of theft during the hours the city slept.

In the 1700s Philadelphia used a watch and ward society not unlike the earlier ones in England. Members were conscripted as a part of their civic duty and, if they found it inconvenient to serve, were permitted to pay another man to take their place.

Development of American Police Forces

The early 1800s saw the institution of day watches in Boston and New York, although no coordination existed between the efforts of the day and night forces. Philadelphia, in 1833, founded what is probably the earliest counterpart of our present round-the-clock police force. A bequest from a wealthy citizen, Stephen Girard, provided the funds for establishment of two, twelve-hour shifts, both under the control of a single captain. In this same year the city of New York undertook a study of the relatively new London Metropolitan Police (Scotland Yard) with an eye to adapting its procedures to their use. It would be eleven years, however, before public concern over the so-called "immigration riots" would lead to a consolidated force of some 800 men under a single chief of police in the city. In terms of organization, little significant change has taken place from that day to this as far as metropolitan police departments are concerned. Technological changes, of course, have been many and these will be discussed in a later chapter.

The traditional American distrust of strong centralized government had its effect on early police agencies and, of

Regulation uniforms of New York City police, 1856, showing, from left, the uniform for captain, rain wear, chief, reserve corps, lieutenant, and private.

course, there is today still no national police authority. This attitude carried over even into the area of the appearance of police, and it was not until 1856 that members of the New York department wore uniforms. Against considerable public opposition, uniform hats, then badges, and finally full uniforms were put into use. Not until 1860 did police in Philadelphia succumb to the trend, and today it's interesting to watch the experiments in places such as Menlo Park, California, in "softening" the police image by getting away from the traditional uniform. Whether the blazers worn in this department are actually less representative of implied power than a normal uniform is the subject of much debate, but the principle is interestingly reminiscent of a much-earlier concern.

Further evidence of the fear of concentration of power in police agencies exists in the fact that in the early 1800s most chiefs of police were elected, serving short terms of two to four years. The price paid for this assurance that the city wouldn't come under the control of one man was general inefficiency and lack of control over members of the police force. Chiefs commonly held onto their civilian occupations while in office and, in effect, gave only part-time attention to police work. With few exceptions, police administrators today are appointed on the basis of their experience and proven ability, in open competition. The result has been increased efficiency, and, with the continuing development of professionalism, the feared lack of responsiveness to the needs of the community is less and less evident.

Various forms of civilian control, to assure the desired responsiveness to the community, have been tried over the years. Police Boards were first tried in New York in the 1850s. Effected at levels of government ranging from municipal to state, they have fallen into general disfavor because of the political involvement and the undesirable interference by inexperienced, though well-meaning, amateurs in the professional operation of the departments.

While the municipal police department developed in the cities of New England, the more prevalent county form of government throughout the South resulted in a concentration of police authority in the office of sheriff. Sheriffs and constables (principally in the smaller areas such as townships and unincorporated cities) were and still are usually elected positions. Often their terms are short, as were those of the early chiefs of metropolitan forces, and they are precluded from succeeding themselves in office. Use of the sheriff as chief law enforcement officer of a county survives strongly today, although the constable is becoming increasingly rare.

Overlapping of jurisdiction among various law enforcement agencies has always been a problem of sorts in America, again due to our inherent resistance to centralization of authority. In the old west the United States marshal had authority in the territories and sparsely populated regions. Towns had their own marshals, sometimes constables and even sheriffs. At the beginning of the present century Pennsylvania established the first state police, to be followed shortly by New York. All states now have some form of state police although their basic role is often that of traffic enforcement. With the development of many different federal enforcement agencies, each with a specific and limited responsibility which will be explored in a later chapter, it's not uncommon for as many as five or six agencies to be involved in the investigation of a single specific crime. Today there are over 40,000 separate police jurisdictions in this country: over 3,000 sheriffs; 1,000 municipal departments; 15,000 minor forces in villages, boroughs, and townships; and a myriad of federal and state agencies. While this is often viewed as a weakness of our system (or, "nonsystem" as it is more correctly called) it is also a strength, traceable directly to the basic American desire for local government responsive to local needs.

Technology in Law Enforcement

No overview of development of law enforcement in America would be complete without at least a brief treatment of technological progress. *Communications* is one of the two major areas of such development. From the early British method of communicating between officers by rapping the nightstick on the pavement, it was not much progress to the use of whistles in the same manner. Although the whistle extended the range of communication, the first real breakthrough came in 1878 when the Washington, D.C., department initiated the use of telephones. This was followed in two years by a combination telephone-telegraph call box system in Chicago. Police radios were the next significant milestone beginning in the early 1920s with use of shortwave radios to broadcast from Pennsylvania's state police headquarters to a substation. By 1929 Detroit had radio communication to its patrol cars, but it was several years later before the cars could broadcast back to the station.

In the field of *investigation* the first significant development was adoption of the identification system of French anthropologist Alphonse Bertillon. In 1882 police agencies and prisons began using his system of identifying criminals by recording measurements of specified areas of the body along with a description of identifying marks (scars, tattoos, and the like) and personality characteristics. Even with the subsequent addition of photographs to the system, nagging doubts persisted as to the infallibility of it. These were confirmed in 1903 when a man named Will West was measured upon entry into prison and found to have the same measurements and physical ap-

The West Case

When he was received at Leavenworth, Will West denied previous imprisonment there, but the record clerk ran the Bertillon instruments over him anyway. He knew the reluctance of criminals to admit past crimes. Sure enough, when the clerk referred to the formula derived from West's Bertillon measurements, he located the file of one William West whose measurements were practically identical and whose photograph appeared to be that of the new prisoner.

But Will West was not being coy about a previous visit to Leavenworth. When the clerk turned over William West's record card he found it was that of a man already in the Penitentiary, serving a life sentence for murder. Subsequently the fingerprints of Will West and William West were impressed and compared. The patterns bore no resemblance.

It would be hard to conceive of a more nearly perfect case for refuting the claims of rival systems of identification. Although the two Wests are not known to have been related, there was a facial resemblance like that of twin brothers. The formulas derived from their Bertillon measurements were nearly identical, allowing for slight discrepancies which might have been due to human variations in the measuring process. And finally, there was the crowning coincidence of the similarity of names.

The fallibility of three systems of personal identification —photographs, Bertillon measurements, and names—was demonstrated by this one case. The value of fingerprints as a means of detecting that fallibility was established. [Identification Division of the FBI, "Fingerprint Identification" (Washington, D.C.: U.S. Government Printing Office, 1970), p. 7]

pearance as another prisoner, strangely named William West, already an inmate in the same institution. Fingerprints of the two were made and found to be totally dissimilar, and the superiority of the newer system was established. The validity of fingerprints as identification had been accepted since 1891 when an Argentinian police official and criminologist, Juan Vucetich, introduced a practical way of classifying them and set up a registry of prints for comparison purposes. Many others contributed heavily to the development of fingerprinting (notably Sir Francis Galton and Edward Richard Henry in England, and DeForest in America), but not until 1905 was the Henry system officially adopted in the United States for criminal records. In 1924 the Identification Division of the FBI was established with a bank of some 800,000 prints which has now grown to over 200,000,000. Interestingly, the odds of duplicate fingerprints in individuals are said to be over 64 billion to one, compared with a total world population of only four billion.

The Law Enforcement Responsibility

Today the American criminal justice system increasingly aims at keeping people out of jail rather than on putting them in jail as may once have been the case. The six basic responsibilities of law enforcement agencies shown below have been set forth by the International City Manager's Association in their publication *Municipal Police Administration.* They apply more specifically to police and sheriff's operations than other law enforcement agencies because only these organizations have the full spectrum of police responsibility. State and federal law enforcement agencies may function in some of these areas, but only the grass-roots police agency, with full street policing responsibility, will function in all six areas.

1. *Prevention of crime* is aimed at minimizing *intent,* one of the two basic elements said to be required if crime is to exist. Law enforcers today are engaged in many activities which blend into the social aspects of our lives. Teaching classes in high schools and colleges, giving talks in elementary schools and at community meetings, and counselling juvenile offenders rather than committing them to the courts in every instance of violation are but a few examples of crime prevention programs engaged in by members of law enforcement agencies. The many aspects of this type of activity will be discussed in a later chapter.

2. *Repression of criminal activity* is aimed at the second of the two elements conducive to commission of a crime: *opportunity*. In other words, if both intent and opportunity are necessary for a crime to take place, prevention activity tries to shape attitudes so criminal intent is reduced, and *repression* activity tries to decrease the opportunity for those who retain the intent. Visible patrol in plainly marked police units is one way this responsibility is discharged; by creating the impression that the police are present the perception of opportunity on the part of the criminally intent may be at least theoretically reduced. Another activity, which may seem to overlap with the prevention aspect, is the furnishing of advice to citizens on ways of protecting themselves from crime. For example, the federally funded *Crime Specific* program, which provides for the dissemination of information to citizens on how to protect their homes against burglary, is really aimed at reducing the opportunity for crime rather than the intent to commit it.

3. *Apprehension of criminals* is more traditionally the role of police than the previous two. Little needs to be said about this basic responsibility except that to the extent that the first two activities fall short of their goal, this one becomes more demanding of law enforcement officers.

4. *Recovery of stolen property* is similar to apprehension in that, obviously, as prevention and repression are more effective, the need for recovery decreases. There is, of course, no hope that the need for this activity will ever disappear, but the rising crime rate of recent years gives added emphasis to the need for increased effectiveness in the first two areas of law enforcement.

5. *Regulation of noncriminal activity* covers a range of duties from issuance of citations for vehicle code infractions through maintenance of order at public gatherings. A critical part of this responsibility that is receiving increasing attention today is the intervention in family crises. The family disturbance, as mentioned earlier, is not a police matter in itself except to "keep the peace." It is, however, a source of considerable crime through the process of escalation. Police departments across the country are placing special emphasis on methods of recognizing and handling the "one-thing-led-to-another-and-I-grabbed-the-gun" syndrome. There is some social aspect to this focus on the family crisis in that it is a form of prevention, but it has practical, shorter-range goals as well. The single largest source of injuries to police is the so-called "family beef." Since police are forced to become involved in such situations and

since their traditional authority in them is so limited, it becomes obvious that the manner in which they are handled is critical.

6. *Miscellaneous services* is the final category of basic police responsibility and is a constantly changing one. At one time this description of police activity denoted primarily such functions as provision of escort services for visiting dignitaries. In today's society, however, there is increasing realization that the police are not separate from the community and cannot afford to be so. This realization, coupled with the fact that they are the only governmental body available on a 24-hour basis, results in police being called upon for a wide variety of services which are not within the traditional scope of such an agency. Such things as rendering first aid to injured persons, arranging care for the elderly and young who are unable to care for themselves, even delivering babies frequently become part of the police responsibility. Assisting people who are locked out of their homes, or have become stranded in their vehicles, or even simply require referral to another agency of government are part of the demand on police time. All these and many more responsibilities which don't actually fall into the other basic charge of the police function are performed by them daily.

While the time required to handle such miscellaneous duties is fairly widely accepted as justifiable, such is not the case with all assignments in this category. Again by virtue of their 24-hour availability, relative mobility, and status as an arm of government, police are often called upon for escort duty, deliveries between other arms of government, and numerous other services which are available to and benefit a relatively small segment of the public. In these areas, especially with the increasing need to spend time in the other areas of basic responsibility, there is growing resistance among both police administration and the general public.

The Police Force in America Today

While it has been said so many times in so many ways as to have become almost a truism, the patrol function is the very soul of police work. As a test, consider the image the word *police* brings to your own mind. It's very unlikely that you visualize a man in a business suit sitting behind a desk wrestling with problems of budgetary control or meeting with the city council to attempt funding for increased service to the community. Nor do you probably see the lieutenant abstracting data on crime occurrences, the laboratory technician processing photographs, the communications supervisor coordinating the flow of information through switchboard and broadcast console, or even the detective spending countless hours on the telephone, preparing and reading reports, and conferring with members of the district attorney's staff. Like most people, the word *police* probably creates in your mind a picture of a uniformed patrolman in a black-and-white radio car.

This image of the police function is justified not only by the visibility of the patrol unit but by the fact that to the extent that the patrol force falls short of its total goal, the need for the other functions is created. In other words, if patrol were 100 percent effective there would be no need for detectives to perform their investigative role. To be sure there would still be some need for the administrative function but it would be greatly reduced.

A relatively recent trend to experimentation with *generalization* of the patrol function will be explored in a later chapter but is included here to point up the changing nature of the role. Basically this trend is aimed at expanding the role of the patrol officer into the other two functions. The investigative responsibility is expanded beyond the traditional preliminary limits, and the citizen has increased contact with the patrol officer and less with other members of the department. The exact manner in which this approach is implemented has almost as many variations and names as there are departments trying it. The root cause for all such experimentation, however, is a desire on the part of many police administrators to allow the basic police unit, the patrol officer, greater involvement in the community by letting him handle more of the basic police responsibility. The effect is a *decentralization* of the department into several almost separate departments in different areas of the city. In a sense it is a latter-day application of the original American concept that only by decentralization of government can government be totally responsive to community needs.

It's not our intention to advocate or argue the case for the team approach to police work, but it is an interesting philosophical development in law enforcement which will be with us in many forms for some time to come. In summary, it represents the strongly emerging trend toward realization that isolation of the police from the rest of society is an unworkable situation and that effective police service can be provided only if the goals of police and the rest of the community are brought closer together.

SUMMARY

The need for law arises from the need of man to coexist with his fellow humans and grows into a continuing compromise of personal independence and freedom to the goals of society.

Between the extremes of no government at all (anarchy) and total state supremacy of individual rights (fascism) lie many forms of government by law. Rule by a single person (monarchy) exists in many areas of the world and may or may not be accompanied by some form of legislative body rather than having all laws decreed by the monarch.

Customs are the standards of behavior accepted by any society. Collectively, these customs make up the society's *culture. Sanctions,* or rewards and penalties for following or failing to follow the customs of the society, are always established and the nature and severity of the sanction is one way of distinguishing a simple custom from a *law.*

In our society, government under law is judged as to quality in accordance with the ancient Greek principles that it must *rule for the common good,* be *representative of the community,* and have its *authority derived immediately from the community.*

The goal of primitive law was vengeance, as typically expressed in the concept of *lex talionis.* Enforcement, both in apprehension and judgement, was the responsibility of the family in primitive society. In civilized society law is considered to have two aspects: the *substantive,* or behavior definition, and the *adjective,* or description and placement of responsibility for enforcement of sanctions. Even without significant moral fault or harm to an individual being involved, society may designate actions as illegal if they are held to be harmful to the best interests of the community as a whole.

Imprisonment is a form of punishment unknown to primitive society, which limits its sanctions to physical force or exile. The concept of justice, while more refined in civilized society, has always been the overriding but elusive goal of law.

The earliest known code of law is that of the Babylonian ruler *Hammurabi.* Other significant codes developed in the intervening 4,000 years include the *Draconian Code* of ancient Greece; the *Justinian Code* of the early Romans (still the basis for most European law); the *Napoleonic Code* (the basis for law in Louisiana); and the *English Common Law* (the basis for law in the other states).

The formal codes of law which govern conduct in our society are examples of *statute law;* so-called *case law* is the collection of summaries of how statute law has been applied by judges in various situations.

Violation of the provisions of the *penal code* constitute a *crime;* violations the *civil code* are called *torts* and are subject to adjudication in the civil courts. A criminal act, which is considered to have been committed against society as a whole, may result in punishment in criminal court and, in addition, be the subject of separate judgment against the offender in civil court. Fines in civil court are in the form of damages paid to the offended party; fines in criminal courts are paid to the state. Only in criminal court can imprisonment be set as the punishment.

Crimes are classified as *malum in se* if they are held to be evil in themselves; they are called *malum prohibitum* if they are prohibited because the local legislative body has declared them evil.

Felonies are the more serious crimes, carrying the possibility of both fine and imprisonment in the state penitentiary. *Misdemeanors* can result in fine and/or imprisonment in the county jail. *Infractions* are the least form of violation.

Our systems of law and law enforcement are derived principally for the early English practices. During the Anglo-Saxon period the *shire-reeve* was the law enforcement officer for a political unit equivalent to our county. At the *hue and cry* raised by a citizen who knew of a crime, a *posse comitatus* was formed by the citizenry within earshot to pursue the offender.

During the Norman period the position of *comes stabuli* was created. Later, *bailiffs* patroled the cities by night, assisted by *serjeants.* This system led to the development of two policing shifts called the *watch* (at night) and the *ward.* The *watch and ward* period saw the first permanent, trained police force and the first police courts established. Early in the nineteenth century *Sir Robert Peel* created the *Metropolitan Police* for the area around London and became, in effect, the father of modern police work.

The development of the judicial side of our heritage included progress from the early *trial by ordeal* courts through the establishment during the Norman era of the *vicecomes* position (at the expense of part of the power of the shire-reeve) to the reforms of Henry I which included definition of felony and misdemeanor status of crimes. *Selectmen,* charged with investigation of crimes and the return of a *Vere Dictums,* also developed at this time.

The *Magna Carta* of the thirteenth century contributed heavily to the formulation of our own Constitution, particularly in the area of due process of law.

During the Westminster period freemen were first allowed to invoke the process of law on their own behalf and the concepts of *justice of the peace* and *bail* were developed. The *Star Chamber* courts of this period used torture to obtain confessions from the accused, but at the end of the era the right of *habeas corpus* was established by law.

The European and British influence on our system began with the *schout* and the *rattle watch* in early New York. The watch and ward system carried over in areas such as Philadelphia during the eighteenth century, and it was not until the early nineteenth century that police forces recognizable by today's standards were organized. The first coordinated round-the-clock force was established in Philadelphia through use of private funds. Eleven years later New York installed a force patterned after London's Metropolitan Police. Uniforms were not used by police until twelve years later when they were adopted by the New York Police Department.

Professionalism in police work developed slowly, evolving through early problems caused by many factors including short terms for administrators and interference from politically-oriented review boards.

Communications in police operation achieved its first recognizable progress in the last quarter of the nineteenth century with the installation of telephones and combination telephone-telegraph call boxes. *Radios* were not used until the second decade of the twentieth century, and it wasn't until the thirties that *two-way* radio communication was possible. *Investigation* relied upon the *Bertillon* system of identification until early in the twentieth century at which time *fingerprinting* became the accepted standard.

Law enforcement agencies' responsibility is divided into six areas: *prevention, repression, apprehension, recovery of property, regulation of noncriminal conduct,* and *miscellaneous services.* Organization of the police function is into three areas: *patrol, investigation,* and *administration.* The current trend is to experiment with *decentralization* of police responsibility and *generalization* of the patrol officer's role into the area of the investigation. The avowed purpose of such efforts is to increase involvement of the police department with the rest of the community to help achieve a mutualization of goals.

REVIEW QUESTIONS

Answers to these questions appear on page 381.

1. Are the sanctions provided by laws more likely to be in the nature of rewards or punishment? _____
2. The principles of good government set forth in this chapter provide that it must rule for the common good. They also specify two relationships between government and the community. In your own words, what are these two relationships? _____
_____
3. Of all the goals of law, the most important, and yet most difficult to achieve, is _____.
4. Which of these provisions of Hammurabi's Code is an example of the principle of *lex talionis?*
   a. dismemberment as a sanction for certain crimes
   b. acceptance of women into any of the three classes of citizens
5. *True or false?* English Common Law is so named because it was felt that its principles should be applicable in all geographical areas of early England.
6. Which type of law is the basic law in your state: statute law or case law? _____
7. Can a person be tried in civil court as the result of his criminal act? _____
8. Would a crime such as rape be more likely classified as *malum in se* or *malum prohibitum?* _____
_____
9. The man whose statement of principles for law enforcement most affected today's police departments was _____
_____.
10. The primitive method of determining guilt or innocence, as applied by the Anglo-Saxons, is called _____
_____.
11. The true bill returned by our grand jury is directly traceable to the early English:
    a. *Vere Dictums*
    b. *Vicecomes*
12. The Fifth Amendment to our Constitution, dealing with due process of law, has its roots in what English document? _____
13. The right of the accused to be presented before a magistrate in reasonable time, be apprised of the charge and be freed

on bail to await trial, was formally established in what Act passed in 1679? _____

14. Until the acceptance of fingerprints as the only valid identification system, what system was most widely used? _____

15. Flooding an area with a higher-than-normal number of black-and-white police cars is an example of which of the six basic responsibilities of police? _____

16. Creating the realization in school children that dope is for losers is an example of which area of police responsibility? _____

CHAPTER 2

THE CAUSES AND SCOPE OF CRIME

OVERVIEW

Everyone knows that a police officer shouldn't worry about the causes of criminal activity, that he has enough to do dealing with the effects of it—right? Not necessarily. While it's true that the scope of crime today is such that merely keeping up with treatment of the symptoms often seems impossible, that doesn't mean that we can afford to be ignorant of the causes or refrain from trying to treat them.

Charles Rowan, commissioner of the new Metropolitan Police in London 150 years ago, said, ". . . the principal object to be obtained is the *prevention* of crime. To this great end every effort of the police is to be directed." In the same general order to his department, he went on to state that the objectives of the police establishment are better effected by such activity than by the detention and punishment of the offender after he has succeeded in committing the crime.

Today much attention is given to evaluating the performance of police and other law enforcement agencies. Effectiveness is increasingly seen as being not so accurately measured by the number of arrests, the number of responses to calls for service, or even the number of convictions obtained through diligent police work, as it is by the absence of crime.

It is not our purpose here to divine the ultimate role of enforcement agencies in preventing criminal activity; this fascinating challenge remains for those who directly enforce the laws on the streets of America. In this chapter, however, we will look at the *causes* of criminal activity, the *types of people* involved in it, and the *scope* of its effect on our society. Knowledge of this type is absolutely essential to the ability to function professionally in law enforcement.

THE CRIMINAL RATIONALE

The complexities of the human mind in its decision-making process are so enormous that no one can hope to ever completely understand them. We must, however, make some assumptions in order to provide ourselves with a basis for setting our own course of action.

If we set aside for the moment consideration of those who are incapable of rational thought, we can try to determine what sort of process the criminal goes through to arrive at the decision to commit his act. If we assume that he knows that the act is held wrong by the society in which he lives and that it carries with it negative sanctions, we may draw some conclusions which comprise the classical approach to understanding criminal behavior.

First we can conclude that *he feels the act must be committed.* He may think that he has no way of achieving the desired positive result (in his own frame of reference) by following normally accepted patterns of behavior. This may be because of his own personal inadequacies or it may be (in his mind, at least) because of the inequitable structure of society at the time he is forced to function within it. As an example, let's consider the case of prostitution. In almost all states prostitution is illegal for both the seller and the buyer. Yet it continues to exist as it has since the beginning of monetary systems, and it probably always will.

For any number of reasons, the prostitute decides that her financial needs can not be met by any means other than through rental of her body. She may feel that society is wrong and that she is harming no one but herself. Or she may feel that, right or wrong, there are no options available to her. The same attitudes may exist in the customer. He may believe that "it's going to be legal soon, anyway," or he may just feel that "it seemed like a good idea at the time." In any event, both parties decide that at the particular point in time when they are forced to exist in a society that has declared the act illegal, their needs can only be satisfied by commission of the act.

Since we have assumed that both also know of the negative sanctions society provides for the act, we can also surmise that both feel that the positive rewards of the act (which in their minds are assured) outweigh the possibility of the negative sanctions being enforced. In other words, they think they can *get away with it* or, at least, the probability of their getting caught is remote enough that the negative possibilities are sufficiently diminished to make it worth the risk.

While the example used here is perhaps oversimplified because of widely spread uncertainty about the crime itself, the principles are applicable to any criminal act. But, of course, not all individuals will reach the same conclusions on the need for the act, even when placed in seemingly identical circumstances. So it behooves us to look at these needs and then at some theories as to why some individuals choose to commit an act they know to be criminal.

THE NEEDS OF MAN

The needs of man are generally classified as *physiological* (bodily needs), *psychological* (personal, mental, and emotional needs), or *social* (psychological needs which relate to our feeling of how others see us, as opposed to our personal feelings about ourselves).

Obviously, physiological needs are the most immediately important to sustaining life. These needs are defined in slightly different terms by different authorities, but basically they are the need for air to breathe, food and drink, sexual satisfaction, rest and sleep, comfort (warmth or cold, as appropriate), avoidance of pain, and relief of bladder and bowel tension. Psychological needs of self-respect and confidence, freedom from emotional or mental pressure, and general well-being can become temporarily even more important to an individual than physiological needs, especially if the latter are perceived by him at the time as being highly unsatisfactory. The social needs such as approval of peers, being like others, and in general, that elusive quality of "success," are obviously not as critical as the other two. They can, however, become as important to a given individual under certain circumstances.

As the individual develops through maturation, these

needs all combine in him in varying degrees of importance to shape what we call his "personality." He experiences frustrations as he finds that he is not always able to satisfy his needs as he perceives them, and it is the way in which his personality deals with these frustrations that determines whether he will behave in a manner that may become criminal. The person who is fortunate enough to develop self-control in the face of frustration is obviously less likely to use extralegal means to satisfy his perceived needs. The self-indulgent person, conversely, is more likely to take short cuts to need-satisfaction and, achieving some satisfaction this way, becomes more and more prone to be less and less interested in "technicalities" such as the law.

In other cases, of course, the inability to satisfy needs may seem to be largely thrust upon the individual by outside sources and may not be the result of his own inadequacies. Evaluating these situations is a tremendous (and important) task beyond the scope of this work. It is interesting to note, however, that while the argument that society imposes pressures is irrefutable, the fact remains that not all people are unable to withstand these pressures. Let's now look at the theories on why this difference exists in individuals.

EARLY THEORIES OF CRIMINAL BEHAVIOR

As early as the eighteenth century Cesare Beccaria founded the classical school of theory on criminal behavior, often referred to as the "avoidance of pain" principle. Beccaria held that a certain amount of hedonism existed in all people in that they sought to maximize pleasure and minimize pain, and he believed in the free will of the individual. He advocated publishing the laws and sanctions so that, once everyone knew the rules, violation could be held as a matter of free will and, therefore, the consequences must be accepted. Children and insane persons were exempted from responsibility for the consequences of their acts. It's rather remarkable how modern this early thinker's concepts appear today.

A century later another Italian, Cesare Lombroso, used his profession as a physician and anthropologist as the base for experiments and a theory of his own. By studying physical characteristics of criminals and taking measurements of them, he devised the "born criminal" theory. Similar to the equally invalid phrenology approach, which roughly attempts to predict behavior by size and shape of the head, his conclusion was that criminals were likely to have large jaws and sloping foreheads. He rejected the free-will principle of Beccaria in favor of the idea that such people were, in effect, throwbacks to primitive man and thus likely to behave in primitive ways, that is, criminally.

A student of Lombroso, Enrico Ferri, took a largely opposite view and held that the causes of criminal behavior were mainly sociological rather than biological. He borrowed from both his predecessors and classified criminals as belonging to five types: *born, insane, accidental, occasional,* and *spontaneous* (emotional) criminals.

TWENTIETH-CENTURY THEORIES OF CRIMINAL BEHAVIOR

In the early part of the twentieth century the American Albert Morris departed completely from the "born criminal" concept with his position that criminals develop as the result of their early environmental experiences. He held that, with trained, professional observation of the developing child, it would be possible to detect early signs of incipient, antisocial behavior and correct it, thus eliminating crime.

Around the same time another American, Clifford Shaw, studied occurrence of crime and delinquent behavior in terms of geographical location. Using pin maps in the city of Chicago, Shaw identified the "inner city" concept (although not by that term) connecting high incidence of criminal behavior to decaying residential neighborhoods adjacent to industrial and commercial centers in the city. As the neighborhoods declined as desirable residential centers, he traced changes in ethnic composition which coincided with the affluence of the individual ethnic groups moving into and out of the neighborhoods. He found that, while the ethnic groups changed, the street culture remained and the delinquency problem, both adult and juvenile, remained. Now, nearly a half-century later, we seem to be rediscovering the same principles. Neighborhoods decline in economic value as they become older, and there is always a group which can afford nothing better at the time. As the present residents increase their ability to move out, they do so. Others take their place and are resented as newcomers, with this resentment taking the form of social conflict. The chain continues and the new ethnic groups make war with each other, but the basic street culture, and the basic problems which generate it, remains to be passed on and perpetuated.

More recent theories, such as E. H. Sutherland's theory of

differential association and M. R. Haskell's socio-psychological *reference group theory,* are refinements and clarifications of Shaw's. These men, and others who support the same general point of view, hold that the developing criminal personality acquires its behavior patterns from association with peer groups. In other words, given a combination of influences from the family, the physical and emotional environment, exposure to street subcultures, and the currency and intensity of each of these influences, delicate changes in commitment take place in the individual. Partly due to the frequency of exposure to each of these influences and partly due to the momentary ability to withstand them because of his development and the intensity of the experience, the individual accepts or rejects varying amounts of the street culture. The balance is delicate and dynamic. Once a commitment is made in one direction or the other, simple inertia tends to keep it developing in that direction. When enough commitments have been made in the direction that holds legal codes to be unimportant or unfavorable to his goals, the individual has become a criminal, whether he commits an overt criminal act at that particular time or not. The act will take place at the first perceived opportunity coinciding with a need that is unsatisfied.

The Effect of Heredity

Although no enlightened student of criminality today feels that heredity is the sole cause of criminal behavior, that is, that criminals are born, not made, heredity is a factor which must be acknowledged. Certain traits or tendencies are passed on from parent to child. Glandular makeup of the individual, for example, is inherited and the chemicals secreted by these glands do have an influence on behavior that is measurable. Doctors are able to treat patients, through use of chemicals, to alter the effect of such glands on behavior. This is not to suggest that criminality can be eliminated or even controlled by the application of chemicals. Aside from the moral implications of such a prospect, heredity must be considered as only a contributing factor to the criminal personality. The personality traits passed on through the genes of our parents only combine with environmental conditions to weaken the ability to withstand frustration and make the possibility of criminal behavior more likely. One person may go a lifetime, with a set of personality traits similar to another, without ever encountering the same set of conditions which make the commission of a criminal act seem the most desirable course of action at the time. The other person may encounter such conditions with some frequency and constantly be in trouble with the law. This is the basis of the multiple-cause theory of criminal behavior widely held by criminologists today.

The Effects of Environment

In considering the effects of environment in creating criminal behavior, one must consider not just *physical* aspects such as living conditions, but also the *emotional* aspects such as social, family, and other psychological pressures that surround people and shape their attitudes. These forces don't exist in isolation from each other and can't be identified and labeled in real human beings as neatly as they can on these pages. Every person is a product of a number of forces acting in concert on him each day of his life. But we can and should try to group them into manageable groups so we can look at them as clinically as possible and begin to understand the nature of their effect in creating the problems we deal with daily.

Poverty. Financial deprivation is an obvious source of much criminal activity, but why does it have such a marked effect on the social behavior of some persons and not on others? The answer is, of course, that lack of money in and of itself is not usually the immediate cause as much as the difference in life style that lack of money creates. Certainly everyone can understand the direct cause-and-effect relationship that exists between the stealing of a loaf of bread by a man who momentarily lacks any other perceived means of feeding his family. But this is, fortunately, rare. More common is the variety of behavioral and attitudinal patterns adopted by the man who continually lacks enough money to maintain what we accept as a minimal living standard.

Under these conditions, money (or the lack of it) becomes a preoccupation which robs him of the capability to do the things which would, under more normal conditions, tend to shape the behavior of his family into more socially acceptable patterns. Studies show, for example, that poverty-level families have less time or inclination to express the affection which is considered vital to normal social development in the child. An interesting comparison here is that in many families at the other end of the economic spectrum a similar problem exists and for the same reason: preoccupation with money. Such preoccupation seems to preclude normal family living and is far too common in our society, rich or poor.

The Poor Go To Jail

In mid-1972 LEAA [Law Enforcement Assistance Administration] had the Census Bureau survey this country's 3921 jails, which are "the intake point for the entire criminal justice system." These are some of the things that survey discovered about the 141,600 people who were in jail at that time:

—Mostly "dumb" people go to jail. Seven black inmates out of ten, and six white prisoners out of ten, had not finished high school.

—Mostly poor people go to jail. Nearly half of the blacks, and 42 percent of the whites, earned less than $2000 in the year before arrest. Ninety percent of blacks and 84 percent of white inmates earned less than $7500.

—People without jobs are highly likely to wind up in jail. Two out of every five inmates were unemployed at the time they were jailed and three out of ten had been jobless for more than a year. And of those who had been employed, 60 percent had worked on a part-time basis. [Carl Rowan, "The Poor Go To Jail," *New York Post* (Sept. 25, 1974), p. 37]

Lack of discipline. While this factor was already noted as contributing to antisocial or criminal behavior, it has primarily environmental roots. Poverty, broken homes where the mother must work and is unable to be physically present to provide continuity in the life of the child, and a general lessening of parental control in an increasingly permissive society are strong environmental factors that are identified with above-average frequency in the profiles of persons who turn to criminal behavior to satisfy their needs. Technically, discipline is defined as, "training that corrects, molds or perfects the mental faculties or moral character" as often as it is, "control gained by enforcing obedience to order," or, "a system of rules governing conduct." By any or all of these definitions it is easy to see that when the discipline of the child is provided more by the subculture of the street than by the loving head of the family, the twig is strongly bent in the wrong direction.

Absence of a behavioral model. The behavioral model is an often-overlooked factor of environment that may be lacking even in what would be considered normal home situations. Strict adherence to all laws is virtually nonexistent in the adult population. Everyone drives too fast on occasion, for example, or violates other societal rules of varying seriousness. Perception of such flaws in the behavior of those who serve as models troubles the naturally questioning mind of a young person trying to form his own values. To the degree that this is perceived as hypocrisy by the young person, identification with the always-present counterculture becomes more attractive.

Television and movies. The media today are powerful environmental factors whose effects are often argued and debated. Psychologists take both sides of this issue, but it seems obvious that the potential for negative effects is very real. Crime and violence are constantly featured in the media today. There is also a strong tendency to "tell it like it is" as a departure from the older, stereotyped impressions of criminals as doltish, obviously evil persons. There's no inherent evil in presenting lifelike images, but there is room for argument as to how accurately this is being done. For example, it's not enough to show that the good guys win and the bad guys eventually get caught and go to jail. In the meantime the young viewer sees the criminal spending a good portion of his life free from social restraints and economic want. To a person who perceives his own situation as one of constant restraints on his behavior and constant economic inadequacies, even temporary relief can be very tempting. When the severity of the negative sanctions isn't portrayed adequately, it may seem like not such a bad risk. It's a lot easier to produce a film with an exciting car chase than one which captures the cold, endless sterility of a jail cell. Similarly it is easier, and more profitable, to show the excessive behavior of the criminal and assume that the viewer will somehow know that it is wrong than to show the adverse effects his actions have on the victims. If nothing else, the continued exposure to crime and violence must have the effect of "normalizing" such behavior in the minds of the viewers. Considering the tremendous amount of time young minds are exposed to television, one can well understand the potential effect of the material they see.

Religion. As a formal institution, religion was once a more powerful environmental factor than it has been in recent years.

> ### Violence in the Media
>
> There are, of course, those who maintain that film violence is cathartic, even purgative—that it provides a harmless outlet for normal tensions and aggressions. That may, indeed, be true—with most well-balanced adults and with many well-balanced children. But the testimony of experts is overwhelming on what happens to the emotionally troubled child when he is exposed to film violence:
>
> "For some children, the impact of violence so graphically portrayed and so available may be deeply disturbing. A child who is already struggling with his own aggressive feelings may be unable to cope with the open aggression so portrayed"—Josette Frank, former director of children's books and mass media for the Child Study Association of America; . . .
>
> "Children with borderline psychopathic tendencies may be pushed to overt delinquent behavior by violent entertainment"—Isidore Ziferstein, M.D., a psychiatrist at the Southern California Psychoanalytic Institute, in Los Angeles; . . .
>
> Even the healthy child, whose mind is, nevertheless, in its formative, impressionable stages, may suffer from exposure to film violence. Three years ago, the U.S. Surgeon General's Advisory Committee on Television and Social Behavior warned that violent entertainment "may be contributing, in some measure, to the aggressive behavior of many normal children."
>
> The harmful impact of film violence is at least threefold:
> - It subconsciously makes the child more restive, more aggressive, more hostile.
> - It provides the child with specific behavioral models to emulate.
> - It teaches the child that violence is an acceptable, indeed a preferred means of resolving any problem. [David Shaw, in *Today's Health* (Oct. 1974), published by the American Medical Association.]

Regardless of how one relates the institution to personal needs, it must be recognized at least as being capable of providing positive discipline for many individuals. For many people it provides necessary relief from temporal frustrations and thus relieves a source of pressure to create criminal acts. For others it forms the basis of their conscience and the ability to distinguish right from wrong. While lack of formal religious activity can't really be called a definite contributing factor to formation of criminal inclination, it certainly isn't a favorable condition.

Social Frustrations. Impatience with existing conditions, of course, has always been a strong factor and is increasingly powerful in today's society. As relief from social injustice becomes greater, and certainly no one will doubt that much has been achieved in the last decade, impatience with remaining frustrations increases. What once seemed a misery that had to be endured endlessly now seems agonizingly close to disappearing. It shouldn't be difficult to understand that with the end of many inequities close at hand, the anxieties they create become more acutely painful and the tolerance for slow progress decreases.

Social Mobility. The mobility of our present society serves to feed the negative effects of all these environmental factors. The maturing young person of today has the means to move

Cause or effect? Lack of respect for rights of others manifests itself in many ways, including graffiti which adds to the feeling of despair pervading poverty areas.

away from the influence of the family unit with greater ease than ever before. Similarly, even the restraining influence of his peers can be escaped fairly easily if he finds it too restrictive of his desires. When this decision is reached, it is not hard for him to lose himself in the larger urban areas and be relatively free from responsibility or fear of social condemnation for his acts. Without these restraints on his behavior, and with the ever-present, antisocial behavioral models, the young person who chooses this route is very likely to end up committing criminal acts.

These observations on the causes of criminal behavior are not presented as a definitive work on criminal psychology, nor are they offered as tools essential to work in law enforcement. Everyone who takes up a career in law enforcement, however, will work with the results of the observations made here as he deals with antisocial behavior. Through applied study and observations of the areas discussed above, law enforcers, hopefully, will be better able to contribute to the solution of the problem rather than simply the treatment of its symptoms.

CATEGORIES OF CRIMINAL BEHAVIOR

Recognizing categories of criminal behavior is not merely an academic pursuit. Even though there's no place on a crime report to classify the suspect as a "white collar" offender or a "professional" criminal, your understanding of the causes and scope of crime is furthered by realizing that each of these classes exists.

A drunk lying in a skid row alley is committing a crime. So is the 10-year old who snitches a candybar from a drugstore to prove to his contemporaries that he has "hair." But the former is going to commit his crime every day of his life while the latter may never again commit a theft of any kind. Both, of course, are far removed from the professional who steals cars on order or the addict who hits old ladies over the head for the two or three dollars in their purses.

Unfortunately, most people think crime is committed by a relatively small segment of society. It's not. Even disregarding the petty theft committed daily by "respectable" people who take home pencils from the office or even those who take home items of capital equipment valued at millions of dollars annually, the scope of the crime problem is greater and committed by a larger group of people than is commonly realized.

It is estimated today that one boy in six will end up in juvenile court. A Presidential Commission on Law Enforcement conducted a study which led them to the conclusion that, in one year, *two million* Americans were processed by prison, juvenile facilities, or probation agencies. Although there is no way to verify the accuracy of the claim, another such study estimated that 40 percent of all male children alive today will be arrested for a nontraffic offense during their lifetime. Of equal interest is a study of nearly 2,000 persons which revealed that 91 percent had committed acts which, by law, entitled them to serve time in jail or prison. With this preamble, let's now look at the main categories of criminal activities.

Petty or Casual Crime. Petty criminals are those who infrequently commit minor violations of law. The offenses range from occasional petty thefts through more serious acts such as purse-snatching. In between would be such acts as violation of vehicle code provisions, disturbance of the peace, and common drunk. The magnitude in terms of money is difficult to estimate because of widespread lack of reporting, but it is safe to estimate that several millions of dollars are involved annually. The even greater danger is the escalation that constantly takes place. The purse snatcher, for example, may become angered at resistance of his victim and commit an aggravated assault, or the drunk may take to his car and maim or kill. For this reason the term *petty* is actually misleading.

White Collar Crime. Crimes classified as "white collar" are also difficult to evaluate in financial terms. Millions of dollars worth of office supplies disappear annually, but billions may be bilked from the public by dishonest business practices. Embezzlement, fraudulent advertising and sales practices, and a myriad of similar activities account for unmeasured millions of dollars each year being taken from innocent persons by members of society who often live "respectably" for years before apprehension. Violence is seldom involved, so the perpetrators often rationalize their acts as being simply sharp practice; the crime, however, is real and extensive.

Crimes of Passion. Passionate crimes are those committed by persons who do not have sufficient control to withstand the emotional pressures most people are subjected to during their lives. As mentioned previously, one of the greatest dangers to police officers is the family dispute which often escalates into violent acts against person, with the police officer too often being the victim. Such seemingly innocent activities as political arguments and such noninnocent acts as marital infidelity can and often do result in serious crimes being committed by persons who wouldn't consider stealing.

Psychological Crimes. Psychological criminals are slightly different from those in the above category because the act is usually premeditated rather than being committed in a momentary act of irrationality. The man who carefully plots and executes the death of a parent and other victims in someway connected with the parent is but one example. Others include the compulsive arsonist and the kleptomaniac who steals from lack of control rather than financial need.

Narcotics-related Crimes. Narcotics crime is a category that surpasses most of the others discussed here in terms of its enormity. Estimates run as high as 60 percent of total crime being committed simply to support a habit. The narcotics addict far less often commits a crime while under the influence as he does simply to acquire the means to buy drugs. The drug addict is sometimes compared with the alcoholic in an attempt to minimize the seriousness of his act, but the alcoholic usually ends up as a panhandler begging for the price of a bottle of wine. The addict, however, too often ends up as a prostitute, a purse snatcher, or even a professional car thief working for $25 per car to support his needs which have become physiological as well as psychological.

Professional Crime. The professional criminal comes in two basic varieties: *independent* and *organized.* Without meaning to dignify such persons by likening them to noncriminal businessmen, similarities do exist. The independent professional has a specialty which he has devoted his lifetime to perfecting. Whether it's burgling homes or businesses, conning widows of their savings, counterfeiting money, robbing banks, or stealing cars or art treasures, the independent professional seldom does anything else to support himself. He has made a conscious decision to spend his life in criminal activity and has selected one particular type to concentrate on. Seldom is violence against the person the specialty of this type of criminal although he may, as in the case of a burglar surprised during his crime, resort to it rather than face the consequences of his acts.

The organized professional may concentrate on any of the

various types of crimes listed above. The difference is that he works for an organization rather than being "in business for himself." He seldom shares heavily in the rewards for his efforts (organized thieves, for example, often get as little as $25 for stealing a new Cadillac) but, of course, he gets a full share of the penalty if he is caught. The organization for which he works ranges from localized specialty groups, such as car rings, to large organizations which are engaged in legitimate business as well as criminal activities. In the large organizations, such as the notorious Mafia, specialists in violent crime are used to enforce the rules of the organization. Such specialists may also be used to encourage the desired decision on the part of persons who may be reluctant to do business on the organization's terms. As grotesque and dramatic as they may seem, gang-style executions and extortion are real.

Political Crimes. Politically based criminal operations are extremely limited in the United States. Some, such as Students for a Democratic Society (SDS) and the Symbianese Liberation Army (SLA), claim initially to have political orientation but soon degenerate into common criminal organizations specializing in crimes of terror and violence. While their lifespan is usually short, they unfortunately often inspire imitators during their heyday. Political officeholders who commit crimes, taking advantage of their positions, don't belong in this category; they are more correctly classified as white collar criminals.

Sex Crimes. Sex offenders may be classified as either *neurotic* or *psychopathic*. The neurotic offender seldom does any physical harm to others and acts out his aberrations generally in private. If a fearful person by nature, he may become a *voyeur* or Peeping Tom whose main interest in sex is visual, a *transvestite* who is compelled to dress in clothing of the opposite sex, or a *fetishist* who is attracted to private garments worn by the opposite sex. There are many other sexual aberrations in this category but these are the ones most commonly encountered in law enforcement work.

The psychopathic sex offender generally takes a more aggressive approach to the solution of his sex problems. *Rape* is the most common and serious in terms of its damage to the victim, excluding, of course, homicide which is less frequent but often connected with an act of rape. *Exhibitionists,* who usually limit their activity to exposing their genitalia to their victims without violence, may be classified either as neurotic or psychopathic since they are aggressive in their crime. The *aggressive homosexual* is deemed psycopathic and, in fact, his tendencies quite often lead to crimes of extreme violence including homicide.

Prostitution is not universally illegal in the United States, and is not classified as a sex crime for several reasons. For one, it is difficult to tell who is the victim and who is the criminal in such cases. Excluding the possible disease-spreading aspect of the situation, many persons (including some bar associations and many law enforcement authorities) are on record as favoring its legalization. Forced prostitution, of course, is a heinous crime and should always be considered as such even if voluntary participation becomes legal.

Juvenile Crimes. The juvenile offender is not really a separate category unto himself. The crime committed may be any of those possible by law and the offender may fit into any of the categories described above. Juvenile crime is usually considered a category of its own more because it is generally investigated by officers who specialize in cases involving juveniles (rather than in specific types of crimes) and processed through separate courts and detention systems. The scope of juvenile crime, which has increased so tremendously in the last two decades, also tends to make those interested in law enforcement give it special consideration. Certainly the most fertile ground, in fact probably the hope for any effective crime prevention, lies in the successful reduction of juvenile crime.

Recidivists

The habitual criminal is technically called a *recidivist* because of his tendency to relapse or fall back into his previous form of behavior. The fact that so many criminals fall into this category testifies both to the psychological complexity of the criminal mind and the ineffectiveness of rehabilitation efforts in our correction systems. The crimes involved cover almost the entire range of criminal possibility and though there is a strong tendency to repeat the initial crime, such persons often graduate to more serious crime after each of their terms in the "trade school," as prison is sometimes called on the street.

CRIME REPORTING

Every agency compiles its own statistics on crime within its jurisdiction. In spite of many efforts at standardization, there still remains a lack of uniformity that makes totally valid determination of the scope of crime difficult. In addition, estimates on the number of crimes committed that go unreported run as high as two to three times that of reported incidents.

The basis for intelligent planning by law enforcement agencies and other governmental bodies, however, must be dependable statistics on the volume, extent, trend, and nature of the crime problem. To this end in 1930 the Federal Bureau of Investigation instituted the *Uniform Crime Reports* program to provide a nationwide view of crime. Law enforcement agencies voluntarily furnish monthly reports on forms provided by the FBI for this purpose, and the results are published annually by the Bureau. Quarterly reports, in less detail, are also published for trend identification.

About a fourth of the individual states also have their own central collection systems for crime data, and more are working toward establishment of such institutions along the lines of the Uniform Crime Report. Moneys for this development are provided by the federal government under the *Law Enforcement Assistance Administration* (LEAA) which also establishes strict guidelines for controlling the quality of data gathered. With this trend there seems to be hope for considerable improvement in the quality of statistics available to enforcement agencies at some time in the future. The problem of unreported crime, however, will probably be with us for a long time. Continued education through prevention programs is the best hope for improvement in this area.

The FBI's Uniform Crime Report deals with selected crimes called *Index Crimes.* Formerly called "Part I" crimes due to the fact that they are reported in the first part of the report form provided by the FBI, these are the seven most consistently reported offenses and include (1) murder and nonnegligent manslaughter, (2) forcible rape, (3) robbery, (4) aggravated assault, (5) burglary, (6) larceny $50 and over in value, and (7) auto theft. These crimes are treated collectively and individually by geographical area of occurrence and by nature of the offender to a limited extent (sex, age, and race). The report also includes data on arrests, persons charged, clearances (essentially, solved crimes), police employee data, and numbers of police assaulted or killed. Data on recidivism is presented only on criminals who at some point in their career have become involved in a federal offense. The report is extensive and much of it is of interest only to administrators and planners; however, a narrative section which precedes the tabular data makes interesting reading for anyone involved in, or contemplating, a career in law enforcement. (Copies of the report are available at most public libraries.)

In addition to the quarterly and annual compilation of data to aid local agencies in planning and performance evaluation, the FBI maintains a computerized file called the *National Crime Information Center.* In the data bank are over 4 million listings of such things as cars stolen for longer than 24 hours, license plate numbers, persons wanted for extraditable offenses (generally major felonies which, by agreement between the states, require that a person arrested in one state and wanted for a crime in another is transported to the state of the original crime), and stolen guns or other property valued at over $5,000. Although not all agencies are connected directly to the computer, virtually all have some means of rapid access to the information in the file. Those with computer terminals in the department can retrieve wanted information within seconds.

Amount and Economic Impact of Crime

All the percentage and dollar-value figures in the world are perhaps less significant in evaluating the impact of crime than the suffering and fear it creates in people. For example, studies conducted by a Presidential Commission indicate that in high-crime areas of two large cities, nearly half of the residents said they were afraid to be on the street at night and over one-third said they no longer speak to strangers. The same commission claims that a third of all American citizens express fear for their safety if they have to be on the streets in their own neighborhood at night. Another third admit to keeping firearms in their home for protection, while one-fourth say they keep a watchdog. Philosophically, we can theorize that this fear, which deprives the citizen of the ability to lead a normal life in his community, represents a greater loss than any amount of money that is stolen from him.

We need some evaluation of the economic impact of crime, however. Crime does cost all Americans money, even if they are never the direct victim of a criminal act against their person or property. The costs of maintaining expanded police forces, private protection agencies, and insurance are borne directly by every citizen who pays taxes or consumes products. Knowing the relative economic impact of various crimes helps public officials, in and out of law enforcement, assign priorities to the various efforts they control. The figures you're about to read are admittedly estimates and in some cases may be of questionable validity, but they are the best available right now and must be used until reporting practices are perfected.

Crimes against person (lost earnings and so forth) cost over $800 million annually. Murder alone accounts for $750 million of this total.

Crimes against property, including the Index Crimes of robbery, burglary, larceny and auto theft, and other crimes such as embezzlement, fraud, forgery, arson, vandalism, and unreported commercial theft come to approximately $4 billion.

Organized crime, through narcotics, loan-sharking, prostitution, illegal alcohol sales upon which no tax is paid, and the amount retained from gambling activities

Crimes against property cost Americans billions each year. Even the wheels had to be added to this stripped Volkswagen so it could be towed away.

(not the amount gambled, but the amount they keep), annually takes in about $8 billion.

Law enforcement and criminal justice agencies, including police, correctional institutions, prosecution and defense, and the courts, cost taxpayers an estimated $4 billion each year.

Private costs related to crime such as prevention services and equipment, insurance, and private counsel, bail and witness expense, run another $2 billion.

While these figures are, as stated, estimates, the hard figures on incidence of crime are very real, only the estimates on how much less-than-complete they may be is subject to question. In other words, we know that the following figures are actual because they are reported, but we do not know for sure how many more crimes in each category go unreported each year.

The figures from the Uniform Crime Report for 1972 showed nearly 6 million Index Crimes (total for seven meas-

Violent crimes have continued to escalate; in 1973 there were an estimated 19,510 murders committed in the United States, up 42 percent since 1968.

ured crimes), an increase of 141 percent over the decade. There were over 800,000 crimes of violence (an increase of 163 percent for the ten-year period) and over 5,000,000 crimes against property (up 137 percent for the period). Put another way, these figures mean that during the year there was in Index Crime of some type committed for every 35 citizens in America, a crime of violence for every 250 citizens, and a crime against property for every 40 Americans. If you care to convert that population figure to families, you have the even more chilling comparison of an Index Crime for just under each 10 families, a crime of violence for just under every 70 families, and a crime against property for just over every 10 family units.

While the picture was obviously grim, the figures for 1972 did offer a ray of hope. Total crimes reported for that year were down some 100,000 compared with the previous year. This was due entirely to a similiar decrease in crimes against property, however, as crimes of violence increased slightly. The largest decrease came in the auto theft category, followed by larceny and burglary. While the numbers hardly indicated a need to reduce the size of law enforcement agencies, they did represent a reversal of a trend that had continually risen in prior years. Unfortunately, this brief trend reversed itself in 1973 and crime rose in all categories, bringing things back to "normal." According to the FBI report for 1973, there were 8,638,400 Index Crimes committed, an increase of 5.7 percent over 1972. Violent crimes went up 4.9 percent over 1972, and property crimes rose 5.8 percent. All seven Index Crimes increased, with robbery showing the smallest increase with a 2.1 percent rise and forcible rape showing the highest at 9.7 percent.

It's probably superfluous to say that the figures for coming years will be watched with great interest, hopefully by all citizens rather than just those involved in law enforcement. It has become increasingly obvious that the problem is far too great to be handled by police alone. The reversal in 1972 of the rising crime rate was undoubtedly due in part to increased interest in the problem by all segments of society. The hope for the future is dependent upon this continued interest and cooperation.

As simple and obvious as this thought may seem, it's not all that easily accomplished. The fear expressed by persons living in high-crime areas is real and unrelenting. Fear of reprisal often keeps people from reporting crimes, let alone showing cooperation with police. The fact that so many do cooperate under these conditions is probably the single most

54 THE CAUSES AND SCOPE OF CRIME

encouraging part of the situation. An interesting possibility concerning the rise following the 1972 dip in crime is that increased confidence in police, resulting in part from greater police-citizen involvement, may have brought on an increase in reported crime, rather than increased occurrence.

Using Crime Data

Even assuming accurate data, which as pointed out is not completely available, interpretation of the figures is not the easiest of tasks. There is a very strong tendency to look at crime statistics for one city and compare them with another similar city to evaluate the relative effectiveness of police forces.

The first weakness in such comparisons is that there is a tendency to look mainly to arrests or clearances for measurement of effectiveness. In a sense this latter approach is similar to assuming that because one sanitation department picks up more garbage than another it is doing a better job, even though the busier department might be leaving untold amounts of garbage in the streets. The second, and larger problem, is that no two communities are exactly alike.

Even though interpretation of data and evaluation of performance is an administrative task (and thus beyond the scope of an introductory text such as this) everyone interested in law enforcement should be aware of the complexity of the problem. The FBI has listed eleven different crime factors which affect the amount and type of crime that occur in an area. The first two of these factors listed below have been previously discussed in this chapter. The other nine are presented here with brief comments.

1. *Attitude of the community toward law enforcement problems.*
2. *Economic status and mores of the population.*
3. *Density and size of the community population and the metropolitan area of which it is a part.* You would hardly expect crime to be as great in a bedroom community with a population density of one-tenth that of the inner city. Studies of laboratory animals dramatically show the antisocial behavioral development when population density is increased. Studies of human behavior support this conclusion beyond a doubt. At the same time, no community which is part of a large metropolitan area exists in isolation from the

rest of that area. Especially with the high mobility of today's society, the problems of the inner city can not be kept separate from those of the surrounding communities.
4. *Composition of the population with reference particularly to age, sex and race.* Juveniles, particularly males, are a disproportionately large part of the crime problem. The 15 to 17 age group constitutes only a little over 5 percent of the total population, yet it accounts for over 13 percent of crime in America. Persons under 18 make up 26 percent of the arrested population with the 15 to 16 age group having the highest arrest rate of any. Almost half the serious crimes committed are by persons 18 and under. Considering that 23 percent of our population is under 10 years of age, the potential problem here is staggering. And to the extent that conflicting cultural values are retained by different ethnic groups in a community, racial mix contributes to the demands on law enforcement agencies.
5. *Relative stability of population, including commuters, seasonal, and other transient types.* As discussed earlier under the effect of mobility on the tendency to escape constraints on behavior, a population which has less at stake in a community is more likely to resort to criminal behavior as its perceived needs go unsatisfied.
6. *Climate, including seasonal weather conditions.* Any study of crime statistics by time of occurrence will reveal strong correlations with the weather. Apparently hot, muggy conditions take their toll on the resistance of a populace to the temptation to resort to crime and violence, especially among persons living under crowded, inner-city conditions.
7. *Educational, recreational and religious characteristics.* Tendency to criminal behavior is known to be inverse to the amount of education a person has, and lack of recreational opportunities in a community is widely held to be a contributing factor to delinquent behavior. The positive effect of a formal religious foundation was discussed earlier.
8. *Effective strength of the police force.* The ability of the police force to respond in strength to needs for service is a strong deterrent to criminal activity through reducing the apparent opportunity for success. Simi-

larly, the repressive value of visible patrol units in the field, while not universally agreed upon as to its total effect, certainly contributes to reducing the perception of opportunity.
9. *Standards governing appointments to the police force.* The obvious implication here is that the higher the standards are, the more professional will be the quality of police service obtained.
10. *Policies of the prosecuting officials and the courts.* It is unfortunate but true that crowded court calendars in some areas have forced policies that may not be in the best interests of society. If the courts in an area develop a pattern of softness, the street subculture is quick to make note of it. The effect can also extend to the office of the prosecutor, causing him to refrain from issuing complaints against persons arrested under a widening variety of conditions. The reason for this reluctance is given as, "the courts won't convict on this, so why waste everyone's time?" This behavior, too, is quickly noted by the criminal element and used to advantage.
11. *The administrative and investigative efficiency of the local law enforcement agency.* Not all agencies, of course, are equally proficient in discharging their responsibility. Just as criminals are quick to take advantage of soft courts or reluctant prosecutors, they also react quickly to the increased opportunity afforded by inefficient police work. Worse yet, poor performance will antagonize the good citizens in a community and make it impossible to gain from them the cooperation so critically needed.

SUMMARY

The concept of *free will* holds that the person committing a criminal act does so with the full knowledge that society disapproves of and provides negative sanctions against the act. With this knowledge he decides that the risk of having to pay the penalty is overshadowed by the importance to him of the gain from his act.

All acts of man are committed to satisfy one or more of his *physiological, psychological,* or *social* needs. Frustration at being unable to satisfy these needs within himself may lead a

SUMMARY

person with inadequate self-control or discipline to commit criminal acts.

Early theorists on antisocial behavior included Cesare Beccaria (free will, avoidance of pain), Cesare Lombroso (the "born criminal" approach, physical characteristics), Enrico Ferri (sociological, rather than biological, causes of crime, five classes of criminals).

Twentieth-century theorists include Albert Morris (environment causes crime), Clifford Shaw (the inner city and street subculture), E. H. Sutherland (differential association), and M. R. Haskell (reference group), who work from a base in free will theory into the effects of environment and peer relationships.

Heredity creates tendencies toward certain types of reactions under various conditions. Chemical balances within the body can be altered by administration of chemical substances to alter inherited tendencies, but changing the conditions of environment which couple with heredity to create the criminal personality is the only practical treatment.

Environmental factors which contribute to development of the criminal personality include *poverty, lack of discipline, absence of behavioral model, television and movies,* lack of *religious training, social injustice,* and the *mobility* of contemporary society.

Criminal behavior is categorized as *petty* or *casual, white collar, passionate, psychological, narcotics related, professional* (either independent or organized), *political,* or *sexual.*

Crime reporting provides a basis for planning and evaluation of performance in law enforcement agencies. The basic document on national crime is the *Uniform Crime Report* compiled each month from reports submitted by local law enforcement agencies to the FBI which publishes quarterly and annual reports. The seven *Index Crimes* (also called "Part I" crimes) include *murder, rape, robbery, aggravated assault, burglary, larceny* $50 and over in value, and *auto theft.*

The economic impact of crime is tremendous with estimates on crimes against property running over $4 billion, organized crime over $8 billion, and law enforcement over $4 billion.

Interpretation of crime data is difficult because of the complex nature of the interrelationships between crime factors which include density, composition, economic status and mores, stability, and educational, recreational, and religious character of the population; climatic conditions; strength and nature of the police force; policies of the courts and prosecutors; and attitude of community members.

REVIEW QUESTIONS

Answers to these questions appear on pages 381–382.

1. The person who decides to commit a criminal act usually does so because he: (Choose only one answer)
   a. believes it is the only way he can satisfy his needs
   b. believes there is no chance of his being caught
   c. both a and b
   d. neither a nor b
2. Label each of the following needs as either *physiological, psychological* or *social.*
   _____ a. the need for feeling that you belong
   _____ b. the need for warm clothing in winter
   _____ c. the need for self-respect
3. Did Beccaria or Lombroso propound theories of criminal behavior more closely attuned to modern thinking? _____
4. Essentially, the multiple-cause theory of criminal behavior holds that it results from a combination of _____ _____ and _____.
5. *True or false?* Poverty is a strong environmental factor contributing to criminal behavior mainly because it causes people to steal to satisfy their physiological needs.
6. Lack of discipline is a negative environmental factor because it: (Choose only one answer)
   a. fails to develop a positive moral character in the child
   b. fails to maintain sufficient control over the behavior of the child
   c. both a and b are true
   d. neither a nor b
7. *True or false?* Categorizing various types of criminal activity is more important to understanding the causes and scope of crime than it is to the successful apprehension of criminals.
8. Which category of sexual offender, *neurotic* or *psychopathic,* is more likely to become involved in an aggressive act? _____

9. What is the name of the document published annually by the FBI to detail the extent of crime in the United States? _____

10. The seven most commonly reported crimes which are the principal subject of the annual FBI report are called _____ _____ crimes.

11. Do crimes against *person* or crimes against *property* account for the larger economic loss each year? _____
_____

12. The total cost of law enforcement activity is only half the cost to Americans of the largest single item of economic impact due to crime. This is the money taken through illegal activities by _____ .

13. The age group which accounts for the highest number of arrests is:
    a. 15-16
    b. 16-18
    c. 18-20

14. The greatest difficulty in evaluating performance of a law enforcement agency through analysis of statistical data lies in the fact that:
    a. data is not accurate enough
    b. the factors which cause crime are so complex

PART 2

The Administration of Justice

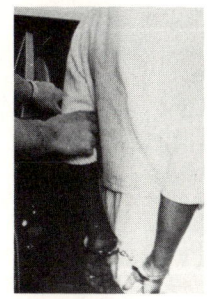

CHAPTER 3

ELEMENTS OF THE CRIMINAL JUSTICE SYSTEM

OVERVIEW

While most people tend to think of the police and the justice system as being synonymous, the law enforcement role is really just one part of our total criminal justice system, the collection of agencies and people which every society must have to enforce its codes of conduct. Ours is a complex system, with many built-in safeguards of individual rights that distinguish it from any other similar system in the world. We need to know and understand all the elements which make up the system—those which handle the prosecution, conviction, sentencing, and correction of those who violate the rules.

The importance of understanding the whole justice system is underscored by a recommendation of the *National Advisory Commission on Criminal Justice Standards and Goals*. In a recommendation for immediate action by all concerned agencies, it suggested on-the-job, cross-training among the members of all criminal justice agencies.

The reasons should be obvious to anyone currently involved in a law enforcement career. Every police officer can tell of dozens of people he took into custody and *knew* were guilty and yet are still on the street because one of the other parts of the system failed to do its job. Similarly, any prosecuting attorney or judge can tell you of an equal number of cases that couldn't be acted upon or had to be thrown out of court because the police work failed to lay a basis in fact for conviction.

The purposes of the system aren't served by finger-pointing or blame-shifting. They can be served well only by understanding the system and its requirements. This chapter, and others to follow, will give you such understanding and point you toward effective functioning within the system.

THE PURPOSE OF THE SYSTEM

The aim of the criminal justice system is to provide an impartial procedure for dealing with those crimes which cannot be prevented and those criminals who cannot be deterred. The system consists of three basic parts. First, the basic role of the *law enforcement agencies,* mainly the police, under these conditions is the detection and apprehension of the suspect. The second basic part of the system is the judicial role of the *courts* which serve to establish the guilt or innocence of the apprehended person and, if his guilt is established, pass sentence upon him as provided by the sanctions of the code violated. *Corrections,* the final part of the system, aims at assuring society that the guilty party will not again violate its codes. This is to be done either by according him special treatment to alter his behavior patterns in some way or, that failing, isolating him from the rest of society.

The roles of each of these three basic segments of the system, while distinct and well defined, aren't separate and can't function with total independence of each other. The courts, obviously, deal only with those the police arrest, and correctional institutions can deal only with those processed through the courts. But the extent to which the correctional institutions are able to rehabilitate convicts directly affects the likelihood of their becoming problems for the police again. It also has an effect on the sentences passed by judges who, in turn, carefully watch the activities of the police, with a direct effect on the way they perform their role.

In dealing with adults, the system follows an *adversary process* which, while it presumes innocence on the part of the person in custody, pits the people of the state against him in an effort to establish his guilt. In dealing with juveniles, a *nonadversary process* is followed in which special courts designed for dealing with young offenders attempt to find a specific course of action to help the juvenile find a way out of his difficulty.

Following the adversary system in simplified form we can see the interplay of the various roles provided. The police, aware that a crime has occurred, proceed to find the probable offender and take him into custody. An important provision of our system which again distinguishes it from others is that the person be promptly presented before a *magistrate.* The facts of the case are presented by the police to the *public prosecutor,* within hours of the arrest, for his determination as to whether the probability of guilt is strong enough to present the person to the court. The magistrate examines the case and, if it is a minor violation, disposes of it at that time; in serious cases the judge holds the accused over for further action and sets an amount of money as bail to be deposited to ensure the return of the person, who is freed until that time, for trial. If the charge is a serious felony, and other criteria are met, it may be turned over to a *grand jury* for investigation that may lead to dismissal of the charges or, if the grand jury believes the charges are well founded, issuance of an indictment.

If the defendant pleads not guilty to the charges he comes to trial. Here his case is presented under supervision of the judge to the jury, if the defendant chooses, or he may elect to have his case heard by the judge only (court trial). He is represented by *defense counsel,* and the people are represented by

Court trial, usually without a jury as here, establishes the guilt or innocence of those who enter the criminal justice system.

the prosecuting attorney who is an employee of the state. If the jury or court finds the defendant guilty, he is sentenced to a term in *prison,* where an attempt is made to rehabilitate him into a useful citizen, or placed on *probation* which means he may live as a normal citizen providing he commits no further violations of law and follows the terms and conditions of probation. If imprisoned, he remains in custody until he completes his term or is adjudged sufficiently rehabilitated to be granted *parole* and allowed to return to society under much the same conditions as if he had been granted probation instead of sentenced to prison.

Such a simplification as the one presented above naturally omits many of the possible exceptions which can, and do, occur every day in the administration of justice under our system. These exceptions will be explored at length in Chapter 4; the overview provided here, however, serves as an introduction to the definitions which follow. In these descriptions an attempt will be made to define the roles of those in the system not only in terms of its classic, or intended scope, but also in terms of the practical way it is performed under the conditions of daily operation in our society today.

THE POLICE

Theoretically, the police role is as it has been defined for generations: *deter* crime or, that failing, *apprehend* those who commit crimes and enter them into the criminal justice system.

In virtually no instance, however, is the role that simple and clear cut. No policeman arrests every offender who comes to his attention and, to that extent, every policeman sets law enforcement policy. In a paradoxical chain of circumstances we can agree that every law enforcement agency must have a set of clear-cut policies and that violation of any of these policies must be held against an officer of that agency. At the same time, no administrator who is honest with himself will deny that he would be in serious trouble if all his officers blindly followed every policy in every circumstance. To do so would actually be an abdication of the responsibility each officer assumes when he accepts his position. He is expected to bring intelligence and compassion to his position, if not creativity, in applying the laws that make up the code. That he must accept the responsibility for his actions if they go wrong and he is found in violation of the policy, is a difficult thing that sort of "goes with the territory." Exercise of personal discretion is performed many times each day by every officer in applying the criminal code which is, in practical fact, a guide to the officer rather than a precise manual for specific action under all possible circumstances.

Examples of this are easy to come by. What constitutes "assault" against person? The law may define it as "an unlawful *attempt* coupled with a present ability, to commit a violent injury on the person of another." But what constitutes an "attempt"? The threat of violence against person—or is it the shove, the actual blow, or the drawing of blood? Regardless of the distinction between assault and actual battery (which is the commission of the act, as opposed to the attempt) any or all of these requirements may be met under differing sets of circumstances and may or may not result in enforcement of the provisions of the penal code against the offender.

Although the policeman is not specifically charged with the duty of administering justice (he is really only responsible for enforcing laws) he does so constantly. Are justice and the community better served by arresting the boy for throwing rocks through the windows of an abandoned house or by merely calling his actions to the attention of his parents? Who are the parents? Can they control him? Or is he a repeat offender beyond their control? Is the extent of this type of crime such in the community that an example needs to be made? What about the upright citizen who leaves a bar and has noticeable difficulty getting his key in the lock of his car door. Do you arrest him before he drives off or wait until you can observe him "driving in an erratic manner" and run the risk of his causing an accident? Is justice better served by giving him an arrest record than by calling a cab for him, possibly in violation of departmental policy and thus exposing yourself to discipline? Thousands of officers decide this one differently every night, each to the dictates of his own conscience and according to his own interpretation of what is best for the community he serves. Such decisions on whether or not to invoke the criminal sanctions provided under the law are a constant part of the policeman's life.

In addition to the complications imposed on his task by the need to arbitrate social values, there is the technical complexity which is due to both court decisions and plain human nature. Court decisions on application of constitutional principles create many difficult situations for the policeman. "Probable cause," the constitutional requirement for detention or arrest, is an increasingly difficult determination. How suspicious must conduct be? What evidence is going to be admissible in court? How must a search be initiated and conducted to avoid losing a case even though the suspect turns out to be unquestionably guilty? Will the witness testify or the victim press charges? A great deal of considerable importance rests upon the individual officer's resolution of such questions in making his decision on whether to act. If he decides negatively, a burglar or rapist may go on unrestrained to commit his act. If he decides positively and has overestimated the seriousness of the situation he may hurt or even kill someone unnecessarily. These complicating factors are pointed up not so much to glorify the role of the police officer as to establish its true breadth and show how he actually must exercise more discretion than is often realized, even to the extent of lapping over into the responsibility of other elements of the system.

THE PROSECUTOR

Following the arrest of a suspected violator the most important role in the criminal justice system is played by the public prosecutor. Usually called the district attorney, his office is an elective one, most often on a county-wide basis. Sometimes several very small counties may elect such an official on a cooperative district basis, and many cities utilize their own city attorney for much of the role. In federal cases this function is performed by the U.S. Attorney but, regardless of the title of the person involved, the role is basically the same.

The prosecutor's office is a key one because he really controls the pretrial events of most cases. He is the one who investigates the evidence gathered by police, and the manner in which it was obtained, and decides whether to press the case or drop it. Technically this function is supposed to be performed by the magistrate but, partly because of crowded court calendars in most jurisdictions and partly because most judges lack an investigative staff, it is in fact performed by the prosecutor. *Plea bargaining,* in which the defendant pleads guilty to a charge which is less serious than that for which he was arrested, is also usually carried out by the prosecutor, again as an aid to courts with crowded calendars.

The basic role of the prosecutor and his staff is to *investigate, file a complaint* (or *information* as it is also called) against the arrested person if the charge appears justified, and conduct the *prosecution* on behalf of the people of the state when the case comes to trial. In cases where secrecy is important, as in a conspiracy where filing a public-information charge against one defendant might prematurely alert others involved, he may seek an indictment through the grand jury if one is available in the jurisdiction involved.

While it might seem that this role is entirely against the accused, the prosecutor is specifically charged with the responsibility of not allowing his office to take such a stand. He must at all times conduct his investigation to see that justice is done, rather than solely to convict. This is a key concept in understanding the role of the office. The fact that in most cases his efforts appear to be directed at conviction should be due to efficient police work in arresting the right person on the basis of evidence constitutionally obtained. It should also be due to the fact that in cases where these criteria are not met by the police, the prosecutor sees to it that the case never appears in court (that is, he declines to issue a complaint against the person arrested).

Unfortunately, the pressure of crowded courts can have adverse effects on the manner in which the prosecutor performs his job. Plea bargaining, mentioned above, is one of these effects. If a person is guilty of the larger crime it seems of questionable benefit to society to allow him to plead guilty to the lesser charge simply to obtain an easy conviction. The theory is basically that the expense of a court trial is saved, an admitted benefit to heavily burdened taxpayers, and the process of justice is speeded to the benefit of both the accused and society.

An additional detrimental effect of crowded court calendars is that some prosecutors will decline to issue a complaint simply because, even though they believe the person to be guilty, they also believe that the courts in their area will not convict on the charge. Not only is this an actual assumption of the court's responsibility by the prosecutor but the obvious extension of this type of thinking could cause police to say, "why arrest for this crime? The DA won't issue a complaint." If this thinking ever becomes common among police agencies, our entire system is in deep trouble.

THE GRAND JURY

A grand jury is a panel, usually of from twelve to twenty-three persons depending upon the population of the county from which the panel is drawn, which examines in private session accusations against persons charged with crime. If the grand jury finds that there is sufficient evidence against the person to warrant bringing him to trial, it issues an *indictment* which is an *accusation,* not a conviction. This is an important point to remember because many people think an indictment is some sort of conviction of guilt and this is not the case. It means that evidence has been presented which suggests that a crime may have been committed; it is simply a *charge* against the person named requiring him to be tried in a court of law. Federal grand juries, as opposed to the more common county grand juries, deal only with alleged federal crimes. Either type of grand jury may deal with misdemeanors as well as felonies although in practice most charges brought before them are felonies.

Grand jurors are selected by drawing from a list of names submitted by judges of the courts they serve. For example, a grand jury serving a jurisdiction containing thirty-six superior courts would be selected from a box containing seventy-two names, two submitted by each judge as being members of the community known to him to be persons of good character. The persons selected may become involved in lengthy investigations or simple brief hearings of witnesses. Service is for a term of one year and the pay is nominal (usually five dollars per day, plus mileage to the session).

As with the prosecutor, grand jurors are specifically instructed that their role is to serve justice rather than simply to indict those presented before them. They are told that they are to screen accusations and only formally accuse those against whom the evidence seems to be substantial.

The grand jury system is currently the target of considerable criticism primarily because of the secret nature of their deliberation. Because there is no right of representation for the accused, and therefore no cross-examination of witnesses, some people liken grand jury proceedings to the Star Chamber courts of early England. Others point to the very high percentage of indictments returned as compared to the number of accusations declined by grand jury panels. The latter criticism is hopefully defensible on the basis of careful preparation by the police and the prosecutors who bring most charges before grand juries (investigations may be initiated by others, including the grand jury itself, but most start with the prosecutor's office). The need for secret sessions can be argued on two counts: (1) the normal information filing by a prosecutor is public record, and (2) an open session might impair the possibility of making a successful case against a large number of

The Grand Jury

Twenty-three pairs of eyes—seemingly cold and distrusting but perhaps merely bored and apathetic—stare at a lone witness seated in a somber chamber behind a locked and closely guarded door.

He fidgets and glances nervously about. There is the man asking him the probing questions—the prosecuting attorney. There is the stenotypist, carefully taking down every word for possible future use.

And there are the men and women behind the 23 pairs of eyes—all his fellow citizens—holding in their hands the fearsome power known as "indictment."

There is no lawyer to sit beside the witness, to give him advice and perhaps ask additional questions of him and other witnesses who may precede or follow. There is no judge to referee. There is no audience to pierce the veil of secrecy.

This is the grand jury. . . .

It has been called a "protective bulwark standing solidly between the ordinary citizen and an overzealous prosecutor"—which, at one point in its evolution, it was.

But hardly anyone believes the grand jury is serving that function today.

To its most severe critics, the grand jury has become a mere "handmaiden" of the prosecutor. . . .

There is, however, heightened interest in grand jury reform, stemming perhaps from:

—The use of grand juries in a Justice Department program of alleged harrassment of political dissidents growing out of the anti-Vietnam war movement of the late 1960s.

—Watergate and all of its ramifications, which focused public attention on grand jury treatment of public officials and political leaders in high places.

—The use of grand juries in an effort to force newsmen to give up their closely guarded confidentiality of sources and in effect become government informers.

—Attacks on county grand jury membership as unrepresentative because jurors are specially chosen rather than selected at random from the public at large.

—Charges that the civil rights of those brought before grand juries are violated, a claimed result of such practices as barring lawyers for witnesses from the jury room and not allowing cross-examination of those who testify against a potential defendant.

Whatever the reason, the time seems ripe for reassessment of the grand jury. [Gene Blake, *Los Angeles Times* (Nov. 3, 1974). Copyright 1974, *Los Angeles Times*. Reprinted by permission.]

people. Narcotics "buy" programs are a frequently cited example. Police may not wish to tip their hand before they have the program sufficiently developed to reach those higher-ups whose arrests would be most beneficial to the community. Filing of a normal complaint by the district attorney early in the program in such cases could easily be harmful to the more important objectives it seeks to achieve. As compared with the public nature of the regular complaint, any grand juror who discloses evidence, or the panel's vote, is guilty of a misdemeanor (unless such disclosure is required by the court).

THE TRIAL JURY

Unlike the grand juror who is selected from a pool of persons recommended by judges who know of their qualifications, the trial juror is drawn at random from the list of registered voters in a county. His qualifications are then examined by oral interview conducted by the attorneys on both sides of the case. Each attorney is usually permitted a certain number of *peremptory challenges* of prospective jurors, challenges in which an attorney can reject or dismiss a juror, before the panel is selected, without giving a reason. In addition, the attorney for either side may dismiss as many jury candidates as he wishes *with cause*. Cause must be demonstrated during the interview as something in the juror's attitude which makes the attorney feel his client will be unlikely to receive a fair and impartial decision from the person in question. Aquaintance with one of the parties to the case, prior formation of an opinion as to the guilt or innocence of the defendant, or any of many such reasons justify dismissal of a prospective member of a jury.

Again in contrast to the grand jury which must decide only that there is enough evidence to warrant bringing the accused to public trial, the trial jury must decide that there is proof *beyond reasonable doubt* of his guilt. The presumption of innocence prevails in the absence of such proof and is an extremely important part of our system.

While the jury is a key part of our system it, like the system itself, is not infallible or unbeatable. It is virtually impossible, for example, to find twelve members of the community in which a crime was committed who are totally devoid of prejudices regarding any type of case. Each of us is the product of an entire lifetime of learning experiences which develop prejudices. If this weren't so we would continually have to learn the same lessons each time we encountered any set of conditions, even to the extent that the burned child would not stop putting his hand back in the flame. Thus, during the selection of the panel from the pool offered for consideration, the attorneys for both sides actually play a very serious game with their examinations. Each tries to avoid panel members who might have prejudices which would be harmful to his side of the case. Each tries through this elimination process to end up with a panel which, more than being fair and impartial, will be favorable to his side. Considered in this light it is really somewhat surprising that any panel of jurors is finally settled upon as satisfactory!

DEFENSE COUNSEL

An extremely important and often misunderstood part of our criminal justice system is that of defense counsel. It's easy to wonder how any moral person could bring himself to defend a person he believes to be guilty of a crime. But the attorney who accepts the role of defender, while also a servant of justice, must not allow himself to be swayed by his own personal opinion of the person's guilt or innocence.

The key concept here is that every person accused of a crime is entitled to legal counsel under our system of justice. Our Constitution specifies that a person may be deprived of life or liberty only by *due process of law.* Unless he is afforded every legal and factual defense available to him, this requirement of the Constitution is not being met. And, while small in terms of percentage, a great many persons are in fact in prison today, in spite of their innocence, because the preponderance of evidence seemed to be against them. It is extremely important for society to have confidence in its criminal justice system, and if a person is convicted merely because of suspicious circumstances and/or lack of a good defense effort at trial, such confidence is seriously eroded.

So important is this concept that the office of *public defender,* equal in rank to that of prosecutor, is established for those who can't afford to hire legal counsel. Advisement of this fact is required by law when a person is arrested. Unfortunately this requirement is considered an impediment by many law enforcement officers and, in fact, if it's not handled properly it can jeopardize an otherwise good case against guilty persons. However, in the long run, if it only serves to ultimately increase public confidence in our system, it works to the benefit of all concerned.

It's also unfortunate that many public defenders, like many public prosecutors, are relatively young, inexperienced at-

> ### A Question of Confidence
>
> Can a lawyer who learns that his client has committed a crime for which he has not been charged keep that knowledge to himself? The question has come up frequently during the past year in connection with the Watergate investigations now unfolding in Washington. Last week the issue was raised starkly in a murder trial in rural Lake Pleasant, N.Y. Two attorneys for a man accused of one killing revealed that they had known for six months of two other murders committed by their client. They had kept silent because they felt bound by the confidentiality of the lawyer-client relationship. . . .
>
> However shocking the two lawyers' silence may have been, it appears to be legally sound. The American Bar Association's Code of Professional Responsibility upholds the confidentiality of the lawyer-client relationship. Almost unanimously, A.B.A. members agree that this "sacred trust" is essential if the attorney is to represent his client properly. "The conduct of the lawyers is absolutely correct," says Hofstra University Law Dean Monroe Freedman. "If they had acted otherwise, it would be a serious violation of their professional responsibility."
>
> Surprisingly, no individuals, not even lawyers, are generally required to report crimes that have been committed (as opposed to crimes in preparation); only if they actually tamper with evidence are they vulnerable to charges of obstruction of justice. Under U.S. law, an attorney's sacred trust belongs to his client, not to the court. [Reprinted by permission from *Time*, The Weekly Newsmagazine; Copyright Time, Inc. (April 4, 1974).]

torneys just beginning their practice. The quality of legal representation sometimes suffers because of this. Hopefully these things balance out to the benefit of society in general. In any event, and even though all parties concerned may be offended by the statement, it is probably true that even a poorly equipped lawyer is better than none at all since the provisions of law are generally unknown to the average citizen.

THE CORONER'S OFFICE

The coroner is usually elected by county, but in some states he is appointed. His duty is to investigate any death which takes place under suspicious circumstances. If a physician refuses to issue a death certificate for any reason, the coroner is required to conduct an investigation and an autopsy to determine cause of death. The finding of a coroner's jury following an inquest does not usually hold the same impact as an indictment, but it may be used by the prosecutor to obtain one. In some states, however, a judge may issue his summons on the basis of the coroner's findings just as though the district attorney had issued a formal complaint information.

In addition to his role of determining cause of death, a coroner qualified in forensic medicine (suitable for use in court) can be of considerable assistance to successful investigation and prosecution of the criminal case. In many cases where the body is unrecognizable, only skillful examination by specialized members of the coroner's office (such as dental examiners) can determine identity of the deceased.

THE COURTS

Under the criminal justice system the obvious role of the courts is to afford trial to those accused of crimes. The various possible routes through the courts will be explored in the next chapter; here we will deal with the various levels of courts and the persons who operate them.

Courts range in authority from the justice courts, presided over by the largely vanishing justice of the peace, through the federal Supreme Court (see Figure 3-1). In previous years, many presiding officers in justice courts had no actual legal background and were elected or appointed as political favors. By contrast, Supreme Court justices are, of course, among the finest legal minds in the nation. Though appointed by the President of the United States, Supreme Court justices are subject to the approval of Congress and some have been the subject of long and bitter debates.

Municipal Courts. Generally, municipal courts are the lowest level of court in operation today. In most jurisdictions the municipal judge hears infractions, misdemeanors, and conducts preliminary hearings on felony charges. If he finds reasonable cause to believe that the charged person has committed the felony he "binds" him over for trial in the next higher level of court available, usually a *superior court* which functions on a county level and hears all felony cases.

The setting of bail, to allow the defendant to go free until

76 ELEMENTS OF THE CRIMINAL JUSTICE SYSTEM

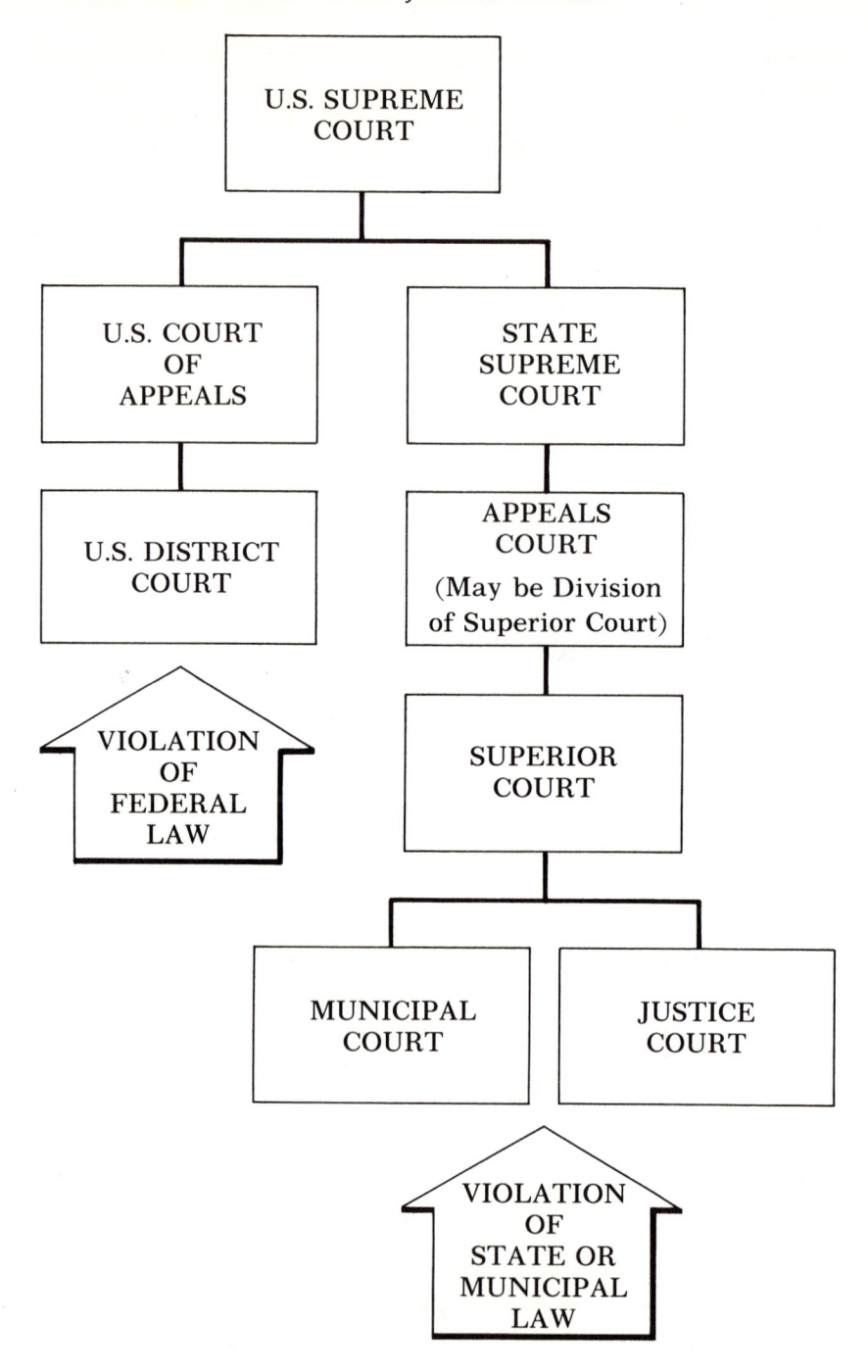

```
                    ┌──────────────┐
                    │ U.S. SUPREME │
                    │    COURT     │
                    └──────┬───────┘
              ┌────────────┴────────────┐
      ┌───────┴────────┐         ┌──────┴──────┐
      │  U.S. COURT    │         │    STATE    │
      │      OF        │         │   SUPREME   │
      │   APPEALS      │         │    COURT    │
      └───────┬────────┘         └──────┬──────┘
              │                         │
      ┌───────┴────────┐         ┌──────┴──────────┐
      │ U.S. DISTRICT  │         │    APPEALS      │
      │    COURT       │         │    COURT        │
      │                │         │ (May be Division│
      │                │         │ of Superior Court)│
      └────────────────┘         └──────┬──────────┘
        ⇧ VIOLATION                     │
          OF FEDERAL            ┌───────┴────────┐
          LAW                   │   SUPERIOR     │
                                │    COURT       │
                                └───────┬────────┘
                          ┌─────────────┴─────────────┐
                    ┌─────┴─────┐               ┌─────┴─────┐
                    │ MUNICIPAL │               │  JUSTICE  │
                    │   COURT   │               │   COURT   │
                    └───────────┘               └───────────┘
                              ⇧ VIOLATION OF
                                STATE OR MUNICIPAL LAW
```

Figure 3-1. THE APPELLATE COURT STRUCTURE

the time of his trial, is the province of any court judge. In theory he takes into consideration such factors as the seriousness of the crime, and the personal situation of the defendant in determining theamount of bail required. In practice this is often an automatic process, carried out in accordance with a fixed schedule for various offenses. Although the Constitution provides that bail must not be "excessive," judges also rightly consider such things as the danger to society of freeing the defendant, the likelihood that he may flee prosecution, and other factors which may lead him to set bail so high that it is unlikely to be deposited on the defendant's behalf. In certain instances the judge may even order the defendant to be held without bail if he feels that it is unlikely he will appear for trial.

Superior Courts. These courts are usually organized into various divisions, according to the types of cases heard and/or by geographical location within a county, including an *appellate division* which hears appeals from the decisions of lower courts. Each division has its presiding judge, usually an elected position (by his peers), and a structure of *nonjudicial* positions to carry out the many necessary functions attendant to the process.

The *clerk* of the court is appointed by the judges to handle the ministerial duties of the court. In most cases this is an administrative position which has among its duties the appointment of *deputy clerks* for each of the divisions. The deputy clerks for each court have various important tasks to attend to ranging from swearing in witnesses to scheduling conferences for the judge with attorneys and maintaining minutes of proceedings.

The *court reporter* records verbatim, as opposed to the minutes kept by the clerk, the trial process. If a transcript of the trial is needed, as for an appeal, the reporter makes this from the notes taken during the original trial.

The *bailiff* is responsible for maintaining order in the court and is a sworn peace officer, usually a member of the sheriff's department of the marshal's office. In addition to maintaining order the bailiff is responsible for the custody of the jury during recesses and deliberation and for guarding prisoners.

The office of *marshal* is the enforcement arm of the court. A sworn peace officer, his duties are primarily civil rather than criminal and include serving court orders to appear, enforcement of judgements, as well as performance of bailiff duties as noted earlier.

> ### The Law Explosion
>
> The simplest way to describe the explosion is quantitatively. The workload of federal district courts, for example, doubled between 1961 and 1971. Filings in U.S. Courts of Appeals increased over 250% in the last decade. Spiraling caseloads have strained judicial organizations to the point that lawyers speak of crisis, legislatures create new judgeships, and scholars propose new tiers of courts. But the law explosion involves more than volume. The scope and complexity of legal conflicts have increased no less dramatically than caseloads.
>
> Examine any recent volume of state or federal reports. The cases calling for informed decision range from the legality of the Vietnam war or the Alaska pipeline to the right of rehabilitation in prison or the wisdom of busing schoolchildren. The jobs of "judges and company" are simply harder. Americans increasingly turn to courts to settle social and personal disputes formerly handled by family, church, school, and other branches of government. . . .
>
> . . . Even though crime in the United States is primarily a state rather than a national responsibility, the President's Commission on Law Enforcement and the Administration of Justice found in 1967 that federal statutes define over 2,800 crimes. A parallel proliferation of crimes also prevails in most American states. [From J. Woodford Howard, Jr., "Law Enforcement in an Urban Society," *American Psychologist* (April 1974), p. 223]

District Courts of Appeals. Beyond the superior court or its equivalent in the various states, lie *district courts of appeals* and finally, the state supreme court. A defendant convicted in one of the lower courts may appeal his case through these courts and up to the United States Supreme Court in many cases. Normally considerably less than one percent of convictions in lower courts go as far as the Supreme Court. Not all convictions will be reviewed by the Supreme Court unless "substantial federal question" of basic application of law is involved. If this criterion is met, however, it is conceivable that even a traffic violation could be thus taken through the entire court system.

The Federal Court System. The United States Supreme Court, the U.S. Courts of Appeals, and the U.S. District Courts comprise this system. While the Supreme Court will hear cases which have traveled through the state supreme courts, the lower federal courts hear only federal cases. That is, they are not available as recourse to those convicted of violating state law unless, again, a matter of federal question on application of law is involved.

The Probation Officer

The role of the probation officer is a dual one. First, as an officer of the court he is responsible for investigating the circumstances surrounding the commission of a crime and making recommendations on sentencing. If his investigation causes him to believe that the chances of rehabilitation are sufficient, he may recommend to the court that the convicted defendant be conditionally released without serving time in county jail. He may also recommend *summary probation,* a short-term jail sentence and early probational release. His second role is that of supervisor of persons released under either provision.

If the probationer behaves himself, reporting regularly to his probation officer for counselling and not committing any act in violation of his probation, he serves his term outside jail walls. If he violates any of the conditions of his probation, the full term of his sentence is put into effect and he goes to jail. The conditions of probation can be so stringent that convicted persons have been known to refuse it, preferring instead to serve their time and be free from the continuing behavioral constraints. Most people, however, are quite willing to do whatever is required to remain outside jail, no matter what the conditions.

The quasi-parental role assumed by probation officers in performing the supervisory part of their work sometimes leads to a philosophical conflict between them and other elements of the system, notably police officers. In order to maintain rapport with their "clients" (and possibly because of their own social orientation) probation officers sometimes adopt appearances and mannerisms much like those they supervise. Partly for this reason, and partly because they may "go the extra mile" with their probationers in an attempt to salvage them through rehabilitation, police officers often question which side of law enforcement they're on. Rightly or wrongly, many police officers feel that it's not uncommon for a probation officer to conceal minor violations of law to keep his clients from becoming in violation of their probation. In any event, the more liberal orientation of the probation officer is often at odds with the traditionally conservative orientation of the policeman.

CORRECTIONAL INSTITUTIONS

Correctional institutions under the criminal justice system are generally of two types: *jails* and *prisons.* Jails are at the city or county level and are used to hold prisoners until trial, if they are unable to post bail for their release, and to confine convicted misdemeanor offenders for the term of their sentence. Prisons are at the state or federal level and are strictly for the confinement and/or rehabilitation of convicted felony offenders. Federal prisons differ slightly in this regard in that they are also used to confine persons convicted of federal misdemeanors. Within the various state prison systems there are different levels of security ranging from prisons without walls to institutions which are isolated geographically from the rest of society.

This final element of the criminal justice system is in itself isolated from the rest of the system. While police, prosecutors, judges, attorneys, probation officers, and parole officers have daily contact with each other, correctional officials seldom have such direct interaction. The public also rarely has contact with or even thinks of its correctional institutions. This is partly because of the physical remoteness of prisons but also because we tend to regard them as a sort of receptacle into which the unpleasant aspects of society are placed for our protection and convenience. Only when the news media feature stories of deplorable conditions or riots do we become consciously aware of the fact that prisons do in fact exist. There are over a million persons, however, whose daily lives are in the control of this part of the system. Two-thirds of these are under the jurisdiction of probation or parole offices, with the remaining third in prisons or jails.

The role of the correctional system is a dual one: *treatment,* or attempted rehabilitation of convicted offenders, is allegedly the major role of such institutions; *custody,* or isolation from the rest of society, is supposed to be the alternative role. In fact, only one-fifth of personnel in prisons have positions which are neither custodial nor administrative, and most jails have only custodial or administrative staff. This is somewhat understandable in the case of jails where a large portion of inmates have not yet been to trial and therefore are not eligible for rehabilitational efforts. But with such a preponderance of effort in prisons being spent on custody, it is hard to say that the general failure of rehabilitative efforts is solely due to the incorrigibility of the inmates themselves.

Clearly there are people who are beyond treatment and require permanent isolation from society. Others, however, could be more useful in society caring for their families that instead are supported by public funds through welfare programs. Unfortunately many of the programs which have been aimed at this goal have lacked the ability to truly rehabilitate the persons they process. The result too frequently has been that people have been released prematurely and have returned to criminal behavior and again become police problems, re-entering the criminal justice system after having learned little more in prison than greater skill at their "trade."

If our prisons may be said to have generally failed in their rehabilitative efforts, the county jails of America can best be described as intolerable. Most have officially been declared unfit for human habitation and yet exist in the same ancient, unsanitary buildings that have housed them for generations. Personnel generally include no professional staff members and often consist of recent graduates of sheriff's academies used as jailers to provide them a break-in period prior to entering their regular duties. No attempt at rehabilitation is made partly because of the nature of the status of those incarcerated, as noted above.

Though most state laws require segregation of male from female, misdemeanor from felony, and juvenile from adult prisoners, a wide variety of offenders is often intermingled in crowded cells and holding tanks. The initial exposure to crimi-

A jail in Washington, D.C. in 1861. Many of the county jails in America today are housed in old, unsanitary buildings, and conditions in many are deemed intolerable.

nal justice thus afforded an 18-year old arrested for a minor offense can hardly be expected to favorably shape his attitudes toward law enforcement and his community in general.

There are over 3,000 county jails and thousands more lockups in smaller cities used only to hold prisoners prior to arraignment. If you described them as all being in approximately the condition described above, very few agencies would be able to successfully prove you wrong. Progress is under way in many states, such as honor farms for minimum-security risks, and though most of it is in facilities for those who have passed their initial detention period, official attention is being focused on the problem. Jails and prisons, however, remain largely punitive in nature rather than rehabilitative and even in the best, the recidivism rate for graduates runs over 30 percent.

The Parole Officer

There is a basic similarity between the roles of the parole agent and the probation officer. Both have a responsibility for supervision of persons convicted of crimes but allowed to be outside of custodial institutions. The difference is that the client of the parole agent has always served at least some time in a state or federal prison and has been released conditionally on the grounds that his rehabilitation is sufficient to allow his return to society. As with the probationer, the parolee is subject to return to custody to serve out the term of his sentence if he violates the conditions of his parole.

Philosophically, at least as far as the police view it, there is also a difference between the two types of supervisors of released persons. Perhaps because his clients are poorer-risks who have started out convicted of more serious crimes, the parole officer may be more aware of the fact that a certain number of his charges are likely to fail. Thus, police feel that he is more likely to report violations rather than extend himself to keep the parolee from becoming in violation.

THE JUVENILE JUSTICE SYSTEM

Separate provisions appear at virtually every stage of comparison with the criminal justice systems for juvenile and adult offenders. This isn't really surprising when you consider that as far back as Hammurabi's Code provision was made for different penalties for offenders 14 and under.

In most police departments, while offenders under 18 are

A juvenile detention facility of 1854 with youngsters working in the laundry room. Juvenile detention facilities of today are constantly under criticism for plant, personnel, and rehabilitative programs.

arrested by the same officers who handle adult crimes, they are shortly turned over to an investigator who specializes in handling juveniles. Since most investigators specialize in type of crime rather than type of offender, this is the first significant difference between adult and juvenile justice.

The second basic element of the justice system, the courts, is also quite different than for adults. The adversary system, an essential part of adult courts, doesn't exist in the juvenile courts. On the premise that there is a basic lack of responsibility on the part of the juvenile and a greater probability of rehabilitation, the juvenile courts aim at protecting the child from separation from his parents if at all possible. Unless it is believed that the child requires protection from his environment at home, the community requires protection from the juvenile, or the property of others is in danger by his freedom, the child will usually remain with his parents. While the theory is not that the juvenile is exempt from the law or the criminal justice system, it is felt that he should be protected from the harsher aspects of it and rehabilitated if at all possible.

Instead of having a prosecutor investigate and decide whether to issue a complaint against the offender, offenses committed by juveniles are investigated by a probation officer on behalf of the court. The investigation goes as much into the background of the accused and the circumstances surrounding the commission of the crime, as it does into the matter of evidence of the crime. The aim of the investigation is to make a decision on whether to petition the juvenile to the court system for processing, to detain him or release him to his parents, or refer him to an outside agency for counselling. There is seldom a question of bail involved in a juvenile case; the child is either detained or released to his parents.

In juvenile court there is no trial as such, but rather a *hearing*. The hearing is informal in nature, in contrast with the formal trial process for adults, and takes place in private session. There is no jury and usually offenders are represented by the public defender, regardless of their ability to hire private counsel. All offenses are considered civil, rather than criminal, with no distinction between what would be felony or misdemeanor offenses for adults. The rules of evidence are also different for juvenile hearings. Whereas the adult on trial must be found guilty "beyond reasonable doubt," the juvenile may be found guilty by a "preponderance of evidence."

If it is determined that the juvenile must spend time in continued custody, he is made a ward of the court and placed in one of the correctional institutions maintained by the county. In theory the thrust in such institutions is solely treatment rather than punishment or custody for isolation purposes. These facilities are primarily trade schools with the goal of rehabilitation and development of a useful trade for the youngster. Too often, of course, the trade learned is the same one for which he was committed to the institution. In such cases graduation really means going from juvenile offender to adult criminal. Not all cases end this way, naturally, but it's felt that an alarmingly high percentage do (concrete data on how many juveniles actually graduate to adult crime are not available at this time).

As with all other elements of the justice system, juvenile procedures are currently under close critical scrutiny. Much criticism is leveled at the informality upon which the court process is based. Some feel that an adversary system like that used in adult courts would better protect the rights of the individual juvenile than the one-sided hearing now used. Increased use of the rights to private counsel is recommended by some as a means to this end. Qualifications of many juvenile court judges are felt to be similar to those of the justice of the peace a few years ago, that is, some actually have no legal background prior to taking their positions. Similarly, in a process which leans so heavily on the social and behavioral sciences for decisions acutely affecting the lives of those before it, many judges are lacking in such training. Juvenile halls and other detention facilities are constantly under criticism in even the most advanced jurisdictions for inadequacies of both plant and personnel. Again, as with its adult counterpart, the juvenile justice system is in the process of reform and progress, though sometimes so slow as to be almost imperceptible.

THE NEED FOR AN INTEGRATED INFORMATION SYSTEM

The need for an integrated, computerized information system throughout the criminal justice system is recognized by virtually every administrator involved in law enforcement. Presently every agency in every jurisdiction maintains its own records in its own way, plus, of course, those records required for state or federal purposes. And, while the thought of national dossiers is repugnant to most people, particularly civil libertarians, the benefits of some controlled form of centralized crime information should also be obvious.

Judges, for example, could pass more intelligent sentences if they knew the history of the defendant in response to treatment in other jurisdictions. Such information is currently buried in countless files and not available in any way that could be considered at all practical. The activities of organized crime could be much more effectively combatted by police if the intelligence information available in local agencies could be pooled, analyzed, and disseminated. Almost all activities of this enormously expensive criminal segment are in some way either national in scope or at least involve several communities. At present, with virtually no communication between agencies for the purpose of sharing intelligence, there is no way to attack organized crime on an organized basis.

The ability to track an arrestee through the criminal justice process after he has been turned over to the courts would be useful to every administrator. By learning what disposition is made of persons his agency enters into the system, he can better evaluate the effectiveness of his and the other involved agencies. Recidivism and graduation from juvenile to adult crime could be analyzed on the basis of hard data rather than gathered impressions. Occurrence of crime and its economic impact could be realistically assessed if the uniform reporting procedures required for an integrated information system were put into effect by all law enforcement agencies.

Virtually everyone in the criminal justice system, from police officers through parole agents, realizes that more information is needed to make the system function on an informed rather than speculative basis. Fortunately, the need is also recognized by those responsible for funding federal and state projects, and such programs are under way in several states.

SUMMARY

The criminal justice system is composed of three basic parts: *law enforcement* (police and other agencies), *judicial* (courts), and *corrections* (jails and prisons). The basic roles of these segments are, respectively, *apprehension, trial,* and *rehabilitation and custody.*

In dealing with adults, the courts follow an *adversary procedure* in which the state attempts to prove the guilt of the accused person who is presumed innocent unless the state is successful in this effort.

Following an arrest by the police the *prosecutor,* or district attorney, examines the facts and issues a public *complaint,* if warranted, against the arrested person on behalf of the state. In complicated cases, or when secrecy is temporarily important, the prosecutor may ask the *grand jury* to return an *indictment* accusing the person of a specific crime.

Defense counsel, either public or private, presents the side of the accused during trial where, if found guilty, the defendant is fined by the judge or sentences to probation, prison, or a combination of these. During a *probation* period the convicted offender is allowed to remain free providing he does not violate the terms of his probation as prescribed by the judge. If sentenced to prison he may become eligible for *parole* at some time prior to completion of his full sentence and be freed under conditions similar to probation.

Police have considerable latitude in enforcing the laws of the penal codes of the state within the policies of the department for which they work. The decision on whether to arrest for a given violation is made on the basis of the officer's judgement of how the needs of the community will be best served. Technical requirements, derived from court application of individual and constitutional law, also govern the officer's decision on whether and when to arrest.

The *prosecutor* and his staff have the role of *investigating* the facts of evidence in a crime, *issuing* a complaint against the person arrested if the facts warrant it, and *prosecuting* the case against him when it comes to trial. The overriding charge of the prosecutor is the serving of justice, rather than merely obtaining convictions, and considerable latitude is exercised ranging from refusal to issue a complaint through reduction of charges via the *plea-bargaining* process.

The *grand jury* meets in secret session for the purpose of examining evidence and hearing testimony from the state to determine if there is sufficient indication of possible guilt to accuse the person of the crime by issuing an *indictment* against him. The accused is not represented by counsel during grand jury hearings.

The *trial jury* has the responsibility of determining the guilt or innocence of the accused during a trial supervised by the judge. Unlike the grand jury, which needs only to decide if there is enough evidence to warrant accusing the person, the trial jury must decide that there is evidence beyond reasonable doubt of his guilt.

Defense counsel has the role of assuring that the accused receives *due process of law,* as provided under our Constitution, regardless of any personal thoughts the counsel may have about the defendant's guilt or innocence. The office of *public defender* is provided by the state to those who are financially unable to hire private counsel.

The *coroner* investigates any death which occurs under suspicious circumstances to determine if there is evidence of a criminal act involved. A hearing into the facts surrounding such a death is called an *inquest* and is heard by a *coroner's jury.* The results of such a hearing do not usually have the same impact as an indictment from a grand jury but rather are used to obtain such an indictment.

Various types of courts exist ranging from *justice courts* at the lowest level to the federal *Supreme Court. Municipal courts* hear misdemeanors and infractions, plus preliminary hearings on felony cases. *Superior courts,* functioning at the county level, hear felony cases and appeals. At the head of each state court system is the *state supreme court,* with intermediate *district courts of appeals* leading to it. In addition to the United States Supreme Court, the federal court system includes *U.S. district courts* and *U.S. courts of appeals* which hear criminal cases.

Staffing of courts typically includes a *clerk* who schedules conferences with counselors and the judge, swears in witnesses, maintains minutes and performs other duties; a *court reporter* who takes verbatim notes of the trial proceedings; a *bailiff* who is a sworn peace officer and maintains order during the trial; and the office of the *marshal,* also a sworn peace officer, who is responsible for carrying out the orders of the court.

Probation officers are officers of the court who are charged with the dual role of investigating the circumstances surrounding a crime (to make recommendations which will be considered by the judge in determining sentence) and supervising the conduct of persons placed on probation as a condition of freedom during the term of their sentence.

Parole officers supervise the conduct of persons who have been conditionally released from prison prior to completion of the full term of their sentence.

Correctional institutions are of two general types for adult offenders: *jail* (at the city or county level) or *prison* (at the state or federal level). Persons convicted of misdemeanors serve their sentence in jail, while persons convicted of felonies serve in prison. In theory the aim of a prison sentence is primarily rehabilitation although it in fact is often little different from jails which are primarily custodial in nature, serving only to isolate the convicted offender from society and punish him as a deterrent.

The *juvenile justice system* is significantly different at all levels from the adult, primarily due to the concepts that the child is not fully responsible for his acts and has greater likelihood of rehabilitation. In most police departments special *juvenile officers* are provided to handle cases involving young offenders. A *probation officer* handles the role which would normally be taken by the prosecutor for an adult case, investigating the facts surrounding the crime and making recommendations as to whether the courts should be involved. The procedure in court is a *nonadversary hearing,* rather than a trial, and no jury is involved. Hearings are held in private with the juvenile represented by a public defender. Detention facilities for juveniles are primarily trade schools which in theory aim at treatment instead of custody.

An integrated information system which will provide uniform records of crime and persons convicted of crime is held to be a high priority need of the criminal justice system.

REVIEW QUESTIONS

Answers to these questions appear on pages 382–383.

REVIEW QUESTIONS   89

1. Label each of the following as either *police, court* or *corrections* depending on the segment of the criminal justice system handling the function.
   _____ a. probation officer
   _____ b. juvenile officer
   _____ c. parole officer
   _____ d. district attorney
   _____ e. public defender
   _____ f. grand jury
   _____ g. responsibility for apprehension
2. *True or false?* The primary responsibility of the prosecutor is to successfully prove the state's case against the defendant.
3. *True or false?* When a grand jury returns an indictment against a person it indicates that the person has committed the crime of which he is charged.
4. If the police wanted to charge a person with a crime without alerting others who may be involved to the fact that an investigation is in process, would they ask the district attorney for a *complaint* or a grand jury *indictment?* _____
5. Label each of the following as being true of a *trial* jury, a *grand* jury, or *both*.
   _____ a. make decisions on basis of evidence "beyond a reasonable doubt"
   _____ b. panel members may be challenged by attorneys for either side
   _____ c. panel members drawn from pool of names submitted by judges
   _____ d. meet in public session
   _____ e. make decisions based on substantial evidence that the person charged may have committed a crime
6. A defense attorney can take a case for a person he privately believes guilty because the constitution specifies that no person shall be deprived of life or liberty except by _____ .
7. If a person dies and no doctor will issue a death certificate,

the death must be investigated by the _____ .

8. A peace officer assigned to take charge of prisoners during court trial and maintain order in the court is performing the duties of the _____ .
9. If required, a verbatim transcript of the proceedings during a trial is provided by the court _____ .
10. Minutes of the proceedings in court are kept by the court _____ .
11. Label each of the following statements as referring to a *justice* court, a *superior* court, or a *municipal* court.
    _____ a. hears felonies
    _____ b. hears misdemeanors and preliminary felony actions in most jurisdictions today
    _____ c. lowest level courts, diminishing in number
    _____ d. first level of appeals courts
12. If a person has been convicted, but instead of going to jail or prison is allowed to stay free as long as he avoids breaking the law, will he report to a probation officer or a parole officer? _____
13. A person whose rehabilitation in prison has been judged sufficient to warrant his conditional release prior to completion of the full term of the sentence, will report periodically to a _____ officer.
14. A person convicted of a felony offense and sentenced to serve time in a state correctional institution will serve that time in _____ .
15. Label each of the following as describing the *adult, juvenile,* or *both* justice systems.
    _____ a. trial by jury
    _____ b. uses public defender
    _____ c. guilt must be established "beyond reasonable doubt"
    _____ d. uses probation officer
    _____ e. bail not involved in most cases
    _____ f. uses private defense counsel if defendant can afford it

CHAPTER 4

THE PROCESS OF CRIMINAL JUSTICE

OVERVIEW

In the preceding chapter you were introduced to the functional elements of the criminal justice system and the people who make them operate. The rest of the story is the process by which justice is served on behalf of both those arrested and the people of the state—in other words, the way in which the system operates.

The process is slightly different from state to state and according to the nature of the crime which has been committed. But basic provisions are similar enough to allow the outlines we'll present in this chapter.

If you're wondering why you need to know all this when most law enforcement officers seldom get involved beyond arrest and booking (other than to testify at trials), consider for a moment your professional status in the eyes of the public. Knowledge of a person's field of endeavor, beyond his immediate role, is always considered a mark of competence. Not that you need to know how to prepare a case for submission to court, but you really should have some idea of what happens after an arrest and the meaning of such terms as *arraignment, plea bargaining,* and the like.

In this chapter we'll take up the various events which

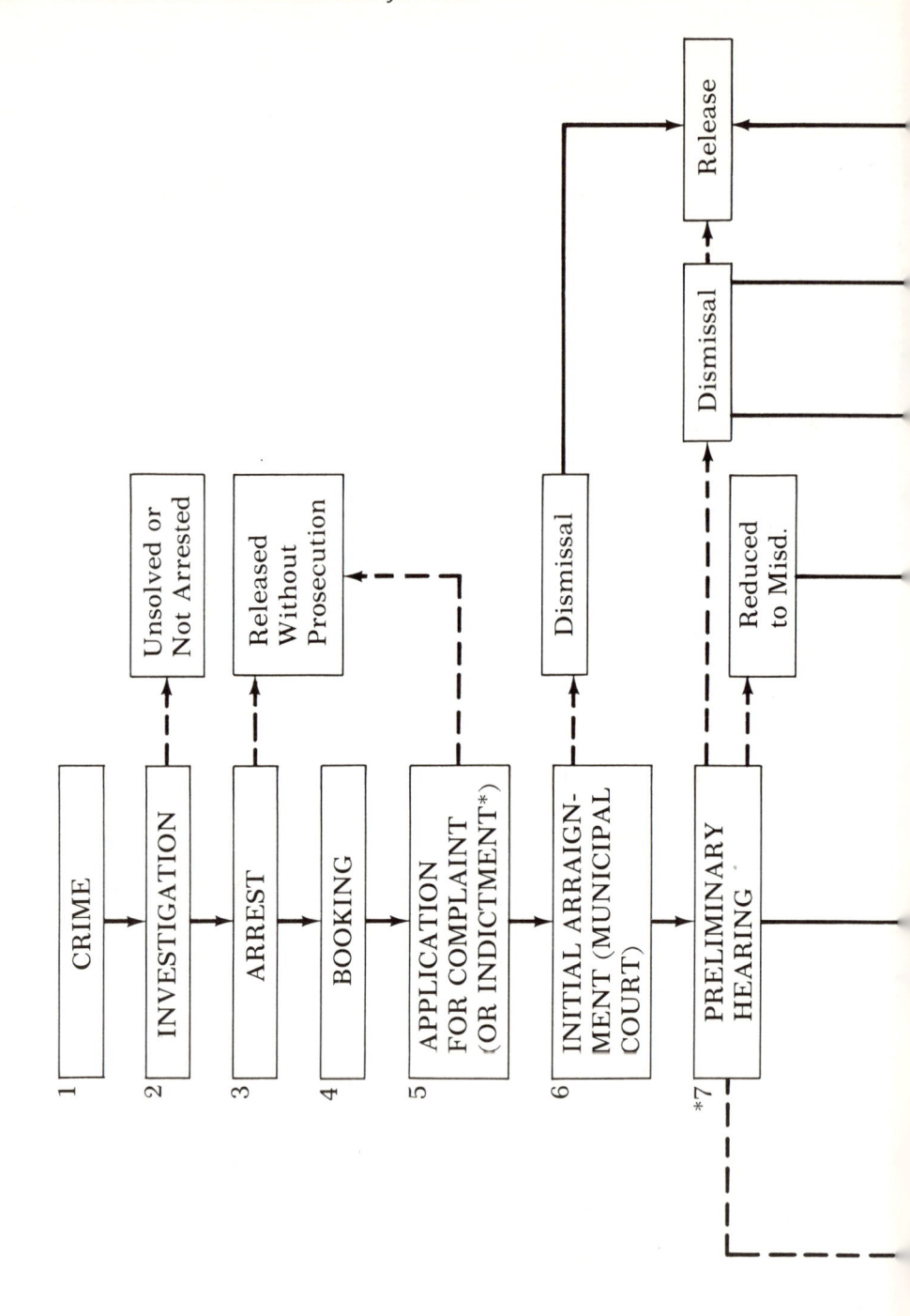

92 THE PROCESS OF CRIMINAL JUSTICE

1. CRIME
2. INVESTIGATION → Unsolved or Not Arrested
3. ARREST → Released Without Prosecution
4. BOOKING
5. APPLICATION FOR COMPLAINT (OR INDICTMENT*)
6. INITIAL ARRAIGNMENT (MUNICIPAL COURT) → Dismissal → Release
*7. PRELIMINARY HEARING → Reduced to Misd. → Dismissal → Release

OVERVIEW 93

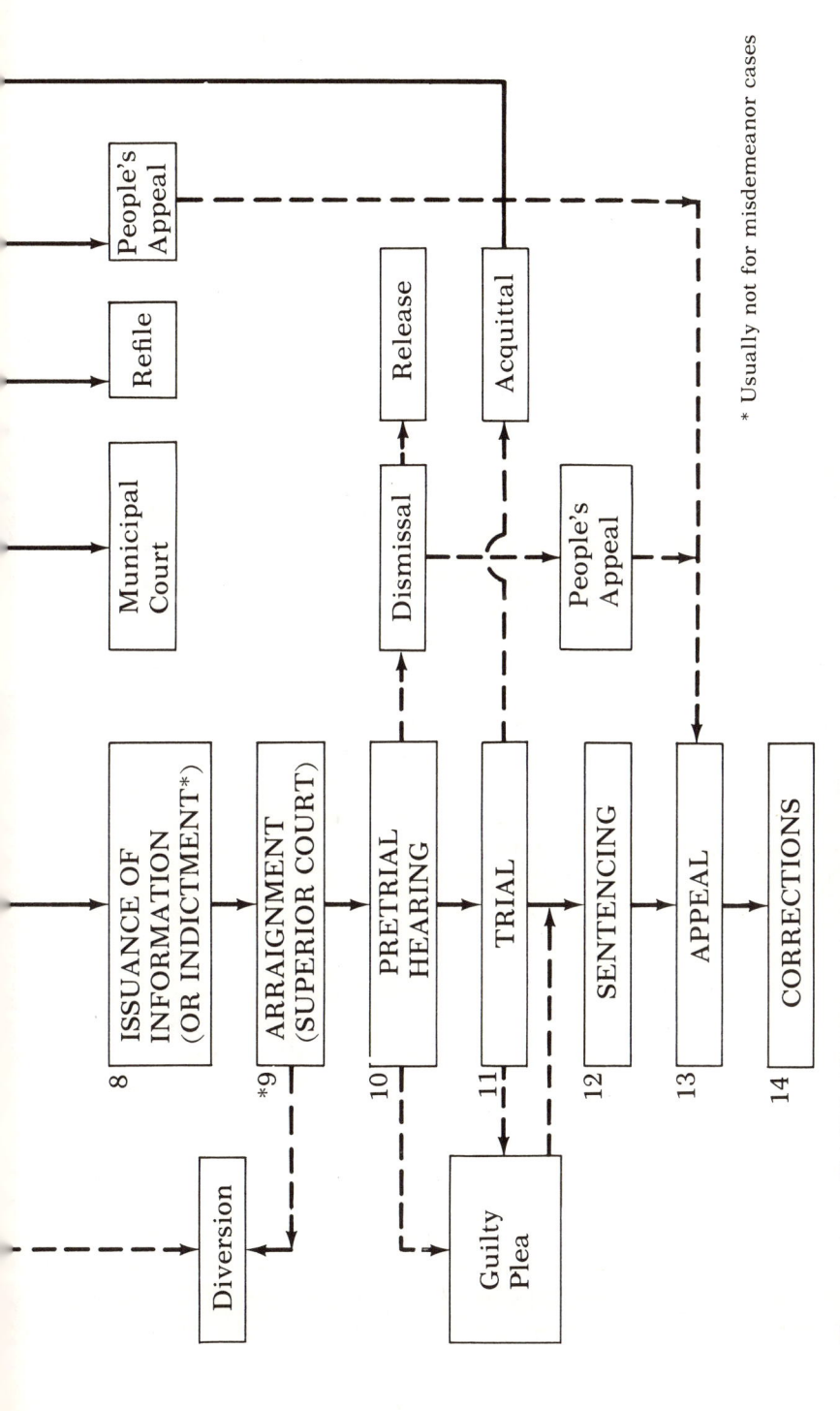

Figure 4-1. BASIC CRIMINAL JUSTICE PROCESS FOR A FELONY

* Usually not for misdemeanor cases

8 ISSUANCE OF INFORMATION (OR INDICTMENT*)
*9 ARRAIGNMENT (SUPERIOR COURT)
10 PRETRIAL HEARING
11 TRIAL
12 SENTENCING
13 APPEAL
14 CORRECTIONS

Municipal Court
Refile
People's Appeal
Diversion
Dismissal → Release
Acquittal
People's Appeal
Guilty Plea

occur during the basic process and then explore some of the alternative routes which may be followed under various conditions.

THE BASIC PROCESS

There are three ways through the criminal justice process according to the type of crime committed: *felony, misdemeanor,* or *juvenile offense.* Figure 4-1 outlines the process for a felony case because it's the most complete. While the process will vary somewhat from state to state, the one outlined here includes the basic procedures usually followed. Most often, misdemeanor offenses are not submitted to the grand jury (as shown in Step 5) and don't require the preliminary hearing (Step 7) or the arraignment in superior court (Step 9). In addition, misdemeanors of a petty nature may skip Steps 7 through 11 and be handled directly by the judge at the initial appearance (Step 6). Juvenile cases are subject to an almost entirely different process as you know, and after we finish examining the felony and misdemeanor processes, we'll take up the juvenile system separately.

The Crime

In order for the criminal justice process to start the crime must of course come to the attention of the law. In relatively rare instances a violation of law may be brought to the attention of the district attorney or the court and the process begun in this way, but normally it begins when the crime is either observed by or reported to a law enforcement agency.

Investigation

As used here the term *investigation* refers to an action by a law enforcement officer to determine responsibility for the commission of a particular crime. It may consist of the response of a uniformed officer to a citizen's call, or it may involve months of detailed work by a plainclothes investigator. Either way this action seeks to connect some particular person or persons with the commission of the known crime incident.

The main purpose of the investigation, of course, is to lead to the arrest of the person guilty of the crime. The investigation may very well not stop with the arrest and, in fact, often continues until the trial itself. Often the investigation fails to solve the crime. Every department has cases which have been on the books for years with no valid suspect identified or arrested. And, of course, identification of the person believed to be guilty of the crime does not invariably lead to his arrest. The latitude exercised by the officer, as mentioned in the case of the juvenile guilty of throwing rocks through the window of an abandoned house, would be one example of such a situation. Another situation would exist in a case where a person is known to have committed the crime but simply can't be found. In addition to the many persons who elude apprehension, there are those who have fled the jurisdiction only to be arrested elsewhere for another crime. It's entirely possible for a person to be convicted and imprisoned, often under an alias, for a second crime with no connection ever made between him and other incidents. This possibility is further evidence of the need for an integrated information system. Many crimes carried endlessly on the case loads of an investigative unit might be cleared if such information were readily available through a computerized information bank.

In addition to the basic need for identifying and apprehending the suspect, the investigation must be carried out in a manner carefully prescribed under the law. In other words, even if the guilty party is found, identified by witnesses, in possession of the fruits of the crime, and arrested, he may be released and never tried for the crime if the evidence against him wasn't obtained constitutionally. This will be covered in greater detail in Chapter 8.

The Arrest

Essentially the arrest occurs when a peace officer decides that he has sufficient reason to believe that the person in question has indeed committed the crime. As with the investigation there are technical points relating to the arrest which, if not properly provided for in the process, can lead to the arrested person being released without prosecution. For our purposes we can assume that an officer takes the suspected person into custody, advises him that he is under arrest for commission of a specific crime, and takes him to police headquarters.

Booking

The booking process is the creation of an *administrative record of arrest.* Fingerprints and photographs are taken of the suspect and a formal record made of his being arrested for commission of the crime.

> ### The Decision to Arrest
>
> The men in blue talk as if they have the least discretion in the system. In fact they have the most, far more than the prosecutors and judges about whom lawyers fret. *The decision to arrest is the critical nexus of discretion in American law enforcement.* Several studies show that police themselves screen out far more legal infractions from the criminal process than do prosecutors or judges, whom police often condemn for permissiveness.
>
> Whatever relevance these findings have for the presumption of innocence, they speak volumes about the decentralization of authority in our legal order. The overwhelming number of social conflicts never become law suits, the overwhelming number of cases are never litigated in courts, the overwhelming number of litigated cases are never appealed, the overwhelming number of appeals are affirmed at state supreme courts or federal appellate courts, and this holds more for criminal cases than for civil cases. . . . Hence, the overwhelming amount of justice in our system is dispensed in the community not by judges and juries but by the police. On the civil side the same is true of social workers. The police are the key to the quality of urban criminal justice. They have more direct power over the lives of our people than any other officials. They are clearly the cities' most important social workers, the major representative of law to the community and, too often, mediators *between* law and the community. [J. Woodford Howard, Jr., "Law Enforcement in and Urban Society," *American Psychologist* (April 1974), p. 225]

At this point in the process, bail may be posted by the arrestee to obtain his temporary release. In most misdemeanor cases the amount of bail is set in accordance with a schedule established by the courts for the crime involved. In more serious felony cases the police may, through the district attorney, request the court to set a higher bail than that set forth on the court schedule, hopefully an amount likely to either assure the appearance of the offender in court for trial or his continuance in custody until that time.

Until such time as bail is posted by the arrested person or his family, friends, or a bail bondsman licensed by the state to make loans for such purposes, he remains in custody. There are options which may effect his release at this point in the process and these will be explained later in this chapter; the normal process, however, is that an arrested person either posts bail or waits in jail until he appears in court.

The Application for Complaint or Indictment

The suspect must be brought before a magistrate within a specified number of hours following arrest (usually 48 hours but varying by state). To begin this movement toward justice a formal complaint must be filed on behalf of the people of the state against the arrested person. This complaint is the first plea of the people to have the case examined by a magistrate. It must be signed under oath by the complainant or a police officer and concurred in by the prosecuting attorney before it can be submitted to the court.

Because of this need for concurrence by the prosecutor's office, some rather confusing terminology has come into use. The phrase "issue the complaint" is frequently used as though it referred to some separate action initiated by the prosecutor. An officer will often say for example, "I had a good case (against the arrested person) but the DA wouldn't issue a complaint." In fact what has happened is that the police have originated the complaint by filing the application but the district attorney, after examining the reported facts, *fails to concur* and thus the complaint never comes before the court. It may be because of lack of evidence (in the prosecutor's opinion) on grounds such as insufficient probable cause at the time the arrest was made. When this happens the person is released without prosecution, and the police can either accept this turn of events or go over the head of the person on the prosecutor's staff. While not often followed, this continued attempt to get the complaint to the court may take the form of further conference with higher-ups in the prosecutor's office or even directly to a magistrate himself.

If the prosecutor agrees that the people have a complaint against the person in custody, the document eventually is called an *information,* which is the basic statement of facts against the person charged with the crime. An information is a matter of public record and, as noted earlier, *indictment* may be sought by either the police or the district attorney if it is felt that the attendant secrecy of grand jury proceedings is more desirable for the people's case. In either event, preparation by the police of the application for complaint completes their role in the process except for continuance of the investigation, consultation with the prosecutor's staff, and possible testimony during the trial.

The Initial Arraignment or Initial Appearance

If the prosecutor concurs with the complaint, a time is set for the initial appearance of the accused in municipal or justice court. This appearance is also called the *initial arraignment* (technically a call to court to answer a charge), and its purpose is for the judge to formally advise the person of the charge against him and his rights under the Constitution. The judge will also require the defendant to enter a plea to the charge and if the plea is "not guilty" he will set the amount of bail, which may be different from the amount set at booking. If the defendant pleads guilty, the sentence can be imposed immediately or the judge may direct him to return for sentencing at a later date.

If the defendant pleads not guilty and the offense is a misdemeanor, the judge may hear the evidence in the case at this stage in what becomes a *summary trial.* In such cases Steps 6 through 11 are combined into a single event and the defendant is either convicted or acquitted. If the judge does not hear the evidence at the arraignment, he will direct the defendant to return at a later date for trial. If the charge is a felony he will set a date for a *preliminary hearing* as described below. (In some states there is a provision for a preliminary hearing in some of the more serious misdemeanor cases.)

The Preliminary Hearing

The purpose of the preliminary hearing in felony cases (and, as noted, in serious misdemeanors in some states) is to test the evidence against the defendant. Held in a municipal or justice court, the result will be to either *dismiss* the charges or *bind over* for trial in a superior court.

If the charges are dismissed the defendant is released and the people have the option of accepting this decision as final, *refiling* the complaint on an amended basis, or filing an *appeal* on a disputed issue of law. In actual practice, however, dismissal of charges almost always results in release without prosecution. When the defendant is bound over for trial in superior court the process continues as below.

Alternative results, such as *reduction to misdemeanor* of felony charges against the defendant or *diversion* into a probationary plan for treatment of the defendant, are possible in the superior court. There is also the possibility that the court will accept a *certified plea* (a plea of guilty, made in open court) in which case Steps 7 through 11 are combined into one.

Issuance of Information or Indictment

Before further proceedings take place in court, the formal issuance of an *information* or *indictment* based on the complaint must occur. In the information procedure, the prosecutor officially files the complaint document marked with the date for the defendant's next appearance in court (as set by the court at the preliminary hearing). If the indictment procedure is followed it will of course be necessary to submit the complaint to the grand jury for its investigation and deliberation. If the grand jury returns an indictment, this takes the place of the information developed in the lower courts and, in fact, takes the place of the preliminary hearing.

In most states the grand jury process is seldom used because of the time requirement. With so many crimes and only one grand jury per county, the process is really a potential bottleneck. Seldom is this route followed, in any state, in the case of misdemeanors. Even with felony cases the usual practice is to use the information approach to bring the people's plea before the court.

Arraignment in Superior Court

Often the only step in the process formally called *arraignment,* to distinguish it from the initial appearance in court, in this step the court hears the plea of the defendant, lets him choose between a court or jury trial, and appoints a public defender if appropriate.

In felony cases, usually the only ones where an arraignment takes place, there is also the possibility that the court will accept a plea of guilty to a reduced charge. This process can take place at any time prior to trial but most often is accomplished at the arraignment or as the result of the preliminary hearing.

The Pretrial Hearing

At the request of defense counsel or of his own volition, the judge may order a pretrial hearing to test the validity of line-up procedures, confessions, or evidence obtained through search and seizure. He may also rule on the acceptability of *discovery motions* (such as recordings or statements of witnesses) made by defense counsel to obtain relevant evidence in possession of the prosecution.

Dismissal of charges is often the result of these hearings since they are frequently held because the judge already suspects there may be a flaw in the people's case. If the case is dismissed, the defendant is released and the people have the right of appeal on an issue of law.

Trial

Once the process has reached this point there are only three basic possibilities remaining: acceptance of a *guilty plea*, a *verdict of guilty,* or *acquittal.* A guilty plea at any point during the trial terminates it and eliminates the possibility of a verdict of guilty or an acquittal. In practice, some 90 percent of all cases terminate in this manner prior to reaching trial.

If the case comes to trial the defendant has the option of trial by jury or the judge alone (called a *court trial*). If a jury trial is chosen a panel of twelve members is selected from the pool of jurors available. A few additional "alternates" are selected in case one of the twelve becomes ill or otherwise must withdraw before the case is concluded. The prosecution and the defense each has the right to ask questions of prospective panel members and may dismiss or excuse any whom they feel would not be able to give the matter a fair and impartial hearing. When the jury is empaneled the case begins with each side presenting its witnesses to give testimony of their knowledge relative to the case. The attorney who calls the witness asks questions on *direct examination,* after which the opposing attorney may ask questions on *cross-examination* in an attempt to overcome any unfavorable (to his client) impression the witness may have given the jury.

When all the evidence has been presented the judge directs the panel to retire and reach a verdict in accordance with the law which he explains to them as it applies to the case and their role. The bailiff conducts the panel to the jury room where they first select a foreman from among their members to be responsible for leadership of all discussions, vote-taking, and liaison between the panel and the court, including deliverance of the verdict when it is reached.

The Juror as Prisoner

The sequestering of jurors—which means keeping them together under surveillance for 24 hours a day—occurs in dozens of flamboyant U.S. trials every year. The goal is to guard the jurors from the influence of heavy media publicity, to shelter them from community prejudice and to protect them from physical threats and intimidation. An American Bar Association poll indicates that two-thirds of defense lawyers and 80 percent of judges favor the practice. . . .

The rules governing the lives of a sequestered jury are usually set by the presiding judge, and they can vary considerably. At a minimum, jurors can read newspapers and newsmagazines only after any information bearing on the trial has been snipped out—and they are not allowed to watch any television news programs. The [John] Mitchell-[Maurice] Stans jurors [were] forbidden to watch either courtroom dramas such as "Owen Marshall" or the Johnny Carson show because a topical joke about the trial could pop out. At the trial of the Chicago Seven, Judge Julius Hoffman ordered that the jurors could not read any newspapers or magazines or watch any television at all, even football games. . . .

Sequestered jurors must live in adjoining hotel rooms, usually in a segregated wing; they must eat all their meals together, go to the drugstore for toiletries together and travel together to and from court. In the Mitchell-Stans trial, all telephone calls [were] "monitored" and the jurors [were] allowed to visit with their families on weekends in a large room, with U.S. marshals present. At the Florida trial of the Gainesville Eight, a juror could be alone in his room with a visitor—so long as the door was open.

Whether all this strain on juror's minds and lives actually contributes to fairer trials is a matter of dispute among lawyers. "I don't know if it works 100 percent, but it helps," says Grant Cooper, who was chief defense counsel for Sirhan Sirhan, the killer of Sen. Robert Kennedy. But just whom it helps and how, they don't seem to know. "Sequestered jurors are bound to be unhappy," says Washington trial authority Ronald Goldfarb. "They can blame the defendant and say, 'Let's hang him and get it over with,' or they can blame the legal process and say, 'Screw the government.'" [*Newsweek* (March 18, 1974). Copyright Newsweek, Inc. 1974, reprinted by permission.]

Sentencing

In misdemeanor convictions, the lower court judge may set the length of sentence within the limitations prescribed by the penal code, most of which specify a maximum of one year in jail and/or a fine of $500.

Upon the defendant's conviction of a felony offense, the superior court judge sentences him for the term prescribed by statutory law. A reviewing body (generally appointed by the governor of the state) then sets the actual length of sentence.

The judge may suspend the sentence to state prison as prescribed by law and grant probation, setting forth conditions which may include a term in the county jail, a fine, or both. Violation of probation or nonpayment of a fine can result in incarceration in state prison in addition to any portion of the sentence served or probation passed up to the time of violation. In cases of suspended sentence, the defendant is free as long as he behaves himself. This is similar to probation in its effect on the person's freedom except that he may not be required to report to a probation officer. In deciding whether to suspend the sentence the judge may lean heavily on the information and recommendations from the probation officer who has studied the defendant's background (family history, marital situation, education, work record and so on).

Appeals

Either party to a criminal action may appeal the outcome of the case based on a question of law. The defendant may also appeal any judgment of conviction except one which is based on his plea of guilty. The right of the people to appeal the decision of the court usually stops (except for a question of law) once the trial has actually begun and the defendant has been placed in jeopardy. This, of course, goes back to our English Common Law heritage that a man shall not be twice placed in jeopardy for one charge.

Generally speaking, appeals from one court's decisions are heard in the next higher court; for example, an appeal from a municipal court decision will be heard in a superior court, one from a superior court will be heard in a district court of appeals, and so on. An appeal from the people in a criminal case does not cause the defendant to be placed back in custody until the appeal is heard. Conversely, an appeal by the defendant will not usually obtain his freedom pending its hearing.

Corrections

The role of the corrections phase of the criminal justice system has been covered extensively already. Little more needs to be said at this point other than to re-establish it as a final step in the process. The form of correctional activity may be probation or imprisonment. If the latter is the case, a *writ of habeas corpus* may be sought by the convicted defendant if he feels he is imprisoned illegally. If the judge reviewing his application agrees there is enough evidence to issue the writ, he may allow the person to be freed on bail until a hearing is held. The judge is not required, however, to free the person until the hearing.

If the convicted defendant is in state prison he automatically comes up for parole at a certain time. If granted, he then may elect to either serve his term or accept the parole. If the sentence is to the county jail, parole is not possible and the full time must be served.

Alternatives to the Basic Process

There are a number of alternatives which may take place to either abort the system or alter its course. Unsolved, undetected, or unreported crimes are examples of possibilities which would abort the process. Similarly, release without prosecution could occur at the time of arrest; following the application for complaint if the prosecutor fails to concur with the police position; at the preliminary hearing if the judge fails to agree with the district attorney and police; or at the superior court as the result of the pretrial hearing if the judge feels that something in the process to that point has been unlawful or that the evidence presented does not support the charge.

Citation in lieu of booking. In some states a citation can be issued for misdemeanor cases. Departmental policy determines which misdemeanors are subject to this treatment and crimes involving sex, theft, or moral turpitude are typical exclusions. When this alternative is used the person is arrested and taken to the station, but the normal booking process is usually not followed. Instead, a citation similar to a traffic ticket is issued and the arrested person is released from custody upon his written promise to appear in court at the time specified on the citation. The suspect must waive his right to be brought before a magistrate (which would normally be within two days), but this is seldom difficult to obtain. Most people would prefer to be free for the five or more day period prior to their appearance in court rather than sit in jail for up to two days under the normal procedure. A copy of the citation is presented to the magistrate or other officer authorized to set bail, and the amount of bail is set. This may be posted by the defendant prior to his appearance in court and, if he fails to appear at the promised time, the bail is forfeited. The judge may then order that no further proceedings be directed against the defendant. At the time a citation is issued, the arresting officer can indicate that he reserves the right to have the person booked at a later time. Unless he indicates this, there is no further need for the arrested person to appear on the matter.

The citation normally is used for minor misdemeanors which, in the opinion of the police, can be treated much the same as a traffic violation. This saves the time which would otherwise be required for booking and for the arrested person avoids the stigma of having a national file created on him. The process does provide for booking at a more convenient time if the police feel it is warranted and that the person can be relied upon to show up as promised. With the heavy load placed on most departments during peak incidence hours, this process is being used increasingly to speed the process of justice and free officers for field duty.

Arraignment without booking. This process is similar to the citation process and is usually used in minor misdemeanors and municipal code violations. For example, an officer may believe that a case can be made against an offender but not at the time of the investigation. Detectives may subsequently develop enough information to take an application for complaint to the prosecutor. If the prosecutor agrees he will ask the officer if he wants a warrant issued for the arrest of the person. In such cases the offense is often of such a nature that a warrant is not requested and the prosecutor simply writes a letter to the defendant advising him to appear for arraignment. No booking is made and no citation is issued, so no formal record of arrest is created. The judge in such instances usually handles the case in the same manner as any other petty offense, either dismissing the matter or accepting a plea of guilty and proceeding directly to sentencing. Bail is not usually involved since the initial appearance (where it would normally be set) is also the final one.

Own-recognizance release. Commonly called "O-R" release, this procedure is another alternative to the bail process.

Any judge or magistrate may, at his discretion, release a person instead of requiring him to post bail. The court may later rescind this order and require bail prior to trial if it decides to do so. O-R release is not a right, as such, but may be sought by any arrested person by applying to the court. Granting such release is the sole prerogative of the appropriate court. A person who is granted O-R release and fails to appear is guilty of a separate and additional felony or misdemeanor depending upon whether his original charge was a felony or a misdemeanor. Release of this type may be made after investigation by a staff person, but it is far more likely to be based on only the judge's impression of the person during the initial appearance, the individual's background, and the nature of the offense.

Plea bargaining. This concept was discussed earlier but it is an important enough part of our present criminal justice system to warrant additional comment. The reduction in charge thus accomplished may result from a simple, hurried meeting outside the courtroom or from a series of elaborate conferences between the prosecutor's staff and defense counsel. The agreement may be made because the prosecutor sincerely believes the lesser charge is the only one justified by the facts of the case or because the court has ten times as many cases as it can handle. In fact, the latter is probably the reason more often than the former. In either event, the charge is reduced in exchange for a plea of guilty from the defendant and the trial is avoided.

Depending upon the stage of the process where the bargain is reached, the arraignment, preliminary hearing, and pretrial hearing may also be avoided. Cost to taxpayers is thus reduced, time of the courts and the defendants is saved, and ability to have a speedy trial is provided to other defendants who would otherwise have to wait for court calendars to clear. Whether the process of justice is improved in terms of quality as well as time is a matter of frequent debate among the legal community. Some complain that the secret nature of the process can result in less attention being paid to the rights of the defendant than in a public trial. The quality of his legal counsel obviously has a great deal to do with the validity of this charge. Others express concern over the fact that in some jurisdictions the practice is officially unsanctioned and yet takes place daily. In such cases the parties to the process are forced to lie to the judge and state that no such bargain was made. The odious nature of this act is self-apparent. Other criticisms are directed at the over-efficiency of the process. A police commissioner of New York City once claimed that of 94,000 felony arrests made in one year by his officers, only 550 came to trial. The rest were either negotiated to sentence without trial or dismissed. Somewhere in this mass of plea-bargaining efficiency it's very likely that many people guilty of serious crimes get off with virtual wrist-slaps. Other people, quite possibly innocent, may have pleaded guilty to a reduced charge to avoid prolonged extension of the horrifying experience of being in jail. And this negative picture doesn't even consider the effect on police or injured citizens who see guilty persons getting off with minimum penalties for their acts. Because of these and other abuses in the process, the Supreme Court has asked that any plea bargaining be announced in court so the judge can either accept or reject the results of the bargaining effort.

Another similar form of negotiated justice practiced mainly in larger eastern cities with crowded court calendars is *sentence bargaining*. In this process the defendant is usually charged with multiple counts of the same or similar offenses and agrees to plead guilty to one count in exchange for dismissal of the others and an agreed-upon sentence. For example, a man may be charged with five counts of burglary. His attorney will offer a guilty plea on one count if the others are dropped and his client is promised "no state time." The prosecutor, feeling he probably couldn't get five convictions anyway, may agree to seek a maximum sentence of one year in county jail instead of state prison. The man then pleads guilty to the felony charge but serves his time in jail, rather than prison, or may even get probation. As with regular plea bargaining, the state is saved the time and expense of a court trial, but the quality of justice is open to question.

Diversion. A relatively new alternative which can occur at the preliminary hearing in municipal court or the arraignment in superior court, diversion in effect is similar to probation except that the defendant has not been found guilty at the time of his conditional release. This process, usually used in cases of narcotics or alcoholic addiction, provides for the defendant to submit himself to treatment and counselling as the condition of his temporary release. The case against the defendant is not considered terminated during diversion but rather is suspended until the outcome of treatment and counselling is assessed by the court. If at any time during diversion the subject fails to comply with the provisions of his release or it becomes obvious that the diversion is not going to be successful, he re-enters the criminal justice process at the point he left it. Not all states have provision for the diversion process and results in those which do are not yet conclusive.

An Alternative to Prison

Under the (Minnesota) program, convicts sentenced for nonviolent property crimes live in a halfway house, take jobs and use part of their earnings to repay what they stole. Says Ron Johnson, supervisor of the Minnesota Restitution Center: "It's one thing to break into a garage. It's another to have to look the owner in the eye afterward. We're building a sense of responsibility."

Started 21 months ago, the program has so far handled 58 felons chosen at random from convicted thieves, forgers and the like in Minnesota prisons. The victim and the convict must work out a written contract. . . .

Once an agreement is made, the parole board releases the prisoner to the halfway house. . . . Counselors help find a job, and initially there is an 11 p.m. curfew. Group therapy sessions twice a week continue for the first six months. Though the debt is sometimes quickly paid off, the inmates must stay in the program until they are fully released from parole.

The convicts are enthusiastic. "I would have spent 18 months in the reformatory," says Steve Norlund, who has been working off $417 in forged checks by assembling freezers. "I know I'll be going back if I screw up. This makes a lot more sense." Speaking for the eleven-member staff, Johnson adds: "When I was a parole agent, I would see my guys maybe once a month. Here we have daily contact." As for the victim, Garage Owner Carl Brown notes, "It's no further risk to me. He's making the payments. Maybe this will straighten him out."

Of course, it does not always work that way; authorities claim only a "modest success" so far. Of the 58 "clients" as they are called, 18 have either disappeared, committed new crimes or bent the rules sufficiently to be sent back to prison. . . . The program will now try to improve results by dropping random selection. Meanwhile, there is special pride in the thief who last month became the center's first graduate. Now completely on his own, he is working full-time as a truck driver. [*Time* (June 3, 1974), Reprinted by permission from TIME, The Weekly Newsmagazine; Copyright Time, Inc.]

Probation subsidy. This experimental program is aimed at rehabilitation of convicted felony offenders. Under this program the person who has been sentenced to state prison, but is considered by the court to be "rehabilitable," is placed on probation rather than parole. Part of his probation may be a term in county jail, but essentially he is considered to be taking part in a community rehabilitation program in the county where he lives. Since the cost of this program must be borne by the county rather than the state, as would be the case if he were serving his prison sentence, the state makes a financial allotment to the county to defray the expense. So far the results of probation subsidy have been unsatisfactory. Community rehabilitation turns into little more than a periodic visit to a probation officer. County probation staffs have been drastically enlarged to handle the increased load and still the net result has largely been to simply return the convicted criminal to the street. Since rehabilitation is generally ineffective, probation subsidy seems unlikely to survive unless new concepts are devised for improving the quality of the basic effort.

Dismissal. Charges may be dismissed in four places during the criminal justice process. Dismissal may occur at the initial appearance, the preliminary hearing, superior court arraignment, or the pretrial hearing. In some instances charges may be refiled by the prosecuting attorney or a people's appeal may be filed. In fact, however, dismissal of charges almost always means just that: termination of the case.

Procedures for Misdemeanor Cases

In addition to the possibility of a summary trial, where a petty offense may be dealt with at the initial appearance, the basic process for a misdemeanor differs in a few other ways from the basic process for a felony.

For one, since there usually is no preliminary hearing, diversion is only possible at the initial arraignment in municipal court. For another, the charge against the defendant is almost always brought through application for complaint and information rather than indictment (since grand juries seldom are involved in misdemeanors). Plea bargaining is involved in misdemeanors less often than in felonies since many misdemeanor cases are already less serious in nature.

Citation in lieu of booking and arraignment without booking are, of course, only possible in misdemeanor cases. Release on O-R, though possible in felony cases, is mostly confined to misdemeanors in practice.

THE JUVENILE JUSTICE PROCESS

More than in the adult criminal justice process, the juvenile justice process varies in detail between jurisdictions. The age of juveniles is not even universally agreed upon; in thirty-three states (and the District of Columbia) juveniles are classed as those 17 and under, while in twelve states they are those 16 and under and in six states those 15 and under. Procedures within a given county are often not uniform except in the most general comparisons. Thus, the procedure depicted in Figure 4-2 presents the essential steps which usually are taken to design individualized treatment for the young person in trouble.

Looking at the individual steps we can see that the first three may be the same as in the adult process—crime, investigation, and arrest. In actuality, these three steps may not exist at all, and the beginning of the process may be a nonpolice referral from sources such as the parents of the juvenile, his school administration, or another agency (such as welfare). In other words there may not be a crime involved at all. The reason for referral may be simply a lack of ability to control the behavior of the juvenile or even the fact that his environment is such that his well-being is endangered. The result may be the same, however, and the juvenile may be made a ward of the court, as if commission of a crime were the reason for his entry into the system. Thus, he may be institutionalized whether he committed a crime or not, although the type of institution to which he is committed may be different. The number of juveniles in institutions for delinquent behavior, however, is about fifty times greater than the number who are there because of their dependent or neglected status. Probably the saddest of the many problems that plague our institutional system for juveniles is the fact that 2 percent of those in it are guilty of no crime other than having parents who are unable or unwilling to care for them, and they are often put into the same hopper with young people working their way into the adult criminal justice system. Many authorities in juvenile corrections believe that incarceration generally does no good and, in fact, does more harm than good. They claim it is not proving to be effective in combating the problem of juvenile delinquency. True or not, there is sometimes no choice but incarceration to protect the community or the juvenile himself.

110 THE PROCESS OF CRIMINAL JUSTICE

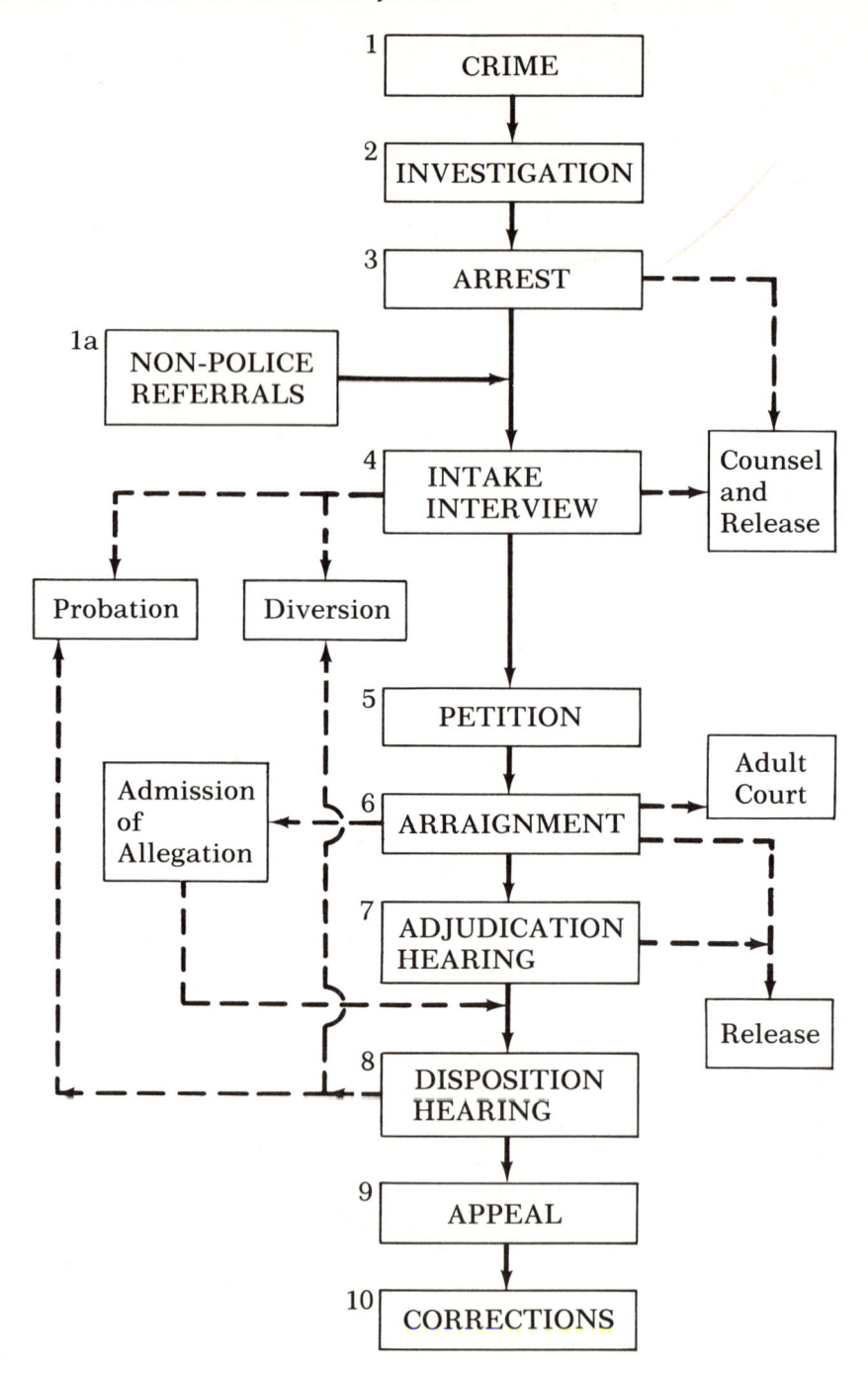

Figure 4-2. JUVENILE JUSTICE PROCESS

The basic steps we're going to look at here are those which would be followed if a crime were committed. As with the adult process, we'll discuss each step briefly in terms of what normally takes place and then look at the alternatives which may occur. We will skip the first three, which as pointed out may not occur at all, and begin with the point where the process first noticeably differs from the adult process.

The Intake Interview

This is the initial interview conducted by someone other than a police officer. Although much of the same ground may have already been covered by the police juvenile officer, this step is usually conducted by a member of the probation department (in some smaller communities it may be a judge) to examine the facts leading to the commission of the crime and the background of the juvenile.

The interviewer decides if court action is required or whether some nonadjudicatory disposition is more appropriate. In most cases the child is either counselled and released to his parents or diverted to some outside agency for counselling and/or treatment. In many other cases, the youngster may already be on probation and the new offense will simply be added to his record unless it is serious enough to warrant new attention by the courts. For example, a simple curfew violation by a juvenile on probation would probably be added to his record and his probation continued. Participation in a felony, however, would usually cause him to enter the court system.

If the decision is to take the matter to court, a *petition* is prepared instead of the complaint application used in adult cases. If the police and the intake interviewer agree that the child should remain in custody, rather than be released to his parents, the petition will request this and a *detention hearing* will be conducted by the court before the process goes any further. In the vast majority of cases, however, the juvenile is released to his parents.

Arraignment

This step is equivalent to the initial appearance or arraignment in adult cases and includes elements of the preliminary hearing. Here the juvenile is advised of the charges against him, interviewed by the judge, and has his first opportunity to admit to the allegation (equivalent to a guilty plea). If an admission is made, the judge will make *disposition* (equivalent to the sentence) at this point, just as he might pass sentence during the initial appearance on petty misdemeanors in adult cases. Bail, set at this point for adults, is seldom involved for juveniles who are usually released to their parents pending court appearance. In exceptional cases, such as homicide, the question of whether the offender is fit for juvenile proceedings or must be tried as an adult will also be decided here.

Adjudication Hearing

This step is equivalent to the trial in an adult case. Usually without counsel for either side, the nonadversary hearing is conducted in private with only the judge, probation officer, the juvenile, and his parents present. While there is never a jury, some states do allow defense counsel and a public defender may be appointed.

The judge decides if the facts support the allegation, but the juvenile is not on trial. Rather, the hearing is to determine the truth of the matter and to prepare the judge for designing

The adjudication hearing for the juvenile offender is conducted in private with only the judge, probation officer, the juvenile, and his parents present; usually, as here, there is no counsel for either side.

a corrective program which will hopefully match the needs of the case.

Disposition Hearing

This is the equivalent of the sentencing step in the adult process. The disposition may be a term of probation (with or without a treatment program) or custody in any of several types of institutions. In either event the juvenile becomes an *adjudicated delinquent* at this point. In many states the judge has the option of committing the juvenile for the specific crime with which he is charged, or merely as a person (or child) in need of supervision, unruly, unmanageable, or incorrigible. This is a further reflection of the fact that every effort is made to treat the young offender as a person with a behavior problem rather than a criminal.

There is an appellate process available to convicted juveniles at this point, just as there is to adults.

Corrections

The corrections phase of the juvenile justice system takes the form of probation more often than not. As with an adult probationer, the juvenile is required to maintain contact with his probation officer and refrain from violating the terms of his probation. Failure to behave, as with an adult, can lead to his incarceration in any of a number of different types of institutions.

The initial phase of any juvenile's incarceration, regardless of the reason for his being there, usually takes place in a *detention center* or a *shelter*. After adjudication he may be committed to a central juvenile correctional authority for subsequent, temporary assignment to a *reception center* or a *diagnostic center*. Usually none of these four types of temporary-custody institutions have full-fledged correctional capabilities. Often they don't even have any education program. They merely maintain custody of the juvenile until his disposition hearing. Males and females are often housed in the same facility for from two weeks to two months.

The detention center is the juvenile equivalent of the county jail for adults. They are relatively small and are administered by local government rather than the state. Shelters are also usually administered locally but are less physically-restrictive than detention centers. They usually have some child welfare services but house suspected delinquents as well as dependent and neglected children. There are private and public welfare agencies which are also used to perform this function in some cases, but the public shelter gets most juveniles at this stage of the process. Dependent and neglected children usually progress from the shelter to public or private foster care agencies. In most cases, adjudicated delinquents begin in diagnostic or reception centers which are operated on a state level. From such centers the delinquent normally is assigned to a *correctional facility* for treatment and reformation.

Correctional facilities may be *training schools,* rural facilities providing work programs such as forestry camps, farms, or ranches, or *urban group centers* such as halfway houses. Training schools are the most common and, accordingly, are the largest. They're also the most physically restrictive, usually providing relatively high security and isolation from the community. Obviously, juveniles whose behavior presents a more serious problem end up in such institutions. The rural facilities have a much greater degree of freedom for inmates and offer more contact with local communities. The halfway houses or group homes are the least physically restrictive. Usually located in residential neighborhoods these institutions are most often converted private residences. Inmates generally leave daily to attend regular schools or work at normal jobs. Individual and group counselling are often available at this level of detention.

Parole is a possibility in the juvenile system just as in the adult. Similarly, violation of parole provisions can result in return to the institutional facility for continued detention.

Alternatives to the Basic Process

Most of the alternatives available in the adult process are also available to the juvenile. Parole and probation have already been discussed as alternatives. Diversion is a common alternative with the juvenile being channelled into public or private agencies for counselling or treatment as the result of the intake interview, the arraignment, the adjudication hearing, or even the disposition hearing. Counselling and release to parents is the most common alternative used with juveniles. In fact, as noted several times, this represents the basic thrust of the system. The counselling may be performed by the juvenile officer at the police department, the probation officer at the intake hearing, the judge, or any of the agencies used in the diversion process.

Some adult system alternatives don't apply to juveniles. For example, O-R release doesn't because there is usually no bail involved and a juvenile obviously can't be released to himself. Plea bargaining is not used in the juvenile process since there are no felony or misdemeanor charges (only allegations made in a civil, rather than criminal manner).

SUMMARY

The first step in the basic adult process, whether for a felony or misdemeanor, is the commission of a crime.

Investigation, the second step, may continue throughout the administration of the process, but it aims primarily at identification of the persons responsible for the crime.

Arrest takes place when the peace officer has sufficient reason to believe that a particular person has committed the crime and is able to physically apprehend that person.

Booking is the creation of a formal administrative record of the arrest. Bail may first be set at this point.

Application for complaint is made by the arresting officer to seek the court's examination of the case against the arrested person. An indictment may be sought at this point if desirable. Concurrence of the prosecuting attorney is necessary if the process is to continue.

The *initial appearance* of the arrested person takes place in municipal or justice court for the purpose of advising the person of the charges against him, advising him of his rights, and setting bail. For minor misdemeanors a *summary trial* takes place at this point, and the case is either dismissed or sentence is passed.

The *preliminary hearing* provides a test of the evidence against the defendant in municipal or justice court. The case is either dismissed or the defendant is bound-over for trial in superior court.

An *information* or *indictment* is filed against the defendant to form the basis of the people's case. An information is filed by the prosecutor in concurrence with the police application for complaint. An indictment is returned by the grand jury.

Arraignment in superior court allows the defendant to make his plea of guilty or innocent, choose between a court or jury trial, and obtain a public defender if he qualifies for one.

A *pretrial hearing* may be ordered by a judge to examine some question about the strength of the people's case (usually on the grounds of the manner in which it has been conducted up to this point).

Trial is for the purpose of establishing guilt or innocence of the defendant. The defendant can choose to have either a trial by jury or by the judge alone, a *court trial.*

Sentencing establishes the nature of the penalty to be paid by the convicted defendant and may yield a suspended sentence, probation, fine, imprisonment, or a combination of these.

Appeals are available to either party in the criminal action. The people's right of appeal is limited to questions of law once the trial has begun and the defendant placed in jeopardy.

Corrections carries out the terms of the sentence as the final step in the basic criminal justice process.

Alternatives to the basic process include *release without prosecution; citation in lieu of booking,* in effect, issuance of a ticket for a minor, wrongful act; *arraignment without booking,* to allow prosecution of the case without creation of a record for the offender; *own-recognizance release,* release without bail upon promise to appear for the initial hearing; *plea bargaining,* reduction of the charge to a lesser offense in exchange for a plea of guilty; *diversion,* channelling the defendant into a treatment and counselling program rather than continuing with the formal justice process; *dismissal* of charges against the defendant; and *probation subsidy,* release on probation of persons sentenced to state prison.

Misdemeanor cases usually are not heard by grand juries nor are they arraigned in superior court. They also don't have a preliminary hearing. O-R release is more common in misdemeanor than felony cases. Citation in lieu of booking and arraignment without booking are possible only in misdemeanor cases.

The *juvenile justice process* may begin with a crime or with a nonpolice referral.

The *intake interview* begins the juvenile process following either arrest or nonpolice referral. The interview is conducted by either a probation officer or a judge to determine the need for court action.

A *detention hearing* is held if the probation officer requests that the juvenile be detained prior to court proceedings.

Arraignment is held for juveniles to provide the same function as the initial appearance for adult offenders—charges are explained and an admission of them may be made by the offender.

The *adjudication hearing* takes the place of the trial. The juvenile is not on trial in this nonadversary proceeding, although he may in some states be represented by counsel.

The *disposition hearing* is equivalent to an adult's sentencing procedure. An appeal may be made from the results of this hearing which attempts to design a corrective program for the juvenile.

Correctional institutions include *detention centers* or *shelters* at the local level (initial detention of all juveniles pending court hearings) and *reception centers* or *diagnostic centers* at the state level for detention of adjudicated delinquents. Custodial correctional facilities may be *training schools, rural work programs,* or *urban group centers.*

Probation is the most common correctional program for juveniles; *parole* is a possibility from any detentional facility.

Counselling and release to parents is the most common alternative to the steps of the juvenile justice process. *Diversion* into a treatment and counselling agency is the next most common alternative. O-R release and plea bargaining do not occur.

REVIEW QUESTIONS

Answers to these questions appear on page 383.

1. *True or false?* The first three steps in the justice process may be the same whether the cause for the process is an adult misdemeanor or felony or a juvenile offense.
2. The first formal administrative record of the arrest is made at the _____ step.
3. *True or false?* The application for complaint is usually prepared by the prosecutor's office.
4. At what step in the adult process for misdemeanors may the summary trial be held? _____
5. In what type of court is a preliminary hearing held? _____
   _____
6. If the judge feels there is enough evidence to warrant taking the defendant to trial on felony charges, what action will he take at the preliminary hearing? _____
   _____
7. At what step in the process does the defendant choose between a court trial and a jury trial? _____
8. If the judge feels there may be something questionable about the way the state's case has been developed, he may explore it at a _____ .
9. Which of the following alternatives is/are designed to allow a person to go free without posting bail?

a. citation in lieu of booking
b. arraignment without booking
c. O-R release
d. plea bargaining
e. probation subsidy
10. The process of reducing a charge from a felony to a misdemeanor in exchange for a plea of guilty to the lesser charge is called _____.
11. The alternative process where a person may be released upon his written promise to appear in court, with the police retaining control over whether or not booking is to be made, is called _____.
12. Channeling a defendant into a treatment program as a possible alternative to further prosecution in the criminal justice process is known as _____.
13. An experimental program which provides for participation in a community rehabilitation plan with the state reimbursing the county for the costs of administering the program is called _____.
14. What is the first step in the juvenile justice process following either the arrest or the nonpolice referral? _____
15. In the blank spaces provided write the equivalent term from the juvenile justice process for the adult process step described.

Adult	Juvenile
a. Initial appearance or arraignment	_____
b. Application for complaint	_____
c. Trial	_____
d. Sentencing	_____

16. What is the most common correctional action taken for juveniles? _____
17. The most commonly used alternative to the full juvenile justice process is _____.
18. Which type of juvenile correctional facility offers:
a. highest security? _____
b. least physical restriction or activity limitation? _____
c. reduced physical restriction plus controlled work programs? _____

PART 3

Organization and Operation of Law Enforcement Agencies

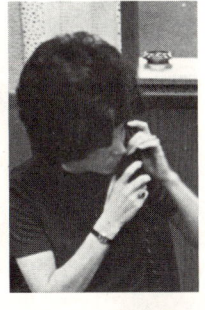

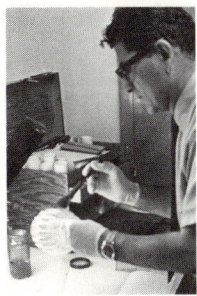

CHAPTER 5

THE AGENCIES

OVERVIEW

If you tell someone you're going into law enforcement, the chances are they will picture you in a black-and-white car patrolling the streets. And maybe that's exactly what you have in mind. Your choice, of course, is far from being such a narrow one even though most people do enter the profession this way.

Thousands of men and women spend their entire working lives in law enforcement without ever being involved in street police work. This chapter is intended to give you a total picture of what is done by and what life is like in city, county, state, and federal agencies of the criminal justice system. To complete the picture we'll also look at private agencies. After reading this chapter you should have a good idea of the range of opportunities available and the duties and challenges afforded by each. The need for qualified people in all levels of law enforcement should be obvious from even a casual reading of the daily paper. The opportunities for capable men and women have never been greater.

MUNICIPAL POLICE DEPARTMENTS AND SHERIFFS' OFFICES

Much of this book is devoted to explaining the organization and operation of police and sheriff's departments, the agencies most people think of when law enforcement is mentioned. Thus, here we will discuss them in terms of their relationships to other agencies in the criminal justice system and examine the life style of each.

Municipal police, as you know, are responsible for enforcing the laws of the city and state within the geographical confines of a particular city. A police officer, however, is a sworn *peace officer* of the state and as such has authority anywhere in the state. As a matter of fact, that authority can even be extended beyond the borders of the state if the officer is engaged in "fresh pursuit" of a person who has committed a felony. The restriction of his activity to the city which employs him is really just a matter of practical limitation of responsibility.

Sheriff's offices, of course, have county limits rather than city boundaries to define their area of responsibility. While their principal responsibility is in the unincorporated areas of the county, they also have jurisdictional rights in the various cities within the county. As a matter of practice they usually leave the cities to the municipal departments in those cities which have them.

Many sheriff's offices provide police service under contract to cities which don't have their own municipal departments. Under this plan, the city contracts for a specific number of patrol units which operate out of the nearest substation but confine their patrol solely to the contracting city. Certain specialized services, such as helicopter patrol, can also be provided under contract to local police departments which don't have their own equipment. If local departments have need of extra power, as in riot control, they can call on the sheriff's department for the needed men. While some sheriff's offices have only custodial duties and others have civil divisions and serve civil processes, the majority provide full-service police functions as described here.

In addition to the normal police functions, most sheriff's departments also provide bailiffs for courts within the county, maintain the county jail facilities, transport and deliver prisoners to court and prison and, in general, perform all law enforcement duties on behalf of the county. As with any agency whose officers are sworn peace officers, sheriff's deputies have authority statewide as well as within the county for which they work.

The primary codes enforced by police and sheriff's departments are, of course, the penal and vehicle codes. They can and often do enforce other codes (such as welfare and institutional codes and even business and professional codes) unless the problem is a civil one. In civil disputes, such as landlord-tenant disputes, family disputes, and disputes between customers and merchants, their primary duty is to keep the peace and prevent escalation of the dispute into a violation of a penal code provision. Local police departments also enforce the provisions of the municipal code within their city.

Life As A Street Cop

Since they provide law on the street, the "clientele" dealt with by the police officer or deputy sheriff is the broadest of any agency. In contrast with an agency which, for example, concentrates almost exclusively on traffic violation (such as the highway patrol) a policeman or deputy is going to see a lot of the lower echelons of society. They get the dopers, child beaters, drunks, suicides, and perverts that most people only know about through news stories. The situations they deal with daily are often not pleasant, and those with faint hearts or weak stomachs are apt to be shocked at least once during any evening's ride with the average officer. Surprisingly, however, sensitivity and compassion are not rare qualities in street policemen. This isn't to say that there are no brutal or sadistic policemen or that "contempt-of-cop" arrests don't occur. But the plain fact is that there's enough real business to make it unnecessary for most policemen to go out of their way to find trouble. Also, they see enough mistreated victims to realize how much suffering one person's action can inflict on another.

While we're dealing with the cold facts of life as a police officer, and before we get into the more technical aspects of it, let's examine the experiences of George Kirkham, a professor of criminology at Florida State University. As recounted in the *FBI Law Enforcement Bulletin,* March 1974, his six-month tour of duty as a patrolman gave him an insight into life on the streets he had never dreamed of as a professor of criminology or as a corrections worker dealing with convicted felons.

> I had always personally been of the opinion that police officers greatly exaggerate the amount of verbal disrespect and physical abuse to which they are subjected in the line of duty . . . as a college professor, I had grown accustomed to being treated with uniform respect and deference. I somehow naively assumed that this same quality of respect would carry over into my

new role as a policeman. I was, after all, a representative of the law, identifiable to all by the badge and uniform I wore as someone dedicated to the protection of society. I quickly found that my badge and uniform, rather than serving to shield me from such things as disrespect and violence, only acted as a magnet which drew me toward many individuals who hated what I represented.

After completing his academy training, Dr. Kirkham's first night of duty brought him into contact with a "large and boisterous drunk" in a downtown bar, arguing with the bartender and refusing to leave. "Excuse me, Sir," Dr.-Officer Kirkham opened smilingly, calling on his considerable experience as a correctional counsellor and mental health worker, "but I wonder if I could ask you to step outside and talk with me for just a minute?" What he got in return was a disbelieving stare and then a round-house swing to start a battle that ultimately cost him a perfectly good uniform shirt and several illusions. Reviewing that and other experiences in the following weeks, Dr. Kirkham later recalled that:

> As a university professor, I had always sought to convey to students that it is a mistake to exercise authority, to make decisions for other people, or rely upon orders and commands to accomplish something. As a police officer myself, I was forced time and again to do just that. For the first time in my life, I encountered individuals who interpreted kindness as weakness, as an invitation to disrespect or violence . . . I found that there was a world of difference between encountering individuals, as I had, in mental health or correctional settings and facing them as the patrolman must: when they are violent, hysterical, desperate . . . as a police officer, I began to encounter the offender for the first time as a very real menace to my personal safety and security of our society.

Dr. Kirkham recalls an incident illustrative of the fear that every policeman comes to know periodically. Pulling alongside a car double-parked in the middle of the street, he asked the young male driver to either park or move on. The driver loudly cursed the officers, drawing a hostile, Saturday-night crowd which he exhorted to help protect him from police harassment. With no way to back down from their responsibility to enforce the law, the man's continued cursing and refusal to move his car left the officers no alternative but to arrest him. As they moved to do so the crowd closed on them, one woman unstrapping Kirkham's revolver and attempting to draw it. "Suddenly," he relates, "I was no longer an ivory-tower scholar watching typical police 'overreaction' to a street incident . . . I was a part of it and fighting to remain alive and uninjured. I remember the sickening sensation of cold terror which filled my insides as I struggled to reach our car radio. I simultaneously put out a distress call and pressed the hidden electric release button on our shotgun rack as my partner sought to maintain his grip on the prisoner and hold the crowd at bay with his revolver." Reflecting later on this experience, Dr. Kirkham wrote,

> How harshly I would have judged (only a few months before) the officer who now grabbed the shotgun . . . I had always argued that policemen should not be allowed to carry shotguns because of their "offensive" character and the potential damage to community relations as a result of their display. How readily as a criminology professor I would have condemned the officer who was now myself, trembling with fear and anxiety and menacing an "unarmed" assembly with an "offensive" weapon . . . but now it was *my* life and safety that were in danger, *my* wife and child who might be mourning. Not "a policeman" or Patrolman Smith, but *me* . . . I felt accordingly bitter when I saw the individual who had provoked this near riot back on the streets the next night, laughing as though our charge of "resisting arrest with violence" was a big joke . . . I found myself feeling angry and frustrated a short time afterward when this same individual was allowed to plead guilty to a reduced charge of "breach of peace."

A person who was raised in a comfortable, middle-class home insulated from the kind of human misery police see daily, Dr. Kirkham found that,

> the often terrible sights, sounds, and smells of my job began to haunt me hours after I had taken the blue uniform and badge off. Some nights I would lie in bed unable to sleep, trying desperately to forget the things I had seen during a particular tour of duty: the rat-infested shacks that serve as homes to those far less fortunate than I; a teenage boy dying in my arms after being struck by a car; small children clad in rags, with stomachs bloated from hunger, playing in a urine-spattered hall; the victim of a robbery senselessly beaten and murdered.

An important truth which we all know but tend to overlook was stated very well by the professor in reviewing his total experience.

> As a criminology professor, I had always enjoyed the luxury of having great amounts of time in which to make difficult deci-

sions. As a police officer, however, I found myself forced to make the most critical choices in a time frame of seconds, rather than days: to shoot or not to shoot; to arrest or not to arrest; to give chase or let go . . . always with the nagging certainty that others, those with great amounts of time in which to analyze and think, stood ready to judge and condemn me for whatever action I might take or fail to take.

Dr. Kirkham recommends his experience to others in the broad field of law enforcement, particularly parole officers and prison counsellors who could, ". . . see their client Jones—not calm and composed in an office setting, but as the street cop sees him—beating his small child with a heavy belt buckle, or kicking his pregnant wife." He further wishes that every judge or juror could see "the ravages of crime as the cop on the beat must: innocent people cut, shot, beaten, raped, robbed, and murdered." He feels, and he must be right, that it would give them a different perspective on crime and criminals. And, as a result of his experiences, Kirkham's esteem of police officers grew:

> In spite of all the human misery and suffering which police officers must witness in their work, I found myself amazed at the incredible humanity and compassion which seems to characterize most of them, a young patrolman giving mouth to mouth resuscitation to a filthy derelict; an officer giving money out of his own pocket to a hungry and stranded family he would probably never see again; another taking the trouble to drop by on his own time to give worried parents information about their problem son or daughter.

He also expresses surprise that the often enormous daily pressures of their work—long hours, frustration, danger, and anxiety—are seemingly taken in stride by most officers. In his own case, though he had always lectured on the importance of "keeping one's cool" (and prided himself on his own ability in this regard), he found himself unable to do so on at least one occasion. Coming off a long, hard shift which ended in a high-speed chase of a stolen car at great personal risk to him and his partner, the pair was headed for breakfast at a local restaurant when they heard the sound of breaking glass coming from a church.

> Spotting two long-haired teenage boys running from the area we confronted them and I asked one for identification, displaying my own police identification. He sneered at me, cursed, and

turned to walk away. The next thing I knew I had grabbed the youth by his shirt and spun him around, shouting, "I'm talking to you, punk!" I felt my partner's arm on my shoulder and heard his reassuring voice behind me, "Take it easy, Doc!" I released my grip on the adolescent and stood silently for several seconds, unable to accept the inescapable reality that I had "lost my cool." My mind flashed back to a lecture during which I had told my students, *"Any man who is not able to maintain absolute control of his emotions at all times has no business being a police officer."* . . . now here I was, an "emotional control" expert, being told to calm down by a patrolman!

On the complexity of the challenge of being a police officer Dr. Kirkham summarized that while he had always considered policemen as sort of paranoid, he found that suspiciousness is actually something a good policeman cultivates "in the interest of going home to his family each evening." He found that he was carrying an off-duty weapon himself and being watchful of who and what was around him at all times. Open doors, persons loitering on darkened corners, dirt-covered, rear license plates all took on new significance to him as his experience as a street cop grew. Even his personality changed (according to his friends), and he now feels that maybe society demands too much of policemen. Not only must they enforce the law but also function in the paramedical, psychological counselling, and social science fields. A good deal of this collateral responsibility is unavoidable, as pointed out earlier in this book. There's simply often nobody else around at the time an emergency arises and must be dealt with. "No one else wants to counsel a family with problems at 3 A.M. on Sunday; no one else wants to enter a darkened building after a burglary; no one else wants to confront a robber or madman with a gun. No one else wants to stare poverty, mental illness, and human tragedy in the face day after day, to pick up the pieces of shattered lives."

In answer to his own question, "Why does a man become a cop?" Dr. Kirkham concludes, "Night after night, I came home and took off the badge and blue uniform with a sense of satisfaction and contribution to society that I have never known in any other job. Somehow that feeling seemed to make everything—the disrespect, the danger, the boredom—worthwhile."

The above recounting of one man's experiences during six months as a police officer should give the reader a better emotional insight into what it's like to be a cop. The relatively short period of time involved doesn't take us into some of the other problems that develop from repeated application of the same experiences over a protracted period of time. The high divorce rate among police, for example, probably arises in part from the anxieties connected with the job, and the higher-than-average alcoholism rate is also probably related to the anxiety level the job creates. But, since most of the real surprises on any job are likely to be encountered during the first six months, what happens in this period probably closely reflects what a new officer may find on the job during his probationary period. In any event, the experiences are interesting and worth putting into the hopper, so to speak, when thinking about your career choice.

Some of the more mundane, but still real-life, considerations one should make in choosing a career are considered below. The need to move one's residence, for example, occurs least frequently in a municipal or sheriff's department. Some agencies require an officer to live within the geographical confines of the area he serves, but this is a diminishing requirement. Even if the agency you consider does have such a requirement, you'll know about it ahead of time and only one move would probably be required during your career. In some state or federal agencies more frequent moves may be required as transfers occur during a person's career.

Assigned territories are usually smaller in municipal or county agencies, giving the officer an opportunity to become involved in the community he serves. Out-of-town travel, a romantic concept to most young, single people (but less attractive as a person acquires a family) is minimal in this type of service. A detective may have to travel to another jurisdiction to transport a prisoner, but this is fairly infrequent in any but the largest city departments.

Promotional opportunity is broader than one might think in even the relatively small (under 100 officers) departments. While it still takes at least a couple of years to make supervisor in even a growing city, there are many specialist possibilities such as motor officer or detective offering opportunity for growth in both experience and pay. These are explored in the next chapter.

Educational requirements are generally lower in local agencies with the most common being a high school diploma or equivalent. Some police departments require two or four year college degrees, but most rely on careful evaluation of each applicant rather than stereotyped impressions of the value of formal academic achievement. Training after hiring is increasing in most agencies, largely through state-mandated programs. While most agencies look favorably upon applicants who have evidenced a continuing interest in police work by pursuing an academic career in police science, they still rely most heavily on their own careful selection of applicants and specific training provided by a curriculum of their own choice (for example, an academy selected by the department).

It's almost impossible to make any definitive statement about pay scale in various agencies because there are so many different ones involved. Besides, with the fluctuating economy of today, any dollar figure we put down may look ridiculous by the time this book gets into print. Pay is important, as anyone knows, but it's not the most important consideration in a career, as anyone who's been around a few years comes to know. One must have enough money to take care of his needs in relative comfort, but beyond that, no amount of money is going to make a hateful job tolerable, let alone satisfying as a career. Police salaries once were at the low end of the scale when compared with general industry. This is no longer true and in most areas policemen are able to live in better-than-average homes and drive better-than-average cars. Part of this is due to the increasing professionalism of policework, part to the increasing awareness of communities that their needs are best met by people who are capable of earning better-than-average salaries, and part to the fact that most agencies require recruits to be able to successfully manage their own financial affairs before they hire them. In any event, the dollar amount of a salary is only relevant to the community in which it is paid, and the interested applicant is advised to query the agencies in which he is interested to determine if the salary opportunities are adequate to meet his needs.

STATE AGENCIES

For each of the allied agencies in law enforcement, we will discuss the terms of responsibility for enforcement of various codes, demands on officers' physical, intellectual, and emotional capabilities, type of clientele dealt with, and any other factors which might normally be expected to affect a person's choice of careers. We'll begin with the agency which is most similar to those with street-policing functions and then cover other state agencies.

State Police

The state police function varies considerably from state to state but some generalizations can be drawn. In a few states, for example, state police officers live in barracks. Such institutionalized living is unattractive to many people, of course, and this accounts for its infrequency. In some states the agencies exercise broad police powers throughout the state, acting in effect as the "super-police" authority on virtually all matters, while in about one-fourth of the states, state police authority is limited to motor vehicle regulation. More typical, however, is the structure followed in California.

The California State Police Division employs some 300 persons in three zones which are in turn divided into twenty areas. The agency is charged with enforcing government, penal, and health and safety codes on state property (such as state buildings, state parks, and state university grounds). Approximately 90 percent of personnel are directly involved in field operations, with the balance in support functions. All positions are open to both men and women and are covered by the Civil Service Act. Of the various allied agencies, state police work most nearly matches municipal or county work in terms of types of cases handled and clientele dealt with. The problems of inner city police work, however, are not encountered.

State police officers, as you might expect, are sworn peace officers of the state with full powers of arrest. Very little out-of-town travel is required by this position, similar to but slightly less than a municipal or county officer. Geographical relocation to another part of the state is possible upon request and may also be required by promotion. Assigned territories vary greatly in size, from one block to as much as forty square miles, depending upon the nature of the assignment.

Many specialist positions, such as aircraft pilot, are available on the basis of qualifications rather than length of service; most persons who advance to line supervision as sergeants do so within five years. Entrance requirements are similar to most regular police agencies: high school or equivalent, 18 to 40 years of age, in good health with normal hearing and vision (20/70 correctable to 20/30), at least 5'7" tall with proportionate weight, and the ability to pass an agility test. Successful candidates are given nine weeks of academy training during which they live at the academy and receive regular pay. Pay is approximately the same as for most police departments or sheriff's offices in the state.

An increasing number of state, county, and local agencies furnish weapons for their members. There are a number of reasons for this including both consideration for the officer and the desirability of uniform weaponry throughout the department for interchangeability of ammunition. In California a court decision has held that if the employer is required to furnish "safety equipment" (such as hard hats) for his employees, a police officer should be furnished with a gun for his protection. This extension of the safety equipment principle includes other items such as the officer's baton (nightstick, or "billy" if you prefer). Uniforms, however, are furnished by the officers themselves, and the department provides an annual uniform allowance which usually covers the cost of one new uniform (about $150).

Information on openings and specific requirements for state police positions are available through the state personnel board in the capital of each state and often through local offices in major cities.

Highway Patrol

The highway patrol is usually one of the largest law enforcement agencies in any state, exceeded in size by only the largest city and county forces. Only the most populous states have any single agency larger than their highway patrol.

The primary responsibility of a highway patrol agency is the enforcement of the vehicle code of the state. In addition, however, they handle violations of penal, health and safety, streets and highway, and welfare and institutions codes. In the rural areas, where a sheriff or highway patrol officer may have up to a hundred square miles of territory to cover, each may cover for the other incidents which demand immediate attention. Thus, a highway patrol officer may carry out the preliminary investigation of a homicide, for example, until a deputy sheriff can reach the scene. In general the highway patrol deals mostly with traffic collisions, drinking drivers, auto theft, and attendant problems. Investigations take from two to three hours and, quite different from those of regular police departments, are usually handled to conclusion before another is begun. Thus, the case load, a common problem in police work beyond the patrol level, doesn't really exist.

Training after selection varies among the states but is usually higher than the minimum required by state mandate. In California, for example, the state-mandated minimum is six weeks (240 hours) while the highway patrol provides sixteen weeks (859 hours). Women are just beginning to gain acceptance in highway patrol work, primarily because of the general need to place only one officer in a car to be able to cover the larger rural territories often associated with the job. At this writing California is training a class of forty women for a two-year evaluation program. They will be assigned statewide for nonspecialized field work and this program will be watched with great interest by other highway patrol agencies.

While the problems of policing inner-city areas don't exist on the same level as the street cop, there are demands placed on the highway patrol officer that can be just as strenuous emotionally and physically. One of the most health-damaging aspects of any police officer's duties is the sudden change from what can often be a boring environment to one which creates great adrenalin flow. Certainly these extremes are encountered by the highway patrol. One minute the officer may be in a situation he's been in for hours, such as patroling a lonely desert or mountain road, and then he may instantly find himself engaged in a prolonged 90-mph pursuit under extremely dangerous conditions. As a matter of fact, almost any patrol officer (police or highway) faces more intense and more frequent danger in his automobile during a pursuit than he faces in situations involving guns. This is perhaps most true for the officer on city streets, where every intersection has a high injury potential in spite of his red lights and siren, but the danger is still extreme on even remote highways. Often the very remoteness of the highway tempts the fleeing violator beyond the limits of his ability or equipment and, in the end, the officer must deal not only with a violation of law but an accident victim as well.

In fact, two of the three most dangerous situations for any police officer are faced more often in highway patrol work than in any other. The single greatest injury potential for policemen remains in the family dispute situation which isn't a common one for the highway patrol officer, of course. The other two, pursuits and the approach to the car during a traffic stop, certainly are. Even a careful officer approaching a car by himself is extremely vulnerable to an occupant who wants to do him harm. Familiarity, of course, breeds at least lack of respect for danger and many, many officers have walked casually up to a car, with their citation book in their gun hand, to meet their death. With the high volume of traffic stops made by anyone who specializes in such work, the potential for carelessness is simply unavoidable. The extent to which one is successful in avoiding this potential is directly proportionate to the degree of likelihood that he'll be spending any given evening with his family.

To complete the picture of life in the highway patrol it must be said that very little out-of-town travel is required by the job (although an assigned territory may range from less than a mile to over 50 miles). Geographical assignment is made upon completion of academy training on the basis of statewide needs. After that, requests for relocation are filled on the basis of seniority. Promotion, of course, may mean relocation since the organization must cover the needs of the entire state. Application may be made through any local office of the patrol or directly to the state director's office in the capital. Pay is generally comparable to other agencies with special compensation added for motorcycle or aircraft duty.

Department of Corrections

As with the other state agencies we've discussed, variation in career opportunities is great between the states. Again as before, we will talk here about the organization in California because, as one of the larger states, the opportunities afforded the entry-level applicant are as representative as any.

In this state there are two basic entry-level positions: *corrections officer* (prison guard) and *parole agent.* There are approximately 2,500 corrections officers and some 600 parole officers. The differences in duties are fairly obvious: the corrections officer deals with the convicted felon while he is institutionalized, and the agent deals with him after he has re-entered society. As might be expected, there are more promotional opportunities for corrections officer. Within the institution itself a person (who may be either male or female) may progress from the traditional role of guarding inmates to become a correctional counsellor, a business service officer (dealing with the business or administrative aspects of the institution rather than the inmates themselves), or through the line organization to become a sergeant, lieutenant, and so on.

The element of physical danger for a corrections officer has increased as it has become more difficult to become a state prisoner. That is, since it now often takes more than one conviction as an armed robber, for example, to do state time (probation and/or county jail time are the frequent alternatives), those who do make it to state prisons are increasingly hard core cases. There are, of course, minimum security prisons but duty in these is awarded on a seniority basis.

Entry requirements and starting pay are higher for parole officer, which requires a bachelor's degree in one of the social sciences or public administration. A year's experience in a related field, such as an institution or in certain areas of social work or probation, is also required.

As is the case for corrections officer, the parole agent is a sworn peace officer of the state. Although entitled as such to carry a weapon, departmental policy in California does not require him to do so. If it becomes necessary for him to physically arrest one of his clients for violation of his parole, he may either do so himself or request assistance from a police officer. In general his clients may be described as antisocial and failure-prone. Their attitudes range from cooperative to very resistive, and one of the greatest emotional demands on the agent is the ability to handle perceived failure and the frustration of lack of obvious success from one's efforts. Physical demands are few on either the corrections officer or parole agent. However, the intellectual and emotional demands of constantly dealing with a variety of complex problems of human nature are considerable. To compound the problem, while most experts seem to agree that a case load of around thirty-five is maximum for effective handling by a parole agent, the average is approximately fifty-nine.

As with any state position, information on specific opportunity and application procedures is available from the state personnel office in the capital or major cities.

Alcoholic Beverage Control

An agency which can have a surprising amount of "real police work" to offer is that which controls the selling of alcoholic beverages in a state. In some states this agency may bear little resemblance to a busy detective, narcotics, or vice squad, but in others that's exactly what it looks like. In some states, over half of the personnel may be in the investigator category. At this time, some investigatory staffs have females, and there are no restrictions as to sex of applicants.

Investigators are sworn peace officers and are armed but not uniformed. District organization is primarily along county lines in accordance with the number of liquor licenses issued in a given area (the average district office covers a territory with approximately 3,000 licenses and utilizes ten to twelve investigators). Basically the agency enforces the provisions of the Alcoholic Beverage Control Act as set forth in the state's business and professions code. Investigators are empowered by the business and professions code—in addition to the broader powers accorded any peace officer under the penal code—to enforce all state laws in any matter involving alcoholic beverages. This, of course, brings them into many situations where vice-control activity is required and a high percentage of the investigator's time is spent in just this type of work.

The work of any ABC agent falls generally into two classes: *licensing* and *enforcement*. In both the length of time for an investigation is considerable, greater, in fact, than the length of the average investigation conducted by a police detective. A licensing investigation explores the *applicant's background* (moral character, disqualifying arrest record, rehabilitation record if he has been convicted of a crime, possible relationship to organized crime, and so on), the *source of funds* to be used in the business venture (again to try to eliminate connections with organized crime), and the *premises* upon which the business is to be conducted (to be sure state and local codes are satisfied).

Enforcement work ranges from a high percentage of alleged violations involving minors purchasing, or attempting to purchase, alcoholic beverages to full-fledged extensive vice investigations. In such cases the investigator works the case on a two-pronged basis. The vice offender of course is arrested and prosecuted in criminal court, but the thrust of the agent's investigation is to gain evidence of management complicity in the vice act, so that a case may be made at hearing against the license itself. Thus a prostitute or a handbook operator working out of a bar will be arrested and prosecuted, but not until after the investigator has made a thorough effort to determine the extent of the bar's management's knowledge of or participation in the activity. Narcotics and dangerous drugs are increasingly traded at establishments dealing in alcoholic beverages, and the ABC investigator becomes involved in this type of work as well.

The clientele dealt with by this agency covers the entire spectrum of society from the working girl and street peddler through international celebrities making application for a license to operate a business. While a good portion of a particular district office's business may be conducted in the inner city, the officer doesn't bear the normal police responsibility for everyday life in that area. Rather his is a more specialized and limited (both in terms of time and responsibility) contact with the unique problems of the population. In practical fact the agency's work is a combination of a very powerful governmental licensing operation, doing business with a very powerful segment of our business community, and the vice and narcotics operation of a police department.

While lacking the dangerous aspects of family-dispute arbitration or the high speed pursuits of traffic patrol, the ABC function is not without its demands for high caliber performance. The mere fact that a goodly percentage of the clientele have been drinking and may well be antiauthority to begin with, demands clear thinking and constant alertness. Considering the fact that the job often requires drinking in order to blend in with the surroundings, it's easy to see that special techniques and skills must be developed if retirement age is to be reached.

Entry into this work is possible at three levels. First is the less-frequently used *investigator assistant* route, requiring only a two-year degree in police science. The more common entry is as an *investigator trainee,* a position comparable in pay to police officer and requiring a four-year degree in criminology or police science. *Special investigator* status, the journeyman rank, may be achieved either by progression through the two already-mentioned positions or by lateral transfer from another comparable agency, with at least two years' experience as an investigator. Training is provided on an individual basis as determined by the training officer's analysis of the trainee's needs and the best local means of providing for these needs. There is no academy available, but arrangements are made through cooperating academies or local colleges offering the needed instruction. Defensive tactics and firearm training are universally provided below the special investigator level.

In addition to the programs for full-time trainees the department conducts an internship program in cooperation with four-year colleges and universities. Under this program the law enforcement student takes a special course during his senior year and works part time (up to 70 hours per month, as his schedule will permit) at the local office as a *student assistant.* The maximum duration of participation in this program is one year, at which time the student assistant either makes successful application for full-time employment with the department or terminates. Student participants are paid on an hourly basis, at quite fair rates, and observe all activities of the office including licensing and enforcement. Depending on the qualifications and background of the individual student, there is also an opportunity to participate, in varying degrees, in enforcement operations. Student assistants are not armed and are not placed in dangerous situations, but the program does afford both the department and the prospective employees an excellent opportunity to get to know each other before a career commitment is made.

Promotional opportunities are essentially line since there are no specialist positions other than auditor, which has little appeal to most who enter the service for its basic work. Transfer requiring geographical relocation is minimum but may be required to accept promotional opportunities, as with any statewide operation. Requests for transfers are handled on the basis of seniority. Out-of-town travel is not unusual in the divisions which have large geographical boundaries (some have more than one county, obviously, if the 3,000 license goal is to be met) but is rarely required during the early part of a person's career.

Fish and Game

Although pretty far removed from street police work (about as far as you can get, as a matter of fact) state fish and game departments are fairly large law enforcement agencies. Primarily, they enforce the fish and game code and crimes against the environment such as pollution but, as sworn peace officers, also work with the penal code if the need arises.

Assigned territories are very large, as a rule, ranging upwards of 500 square miles. The work is mostly out of doors in what most people would consider pleasant surroundings. Some assignments require scuba diving for which additional compensation is granted.

Requirements for entry are two years of college in the biological sciences, fish and wildlife management, conservation, or police science, but experience in comparable state or federal work or public law enforcement may be substituted for the educational requirement. Ten weeks of basic peace officer training is provided upon entry.

Travel requirements are obviously heavy and assignment may be to any area of the state, with reassignment fairly frequent as the needs of the department change. Promotional opportunities are strictly through line progression which is relatively slow (four years to lieutenant, the first step above warden, is about minimum). At present this agency uses only male wardens, but with the constantly changing nature of all law enforcement positions with regard to sex, there is no way of anticipating how long this will be true. Applications should be directed to the state personnel director.

Other State Agencies

There are many other state agencies which are similar to those described above, and examination of the others in detail begins to repeat what we've already covered. The state department of justice, for example, has a considerable investigative force, in California, divided into two main enforcement divisions: *criminal* cases and *narcotics* cases. The number of sworn positions is relatively small, numbering about 200 (99 percent male at this time) for both divisions, but the total number of departmental opportunities is almost ten times this figure. Most of the other positions are in identification and information work, laboratory technicians or crime analysts. These of course are services provided by the department for all agencies in the state.

Much of the criminal investigation of the state justice department involves homicide cases where the state has become involved because of the multiple number of jurisdictions in the case (for example, where occurrences seem to emerge in several areas, as in the "Zebra" killings which attracted so much attention in 1974). Similarly, many smaller agencies which don't have the extensive laboratory facilities of the department will call on it for any homicide investigation where the suspect is not known.

Narcotics investigations conducted by the justice department usually involve only larger dealers. Because of local agencies' need for more expertise (or more cash to make a large buy) they may request help from the state. Entry requirement is a four-year degree (with up to two years subsitution for experience) and salary at entry is somewhat better than average for other agencies. An unusual training program is afforded selected applicants. Over a period of seven months the new officer alternately attends academy classes and works in a division office where he may apply the knowledge gained in class. Most entry-level candidates selected by this agency have a prior background in a law enforcement agency.

There are quite a few still smaller and more specialized agencies such as fire marshal, motor vehicle inspector, horse racing board investigator and the like. All of these positions come under the office of the state personnel director and information on them should be available from any branch office.

COUNTY AGENCIES

When one thinks of county law enforcement agencies the natural image which comes to mind is that of the sheriff. And, of course, this is the chief enforcement officer of the county. The *county marshal's* office, as explained previously, functions as an arm of the court and primarily handles civil aspects of law enforcement. Deputy marshals are sworn peace officers of the state, of course, and thus are armed and uniformed, with full power to make arrests in any appropriate situation. For example, while most people think of the marshal as serving *sub-*

poenas (calls to appear in court), *summonses* (demands to present a position against a legal action), or *declarations* (notifications of actions in small claims courts), they also serve *warrants* requiring physical arrest. In fact, if asked about the heaviest demands placed upon a deputy marshal by his job, the respondent may well tell you that they are emotional rather than physical. "When a policeman responds to a call," he may say, "the reporting party is at least glad to see him because there's a chance he'll be able to help. But nobody's glad to see the marshal because he never brings good news . . . he's always there to take something away, and the people seldom react favorably to his presence. It takes a lot of cool to get the job done right without getting into it with the people you call on."

The largest agency of this type in the country is in Los Angeles County where some 600 sworn deputies are used. At present less than one percent of these are female but the number is beginning to grow. A newly-hired deputy is given sixteen weeks' academy training in many of the same skills and knowledges required for regular police work plus considerably more civil law and procedure. Such subjects as traffic and accident investigation are not covered, of course, since a deputy marshal would not become involved in this work even though he is legally entitled to. Just as the duties of a marshal will vary across the country, so will his conditions of work and pay. Although established by state law, the marshal does function at the county level so inquiries relative to employment should be directed to the office itself or the county personnel office.

Another county law enforcement agency that's often overlooked as a career opportunity is that of the *district attorney's Bureau of Investigation*. In Los Angeles county the district attorney's investigative staff has some 250 sworn peace officers with 97 percent of the positions filled by male officers. The range of investigations conducted for the district attorney and his staff is rather surprisingly large. Pretrial investigations include locating and serving subpoenas on prosecution witnesses for superior court criminal cases. Another section deals with *welfare crimes* covering theft or misuse of welfare funds, false claims for services, and internal thefts by county employees. A general assignment section investigates pretrial matters to aid the staff in developing the people's case. It also lends assistance to other agencies requesting help from the district attorney's office, handles specialized bribery and extortion cases, perjury claims, falsification of evidence and intimidation of witnesses as referred by the courts, jail interviews with prisoners, applicant background checks, and even election code violations. Other sections specialize in fraud, embezzlement, bunco, corporate securities, organized crime intelligence, public disorder intelligence, and malfeasance in public office (including claims of police brutality).

One of the larger agencies of this type in the country, this office hires about twenty-five sworn personnel each year and provides them with twelve weeks of specialized investigation training. Entry level requirements are either two years' nonmilitary law enforcement experience with a police or criminal investigation governmental agency, coupled with a college degree or two years of college in police science, or a college degree in police science, police administration, criminology, or administration of justice. Entry level pay is at the high end of the range for police agencies, with room for development in nonsupervisory positions. Information on application procedures is available from the local district attorney's office, Bureau of Investigation.

FEDERAL AGENCIES

If the sheriff provides the image for county law enforcement, and the policeman in a patrol car for law enforcement in general, surely the Federal Bureau of Investigation provides this image at the federal level. With the extreme popularity of the bureau as a subject of movies and television programs it's probably unnecessary to tell anyone what the FBI does. For the record, however, we will review the functions, requirements, and responsibilities of this and the other major federal agencies.

The major federal agencies are under the jurisdiction of either the United States Treasury Department or the United States Department of Justice. Under the Justice Department are the FBI, the Immigration and Naturalization Service, and the U.S. Marshal and the Drug Enforcement Administration (formerly called the Bureau of Narcotics and Dangerous Drugs). The Treasury Department contains the Secret Service, the Customs Service, the Bureau of Alcohol, Tobacco and Firearms, and the Internal Revenue Service Intelligence Division. Information regarding application may be obtained on these agencies by writing the civil service commission or the individual agency in care of its department (Justice or Treasury), Washington, D.C., 20535.

Federal Bureau of Investigation

Perhaps contrary to its popularized image, the FBI is not a national police force. Rather, it is a large (8,500 special agents), fact-finding arm of the office of the Attorney General within the Department of Justice. As such it investigates violations of specified federal laws *(only)* and reports the results of these investigations to the Attorney General. Agents may make arrests when they hold a warrant, when they observe a federal offense being committed, or when they have reasonable grounds to believe that the person to be arrested has committed a felony violation of United States law. Generally speaking, the FBI is charged with enforcement of every federal law not specifically assigned to some other agency. This amounts to some 170 different violations at recent count. Best known, of course, are bank robbery, kidnaping, extortion, and interstate transportation of stolen goods. Domestic intelligence is also the charter of the Bureau on matters relating to espionage, sabotage, and subversive activities.

"G-Men"

In the early morning hours of September 26, 1933, a small group of officers surrounded a house in Memphis, Tennessee. In the house was George "Machine-Gun" Kelly, late of Leavenworth Penitentiary. He was wanted by the FBI for kidnaping. For two months FBI Agents had trailed the gangster. The FBI men, accompanied by local law enforcement officers, closed in around the house, and entered.

"We are Federal Officers . . . Come out with your hands up. . . ."

"Machine-Gun" Kelly was so frightened he could barely talk. "Don't shoot, G-Men; don't shoot!"

This was the beginning of a new name for FBI Agents. By the time Kelly had been convicted and had received his sentence of life imprisonment, the new nickname, an abbreviation of "Government Men," had taken hold throughout the criminal underworld. [*The Story of the FBI* (Washington: U.S. Government Printing Office, 1973), p. 4]

Agents must be college graduates (either male or female) between the ages of 23 and 35 at the time of their appointment. Good physical condition is naturally required but, interestingly enough, the vision requirements for FBI appointment are considerably more liberal than most other agencies. The Bureau requirement is 20/200, corrected to 20/20, while most agencies limit acceptable, uncorrected vision to around 20/70 (many now accept corrected 20/30). Color blindness in an applicant precludes his consideration by the Bureau, as it would with most agencies.

The traditional requirement of a baccalaureate degree in accounting or law has now been expanded to include other disciplines as needs of the Bureau have developed. Most successful applicants, however, are between 25 and 30 years of age with majors in accounting or law. Many have three years' or more experience in law enforcement. A fourteen-week academy training program is provided for all agents. Upon completion of this course they may be assigned to a field office anywhere in the United States or Puerto Rico. Geographical relocation after this is primarily due to promotion or special assignment; it may, however, involve moves of considerable distance since the whole country is the jurisdiction of the agency.

Any law enforcement agency runs a background check on all applicants who do well enough on testing to be of interest to the department. Arrest record, traffic record, and credit history are all reviewed, and interviews with neighbors and family members are conducted. As you might imagine, the FBI is no exception to this rule and has the ability to make a thorough investigation of applicants in whom it is interested. Special agents with the FBI are the only officers of a major federal agency who are not civil service appointees. Applications must thus be directed only to the agency itself.

Immigration and Naturalization Service

In terms of a law enforcement career, this service is the border patrol. There are, of course, many other functions filled by this important agency, such as determination of which alien citizens may enter the United States, but the patrol inspector, who checks incoming cars and trains at borders, travels along river beds in a four-wheel drive vehicle, or patrols vast desert stretches in aircraft, is the equivalent for this agency of the street cop. The basic charge of this function is obviously to prevent illegal entry of aliens. And, while this would normally be thought of in terms of a border assignment, some of the 1,700 officers in this service are also assigned to such exotic locations as Bermuda and Europe where they check entry eligibility of persons boarding airplanes or ships for the United States.

Entry requirements are more liberal than for most law enforcement agencies. There is no educational requirement and no upper age limit. For practical purposes, however, fifty might be considered an upper limit of sorts, for there is mandatory retirement at age seventy. Entrance is by examination which is open to both men and women (although at the time of this writing there were no female patrol inspectors in service; there are, however, female trainees in both inspector and investigator classifications). Appointed applicants are given sixteen-weeks' academy training, which includes Spanish language instruction, and then assigned to one of the patrol stations along the Mexican-American border. Patrol inspectors are probably subject to more travel requirement than most other federal positions, primarily because of the large territories to which they're assigned. The physical demands of the job are considerable due, in large part, to the nature of the territory.

United States Marshal

Nearly 100 persons (one for each federal judicial district) are appointed by the President to four-year terms of office as United States Marshal throughout the United States and its territories. While the various district marshals serve at the pleasure of the President, the 2,000 deputy marshals do not. They're sworn federal peace officers and a part of the civil service system. Open to both men and women, the vast majority of deputy positions are currently filled by men. There is a drive at present, however, to increase the number of female deputies.

The duties of the U.S. marshal are roughly equivalent, on a national scale, to those outlined for the county marshal earlier. Deputies make arrests primarily for federal offenses (as outlined for the FBI special agents) but may also enforce the provisions of state, county, and local codes as appropriate. They transport prisoners to and from federal courts and prisons; provide protection for witnesses at federal trials and for visiting officials from other nations; act as bailiff at federal court; seize and auction property, business assets, and maritime vessels at the direction of federal courts; and perform a variety of other noninvestigative duties such as riot control.

There is a special operations group within the structure of the marshal's agency which is specifically charged with control of unusual occurrences such as riots. However, when a major event such as the Indian uprising at Wounded Knee occurs, deputies from all over the country are assigned to the involved jurisdiction on loan. Thus, while a deputy might well expect to spend most of his time in his assigned territory without having to travel extensively, he may find an emergency requiring his temporary reassignment to such places as Yosemite National Park (as was the case a few years ago to control a hippie invasion), Alcatraz prison, or even Puerto Rico. It's not an everyday thing, but it is possible. About one-third of the United States is government land so the potential for involvement of the marshal's office is considerable.

Entry requirements include a college degree with a minor in law enforcement and high placement on open competitive examination. Various combinations of specialized or general experience (law enforcement or experience in dealing with the general public) with educational achievement may be made to satisfy the provisions of the civil service commission and interested applicants should contact the local office of the agency or the civil service commission for current requirements. After appointment, deputies are given thirteen-week's training at the department's academy in Washington, D.C.

Drug Enforcement Administration

This rapidly expanding agency was previously under the Treasury Department but is now an arm of the Justice Department. Formerly called the Bureau of Narcotics and Dangerous Drugs, DEA uses some 2,200 special agents in its criminal section and another 300 investigators in its compliance section. Unlike the special agents, investigators are not armed and work with people in the United States who are legally entitled to grow or manufacture "controlled substances" (narcotics and drugs as defined in the U.S. Criminal Code). Some 30 percent of investigators and 2 percent of special agents are currently female with the number growing constantly under concerted effort by the agency, which also has a high percentage of minority group agents.

Unlike narcotics officers in local agencies, DEA agents don't usually have to emulate the scroungy appearance of the street-culture drug addict because the DEA agent deals with people who sell dope rather than use it. Their clients look like business men—which they are, albeit a deadly sorrowful business. An interesting statistic in this regard is that of the several thousand arrests made by DEA in 1973, less than 2 percent were users themselves. Conversely, some 25 percent of persons in federal prison are there for drug violations. DEA agents aren't involved in the small, day-to-day marijuana traffic. They deal with the heroin and cocaine markets at high levels. Investigations may be initiated within the agency itself or by local or state agencies cooperating with each other. Like the state attorney general's investigative staff, described earlier, the DEA may be asked to participate for its expertise, its larger capital for big buys, or both. Its special agents are sworn federal peace officers with full powers of arrest but specifically charged with the responsibility of enforcing the federal drug laws as established in the U.S. Criminal Code.

Currently, entry requires any one of three possible combinations of experience and education totaling "5." That is, an applicant may have five years' specialized experience in the field he is attempting to enter, a two-year degree plus three years' specialized experience, or a four-year degree plus one year of either specialized experience or professional experience as defined by the civil service commission. Selected applicants are given twelve weeks of training at the academy in Washington, D.C. and then assigned to duty in one of the larger districts for about two years. During this time there usually isn't much travel, but ultimately there may be a considerable amount. For example, an agent assigned to a case in Omaha may well follow that case to its conclusion in Argentina. There are at present some sixty-seven offices of the DEA in the United States, and another fifty-three in seventeen countries overseas. Information on career opportunities may be obtained from any office, from the Civil Service Commission in Washington, or from most Post Offices.

Secret Service

This curiously-named agency operates under the Treasury Department. The name would seem to imply some sort of espionage activity or middle-of-the-night door-banging to drag people off to internment camps. In actuality, of course, the agency is charged with the responsibility of protecting the persons of the President and Vice President and their families and investigating counterfeiting activity, stolen government checks, and forged government obligations (treasury notes, bonds, stamps and the like). A moderate-sized agency (1,200 special agents, with about one-half percent women at this time) it draws its personnel from the same pool as all other Treasury Department operational units. Successful candidates attend two schools (as do all Treasury agents) after hiring. The first is the Treasury Law Enforcement Officers' Academy in Washington, D.C. which lasts for six weeks; the second is the agency's own academy which teaches recruits the specialized skills required for Secret Service work.

Assignment after graduation from the academy may be to any part of the United States or its territories. There is considerable travel involved in being a Secret Service Special Agent, especially if assigned to the White House Detail. Those assigned to this detail are given further specialized training as demanded by their somewhat awesome responsibility.

Entry requirements include a four-year degree with at least a minor in some law enforcement related field, plus related investigative experience. Experience may be substituted for formal education in the same manner described earlier, but most successful applicants are currently possessed of at least a two-year degree.

Customs Agency Service

Career opportunities in this agency include three basic positions which make up a national total of some 7,000 persons. The *customs investigator,* the smallest of the three categories at about 1,000, performs investigatory duties in the manner of a detective, if you will, as opposed to the uniformed personnel in the other two positions. The *customs inspector* is stationed at a port of entry into the United States (airport, seaport, or border crossing) and seeks to determine if those entering have any contraband material with them. Contraband material is primarily narcotics these days, with firearms and gold in second place, but includes such exotic and unlikely prizes as parrots and cancer "cures." There are roughly 3,000 customs inspectors in service and a like number of *customs patrol officers* who operate between ports of entry in the manner of the border patrol. The primary difference is that the border patrol is looking for illegal entrants, where as the customs people are looking for illegal material.

While the customs agency is responsible for enforcing some 200 laws for forty different agencies at ports of entry, they are no longer in the narcotics investigation business. This function has been transferred (along with some 500 investigators who were involved in the work) to the Drug Enforcement

Agency as outlined earlier. In addition to the three positions described above, all of which are armed officers, there are import specialists who, while they deal with paperwork such as invoices and bills of lading, are involved in law enforcement in that they commonly discover cases of fraud which lead to investigation and arrest.

Entry requirements for customs patrol officers are a minimum of two years' experience in government, education, business, or military service. For customs inspectors the minimum is three years' experience. College training may be substituted for experience. After acceptance, recruits are given the six-week Treasury Law Enforcement Officer Academy course in Washington, plus a six-week Customs Academy course in New York. Assignment may be at any port of entry in the United States or territories.

Bureau of Alcohol, Tobacco and Firearms

The Bureau has recently been accorded autonomous status rather than its former divisional status under the Internal Revenue Service. The work of the Bureau remains essentially the same, however, and includes enforcement of the provisions of federal gun control statutes and control of the manufacture of alcoholic beverages including, of course, collection of taxes due the goverment in connection with such manufacture. The tobacco aspect of the Bureau's work is essentially similar to the compliance section of the Drug Enforcement Administration. That is, rather than being concerned with criminal violations, the investigators assigned to this work deal with the legal manufacturers and growers of tobacco to see that the provisions of the law are complied with, especially the collection of taxes.

Traditionally the image of the ATF agent is that of the "revenuer" stalking the hills of the southeastern states in search-and-destroy operations on illicit distilleries. In fact, until recent years, this was the main emphasis of the agency's work and the one that earned it the reputation of having more fatalities than any other federal law enforcement agency. Today this is still an important part of the agency's enforcement activity, but the main thrust is in firearms and explosives. Under the Federal Firearms Act and the National Firearms Act (both as modified by the 1968 Gun Control Act), the category "destructive devices" includes such items as machine guns, hand grenades, molotov cocktails, bazookas, cannons, sawed-off shotguns and rifles, and other offensive weapons and comes under the purview of the ATF. Guns in this category must be registered with the Bureau and their resale requires Bureau approval of the purchaser and purchase of a $200 tax stamp. The sale of guns to a private party in a state other than that in which the seller resides (in other words, mailorder gun sales) also is under the control of the Bureau.

This medium-sized agency (1,500 special agents, predominantly but not exclusively male) takes pride in the latitude afforded its agents in developing their own cases for submission to the Attorney General. Because of this there is considerable travel connected with the job, especially in the southeastern part of the country (because of the backwoods nature of the illict stills' locations) and in the smaller district offices (because they cover relatively large territories per agent). A bachelor's degree is required, in any discipline, along with high placement on the Treasury Enforcement Agent examination. Training after hiring includes the standard six-week Treasury Department Academy in Washington plus another six-week stint at the agency's own academy, specializing in ATF violations.

Internal Revenue Service, Intelligence Division

While the smallest of the three arms of IRS (the others are Collection and Audits) the Intelligence Division is the one most likely to appeal to persons interested in a law enforcement career. Special agents investigate tax cases where criminal fraud is suspected and attempt to develop a case which will warrant indictment. They have sometimes been successful in removing criminals from the national scene (notably Al Capone) where other agencies have failed. With the increasing involvement of organized crime in legitimate business operations, IRS Intelligence offers one continuing opportunity for countering this growth. IRS investigation of organized gambling, while still a part of the Division's work load, is smaller now that the Organized Crime Strike Force has been formed to work primarily on such cases.

As with other Treasury Department investigative offices, applicants for IRS Intelligence should have a four-year college degree, ideally with the major in accounting or finance and a minor in law enforcement of some sort. Specific requirements are available through the agency or civil service offices. Open

150 THE AGENCIES

competitive examination is required and successful applicants are provided with standard Treasury Officer academy training plus specialized training for work within the Division.

PRIVATE AGENCIES

The evolution of private police agencies has been examined in the first chapter of this book. As a career opportunity private police work is probably vastly misunderstood. To put things into perspective, let's look at the range of positions available and briefly talk about the requirements for each.

At the bottom of the range in terms of entry requirements, pay, and demands on the individual, is the *guard* or *watchman* position. This position is often filled by retired persons, students or others seeking temporary work, or people who want to get into a law enforcement career but are unable to qualify for a position with a public police agency. For all of these reasons the pay is usually low, often just above the minimum wage. While there may be exceptions to this statement, it is fairly safe to say that there are no minimum requirements beyond reasonable health.

Private guards, increasingly unarmed, perform more of a service function than security in many companies.

Private patrol officers are essentially the same as guards or watchmen except, of course, they move from location to location as would a patrol unit in a police agency. Both private patrol officers and guards may be employed by a single company or by a private police service such as Burns, Pinkerton, or Wells Fargo to name but a few of the better-known agencies.

Private investigators, unlike the previous two categories, must be licensed by the state. The majority of persons who go into private investigation agencies are former officers in public law enforcement agencies who, for a variety of reasons ranging from dismissal to retirement (and including, of course, simple personal preference), wish to pursue a career in private police work. Seldom does a person begin his career in law enforcement as a private investigator; more often he will continue or conclude his career in such an agency.

The private investigator, far from the media-created image of the private eye, usually investigates marital infidelity to develop divorce action for his client. On a higher plane he also becomes involved in investigation of suspected insurance frauds and, occasionally, in development of the defense's case for an attorney.

Industrial security offers probably the highest calling in private police work. While the general title can and does include the uniformed positions of guard or patrolman, it also includes investigative positions which provide enough challenge for anyone interested in law enforcement. The administrative positions are often filled by persons recruited from public law enforcement. Investigators are also often drawn from public agencies but may be recruited directly from colleges and universities or developed within a company's own personnel. The number and types of companies and institutions employing private security forces, either as a staff function or on a contract basis, are so large as to make any attempt at listing them ludicrous. Virtually any company or institution of medium or large size needs and uses such an agency.

The function of the guard or private patrolmen is often to meet the requirements of a company's insurance carrier who is interested in early detection of fires. Of course, there is also the traditional responsibility of controlling passage through gates to both general and restricted areas and attempting to minimize theft and burglary.

Industrial security operations include the guard function, as already described, and the more sophisticated investigative function. Investigations can be quite exhaustive and range from screening of applicants for employment to complex theft schemes. Fraud, shoplifting, vandalism, and even company liability in lawsuits fall within the purview of industrial security. The power to arrest is the same for a private policeman as it is for a private citizen. That is, he may effect the arrest of the person he believes guilty, but he must then arrange for a public peace officer to accept the arrested person into custody. For this reason, an industrial security special agent will often do the investigative work, identify the suspect, and then present his facts to a local public agency and ask them to make the arrest. The public agency, on the other hand, may be reluctant to make an arrest based on alleged facts not developed by their own people. In such cases they will insist that the company investigator make a private person's arrest and then accept the suspect into custody. Often a public agency will work a good case jointly with an industrial security group and then make their own arrest. As indicated by their lack of power to arrest, other than as a private person, special agents or private police have no sworn standing in the eyes of the state (except in cases where they may coincidentally be members of reserve units of official law enforcement agencies). Thus they have no authority to carry concealed weapons, except on their employer's premises. Weapons which they are entitled to wear on the job may be worn to and from work, provided they are on the outside of the uniform. Private investigators, being licensed by the state, may be issued concealed weapon permits. The lack of a licensing requirement for private security officers is not universal and, in fact, a trend may be developing to subjecting such positions to licensing practices. If this does develop it will go a long way toward increasing the professionalism of private police.

SUMMARY

The two law enforcement agencies with full street-police function are *municipal police* departments, which have jurisdiction within the geographical limits of the various cities of a state, and the *sheriff's offices* which provide a similar function on a countywide basis. Both are manned by *sworn peace officers* of the state, as are all public agencies other than federal.

State police may be the ultimate police authority within a state or, more commonly, restricted to some special function such as motor vehicle code enforcement or enforcement of law only on state property (such as parks, universities, and official offices).

Highway patrol agencies operate on a statewide basis enforcing primarily the provisions of the vehicle code of the state. They are usually one of the largest single agencies in any state, surpassed only by the municipal and sheriff's departments in the very largest cities and counties.

The *Department of Corrections* in any state is that agency which has responsibility for persons convicted of crimes and sentenced to prison. *Corrections officers* (prison guards) and *parole agents* function within this department.

Alcoholic Beverage Control agencies in the various states investigate applicants for liquor licenses and enforce the provisions of any code violated in connection with liquor. Considerable vice investigation is conducted in this agency.

Fish and Game departments offer the opportunity for a career in law enforcement primarily out of doors in pastoral and wilderness settings.

The *State Department of Justice* investigates cases which overlap jurisdictional boundaries of several agencies or where they have been requested to investigate because of their expertise in a particular area lacking in the local agency.

Other state agencies which have some degree of involvement in law enforcement include such diverse entities as *fire marshal, motor vehicle department,* and *horse racing board.*

The *county marshal* is the principal county law enforcement officer except for the sheriff. The marshal's duties involve primarily the enforcement of the civil code, but he is empowered to make arrests and does so, primarily on serving of warrants.

The *District Attorney's Bureau of Investigation* handles a wide range of duties for the district attorney and his staff ranging from pretrial investigations to jail interviews with prisoners.

The *Federal Bureau of Investigation* is not a national police force but rather a fact-gathering arm of the Department of Justice. Its special agents enforce all federal law not specifically assigned to some other federal agency.

The *Immigration and Naturalization Service* functions as the border patrol and checks eligibility for entry into the United States of persons boarding United States-bound planes and ships at many points around the world.

The *United States Marshal* performs, on a national scale,

a somewhat similar function to the county marshal. Deputies enforce any existing code (federal, state, or local) which is violated on federal property and enforce the decisions of the federal courts.

Drug Enforcement Administration is the federal agency which combats, on a national level, drug violations. Rather than the individual addict or small-time pusher, this agency works at the levels of the importers and national distributors of mainly heroin and cocaine.

Secret Service agents are charged with protection of the families and persons of the President and Vice President and investigation of counterfeiting, theft of government checks, and forgery of government obligations.

Customs Agency Service employees are responsible for preventing entry of contraband material into the United States. In the course of dispatching this obligation they enforce some 200 laws in behalf of forty different agencies.

The *Bureau of Alcohol, Tobacco and Firearms* is responsible for enforcement of federal law and collection of taxes due in connection with the production of alcoholic beverages. It also is responsible for the control of certain firearms and destructive devices as provided by the Gun Control Act of 1968.

The *Internal Revenue Service, Intelligence Division,* investigates cases of possible criminal fraud in connection with payment of federal taxes.

Private police work is classified as either *guard, patrol, private investigator,* or *industrial security*. Guards and patrol officers are concerned primarily with protection of premises. Private investigators work primarily at development of evidence for court cases in divorce actions, insurance frauds, or defendants in criminal actions. Industrial security includes both the functions of guard and patrol, usually, plus the investigative function for a variety of legal actions involving company property or employees.

REVIEW QUESTIONS

Answers to these questions appear on pages 383-384.

1. A person seeking a career in law enforcement which would provide him the broadest possible range of experience would probably apply to one of which two types of agencies? _____

2. In the space provided, write the name of the state agency which is most likely described by the statement given.
   _____ a. Responsible for incarcerated persons and those released on parole
   _____ b. Enforces all codes violated on state-owned properties
   _____ c. Investigates cases involving multiple jurisdictions, or when requested to do so by a local agency
   _____ d. Works vice and narcotics violations if connected with establishments which sell liquor
   _____ e. Enforces primarily provisions of vehicle code and investigates accidents
   _____ f. Works primarily in wilderness and recreational areas
3. At the county level:
   a. the chief law enforcement officer is the _____ ;
   b. the enforcement arm of the court, particularly in civil matters, is the _____ ; and,
   c. investigations preparatory to presenting the people's case in court are conducted by the _____ office.
4. Beside each of the statements below, indicate the name of the federal law enforcement agency referred to.
   _____ a. Operates against high level narcotics violators
   _____ b. Works at the borders to prevent entry of illegal aliens
   _____ c. Responsible for enforcement of all federal law not specifically assigned to another agency
   _____ d. Works at the borders to prevent entry of contraband materials
   _____ e. Enforces decrees of federal courts

156 THE AGENCIES

_____ f. Responsible for protection of the President and his family

_____ g. Attempts to develop information to support claim of criminal fraud in federal tax cases

_____ h. Investigates counterfeiting cases

_____ i. Investigates illegal distillery operations

_____ j. Investigates cases of espionage or sabotage

_____ k. Controls possession and sale of certain weapons

5. In the space provided, indicate the phase of private police work described by the statement.

_____ a. Responsible for investigation of internal theft or fraud within a single company

_____ b. Responsible for control of entrance to premises of a single plant or building

_____ c. Handles investigations such as insurance fraud

_____ d. Responsible for security of premises at several different plants or buildings on separate locations in a city.

CHAPTER 6

LINE OPERATIONS

OVERVIEW

In the preceding chapter we discussed what life is like in some of the more significant (in terms of employment opportunity) law enforcement agencies. Now we're going to see how police departments are organized and go into what the work is like in some of the units within the organization.

Police departments, like any other operational unit, be it military or industrial, are organized in two basic ways. There's the chain of command or vertical organization starting at the top and working down to the entry level positions, and there's the specialization or horizontal distribution of the work by type. In the latter approach the work of the total unit is divided into operational groups, each with its own structure of command.

In this chapter we're going to deal with what is normally called the *line* organization in police work. This is the work the department is "really organized to do," if you prefer to look at it that way. We'll also talk about basic command organization to point out the responsibilities of each level of authority.

THE LINE CHAIN OF COMMAND

Every organization has a chain of command, both overall and within the various functional units. The *chief* obviously is the top command officer. His work is removed from the particular demands placed on the street cop (the source of at least occasional nostalgia on his part), but he is never completely free of them. His responsibility is to utilize the men and equipment of the department to serve and protect the citizens of the community efficiently, economically, and in a manner which will satisfy at once the needs of the government of his political subdivision, the citizens, and the men and women of his department. While this takes a different set of skills from those he used when he rode in a patrol car, he obviously can't afford to forget what that experience was like. The job remains, however, an administrative one and anyone with complete lack of interest in administrative affairs would be well advised to set different goals for himself than chief of police.

The *deputy chief* can serve in at least two capacities. He can run the department operationally (if the chief is primarily occupied with the administrative and politically-oriented aspects of his job), or he can be in a staff position which amounts roughly to carrying communications to and from the chief and the other command personnel. In between these two extremes are many possible combinations of these roles, but most frequently the job tends to one end or the other of the scale.

Captains normally head one of the functional divisions (field operations, investigation, or services) within the department. As such they are completely responsible for the proper functioning of their unit in accordance with the goals set by the chief. They also have staff duties to perform, so theirs is really a dual role. To illustrate, the captain of the investigation division is, in effect, the chief of detectives. He may not be the best detective and, in fact, may very well never have been a detective himself. But he will have had administrative experience and several years of police experience so he will be qualified to administer the work of a detective unit in a police department. Part of this function will be the preparation and operation of such mundane but essential things as budgets. The chief has to make a budget to submit to the governing political body; the captains have to submit budgets to the chief. So, while the captain is the operational head of a line organization of his own, he still functions in both a line and staff position with relationship to the chief.

Lieutenants generally head operational units within a division, as in patrol. In this case, each *watch,* or shift, will have a lieutenant as its commander. The watch commander will have full operational responsibility for all police functions during the eight-or ten-hour period his officers are on duty. Lieutenants functioning as watch commanders in patrol would probably be considered the "most line" of all lieutenants since patrol is the basic function of the police department. Many straight staff positions, such as training officer, planning and research officer, community relations officer and so on require such skill and experience levels that they are manned by lieutenants in even medium or small departments.

Sergeants are the first-level supervision of any department large enough to have a layer of command between chief and patrolman. In some agencies, of course they may be the only layer of command and as such may head functional groups as described here for captains. In all but the smallest departments, however, the sergeant is in charge of a group of officers and reports to a lieutenant. In the average, small-to-medium agency patrol division a sergeant may be assigned to either the field or the desk. The field sergeant tours the various patrol districts during his watch, observing performance of the officers, advising when requested to do so, and handling situations which require his extra experience. The desk sergeant supervises station personnel not assigned specifically to other supervisors and usually handles personal public contact. He may also act as watch commander at least two days a week unless there is an extra lieutenant who floats between the watches to command them on the regular commander's day off. Sergeants may also function in staff capacities as described above for lieutenants.

Promotion to sergeant is in some ways one of the most difficult transitions any police officer will have to make. Changing roles from "one of the guys" to "boss" is difficult in any organization but particularly so in police agencies where extremely close relationships very often exist. Some sergeants end up not making it—going back to patrolman either at their own request or the department's—simply because they cannot handle the transition. The plain fact is that with the stripes goes the responsibility to assume a new role in life and to some people it just isn't worth it. The same thing applies, of course, with each promotion to a new level but the first step is probably the toughest.

SPECIALIZED OPERATIONAL UNITS

At one end of the specialization-generalization spectrum is the one-man department in the smallest hamlet. He does everything and if he gets in over his head he calls on a county or state agency for help. At the other end of the spectrum is the super large municipal or county agency with a chief, a sprinkling of deputy chiefs, fifteen or twenty division commanders, inspectors, and specialists for everything from fingerprints to press relations.

All of this emphasis on specialization began simply enough when the need to conduct follow-up investigations grew so great in London that it was taking too much patrol time away from the officers on the street. In order to be able to predict with some degree of accuracy how many officers would be available for street patrol at any given time, the position of detective was created and charged with the responsibility of investigating those cases which could not be solved at the scene. This is still the basic function of the investigative unit of any police department. As we said earlier, you can look at it as, "if the patrol function were 100 percent effective there would be no need for detectives." They can't, of course, and follow-up investigations take hours or even months, making it impossible to have the patrol officer follow through on every call he handles.

This degree of specialization, which began in the mid-nineteenth century, was enough for police work until the automobile began to show its potential for problem-creation in the 1920s. Traffic units were then created, to be followed shortly by narcotics, vice, and juvenile units. Presently, the degree of specialization in a department depends on many things, principally the demands of a given community for particular types of service. A rural community may have little need for many of the specialized services of the metropolitan areas, and vice versa. The number of cattle-rustling calls in New York City, for example, hardly warrants the formation of the special units that exist in some much smaller western jurisdictions. The Rio Vista department, on the other hand, can probably get by quite nicely without the services of a full-time polygraph specialist or a drug diversion counsellor.

The conditions which led to specialization repeat themselves with agency growth in an endless recurrence of the same cycles. A small agency is formed and grows as population and crime climb. As crime spirals, the need for specialization increases. At first it is possible to use the part-time services of larger nearby agencies which have staff specialists. As need for the specialist's services continues to grow, a staff position is created or an officer is sent to school to learn to perform the specialized function when needed. Then, partly because there is a tendency to find a need for a new capability and partly because the newly-trained specialist tends to want to concentrate on his speciality, the demands for the special service increase to the point where it becomes a full-time need.

At any rate, even with the present trend to increased generalization, the need for specialization will always be with us, and it's probably a good thing from the standpoint of morale. Progression through the line command positions is available to only a certain number of officers each year, and the ability to grow into specialized positions thus becomes more important. It's very human to want to progress in your work and specialization affords an additional opportunity for such growth within every police department.

On the other hand, there is some risk that over-specialization can impede normal progression through the ranks. A man may become so valuable in his field of speciality that management is reluctant to promote him, and after a long period of time in a specialist position, an officer may be considered to have too narrow a range of experience for regular promotion. All of these factors must be given individual consideration in evaluating a career-development plan for any officer in his own agency.

Patrol

As everyone should know by now, patrol is the heart, backbone, or whatever characterization you want to accord it, of the police force. It is, in fact, the basic fiber of any law enforcement agency with a street policing function. The theory of repressive patrol has long been that, by creating the feeling among the non-law-abiding element that "the police are everywhere," crime will be reduced. In spite of the very reasonable challenges to this philosophy being made today (a cop on every corner wouldn't stop such crimes as murder among family members, and so on), there is obvious importance to field patrol.

By dividing the city into patrol districts and deploying motorized units into these districts in numbers proportionate to the experienced need for police service in each, *response time* to calls for police help can be minimized. In other words, if a car has only a few blocks to patrol and can stay in that area, a radio dispatcher can send help to the scene faster than if a car had to be sent from central headquarters. And, of course, the ability to observe potential crime situations depends directly on being in the field, where such situations occur. Traffic enforcement of laws depends entirely on patrol units or their equivalent (motorized traffic units in many agencies are not assigned specific patrol responsibility other than traffic violations).

Most patrol officers feel that theirs is the only real police work and that other functions of the department are carried by them. Patrol is, after all, everyone's image of the police. It's where officers come in daily contact with virtually every aspect of police work, where the uniforms are worn and everyone knows your role in life, and where most of the excitement is. They gripe about the shift work, which most commonly is rotated on a three, four, or six-month basis, about the boredom of the slow hours on whatever shift they don't happen to like, about not getting their preferred days-off while the detectives always have weekends off, and so on. But there is an esprit de corps in patrol that is seldom seen in other organizations and even seems to exceed that at most other functional groups within the department.

Patrol is the largest manpower group in any full-service agency, and the one which gets the new personnel and from which most promotions are filled. New officers are assigned to patrol first because of the greater opportunity for gaining broad experience in a relatively short time and because they can be easily placed with an experienced officer.

The responsibilities of the patrol officer vary somewhat with departmental policy but are traditionally divided into three categories: *preventive patrol* (the visible patrol of the city in plainly marked units); *called-for services* (responding to citizens' need for help); and *inspectional services* (visual examination of premises which have a high probability of need for police service such as liquor stores, closed business establishments, and empty homes). Investigation of crime scenes normally involves only the preliminary stages for patrol officers. They get the facts of the incident from victims and witnesses and attempt to capture the suspect if he is believed to be in the vicinity. Beyond this, however, in most agencies the investigation is turned over to the detectives. Under the many forms of generalization now being experimented with, the scope of the patrol officer's investigation activity is being broadened to varying degrees (see Chap. 13). If the patrol officer saves time by turning investigations over to specialists, it is often lost again to report writing. While he may spend twenty minutes investigating a burglary scene and taking statements from victims, it may easily take the patrol officer up to twice that amount of time to prepare the various reports required. Most agencies are currently working toward reducing the amount of report time required of patrol officers in an effort to free them for more field time. Some of the steps being taken in this area are treated in the final chapter of this book.

Investigation

The general scope of responsibilities for the investigation section have already been outlined in relation to the patrol officer's role. The manner in which investigators are used varies considerably in different agencies ranging from round-the-clock deployment (in order to be able to begin the investigation of a crime immediately) to single, 8-hour shifts during each of the five normal workdays. In the latter instance, which is by far the most common, the detective doesn't become involved in most cases until the patrol officer has completed his preliminary investigation, often the next day unless the crime is unusually serious or complex.

The work of the investigative section is usually divided by type of crime, except for those investigators who specialize in handling juvenile cases. Adult follow-up investigations are typically handled by specialists in such fields as checks, auto theft, burglary, and so on. Entry into detective units is always from another functional unit, usually patrol. Typically an investigator will be paid a rate between patrolman and sergeant, and assignment into investigation is considered a promotion. In some agencies, however, officers are rotated through the detective bureau, and any pay differential is granted only for the duration of the assignment.

Training for the specialized assignment is almost always on the job as far as the department is concerned. Officers who want to prepare themselves to follow a career plan they've laid out for themselves can take classes at local colleges and universities which will be relevant to the job as it exists in their particular department. Typically a man is selected from the patrol bureau on the basis of collective recommendation of the field sergeants and assigned to work for a couple of weeks with an investigator already in the specialized field he'll enter. The case load for almost all detective units is so far in excess of what it should be that there is usually only time for this amount of training. That is, a man is seldom trained on the job in more than one specialty area before he is put to work.

While the public image of the police officer in general is pretty clearly focused on the uniformed patrolman, this clarity of image doesn't exist for detectives. Most people realize that the Sherlock Holmes image isn't realistic but have rather vague ideas of what plainclothes work is like. The very term suggests undercover work to most civilians, and yet a very small percentage of police work falls into this category. In fact, undercover work, when it does exist, is not the task of detectives but rather vice and narcotics officers who are usually under another administrative office.

The detective deals in questions. He works endlessly at seeking out more information relative to crimes. He interviews people who are victims and makes reports. He talks to witnesses and makes reports. He confers with members of the public prosecutor's office to help them get ready to take the case to court, and he makes reports. When a suspect isn't known, the detective asks questions of victims and witnesses to establish an identity. When the identity is known he asks questions of people who may know the suspect to try to establish his whereabouts. When the whereabouts are known he asks questions of the suspect to establish his guilt or innocence. When the suspect's guilt is established in the detective's mind he makes an arrest and asks more questions so he'll be able to establish that guilt in the eyes of the court. And then, when the case comes to trial, he appears as a witness for the state and answers questions from the people's attorney, the defense attorney, and even sometimes the judge.

A good portion of the investigator's time is spent contacting other law enforcement agencies. He reads teletypes looking for suspects who may be in custody elsewhere who could be tied to cases he has in which the suspect is unknown. Often he'll call nearby agencies and talk to their detectives handling the same type of case he does. The intent is to keep current on the types of incidents occurring in neighboring communities because criminals will often work one area for a while and then move to the next town. By exchanging information between neighboring agencies on crimes of a given type it's often possible to put together such clues as partial license plate numbers or descriptions and come up with an identification of a suspect.

Detectives complain about cases they are assigned that are

Investigation

"I don't know what you think detective work is like," Delaney said, staring at the man in the bed. "Most people have been conditioned by novels, the movies, and TV. They think it's either exotic clues and devilishly clever deductive reasoning, or else they figure it's all rooftop chases, breaking down doors, and shoot-outs on the subway tracks. All that is maybe five percent of what a detective does. Now I'll tell you how he mostly spends his time. About fifteen years ago a little girl was snatched on a street out on Long Island. She was walking home from school. A car pulled up alongside her and the driver said something. She came over to the car. A little girl. The driver opened the door, grabbed her, pulled her inside, and took off. There was an eyewitness to this, an old woman who 'thought' it was a dark car, black or dark blue or dark green or maroon. And she 'thought' it had a New York license plate. She wasn't sure of anything. Anyway, the parents got a ransom note. They followed instructions exactly: they didn't call the cops and they paid off. The little girl was found dead three days later. *Then* the FBI was called in. They had two things to work on: it *might* have been a New York license plate on the car, and the ransom note was hand-written. So the FBI called in about sixty agents from all over, and they were given a crash course in handwriting indentification. Big blow-ups of parts of the ransom note were pasted on the walls. Three shifts of twenty men each started going through every application for an automobile license that originated on Long Island. They worked around the clock. How many signatures? Thousands? Millions, more likely. The agents set aside the possibles, and then handwriting experts took over to narrow it down.

"Did they get the man?" Evelyn Case burst out.

"Oh sure," Delaney nodded. "They got him. Eventually. And if they hadn't found it in the Long Island applications, they'd have inspected every license in New York State. Millions and millions and millions. I'm telling you all this so you'll know what detective work usually is: common sense; a realization that you've got to start somewhere; hard, grinding, routine labor; and percentages. That's about it. . . ." [Reprinted by permission of G. P. Putnam's Sons from *The First Deadly Sin* by Lawrence Sanders. Copyright 1973 by Lawrence Sanders.]

unsolvable—the burglary cases with no known suspect. Over 80 percent of such cases are never going to be solved (as opposed to assault cases where only about 30 percent are unsolved or murder with only about 15 percent). Yet an investigation is required, reports must be filed, and the case load gets ever bigger. They tolerate the pick-and-shovel, in-custody cases which are turned over to them by the arresting patrol officers for routine follow-up and preparation for court trial. But they get their satisfaction from the unknown-suspect cases that have enough information to give them a start and in which they are able to turn up and arrest a suspect who may well be responsible for a whole series of similar crimes in the area.

Detectives feel that theirs is a desirable position, carrying with it a certain amount of prestige. Other officers look at it much the same way. There's not the same closeness and spirit in detective work as there is in patrol, though, and the same sorts of bonds don't develop. Whereas patrol officers are constantly backing each other up and learn to depend on this relationship, detectives work largely alone, isolated by their own specialization within a specialized unit. At most a detective will work with one partner on a regular basis, and the need to depend on other detectives doesn't exist to the degree it does in patrol.

Juvenile

Juvenile officers, as already pointed out, usually work within the investigation division and specialize in one type of client, the young offender, rather than one type of criminal act. Juvenile officers must be of a special cut. For one thing they must be able to relate to young people. The frustrations of such work are many. Most kids who get into trouble are released to their parents after counselling, and the abuse heaped upon an officer by a street-wise 15-year-old who knows what's happening can make this pretty tough to take. At the other end of the scale there are the youngsters who get into trouble because of their inablity to cope with peer pressure and for whom this single experience with the potential consequences of antisocial behavior is fully corrective. Here the juvenile officer sees, or at least senses, a positive result of his efforts.

In all but the largest agencies the juvenile officer works the same basic hours as the rest of the investigative division. To match the hours when court is in session, these are the hours of the daylight shift. Because so many of his clients don't match their schedule to this criterion, however, juvenile officers are subject to frequent calls during the evening and night hours. Normally this assignment consists partly of investigation (usually the background and family situation of the offender who was taken into custody by patrol) and partly of counselling the juveniles and their parents. Court appearances are required as frequently as for adult follow-up investigators. This is due to the nonadversary nature of the juvenile justice process and also to the fact that a high percentage of those taken into custody don't go to court at all.

The juvenile officer works extensively with the probation department in determining whether to petition the court to detain the young person or not. He also spends considerable time preparing case material on those offenders who become the subject of petitions. Television hasn't yet discovered the juvenile officer so the public, beyond the parents of those children unfortunate enough to become his clients, has no image of him. His fellow officers don't regard his assignment with particular envy, although many may wish that they had more of the personal qualities which enable him to perform this difficult and sensitive role. Advanced training is provided those whose interests and profiles lead them to juvenile work. Mandated in some states, such as Michigan and California, more agencies all the time are upgrading the requirements and training for juvenile officers. There are courses available in most colleges and universities which will help prepare the interested officer for his eventual assignment in this field.

Traffic

In most agencies a traffic assignment means motorcycle duty. There are a number of reasons for this, most relating to the greater mobility of motorcycles as compared with cars. Of course, every field operations officer is responsible for enforcement of the vehicle code, but the traffic unit has this as their primary responsibility. They aren't assigned a patrol district in the same sense as normal patrol units but do work in general areas. Whereas a patrol car will try to make it through every street in the beat at least once per shift, the motor officer will usually spend most of his time on the busy streets and at selected intersections where his appearance can have a preventive effect on violations.

Because motorcycle riding is admittedly hazardous duty,

168 LINE OPERATIONS

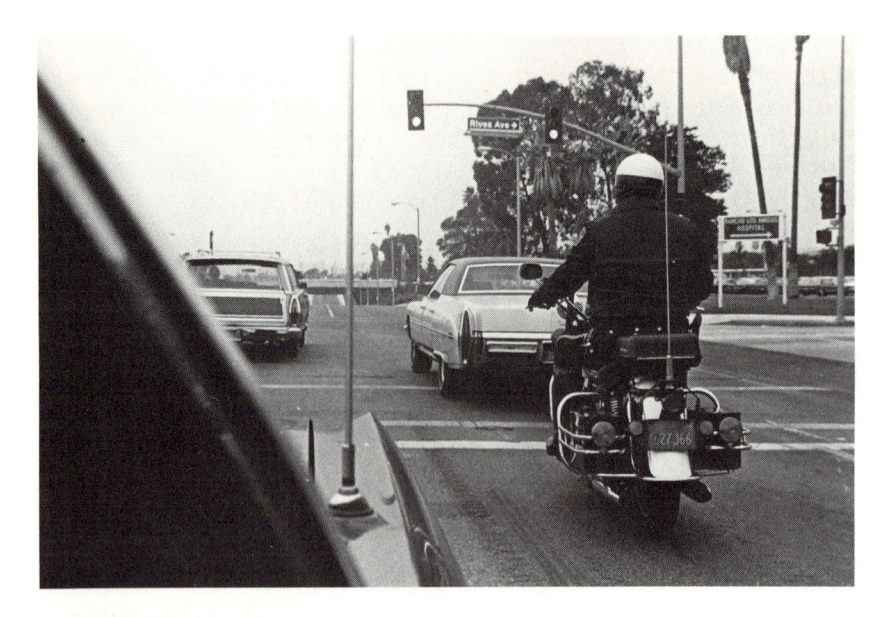

Traffic officers typify the police effort to most people. In spite of the hazards involved, the assignment is coveted by many officers.

extra compensation is usually granted for this assignment. The fact that it is more dangerous to patrol the streets on two wheels than four doesn't deter many officers from seeking this assignment. In fact, maybe even because of this added risk, motor officers almost invariably consider themselves an elite corps. And, as if in testimony to the validity of this feeling, motorcycle units will often be rolled into a situation where intimidation is the goal, as in riot control. There is something about the visible effect of the long-booted, leather-jacketed motorcycle officer that transcends the effect of logic which might emphasize his vulnerability compared with the steel-encased patrol unit.

Because *selective enforcement* (applying the most manpower to the times and locations of most need in terms of traffic violations and accidents) is the basic technique of traffic, working hours can be unusual. Not many agencies still practice the split-shift approach to matching manpower and need, but heaviest distribution of traffic personnel often overlaps normal patrol shift hours. Weekends are usually a little tougher to get off in this division because there are more cars on the roads on weekends and thus more accidents and violations.

Most motor officers enter the assignment from patrol and are already familiar with provisions of the vehicle code. Their initial training concentrates on learning to be a safe and proficient operator of their new means of transportation. Large departments provide their own instruction, but most take advantage of state or county training programs. Another factor of the job that appeals to most policemen is that there is less report writing than for any other assignment in field work. Unless the job entails primary responsibility for accident investigation as well as traffic enforcement, most incidents require only completion of the citation form. Occasionally someone will refuse to sign a citation, in spite of all reasoning and explanation of the meaning of the signature and the consequences for failing to do so, and have to be taken in under arrest. In such cases arrest reports are required, but this is rare. Arrests for drunk driving, however, are quite common.

Accident Investigation

Only in relatively large agencies is this a specialized unit. In most cases all patrol officers must be capable of and have direct responsibility for conducting and reporting a thorough investigation of traffic accidents. But the work must be done in every department, so we will treat it here as a separate, specialized section of a large, full-service agency.

Whereas the normal patrol unit has responsibility for an area that is a small subdivision of the city or division, and the traffic officer usually has an area overlapping several such beats, the accident investigator operates more on a demand basis. In the smaller city he'll have the whole thing as his territory; in the large metropolis he'll work two or three divisions as if it were his "city."

As you might expect, the work is often gory and each investigation can take a relatively long time (an hour is not unusual for multiple-car collisions with injuries) under hazardous conditions. The mere presence of flares and police cars with flashing red lights is no assurance that a drunk or curious driver won't drive right through a wreck and the assembled people. Some of the considerable pride which the A-I men feel for their assignment derives from the complexity of a good investigation. Skid marks need to be interpreted and recorded, a much more complex skill than most realize. Interviews need to be skillfully conducted at a level equal to that of most investigations of criminal cases. And, of course, lives need to be preserved, and a considerable financial impact on the parties to the accident hinges in large part on the quality of the investiga-

Accident investigation includes analysis of type and length of skid marks to determine conditions leading to the event.

tion the officer conducts. Since violation of a provision of the vehicle code is usually involved in determination of which party is the primary cause of the accident, thorough knowledge of the provisions of this code is required.

We've mentioned that A-I men take pride in their selection for this assignment. That their fellow officers view it in a like manner is attested to by the fact that in agencies which have such units there is usually a two- or three-year waiting list. In such agencies all officers are given basic training in accident investigation, but those who are assigned to the special unit are given advanced training before beginning their new duty. It is unusual for civilian educational institutions to offer training in this work other than as part of basic level instruction. Departments with specialized units normally have their own procedures they want followed and will not accept outside training as a substitute for academy training in these procedures. Entry into A-I work is usually through the motor officer route or regular patrol. A person with a definite career plan for himself, however, may try for the assignment at any stage of his career he wishes (though it would be strange to do so after making sergeant).

Vice

Vice units investigate liquor, gambling, and sex violations in a community. Many cities don't have vice units or, if they do, combine them with narcotics, intelligence, or both. The reasons for this alignment are that definitions of vice vary from community to community and in most cases there isn't enough of it (from the majority community viewpoint) to cause general alarm. The side effects usually are of more direct interest to police administrators: organized crime involvement in liquor sales, loansharking arising out of gambling, strongarm robbery linked to prostitution. These are activities that no community will tolerate and which can usually be worked by patrol or regular investigators. The most common exception is where organized crime becomes involved and the special skills of an intelligence unit are required.

In the larger agencies, which operate decentralized geographical divisions, there will usually be decentralized vice units under the coordinating direction of a centralized vice operation. The central operation coordinates, supports, and monitors the operation of the local units, a concept not always entirely popular with the highly specialized operational units. The extremely sensitive nature of their assignment often requires members of these units to assume unpolicelike appearances and/or lifestyles. Primarily for this reason they tend to become isolated from the rest of the agency. Because they have to operate in an atmosphere of unconventional discipline, the strain on their social life far exceeds that of being a policemen in general duty. It takes an understanding wife, for example, to put up with the special demands of this assignment. And the apparent habits of her son-in-law have dampened more than one mother-in-law's enthusiasm for her daughter's choice of a marital partner.

Vice officers usually regard their assignment as a challenging one offering more than the average share of unusual and exciting situations. Considerable special skills, not the least of which is the ability to give the appearance of drinking extensively without losing your ability to function, are required and special training is provided all selected. Larger agencies again provide their own training while smaller ones usually rely on state or federal agencies for this function.

Narcotics

As already noted, narcotics in smaller agencies is usually worked in conjunction with vice and/or intelligence. While vice is often extensively involved with narcotics, there are differences in the roles played. For one thing, while some communities are more tolerant of some vice activities such as prostitutes (even encouraging them for the extra business they can bring in the form of conventions and the like), no community is in favor of uncontrolled narcotics traffic. This at least assures the cooperation of the entire "good citizen" population, a luxury not enjoyed by all vice investigators. Another difference is in the demands placed on the officers themselves. While it's possible for an officer to work many vice operations while maintaining a normal physical appearance, such is not usually the case with street narcotics operations. If the mother-in-law of a vice officer objected to his carousing ways, she would come unglued over the scroungy appearance he takes on for a narcotics assignment. The high-level narcotics officer, as noted in the preceding chapter, can give the appearance of a business person and get by. The street "narc," however, is obliged to take on the appearance of those he deals with and thus goes unshaven, unshorn, and sometimes unwashed. An interesting observation here is that even with these cosmetic disguises, only

Narcotics officers, understandably reluctant to be photographed, have a lifestyle and appearance sharply in contrast with their fellow police officers.

a doper would really be fooled by the average narcotics officer's appearance for he retains, in spite of his hirsute adornment and native costume, a look of health and alertness that has long-since departed the true devotee of drugs. It's sad testimony to the effect of drug abuse that any narcotics officer can tell you of many dealers he's arrested not once but several times, each time making a buy before making the arrest.

From this it should be fairly obvious that the narcotics officer deals with far from the cream of society, even criminal society. Yet users and purveyors alike come from every social and economic stratum and seem to now come in all ages from junior high school up. The satisfaction for the narcotics officer comes from the fact that each time he is able to put away a seller, the spiralling effects of drug abuse slow a little, if only momentarily. Even the arrest and conviction of a user provide relief for society in spite of the popular "victimless crime" theory. The cost of drug-related shoplifting alone is estimated by some to amount to $1 billion annually. And there is virtually no way to estimate the suffering inflicted on mugging and armed robbery victims who have to pay with their own pain for someone else's habit.

In spite of the negative aspects of the job, most police officers regard a narcotics assignment as a prestigious one. Selection is made carefully, as it is for vice or intelligence, on the basis of not only the officer's personal abilities but his family situation as well. It's a wasteful move to put someone in a job like this if his family will be unable to put up with the special demands. Often an administrator can't tell in advance how a family will react, and when a situation turns bad there's nothing to do but reassign the man involved with no stigma attached.

Intelligence

Intelligence, in the military or police sense, is the knowledge gained from collective consideration of all available information on a given subject. Seemingly meaningless and unrelated bits of information, when processed by testing for validity, relevance, and integrated into the larger picture comprised of other information on that subject, provide intelligence that can lead to solution or prevention of crimes.

The object of police intelligence can be anything that poses a threat to the community. Usually it is organized crime or some activity that threatens order, such as the violence-oriented groups that spring up constantly across the country. Some adjuncts of organized crime, such as gambling, seem to be more within the purview of a vice operation (and that is one reason for the frequent combination of vice and intelligence operations in all but the largest departments) but others, such as extortion on a community wide basis, don't involve vice at all.

The intelligence officer works cases by gathering information. In most cases he doesn't make arrests; he gathers information which he uses to derive intelligence that will allow someone else to make the arrest. In fact, strange as it may seem, this very fact often enables an intelligence officer to gather information that would otherwise be denied him. An officer who is known to be intelligence can often sit down in conversation with a subject and be told things that would never be told to an ordinary detective. The psychology of this relationship is not entirely clear, but there seems to be something in the nature of a game involved. The criminal will reveal information to the intelligence officer partly because he knows an immediate arrest is not at issue. There may be some element of ego involved as well, since he's not talking to just another cop but a member of an elite group, or it may be that there is an implied element of confidentiality involved. In any event, the intelligence officer is almost exclusively an information-gathering agent and, as such, either does his job exceedingly well or virtually not at all.

The function of intelligence is primarily surveillance rather than infiltration or undercover investigation. Thus there is usually no need to affect the appearance of the counterculture (which might even be counterproductive in many if not most cases). This is one reason that intelligence combines better with vice operations than narcotics in small departments that can staff at only minimal levels. The work requires the ability to play many roles, however, and may require talking to street people in the morning and having lunch with high-level business executives at noon, with the need in both cases to have the person identify with the officer sufficiently to want to talk to him.

The assignment is both prestigious and difficult. Officers are selected for their intellectual capacity and also for clearly established loyalties, outgoing personality, emotional security and, even more strictly than normal police officers, an impeccable family and financial situation. The exposure to compromise is high in this position and the potential in the officer must be correspondingly low. The work can be tedious and often routine to the point of boredom. Making endless notes of such unglamourous events as seeing a subject on a given day at a given intersection driving a car of a particular make isn't exactly work in the mold of the television super-detective. But, when pieced together, months later with a dozen or so other seemingly bits of trivia to make a case against an organized ring of extortionist operating on used-car dealers, it has its rewards. The lack of immediate reward in the form of arrest at the conclusion of the investigation is somehow compensated for by the overall impact on community life.

The training required for intelligence work is so highly specialized that it's hard to prepare for the assignment in advance of selection for it. Attorneys general, at the state level, most commonly provide the training for local agencies. Large agencies, such as those in major cities and counties, may provide their own training in addition to or instead of this program.

Evidence Collection and Analysis

All but the smallest agencies have some special expertise available to them for collection and processing of evidence. Some departments train all incoming officers in the basic techniques of collecting and processing evidence, aiming at reaching the point where all officers are generally able to function appropriately in this important area. Others select certain patrol officers and provide them training as evidence technicians. This is aimed at having a quasi specialist in crime scene examination available around the clock. As the size of an agency nears 100 officers, full-time specialists in this category are usually employed to locate, collect, and preserve physical evidence at the crime scene.

In the still larger agencies, full-blown crime laboratories, staffed with highly trained evidence technicians and criminalists are used, often on both a centralized and mobile laboratory basis. Another class of evidence specialist is the identification (ID) technician who, like the evidence technician, is a specialist in finger printing and other forms of gathering evidence. But unlike the evidence technician, the ID technician is usually also directly responsible for photography and darkroom work and often even property and evidence storage and retrieval. Various combinations of these roles are found in different departments, but these are the basic elements.

176 LINE OPERATIONS

The criminalist is usually a civilian with a baccalaureate degree in forensic chemistry, criminology, or a combination of these fields. He probably is paid around the level of a lieutenant and works days. The type of investigatory evidence he supplies isn't usually such that a person's detention or freedom waits for his analysis. His analysis is usually to determine such qualities as narcotic or non-narcotic nature of a substance or alcohol content of blood or urine. These high-volume tests are usually made by a technician working a two- or three-shift program at the local agency level. The criminalist makes exotic determinations requiring spectrographic and neutron activation analyses of paint fragments, dirt samples, glass shards, and the like. These can normally wait until he comes to work in the morning, whereas the other determinations mentioned need to be made immediately to establish whether a suspect is to be detained or released.

The technician, either evidence or identification, can prepare for the position by taking classes at the college or university level but more generally is given academy and/or on-the-

Identification technicians perform functions most people associate with detective work, such as the fingerprint analysis being performed here.

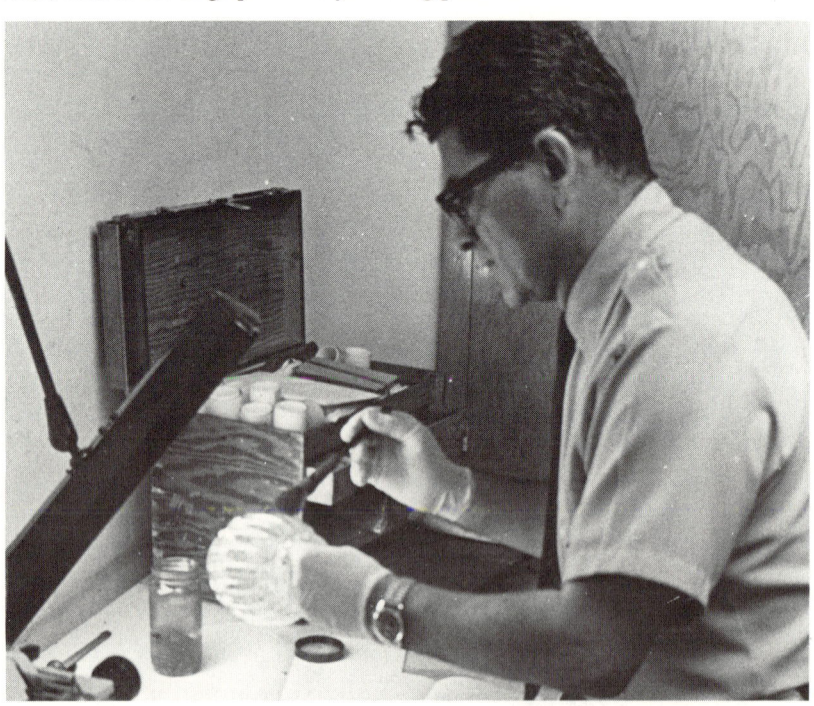

job training after selection. In most agencies the ID technician is not a sworn position and progression into line police work is relatively rare. That the technician is an essential part of the investigation team, however, is not in doubt. Most detectives or prosecuting attorneys will admit that regardless of the quality of job he might do in identifying a suspect and the evidence against him, the successful prosecution of a case depends considerably on the quality of the job done by the evidence or identification technician. For example, an unfortunately too common sight at the scene of a crime is an inexperienced officer allowing the area to be trampled by civilian onlookers and even other officers before it's decided that items such as tire prints, footprints and even fingerprints might help the case. Bits of evidence as seemingly insignificant as scraps of paper or cloth may, because of the trained technician, become keys to successful identification and prosecution of a suspect. Even the value of such obviously important items of evidence as a gun at a murder scene may be diminished through improper handling by inexperienced or unknowledgeable officers. Avoidance of such errors of omission and commission is the specialty of evidence and identification technicians. An experienced and alert technician can sometimes put together a web of logical evidence that has been overlooked by an investigator, taking the case out of the realm of "knowing" a suspect is guilty and putting it into the category of provable cases.

SUMMARY

Line command structure within an organization is the vertical distribution of power beginning at the top with the chief and progressing downward through such positions as deputy chief, captain, lieutenant, and sergeant.

Specialization refers to the horizontal distribution of the department's work by organizing it into general types such as field services, investigation, and administration. Each specialized area of an organization has its own command structure within the general structure of the agency.

Patrol, within the field services division, puts uniformed officers into the field to perform *preventive patrol, inspectional,* and *called-for services.* Deploying patrol personnel into assigned districts throughout the city according to the experienced percentage of need for police service in each district, aims at minimizing response time to calls for service and maximizing the impression of police presence and the ability to observe potential crime situations.

Investigation is an area of specialization created to increase the amount of time a police officer has for patrol. After the responding officer makes the initial investigation and a report of all known details, the investigator or detective conducts the follow-up investigation to identify, locate, and arrest suspects. Work within the investigation division is usually divided by type of crime; the exception is juvenile work which is handled by officers specializing in this type of investigation, regardless of the nature of the offense.

Juvenile officers not only identify suspects and take them into custody when possible but also conduct investigations into the young offender's background to determine if he should be recommended for detention and processing through the juvenile justice system or counselled and released to his parents.

Traffic specialists usually work within the field services division on motorcycles. They don't have assignments on the same geographical basis as other patrol officers but generally concentrate their efforts on those times, intersections, and streets which are the biggest contributors to traffic accidents. This technique is called *selective enforcement.*

Accident investigation, as a unit, is responsible for investigation, determination of responsibility for, and reporting of all accidents in which vehicles are involved.

Vice investigates liquor, gambling, and sex violations within a community. In many departments vice may be combined with *narcotics* and/or *intelligence* operations. Narcotics investigates illicit sale or use of narcotic and dangerous drugs. Intelligence gathers information relevant to any specified criminal activity in a community but generally concentrates on those involving organized crime or violence-oriented organizations.

Evidence collection and analysis is performed by technicians for the high-volume, immediate-need items of evidence such as narcotics content or blood-alcohol level. For the more exotic determinations evidence is collected by technicians and submitted to crime laboratories for analysis by *criminalists.*

REVIEW QUESTIONS

Answers to these questions appear on page 384.

1. *True or false?* Chain of command requires that the chief be better at each of the specialty administration tasks supervised by his captains than they are. The captains, in

turn, must be better at the specialty positions under their command than the officers who perform them.
2. Within the patrol function, the officer in charge of police operations during a particular shift, regardless of his rank, has the title of _____.
3. The position described in the preceding question:
   a. is *usually* filled by an officer with the rank of _____;
   b. is next-most frequently filled by an officer with the rank of _____.
4. The first type of specialization within police departments was the creation of what position? _____
5. The responsibility of observing potential crime situations, responding to citizen calls for police service in a timely manner, and creating the impression of police presence throughout the city, belongs to what functional division of the department? _____
6. How is the workload of cases within the investigation division most commonly divided? _____
7. The most common exception to the rule expressed in the preceding question is what type of assignment? _____
8. *True or false? Selective enforcement* is a term describing the common practice in traffic work of concentrating the policing effort at certain intersections and along certain streets.
9. Two kinds of police work are involved primarily with vehicle code violations. What are they? _____
10. Three types of police work are often combined in one way or another in smaller agencies.
    a. What are these three functions? _____
    b. Which of the three frequently requires an appearance change on the part of the officer? _____
    c. Which type of assignment least frequently involves direct arrests by the investigating officer? _____

CHAPTER 7

SUPPORT SERVICES

OVERVIEW

While the line organization of the police department is set up to take care of the needs of the community, the *support services* organization is set up to take care of the needs of the department. These functions are no less important than street police work or investigation. Yet that's the feeling most people would admit to if pressed for their honest impression.

The tasks range from broadcasting crime information to washing cars, from pushing pins in a map to investigating possibly corrupt policemen. To say that each one is important is almost patronizing; if the work weren't vital to the operation of the agency it wouldn't be done because budget dollars aren't that easy to come by. What's more relevant here is the way each contributes, and we'll look at each of these supportive operations and see how they make the job of the street cop easier, more effective, and maybe even possible!

RADIO-TELEPHONE COMMUNICATIONS

This support service is probably the most easily recognized contribution to the success or failure of the street police function. Haphazard work on the radio desk can make a critical difference in the ability of the patrol officer to apprehend a criminal. It can even cost an officer his life. Think about any crime that comes to mind—a liquor store robbery, for example, an extremely common crime and one in which seconds make a tremendous difference in the probability of apprehending the suspect. It's only in the movies that the cops start out five minutes after the robbers and catch them. Especially with the availability of high-speed highways in most cities and towns, a one- or two-minute lead time means some other officer in some other town may catch him, but not you. An incorrect or incomplete initial crime broadcast can easily result in the suspect driving right by an officer who waits in frustration for the broadcast to tell him what he needs to know: what happened, what the suspects look like, and where they might be. Too often he finds out just in time to realize they passed him thirty seconds ago, going the other way. Or consider what might happen to an officer who receives the information that the robbers have fled several minutes ago, but not that there were three of them, all armed. If he finds the suspect car, with only two occupants in the front seat, the surprise on the floor in back may be his last. The organization of the radio-telephone communications section is basically the same in all but the very smallest agen-

Communications operators link incoming calls and the field force.

cies: there's a *complaint* position which receives calls from citizens, and a *broadcast* position which transmits and receives calls over the radio between the field force and headquarters. In the smallest agencies both positions may be handled by one person, but this is a very difficult task with more than one or two cars in the field. In medium-size agencies the complaint position will be divided between a *desk* function (usually handled by a uniformed officer to receive complaints personally from citizens) and a *PBX* or telephone position. The telephone position may be manned by either a sworn officer or a trained, professional civilian. If the competency level of the civilian is adequate, this is a preferable arrangement because it frees a police officer for field duty. In many cases a trained civilian works out better because he considers the job as a career position as opposed to a policeman whose main qualification may be that he's been injured on duty and is doing this until he gets well enough to go back in the field.

In the largest agencies there may be dozens of *radio-telephone operators* (RTO's) doing the broadcasting of calls received by a complaint board which is manned by a corps of experienced and specially trained police officers. The complaint board will take calls from all over the city and pass them to a supervisor who knows every district and assigns the call to the appropriate RTO, who in turn broadcasts it to the right car. The RTO has to not only know each beat in the district but also which cars are in service, which are out for investigation or on a meal break, and so on. Some cities, notably Chicago, have exotic control boards which show the status and location of every car in the city at all times. Others, such as Los Angeles, rely on manual systems worked by both the RTO and the supervisor. Either way, the excitement of a pursuit is almost as great in the radio room of a large agency as it is in the cars involved. Special link operators, trained in the peculiar problems of pursuit broadcasting, may take over and block normal, nonemergency transmission as the pursuit crosses district and even city boundaries. The communications center takes on the atmosphere of a war room until the pursuit is terminated and radio traffic goes back to normal.

In addition to receiving citizen complaints and broadcasting calls on the radio, communications center personnel get involved in many other information gathering and transmission activities. Teletypes are used to transmit and receive warrants and records. At officers' requests, centralized computer data-banks are queried for the specialized information they contain (stolen property, wants and warrants, vehicle registration, and so on). Silent alarm systems are monitored and notifications made when the alarms are activated. In some agencies personnel also interact with electronic report-taking equipment to transcribe reports telephoned from the field.

The communications operator position, another term for either complaint or broadcast functions, is one often filled exceptionally well by women. The reasons are many and include such considerations as the fact that callers are often excited to the point of near or actual hysteria and a woman's voice can have a soothing effect in such situations. The opposite can be just as true, of course, and some callers prefer to hear a masculine voice when they call for police help. In any event, when a woman fills this position in a smaller agency she is very often the only female on duty when the need arises for a policewoman. Under these conditions the job can take on aspects that are vastly different from information communication, and this is probably one of the reasons so many young women find the job attractive and rewarding. Male or female, communications operator is a job that demands more skill and offers more challenges than many people realize.

RECORDS

As you might expect, the records section of any police agency is responsible for information storage and retrieval. The value to the street or investigatory function can range from invaluable to valueless. The difference is not in the type of information stored but in the retrievability of it. A dramatic comparison of two similar-size departments located within ten miles of each other comes instantly to mind. In one, every case ever handled in the city is still on file. Large, electrically-transported file drawers bring records to a half-dozen scurrying clerks at the touch of a button, yet detectives have grown so weary of being unable to get any information, or complete information, that they sometimes don't even ask. In the other department a lone clerk works calmly among less than a half-dozen vertical files retrieving information that's no more than five years old and usually less than three. Older records are microfilmed or destroyed. The real difference is in the design and organization of the retrieval system. Detectives never have missing documents, never have partial files, and can always get the information they want. They rely on the files and use them as a law enforcement tool.

To a great extent the type of information available from records varies with the size of the department and, accordingly, the amount of money available for developing files. Typically, however, such records as arrest, stolen property, pawn tickets, crime reports, photos, fingerprints, method of operation, alias and the like will be used for criminal investigation and identification. Information in such files can also be sorted by time of occurrence, place, and even day of week to help distribute personnel to the different shifts during a day and deploy them into appropriate areas of the city. Other files on traffic citations and accidents can provide information that will allow effective deployment of traffic units to reduce accidents.

With computerization the data needed by any administrative officer can be sorted according to his individual requirements in a fraction of the time that would be required by manual systems. This, of course, is a concept long embraced by larger business concerns, and with the spread of batch processing and shared-time computers, even relatively small law enforcement agencies now can and do avail themselves of the benefits of computerized data banks. The impact of this developing trend has been to accelerate use of civilian specialists to staff record operations. Clerical personnel have long been civilians, but staff-level work has been done largely by police officers. The volume and complexity of data gathered and demanded now requires a specialization of knowledge that is making it necessary in many cases to turn to industry-trained personnel rather than to retrain policemen.

Records section in smaller agencies is also involved in issuance and documentation of warrants, recall of warrants when the subjects are arrested, creation of state and federally-required reports, issuance of subpoenas and, in general, the office function of most departments in the small-to-medium-size range. The function, staffed mostly with female employees, operates three shifts every day, including weekends, as do communications and any other function involved with patrol.

EQUIPMENT MAINTENANCE

A patrol officer spends two-thirds of his working life in a car. It's no exaggeration to say that the safety of the city depends to a large degree on the quality of the transportation he has available to him in an emergency. Brakes that fail during a pursuit are an obvious danger to life and property of not only the officer but any citizen nearby. A radio that doesn't work can be just as important if the failure occurs at a critical time, and critical times occur constantly. Many cities contract with private concerns for maintenance of vehicles and other operational equipment, but others maintain their own repair facilities. Often the police department will share such a service with other governmental service agencies such as public works. Larger departments with a hundred or more vehicles usually maintain their own police garage because they can't afford to take their chances on priorities assigned to their needs by someone out of their control. Staff in such operations is usually made up of male civilians, and some service is usually provided around the clock although the bulk of the work is done during the days.

PROPERTY

Every police agency regardless of its size handles a veritable mountain of property that isn't theirs: *contraband* taken from arrestees (weapons, drugs and the like), *evidence* to be held for trial, *recovered property* to be returned to owners or disposed of in some other way if that's not possible, *found property* turned in by citizens, and property which belongs to arrestees

Property rooms in most police departments could easily stock a small store with anything from tape decks to house plants.

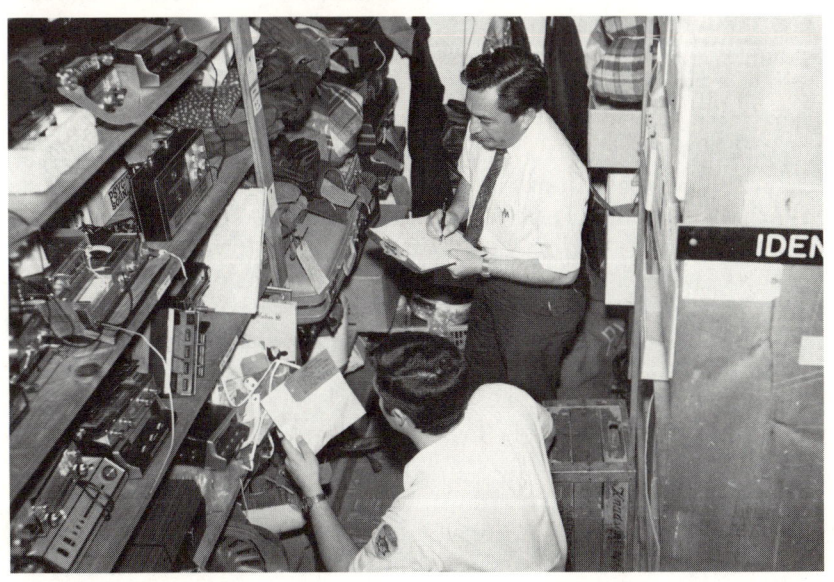

and will be returned to them upon their release or go with them when they are transferred. It amounts to literally tons in most agencies and it's both a responsibility and a major problem. Many departments have to rent space to store the goods they're forced to handle. And with diversion programs now becoming so prevalent, property that may some day be used in a criminal trial (if the person fails to meet the goals of his diversion program) must be stored for indefinite periods.

Not only does the system require security for the goods but also a retrieval system and dependable records to account for the whereabouts of the property at all times from its entry into the system until its ultimate disposal. Typically movement through a system following booking of a prisoner can involve part of the property being returned to him (or sent with him as he is transferred to a larger detention facility, and then returned to him if he is bailed out of that facility prior to arraignment) and part being retained for presentation at trial. If he is convicted and does time, some of the property may be destroyed after a period of time and other parts may be held for return to him upon his release, and so on; it's not a simple task.

Traditionally a job handled by sworn peace officers, there is a definite trend to civilianization of the function. Large cities such as Dallas and Los Angeles have or are in the process of utilizing civilians at all levels of the property operation from administration down to clerical. Smaller cities have experimented with using civilians from antipoverty programs and have experienced varying degrees of success, generally less than in the programs initially aimed at turning the function over to career civilians.

The property section is sometimes combined with the supply function and made responsible for maintaining departmental operating supplies. In some agencies the entire operation is placed under another administrative or technical services operation, such as ID technicians, and made the part-time responsibility of police aides. With the growing size of the problem, however, there is a strong trend to full-time responsibility by career people.

PRISONER CONTROL

"Prisoner Control" may sound like government jargon for "jailer" but there is a necessary distinction. Every agency has some sort of prisoner control, whether it is simply a matter of booking arrestees and putting them into a holding cell before transporting them to a jail in another city or housing them in the agency's own jail for thirty days after conviction. There's a big difference in the type of operation required for these alternative systems because the holding facility operation doesn't need to be concerned with such problems as meal preparation and the like. Their guests will only be with them for a couple of hours so they can wait for their meal until they get to the next hotel.

Then there is the matter of supervision. A jail requires a 24-hour-a-day supervisor, while a holding facility may be monitored by a television camera or even a microphone. The jail requires full-time jailers who may or may not be sworn peace officers. As with most police functions not directly related to patrol or investigation, there is a growing trend to use non-sworn personnel as jailers. Special training is required and uniforms are worn, but the need for police officer training and experience is not evident if you examine the role carefully.

There is a definite trend (in fact a goal recommended by the national Task Force on Police) to centralization and civilianization of jails in municipal agencies. The Task Force has recommended that by 1982 all municipal agencies turn over their detention and correctional functions to county and state agencies. They also recommend that agencies which anticipate requiring full-time detention employees after 1975 hire and train civilian personnel to handle the function. If achieved, this goal will mean the end of jail facilities in municipal agencies which will then have only the temporary holding facilities described above. If you subscribe to the theory held by many that the police role of arrest aimed at prosecution is incompatible with the detentional role of care and custody of the accused, this movement seems to make sense. It is a wise move in any event if you consider the availability of sworn police officers for other duties made possible by civilianization of the function.

PERSONNEL AND TRAINING

These two functions are often combined in all but the largest agencies. Unless the agency maintains its own academy, training is largely a matter of planning the continuing *roll-call training*. A topic is selected for discussion at each briefing session prior to the oncoming shift taking the field (sometimes less-frequently). Subjects are naturally police job topics. Typi-

188 SUPPORT SERVICES

Roll call training, with or without supplemental materials such as the videotape being used here, comprises the bulk of police inservice training.

cally the sergeant may take care of the notices for the day, make any assignment changes required for the upcoming shift, advise of special situations existing and how they are to be handled, and then introduce the topic. "Komrosky, suppose you roll on a 211 silent to the Banner market and when you get there you see two dudes inside going through the register. Manager's on the floor and so're a bunch of customers. What're you gonna do?" No matter what Komrosky answers, he isn't told if it's right or wrong. The sergeant just asks somebody else what they think about the answer. And so on around the room it goes. At some point the training officer gets into it and evaluates the different approaches suggested by each officer. Then it's time for more questions and the session is over.

That's about the extent of roll-call training in most agencies, and it's not all that bad. Many departments now have more sophisticated facilities such as videotape equipment and take advantage of materials put out by state and federal enforcement offices. The tapes are played and then discussions are held. Still other agencies are developing their own tapes to promote special department policies for handling specific types of calls and even promoting management programs. The function of roll-call training is not to develop recruits to basic police officer proficiency; that's the job of the academies. Roll call is to keep the fine edge on the skills of officers already trained and experienced. Everybody forgets basics a little as time goes on and this forgetfulness can get you into trouble.

Administration of a *career development program* usually means taking a survey of the police-related subjects offered by public schools and colleges in the area (and private universities and colleges as well, although the expense of these often rules them out) and coordinating it to development programs for individual officers. The role of the training officer then becomes that of counsellor and administrator of whatever reimbursement policy the department has for officers who are attempting to further their careers with formal education.

Typically the training officer may notice that a particular officer has applied for and received reimbursement for several classes completed in job-related subjects, but the courses taken may lack direction toward any apparent goal. Noting that more courses fall into one area than another, he may talk to the officer to see if he has any particular goal in mind. Finding that he does, the TO might suggest that certain courses would get him closer to the goal he's after. Failing to find a goal or direction, he may try to help the officer set one so his classwork will be more productive for him.

Another function of this position is the laying out of training programs for desired department specialization. If the department decides to set up a certain specialty position, the training officer will outline a training program for the selected officer to meet the state and department requirements. Part of the training may be on the job, another part in the academy of a larger local agency, still another at a state or federal academy, and yet another at some public or private college or university. As important as these functions are, they're seldom required frequently enough to keep a person occupied full time in most agencies. This accounts in part for the customary combination of the function with that of personnel.

Recruitment usually also falls into the personnel organization. Not many agencies do nationwide recruiting but some of the very largest municipal and county departments have occasionally done just that. Most agencies receive inquiries from officers presently employed in other departments and wishing to relocate and from applicants in other cities and states. Personnel of course responds to these. Testing applicants as part of the selection process is another personnel function, as is the background check run on applicants who pass the initial selection steps. Arranging for or conducting polygraph tests may also be done. Maintenance of files on all personnel within the department throughout their careers is another personnel responsibility.

Administration and recruiting, as personnel functions, are normally handled by staff police officers, captains or at least lieutenants. Examinations, background checks, and training are usually handled by sergeants while the clerical functions are usually performed by civilian personnel. There is no widespread trend to increase civilianization of these functions with the possible exception of the training area. Use of educational technologists on a consultant basis has had some application in the larger departments. Notable among these is the Los Angeles Police Department's M.I.L.E. project (Multi-media In Law Enforcement) which developed self-instructional materials for much of the academy curriculum.

RESEARCH AND PLANNING

Usually performed by police officers under a lieutenant or sergeant, this staff function is the one through which all new programs considered by the chief are initially run. The range of assignments is virtually limitless. The unit may be asked to look into the use of new weapons, a new kind or brand of patrol car, the advisability of generalization as opposed to specialization of the patrol and investigation functions, new plans for distributing and deploying personnel, how to increase the amount of preventive patrol time available to officers, and so on ad infinitum.

For some officers it would be considered a dull job—lots of research and not much action. But for others it's an exciting challenge: a chance to find out what other agencies are doing and how it's working out, and a constant opportunity to look into new ways of doing the job and trying them out. It is not a job for people who want to maintain the status quo but for those who like to get to the bottom of things and find out as much as possible about a subject. It's an important job, for obviously, if it weren't for research and planning activity, whether or not it was done by a unit with that title, policemen would still be communicating with each other by banging their night sticks on the pavement.

The pick-and-shovel aspect of research and planning is in the documentation of the research and testing effort. Reports have to be written and manuals developed. This part of the job appeals to a still smaller percentage of police types than even the research, but it has to be done. Fortunately, as with so much of support service there is an increasing amount of the work being done by civilians, and preparing manuals and documents as well as much researching and developing the information can be done by civilians trained in this specialized field.

STATISTICAL ANALYSIS

Development and analysis of statistical bases for management decisions is a huge field of specialized endeavor in industry and a burgeoning one in law enforcement. In police work it can be a part of records, personnel, or research and planning. Increasingly it is a separate function which develops statistics and either analyzes them, as a service to other sections of the organization, or turns them over in raw or sorted form for analysis by the requesting party.

Typical of the types of data requested is crime occurrence by district, time of day, day of week, and month of year. From this information the patrol division is able to assign men to each of the different watches, each of the patrol districts and, hopefully, even control days off and vacations somewhat in harmony with the principles of proportionate need.

Another obvious example of need for statistics in police management is in traffic enforcement, as mentioned earlier. Performance evaluation, comparing actual performance of individual officers and organizational units with some pre-established goal, is also dependent on good statistics, as are reports required by state and federal governmental agencies.

Most agencies are now using or at least considering civilian personnel, especially those with experience in computer systems technology, for statistics gathering and analysis functions. These are relatively high-paid positions, open to men and women equally.

COMMUNITY RELATIONS

The title of this operational unit conjures up at least two separate, if not distinct, images. First there's the relatively slick image of the department spokesman: gray at the temples, perhaps, or crew-cut and wide-eyed, depending on the popular style of the moment. In either event he meets with members of the media, handing out prepared statements in defense or praise of whatever action of the department has the public interest. This particular stereotype of community, or press, relations is likely to be found in only the largest metropolitan agencies. There he'll be a captain or a commander chosen for his ability to think on his feet and keep them out of his mouth.

Most community relations functions are more directly aimed at accomplishing police objectives rather than defending or publicizing them. As has been mentioned earlier and will be enlarged upon again later, community and police goals are now almost universally recognized as needing to come closer together if either is to be achieved. The fact is probably that they already are identical, or nearly so, and any apparent difference is due to poor statement of their goals by both parties and failure to communicate. To this end the activities of the community relations officer are directed.

The basic premise of police–community relations activity is that, since the goals of police and community must be about the same, police can best communicate this fact by increased exposure of their people and operation to the public. In other words, if they have nothing to hide from the public and are really not at any cross-purposes with them, the best way to demonstrate that is to get out among them on other than a called-for or ticket-issuing basis. Either of these two public contacts for police is on a purely professional basis and does nothing to enhance the image of the policeman as a human member of the community at large. In these contacts he is a member of a different community, the police community, and this divides goals rather than unifies them.

The community relations section of the police department does such obvious things as sponsor and participate in community-service operations such as youth organizations and service clubs. Speakers are furnished for church and school programs. Demonstrations and lectures are provided for safety council and citizen meetings of all types. Open houses are held at the police department and ride-along programs are encouraged for not only police-oriented kids but those who are willing to express doubts about the police role as a "community helper" and friend. Police science classes are taught in local high schools and community colleges and officers are furnished, sometimes almost as fodder, to answer questions for sociology classes.

Other programs are less showy, perhaps, and more directly concerned with particular crime problems in the community.

Property identification programs, where the police department loans tools to citizens for the purpose of engraving some identification number (such as their drivers license or social security number) on personal belongings to combat burglary. Such identification on an item reduces its value in pawnshops, and a widespread program of this type eventually leads to discouragement of burglars who don't have an established organization available to them for conversion of property.

"Block clubs" are encouraged by some departments to develop a cooperative, watchdog network among the citizens of a given area. The goal is to increase early reporting of suspicious activity of a special type (usually burglary). Meetings are held with the block organizations where policemen tell about and demonstrate ways of protecting the home against crime. Perhaps more important than the technical aspects of such meetings is the opportunity to meet with citizens on a less formal basis, though still professional, than in the emergency or violation situation.

The goal of all this activity is a broad one and difficult to assign as supportive to any particular line function. To the extent that it succeeds in reducing crime, rather than making investigation or apprehension more effective, all other activities of the department are made easier. This particular support service, because of its fundamental goal of increasing police exposure within the community, has to be performed by policemen rather than civilians. It's a role that is increasingly being performed by women and men together, however, and presents a good specialization opportunity for minority-race officers.

INTERNAL AFFAIRS

This unique function, which investigates possible misconduct of officers, is called many things by policemen with "headhunters" being perhaps the most charitable and printable. The role of policing the police is at once regarded with a chill and a feeling of some pride by the officers of the agency. Only effective internal discipline can eliminate corruption and individual malfeasance in a police organization, and probably the most productive form of such disipline is the peer pressure that comes from pride in belonging to a flawless unit.

In the large agencies, which are the only ones with full-time need for an internal discipline unit that has no other duties, there is a certain amount of honest fear engendered by the operation. It's not a matter of having anything in the closet to be afraid of, but more a matter of the dispassionate, methodical tenacity with which an internal affairs investigation is often conducted. If an agency is large enough to have a full-time unit investigating possible misconduct among its officers, it's also big enough to have had a few cases of proven misconduct. The people in the investigating unit, aware of this very real possibility of a fellow-officer having done something that will reflect badly on hundreds or thousands of other officers who haven't earned a bad name, lack compassion until it's clearly established that the accused officer is innocent. If that

---

Policing the Police

A patrolman caught on the take used to be prosecuted quickly and forgotten; now he is often "turned" and used to trap higher-ups. The spread of uniformed informers is matched by the proliferation of bugs planted everywhere but inside badges. A blizzard of accountants and other financial sleuths now trace credit cards and checking accounts because, says Jonathan Goldstein, U.S. prosecutor for New Jersey, often "it's just a matter of finding the money."

One internal police-investigation unit is currently running its own "pad"—a list of undercover cops getting quite real and regular bribes from gamblers. The idea is to see which other officers come sniffing around to get on the pad. (Afterward, the gamblers will be prosecuted as well.) Suspected cops are also given access to controlled amounts of drugs to find out what they will do with them. In another bit of "integrity testing" that comes tantalizingly close to entrapment, 51 New York police were recently given "lost" wallets containing money; 30 percent failed to turn them in and drew administrative penalties.

The success of these ever more mechanized, computerized, organized methods of fighting graft has prompted a new sense, as Houston Prosecutor Robert C. Bennett Jr. notes, that "something can be done about it." There are signs of a change in attitude among cops too. Michael Armstrong [Queens County District Attorney] . . . says that among Queens police, corruption was once so fashionable that some cops used to exaggerate their "scores" in locker-room bull sessions. Now, says Armstrong, "you've got rookies giving oldtimers a hard time about corruption." [*Time* (May 6, 1974). Reprinted by permission from TIME, The Weekly Newsmagazine; Copyright Time Inc.]

sounds like "guilty until proven innocent" and smacks of unconstitutionality, you can understand a little of why good, clean officers have mixed feelings about the internal affairs unit.

In smaller agencies the need for internal discipline is no less real than in the larger ones, but the numbers involved make it impractical or unnecessary to have a full-time investigative unit. Investigation of a citizen complaint against an officer or the malfeasance suspected within the department itself may be assigned to the commander of a unit or to a staff level officer. To avoid the stigma of perpetual duty of this type, the assignment is usually rotated periodically. In the full-time units, duty is usually limited to a specified number of months to avoid both the stigma and the possibility of establishing a gestapo-type organization within the department.

The ultimate decision on matters of internal discipline must lie with the chief. He makes the decision based on as many facts as he can obtain and without the formality of a courtroom-type proceeding. There may be a trial board which examines the case. Members of the department, peers of the officer being investigated, will sit on such a board and examine the evidence, but the final decision will still be made by the chief.

SUMMARY

The *radio-telephone communications* section has two basic positions to provide the link between citizens and police patrol: *complaint* and *broadcast*. The complaint position takes citizens' requests for help either in person at a desk or, more commonly, over the telephone. The broadcast position communicates with the field force by radio-telephone.

The *records* section stores and provides all police records which provide investigative or administrative assistance to the department.

The *equipment maintenance* function keeps departmental rolling stock and communications equipment in operating condition.

The *property* section maintains records and control over all property that comes into police possession whether it is contraband, evidence, recovered property, found property, or property belonging to arrestees. In smaller agencies it may also handle procurement and distribution of departmental operating supplies.

Prisoner control involves either temporary detention of an

196 SUPPORT SERVICES

arrestee in a *holding facility* and subsequent transportation of him to a centralized jail facility, or custodial detention of him in a *jail* operated by the agency.

Personnel and training are often combined in a single unit with the training function consisting of on-going, in-service training at roll-call sessions. Career development counselling and coordination are also handled in such an operation; recruitment, applicant testing, background checks, and maintenance of personnel records are the normal personnel functions.

Research and planning conducts studies of proposed departmental changes and reports findings to the administration. Manual preparation for the department is also often handled by this unit.

Statistical analysis units have responsibility for development and analysis of statistical bases for on-going operations of the agency.

Community relations may involve handling press relations but covers all departmental activities aimed at improving the image of police and the understanding of their goals by the community of which they are part.

Internal affairs is the function of an agency which has responsibility for investigating reported or suspected instances of police misbehavior.

REVIEW QUESTIONS

Answers to these questions appear on page 384.

1. If you were a police officer and had each of the needs described below, with which of the support service sections described in this chapter would you become involved:

    _____ a. You're on patrol and want to request a meeting in the field with your sergeant.

    _____ b. A citizen stops you as you drive past his house and gives you a bicycle someone has abandoned on his front lawn.

    _____ c. You're going to start night school to get yourself ready for the sergeant's exam in a couple of years, but you don't know what kind of courses to take or where to go for them.

_____ d. You've interviewed a person you found loitering on the street near the school at night and found that he has no warrants outstanding for his arrest. You still think you know him from somewhere so you want to find out if he's been involved with the department before.

_____ e. Your radio isn't working right.

_____ f. You've arrested a burglary suspect and need to get him booked.

_____ g. A citizen complains to the chief that two officers roughed him up during an arrest for drunken driving. He claims you were one of the officers.

_____ h. A local high school is going to offer a class in traffic safety and is looking for an instructor from the department. This is not your specialty but you'd like to do it.

_____ i. You are something of a weapons expert and the chief is going to transfer you out of patrol for as long as it takes you to complete a study on whether or not the department should convert from revolvers to automatics.

_____ j. You need to know what the trend in burglaries of a given type has been in a particular area of town during the last five years.

PART 4

Role Expectations within the System

CHAPTER 8

THE CONSTITUTION AND THE COURTS

OVERVIEW

Today's law enforcement officer operates in a complex web of constraints applied by the courts he serves, the community in which he lives, and the growing drive within his own ranks to achieve recognition as a "professional person."

The three chapters in this section will deal in turn with the effects of each of these major factors in the determination of how the policeman does his job. In this first chapter we'll look at how the courts, through their decisions, have modified police conduct.

While there is neither time nor space to cover all the cases involved or the many ways in which they have affected the lives of police officers, we'll discuss those which have had the broadest and most far-reaching effects. We will discuss each case from both the point of view of the court in reaching the decision and the police in applying it.

The purpose of this chapter is to put into perspective the causes and effects of these landmark cases. It's too easy for the preservice or young inservice person to adopt a semicynical attitude regarding what may seem to be an unsympathetic posture of the courts on these decisions. The often-expressed, but perhaps careless, opinion of some police officers is that "I thought these guys were supposed to be on our side." Such an attitude is really self-defeating, and when the cases are examined the reasons usually take on a different light. The effects are also not as debilitating as a casual consideration might indicate. In any event, they are a part of real life for every person going into law enforcement, so you should be knowledgeable of them.

THE CONSTITUTION AND THE BILL OF RIGHTS

The "trouble," if you care to look at it that way, started not with any particular Supreme Court decision in any particular case, but with our founding fathers. They had a preoccupation with the rights of the individual and a built-in distrust of unchecked authority. They assumed that humans would occasionally let their zeal for good deeds override their moral conscience, at least temporarily, and they provided against that probability. They did so by giving us the Constitution, a document people all over the world agreed was a thing of true governmental beauty, and the Bill of Rights, the first ten amendments to the Constitution.

Exterior of the United States Supreme Court Building, Washington, D.C.

But, little by little, the people who stood most to gain from the provisions of the document chose to ignore certain of these provisions in the interest of expediency. As the pressures of various crises seemed to become unbearable and dire consequences seemed about to engulf us, countless "good deeds" were committed on an expedient basis by well-meaning people in and out of police service. While the phrase was probably not used out loud, there can be little doubt that most of the time the deeds were done in what was sincerely felt to be the "overriding interest of the good of the community." The small step from this thinking to a Watergate situation now seems painfully obvious, but at the time it was very likely invisible. For example when a man is guilty and you know he's guilty, what difference does it make if he sees an attorney *before* or *after* he gives you his confession? And if you don't have to go out of your way to avoid the complications of the attorney's presence (because the guilty person doesn't know he's entitled to one), so much the better. The community gets justice, at a reduced cost, and the streets are a little safer for awhile. What's the harm? Well, let's see if we can find out!

Gradually, around the time of the first World War, and then increasingly as the pressures of wars and depressions were lifted from our social consciences, more people began to wonder about the way results were obtained as well as what the results were. They began to compare these ways with the rules set out in the Constitution. When they did they found that every so often we came out long on good intentions and short on strict adherence to either the letter or the spirit of the rules.

At about the time this trend to examination of procedures was developing into a social force, the makeup of the courts was developing what would be called a *liberal* attitude by most people, although it may well turn out that in the eyes of history this development may be termed *conservative* in terms of interpretation of constitutional doctrine. In any event, as succeeding decisions came down from higher courts (many limiting police behavior to a considerable extent) the police community sincerely believed that it was going to be next to impossible to catch or convict criminals under the new rules. When people who were in fact guilty of crimes up to and including murder were turned back onto the streets because they had been convicted on the basis of technically illegal proceedings, it often seemed that the end of orderly society must be near at hand.

In spite of the intense frustration, however, most of the dire predictions haven't come true. The constraints remain, largely, as do the many of the frustrations. Any policeman can tell you of genuine injustices worked upon him and the community by actions of the prosecuting attorney's office and the courts. But if he's honest with himself, he can probably also tell you of similar results that are due to nothing more sinister than sloppy police work. And if he's really honest with himself he will probably admit that one or two of the times he's been "wronged" by the courts or the DA there has been an element of sloppy police work that contributed to the downfall of the case. As a matter of fact, the quality of professional police work has improved under the stricter rules and the cause of police professionalism has been advanced, rather than impeded.

To most people, "Miranda" and "rights" are synonymous. This is because when a policeman reads an arrestee a statement of his constitutional rights he does so from a card which references the Supreme Court decision in the case of *Miranda* v. *Arizona*. But *Miranda* was only one in a long string of cases in which the state courts and the Supreme Court examined police procedure in terms of constitutional provisions. We will look at these cases in chronological order and discuss each briefly as to its affects on specific philosophical and technological aspects of the law enforcement officer's job.

The Constitutional Amendments

Learned men argue endlessly about interpretation of the provisions of the Constitution. We don't intend to get into such a debate here, but there is need for some statement of what the Constitution deals with in the amendments cited in the decisions. We'll review those amendments to the Constitution, the Fourth, Fifth, Sixth, and Fourteenth Amendments, which have been directly involved in and have been cited in summaries of the individual cases we're about to examine.

The Fourth Amendment deals with *search and seizure*. It says, in essence, that people have the right to the privacy of their *persons, houses, papers,* and *effects* against *unreasonable* search or seizure. In simplistic terms it means that no one can search or seize your person, your home, or your property unreasonably. It also states that a warrant must have *probable cause* to be issued and must *describe* the place to be searched and the persons or things to be seized.

The Fifth Amendment deals with *self-incrimination.* It states that in a criminal case a person *can't be compelled to testify against himself.* This Amendment further considers *due process of law,* stating that *no person can be deprived of life, liberty* or *property* without it. (The Fifth also deals with other important rights which aren't pertinent to our present discussion and thus won't be taken up here.)

The Crucial Amendments

Amendment IV (1791). The right of the people to be secure in their persons, houses, papers, and effects, against unreasonable searches and seizures, shall not be violated, and no warrants shall issue, but upon probable cause, supported by oath or affirmation, and particularly describing the place to be searched, and the persons or things to be seized.

Amendment V (1791). No person shall be held to answer for a capital, or otherwise infamous crime, unless on a presentment or indictment of a grand jury, except in cases arising in the land or naval forces, or in the militia, when in actual service in time of war or public danger; nor shall any person be subject for the same offense to be twice put in jeopardy of life or limb; nor shall be compelled in any criminal case to be a witness against himself, nor be deprived of life, liberty, or property, without due process of law; nor shall private property be taken for public use, without just compensation.

Amendment VI (1791). In all criminal prosecutions, the accused shall enjoy the right to a speedy and public trial, by an impartial jury of the State and district wherein the crime shall have been committed, which district shall have been previously ascertained by law, and to be informed of the nature and cause of the accusation; to be confronted with the witnesses against him; to have compulsory process for obtaining witnesses in his favor, and to have the assistance of counsel for his defense.

Amendment XIV, Section 1 (1868). All persons born or naturalized in the United States, and subject to the jurisdiction thereof, are citizens of the United States and of the State wherein they reside. No State shall make or enforce any law which shall abridge the privileges or immunities of citizens of the United States; nor shall any State deprive any person of life, liberty, or property, without due process of law; nor deny to any person within its jurisdiction the equal protection of the laws.

The Sixth Amendment deals with the defendant's *right to counsel.* It says that the accused in all criminal cases is entitled to speedy and public trial by an impartial jury in the state and district where the crime was committed; to be *informed of the nature of the charge* against him; to be confronted by the witnesses against him; *to power of subpoena* to bring to court witnesses in his favor; and to *assistance of counsel* for his defense.

The Fourteenth Amendment provides *equal rights* for all persons *born or naturalized* in the United States. Passed in 1868 (the others discussed here were part of the original ten amendments adopted in 1791), it was part of the group of three reconstruction amendments aimed at giving slaves freedom, citizenship, and the right to vote. A provision of the 14th Amendment, which *forbade any state* to make or enforce any law *to abridge the privileges or immunities of citizens of the United States* could be an example of legislation that was greater, and more effective, than many of those who enacted it realized.

There's no way of knowing this with certainty, of course, some 100-plus years after the fact, but it does seem that the main thrust of the legislation was toward the slavery issue. Its effect on nonslavery issues in later years will become apparent as the cases to follow are examined.

WEEKS V. UNITED STATES (1914)

In this case Fremont Weeks was suspected of using the mails to defraud—specifically, selling lottery tickets. A police officer, without a warrant, arrested him at his place of employment. At about the same time other officers went to his home and got a key to his house from a neighbor. They had no warrant. Once inside they scooped up all his books, letters, money, papers, notes of indebtedness, stock certificates, insurance policies, deeds, abstracts, other evidences of title to properties, and even his clothing and some candy. All of this property was taken into possession by the district attorney and marshal of the U.S. court for use as evidence at his trial. Later in the same day the officers returned, this time with a U.S. marshal who thought perhaps the officers had missed something (which, considering the inventory of the first search, seems unlikely!). The marshal did find some letters and envelopes in a dresser drawer and took them into his possession, again without a warrant. Mr. Weeks, feeling that his rights of privacy and due process under the 4th and 5th Amendments had been violated by the lack of warrants, sought to have his property returned, prior to his trial. The district attorney refused and the court ordered those items of property which were *not pertinent to the charge to be returned,* which they were.

After the jury was sworn, but before any evidence had been given, Weeks again sought to have his property returned, apparently feeling that if part of the search was illegal under the Constitution, all of it was illegal. His request was denied by the court. He objected again when the papers were introduced into evidence at the trial and was overruled. Weeks was convicted in 1912 and in December of 1913 his case was submitted to the U.S. Supreme Court. In February the following year the justices reversed the lower court's ruling, citing the 4th Amendment. Their ruling was that the defendant, having been *unlawfully deprived of his property* and applying for its return prior to his trial, was *unlawfully tried on the basis of that property being used as evidence* against him.

This was the start of the *"Exclusionary Rule"* of evidence and is in direct contrast to the former belief that if the evidence was pertinent to the case it didn't matter that how it was obtained, even if illegally.

SILVERTHORNE LUMBER CO. V. UNITED STATES (1920)

The Silverthorne Lumber Co., a corporation, was the subject of an indictment for violation of a provision of the U.S. code and had been ordered to produce the books of the company. Fredrick W. Silverthorne and his father refused on the grounds that it would violate their 4th Amendment rights, and they were arrested at their homes and detained in custody. During this detention, representatives of the Department of Justice and the United States marshal went to the office of the company and made a clean sweep of all the books, papers, and documents found there. All employees were taken or directed to go to the office of the U.S. district attorney, where the confiscated records and documents were also taken. All of this action was without authority of warrant.

The Silverthornes immediately sought return of their property and were opposed by the district attorney who claimed that he had found evidence against them and was submitting it to the grand jury. Besides, he claimed, the act of seizure wasn't illegal, even if the officers had no warrant, because he held a subpoena for certain documents relating to the charge in the indictment.

Photographs and copies of the papers taken were made and

a new indictment was drawn up against the Silverthornes, based on the evidence obtained from the confiscated papers. The district court ordered the originals returned to the Silverthornes, but impounded the photographs and copies. Subpoenas were then served to force delivery of the originals and the Silverthornes refused. The court then ordered that the subpoenas be complied with even though it found that the papers had been seized in violation of their Constitutional rights. This put the government in the position of saying that it recognized that the seizure was illegal and was returning the seized property because of this illegality, but, on the other hand, it was proceeding against the owners of the papers on the basis of information it would not have had if the papers hadn't been seized.

The Supreme Court ruled for the Silverthornes on the basis of the 4th Amendment and established the "Fruit of the Poisoned Tree" concept. This concept holds that evidence obtained illegally not only can't be used against the defendant in the matter at trial, but it can't be used against him at all. It expanded the exclusionary rule from *Weeks* into what is now technically called the "Derivative Evidence" rule—if the tree is poisoned, so is its fruit. Some nineteen years later, in *Nardone* v. *United States,* the court ruled on a wiretapping case and summed up this attitude by saying that forbidding the direct use of evidence thus obtained, but failing to put curbs on indirect use, would only invite use of the methods.

GITLOW V. NEW YORK (1925)

The case of Benjamin Gitlow may seem a strange one to include here because it deals with 1st Amendment provisions guaranteeing freedom of speech and not with provisions of the 4th, 5th or 6th Amendments. However, it is definitely a landmark case for it was here that the due process clause of the 14th Amendment was held to absorb provisions of the Bill of Rights. In other words, with the *Gitlow* case the Supreme Court first held that state power was limited by the Bill of Rights as much as national power. This was a revolutionary concept that had far-reaching implications as we'll see when we look at other cases in this chapter.

Gitlow was a member of the Left Wing Section of the Socialist Party in New York. He was a member of the board of directors and business manager of *Revolutionary Age,* the party's official organ. He traveled about the state speaking to branches of the party and advocating adoption of party principles. New York had a law which made it a felony to advocate overthrow of organized government by force or violence either by word of mouth or writing. The trial court, and the appellate court, held that "The Left Wing Manifesto" as published in the organ of the party, did indeed advocate the overthrow of the government by violence, or by unlawful means.

There was no evidence presented by the state that the publication and circulation of the manifesto had any effect. The Supreme Court ruled that it did not question the correctness of the verdict as submitted to the jury and it did not find fault with New York's criminal anarchy act since it was a "reasonable limitation punishing behavior inherently unlawful under a constitutional government." It did, however, rule that since there was no effect from the publication and distribution of the manifesto and no evidence that there was likely to be any effect, ". . . the statute *as construed and applied by the trials court* penalizes the mere utterance, as such, of 'doctrine' without regard to . . . the likelihood of unlawful consequences." This the Court held to be in violation of 1st Amendment free speech guarantees. It decided these were binding upon all states because ". . . the 'liberty' protected by the 14th Amendment includes the liberty of speech and of the press." It was this precedent that subsequently led to the application of the rest of the Bill of Rights to limit the states' powers and brought about a considerable change in the federal system.

BROWN V. MISSISSIPPI (1936)

This was a case where three negroes were accused of murdering a white man. The illegal acts of law men on the case are bad enough in their own right but worse when it's realized that they didn't even bother to try to deny them, indicating that they fully expected to have their actions condoned by the court which, in fact, they were. Shortly after the murder was discovered a deputy with a mob took one suspect to the victim's home for questioning. There he was hanged, cut down, hanged and cut down again, and finally tied to a tree and whipped to obtain a confession. Failing in this the mob sent him home. Later he was arrested by the same deputy and whipped until a confession was obtained. The other two suspects were taken to jail where they were stripped, laid over chairs and whipped until they confessed in detail as dictated by each member of the mob assembled.

On the third day after the crime, the official confessions of the trio were taken by a sheriff who, though he admitted having heard of the beatings, denied firsthand knowledge of them. He did notice that one prisoner limped and couldn't sit down (which the prisoner claimed was due to a flogging) and that another prisoner had clearly visible rope marks on his neck. Nevertheless the sheriff and several others present solemnly took the confessions and testified in court that they were freely and voluntarily given, over the objections to the contrary of the defendants. The next day the court ordered the grand jury to convene which it did, returning indictments against the three for murder.

They were arraigned that afternoon and when the court asked if they had counsel they replied negatively, adding the realistic appraisal that they didn't suppose one would benefit them much. The court appointed counsel and set trial for the following morning, the seventh day after the crime was discovered, and the trial concluded with death sentences for the convicted defendants. It's interesting that the deputy who did the whipping also served as court deputy for the trial and, when put on the stand to rebut the defendants' claims of torture, he admitted it, saying he would have done worse if it had been left up to him.

In spite of the undenied use of torture to elicit confessions, conviction was obtained in the trial court and upheld in the Mississippi Supreme Court, albeit with two judges dissenting. The defendants' appeal was based on the fact that all the evidence against them was obtained illegally and that they had been denied opportunity to obtain good counsel and confer with him, depriving them of their 5th and 6th Amendment rights as guaranteed by the 14th. The U.S. Supreme Court, in ruling against the state, did so on the basis of the due process provision of the 14th Amendment, and for the first time in history set aside a state verdict solely because of mistreatment of defendants. In subsequent decisions, citing this one, psychological mistreatment was to become as important as physical.

McNABB V. UNITED STATES (1940)

The McNabbs, four brothers and one cousin, were moonshiners in the hills of Tennessee, none of whom had more than a fourth grade education or had ever been more than 21 miles from home. Acting on a tip, four agents of the Alcoholic Tax Unit surprised the McNabbs in the act of loading cans of their "white mule" into their car near a cemetery one night. While the McNabbs fled into the cemetery the revenuers set about pouring out the contents of the cans until a large rock landed at their feet. Thereupon one officer ran into the cemetery in pursuit. Finding nothing but some more cans of illegal whiskey, he proceded to empty them and was shot, fatally, by persons unknown (he died without identifying his killer).

Shortly thereafter (early Thursday morning) the officers arrested three McNabbs and took them to the Federal Building at Chattanooga. They were not brought before a U.S. commissioner or a judge. Instead they were kept in a detention room for some fourteen hours, until Thursday evening. They were not permitted to see relatives and friends who attempted to aid them. They had no lawyer and there is no evidence that they asked for or were told that they were entitled to one. A fourth McNabb, Barney, had been arrested by local police early Thursday and turned over to federal authorities. He was placed in a separate room from the others, questioned briefly, taken to the scene of the crime, brought back for further questioning, and then jailed.

That same morning the case had been taken over by the district supervisor of the Alcohol Tax Unit who spent the day studying the case before starting interrogation of the prisoners. At no time during his questioning was a lawyer or member of the family allowed to be with the McNabbs. The interrogator advised the suspects why they were being questioned, who was doing it, and informed them that they did not have to make a statement and that if they did it would be used against them. He told them that they need not fear force and that they didn't have to answer questions unless they wished to do so. They were interrogated singly and in groups, sometimes for a half-hour at a stretch and sometimes for up to two hours, over a seven-hour period ending at one o'clock in the morning.

At about the same time questioning was being resumed the next morning, the fifth McNabb, Benjamin, voluntarily surrendered. Like the others, he was not taken before a judge or magistrate but was questioned for about six hours. Finally he was advised that the others had named him as the one who fired the shots which killed one agent and wounded another. He then admitted the first shot but denied the second. Because of the discrepancies in their stories the questioning continued until two o'clock Saturday morning, a total of two days of questioning without attorney or arraignment.

The McNabbs contended that their 5th Amendment right

to freedom from compulsion to testify against themselves and due process had been denied. The government countered that the confessions were voluntary and thus not in violation. The Supreme Court admitted that it had in previous cases decided against confessions ". . . secured by protracted and repeated questioning of ignorant and untutored persons, in whose minds the power or the officers was greatly magnified," and in cases where defendants had been, "held incommunicado, without advice of friends or counsel." However, the Court held that this case did not have to be decided on those constitutional grounds because the officers had ". . . assumed functions which Congress has explicitly denied them" in not taking the McNabbs immediately "before the nearest United States Commissioner or judicial officer for hearing, commitment, or taking bail for trial." So, in fact, while avoiding a constitutional confrontation the Court did set a precedent which is not yet applied directly to the states but has resulted in changes in anticipation of that happening. The Court clearly said a defendant must be taken before a magistrate to determine the sufficiency of the justification for his detention, rather than holding him over until a confession can be extracted from him. The states heard this and, with the previously established precedent for application of the Bill of Rights to the states through the due process clause of the 14th Amendment, most moved to provide for prompt arraignment in their own penal code.

PEOPLE V. CAHAN (1955)

This is a California, rather than United States, Supreme Court case. In it we see the exclusionary rule applied to a state case for the first time. It came just forty-one years after the *Weeks* case which set the same principle for federal cases.

Charles Cahan was convicted of bookmaking and sentenced to five years' probation beginning with ninety days in jail and a fine of $2,000. His appeal was based on his contention that most of the evidence against him had been obtained illegally, and it seems it was. In what was described by the court as "flagrant violation of the 4th and 14th Amendments" in which officers admittedly broke and entered not one but several (there were sixteen defendants) residences, seized evidence and/or planted listening devices and made recordings of conversations over an extended period of time.

In reversing the lower court's conviction the state court first addressed itself to the meaning of the Constitution. It was held ". . . emphatically clear that important as efficient law enforcement may be, it is more important that the right of privacy guaranteed by these constitutional provisions be respected. Since in *no* case shall the right of the people to be secure against unreasonable searches and seizures be violated, the contention that unreasonable searches and seizures are justified by the necessity of bringing criminals to justice cannot be accepted."

It then took recognition of the current, popularly held attitude toward the exclusionary rule as it applied to states: ". . . [the] Fourth Amendment as it applies to the states through the Fourteenth does not require states like California that have heretofore admitted illegally seized evidence to exclude it now. The exclusionary rule is not 'an essential ingredient' of the right of privacy guaranteed by the Fourth Amendment, but simply a means of enforcing that right, which the states can accept or reject. . . ." It further ruled in regard to the opinions of scholars and judges on evidence that "The rules of evidence are designed to enable the courts to reach the truth and, in criminal cases, to secure a fair trial to those accused of crime. Evidence obtained by an illegal search and seizure is ordinarily just as true and reliable as evidence lawfully obtained. The court needs all reliable evidence material to the issue before it, the guilt or innocence of the accused, and how such evidence is obtained is immaterial to that issue."

In this landmark case, the court finally decided that, "Despite the persuasive force of the foregoing arguments, we have concluded . . . that evidence obtained in violation of the constitutional guarantees is inadmissible. . . . We have been *compelled* to reach that conclusion because *other remedies have completely failed to secure compliance with the constitutional provisions on the part of police officers* with the attendant result that the courts under the old rule have been constantly required to participate in, and in effect condone, the lawless activities of law enforcement officers." The italics here are added for emphasis of what is probably the single most important phrase printed in this chapter. It's worth rereading and remembering, not in words, but in thought.

MAPP V. OHIO (1961)

Influenced in good part by the action of California in *Cahan,* the Supreme Court in *Mapp* made the exclusionary rule binding upon all states.

214 THE CONSTITUTION AND THE COURTS

Dollree Mapp, the defendant, was convicted of possession of obscene material. The search that uncovered these materials began when police officers received a tip that a person wanted for a recent bombing might be hiding at the residence and there also might be policy paraphernalia hidden in the home. When they knocked on the door Miss Mapp telephoned her attorney and refused to admit them without a search warrant.

After a three-hour surveillance the officers again sought admittance and were denied, whereupon they broke down the door and entered. Meanwhile, Miss Mapp's attorney arrived and was denied entrance to the house or access to Miss Mapp. When she demanded to see the warrant, a paper was held up by one of the officers and she grabbed it, placing it in her bosom. A struggle ensued, during which the "warrant" was retrieved and Miss Mapp handcuffed, for being "belligerant" (quotation marks are the Court's). A search of her bedroom, which then spread through the house and into the basement, yielded personal papers and, from a trunk in the basement, the obscene material for which she was convicted.

At the trial no search warrant was produced by the prosecution, nor was the failure to produce one explained or ac-

Interior of the United States Supreme Court where the nine Supreme Court Justices sit and decide on far-reaching issues affecting the administration of justice.

> ### Government Integrity
>
> In 1928 the Supreme Court ruled in *Olmstead* v. *United States* that messages passed over telephone wires were not within the protection of the 4th Amendment (since reversed). Justice Louis Brandeis wrote a separate opinion in which he emphasized the necessity for government to act within the law:
>
> "Decency, security and liberty alike demand that government officials shall be subjected to the same rules of conduct that are commands to the citizen. In a government of laws, existence of the government will be imperiled if it fails to observe the laws scrupulously. Our government is the potent, omnipresent teacher. For good or ill, it teaches the whole people by its example. Crime is contagious. If the government becomes a law breaker, it breeds contempt for the law; it invites every man to become a law unto himself; it invites anarchy. To declare that in the administration of criminal laws the end justifies the means—to declare that the government may commit crimes in order to secure the conviction of a private criminal would bring terrible retribution. Against that pernicious doctrine the Court should resolutely set its face." And so should every law enforcement student, practitioner, supervisor, and administrator.

counted for. The court expressed considerable doubt, "at best," that one ever existed. The state contended that ". . . even if the search were made without authority, or otherwise unreasonably, it is not prevented from using the unconstitutionally seized evidence at trial," citing *Wolf* v. *Colorado,* an earlier Supreme Court decision which held that the 14th Amendment did not forbid admission of such evidence in a state court.

The Supreme Court, acknowledging the possibility voiced earlier by Justice Cardozo, that under our constitutional exclusionary doctrine, ". . . the criminal is to go free because the constable has blundered," admitted that in some cases this will undoubtedly be the result. They concluded, however, that: "The criminal goes free, if he must, but it is the law that sets him free. Nothing can destroy a government more quickly than its failure to observe its own laws, or worse, its disregard of the charter of its own existence." It also cited the words of Justice Brandeis in 1928 on the example government must set for all its citizens. The judgement of the lower courts was reversed, and the provisions of the 4th Amendment were applied to all states under the 14th.

GIDEON V. WAINRIGHT (1963)

This case was felt by Chief Justice Earl Warren to be one of the three most important cases to come before the Supreme Court during his tenure (1953-1969). Considering the magnitude of the others submitted to that body during his sixteen-year service, this evaluation has to be given considerable weight. The other two cases he held most important, *Escobedo* and *Miranda,* follow this one.

The details of the case are not highly important here, since performance of police is not at issue. Rather, it was the simple concept of Court application of basic constitutional rights that was the contention, and the decision was, indeed, far-reaching.

Clarence Gideon was tried and convicted in Florida courts of breaking and entering a poolroom with intent to commit a misdemeanor. This is a felony offense under Florida law. Being without funds to hire a lawyer, he asked the court to appoint him counsel as provided by the 6th Amendment. The court denied his request because, under Florida law, counsel was not required to be provided indigents unless the charge was a capital crime. The Florida Supreme Court, without opinion, denied his appeal.

Overruling a 1942 Supreme Court decision that the necessity of providing counsel to indigents depended on the "totality of circumstances" in the case, the Court in this case decided that the 6th Amendment's provision that in all criminal prosecutions the accused was entitled to assistance of counsel for his defense was made obligatory upon the states by the 14th Amendment.

ESCOBEDO V. ILLINOIS (1964)

In the second of the three important cases on right to counsel under the Warren Court, Danny Escobedo was arrested, without a warrant, for the murder of his brother-in-law and interrogated. He made no statement and was released the same day on a writ of habeas corpus obtained by his attorney. Three weeks later another man, then in police custody (and later indicted along with Escobedo for the crime) identified him as the killer. Re-arrested, along with his sister, Escobedo was taken back to police headquarters and, en route, was told by detectives that he had been named by the other man and that, in Escobedo's words, "they had us pretty well, up pretty tight, and we might as well admit to this crime." Escobedo replied that he wanted advice from his lawyer. He was told that although he was not formally charged, he was in custody and "couldn't walk out the door."

Shortly after they arrived at headquarters, Escobedo's attorney arrived and asked to see his client. He was denied this by a series of officers up to and including the duty chief who told him he couldn't see him because they hadn't completed questioning. Able to see and wave to his client at one point, the attorney was still denied access to him and was told he'd have to get a writ of habeas corpus. Escobedo testified that he repeatedly asked to see his attorney and was told that his attorney "didn't want to see him."

A police officer who grew up in Escobedo's neighborhood and knew him and his family, interrogated him alone and, according to the defendant, told him in Spanish that "he would see to it that we would go home and be held only as witnesses, if anything, if we made a statement. . ." against the other man. Escobedo claimed that he then made that statement, based on this assurance. The officer denied having made such a statement. Having thus admitted at least some knowledge of the crime (for the first time), the prisoner was then interrogated by an assistant state's attorney who took a carefully worded statement, designed to assure admissibility, but did not advise the prisoner of his constitutional rights. It remains undisputed that no one advised him of these rights during the entire interrogation, and this was the basis of his motion both before and during the trial, to suppress the incriminating statements he made. These motions were denied and he was convicted of the crime, which he appealed.

The Illinois Supreme Court first held the statement inadmissible and reversed the conviction. The state petitioned for a rehearing and, granted it, won affirmation of the earlier conviction on the basis that the officer who allegedly made the promise denied it and the court believed him, ruling the confession voluntary.

When the case came before the United States Supreme Court it held that "At the time of his arrest and throughout the course of the interrogation, the police told petitioner that they had convincing evidence . . . without informing him of his absolute right to remain silent in the face of this accusation, urged him to make a statement. . . . It cannot be doubted that, placed in this position in which the accused was when the statement was made to him that the other suspected person had charged him with crime, the result was to produce upon his mind the fear that *if he remained silent* it would be considered an *admission of guilt. . . ."* (italics added here and below to emphasize key points). The court added that Escobedo, as a layman, ". . . was undoubtedly *unaware* that under Illinois law an *admission of 'mere' complicity* in the murder plot was legally as damaging as an admission of firing the fatal shots. . . . The *guiding hand of counsel* was essential to advise petitioner of his rights in this delicate situation. . . . This was the stage when legal aid and advice were most critical to the petitioner."

The sum and substance of the Supreme Court reversal here is that when a man is in jail and asks for his lawyer and his lawyer is available he is entitled to have him there when he is questioned.

MIRANDA V. ARIZONA (1966)

"Miranda," as it's popularly called, was in reality four cases involving four separate petitioners, tried at once before the Supreme Court. All dealt with the admissibility of statements obtained from an individual who is subjected to custodial police interrogation, and the necessity for procedures which assure that the individual is accorded his privilege against self-incrimination under the 5th Amendment.

Ernesto Miranda was arrested by police and taken to a

The Miranda Card

Admonition and Waiver of Rights.

1. You have a right to remain silent.

2. Anything you say can and will be used against you in a court of law.

3. You have the right to talk to a lawyer before we talk to you and to have him present while we talk to you.

4. If you cannot afford to hire a lawyer one will be appointed to represent you before any questioning, free of charge.

5. Do you understand each of the rights explained to you?

6. Do you want to talk about this case or not?

7. Do you want a lawyer or not?

special interrogation room where he signed a confession which contained a typed paragraph stating that the confession was made voluntarily with full knowledge of his legal rights and with the understanding that any statement he made might be used against him. On the basis of this confession he was convicted of kidnapping and rape.

The other three cases involved convictions of kidnapping, robbery, rape and murder. In all four cases the Supreme Court reversed on the grounds that the defendants were either not advised of their rights to remain silent and/or to have counsel before questioning by police, or did not "intelligently waive" these rights. In none of the cases did the Court specifically concentrate on the facts of the cases themselves beyond these issues of constitutional rights.

The significance of *Miranda* hinges on the terms "custodial interrogation" and "waiver" of rights. *Custodial interrogation* is questioning initiated by law enforcement officers after a person has been taken into custody or otherwise deprived of his freedom of action in any significant way. A defendant may *waive* (give up) his rights to remain silent and to be assisted by counsel at a custodial police interrogation, provided the waiver is made *voluntarily, knowingly,* and *intelligently.* This is why, when an officer reads from the "Miranda" card, and advises the arrestee of his rights, he must also ask him if he understands these rights and if he wishes to give up these rights.

Chief Justice Warren, in commenting on this case in later years, said that it simply established that when a man is first separated from his family and friends for the purpose of putting him behind bars, at that point in time he is entitled to counsel.

CHIMEL V. CALIFORNIA (1969)

Ted Chimel was arrested by officers for burglary of a coin shop. Incidental to the arrest the officers conducted a search of his entire three-bedroom house, including the attic, the garage, a small workshop, and various drawers. Over his objection, various items, primarily coins, which were found in the search were admitted as evidence against him at his trial; he was convicted and the conviction upheld by an appeals court and the California Supreme Court.

In their landmark decision reversing this case the Supreme Court held that since this search was *incidental to an arrest* (as opposed to a search by warrant) the 4th and 14th Amend-

220 THE CONSTITUTION AND THE COURTS

ment rights of the defendant were violated when the search went *beyond his person and the area from within which he might have obtained a weapon or* something that could have been used as evidence against him.

EFFECTS OF COURT RULINGS

So there you have it—ten cases out of the thousands decided by the Supreme Court since *Weeks* and one case where a state took the initiative on its own to change the way in which law enforcement operates. Now let's look at what some of the operational changes which have resulted from these decisions. They come down to two basic areas: *search and seizure* and *confessions* which we'll review separately, even though there may be a little overlap.

Search and Seizure

Beginning with *Weeks* in 1914 the Supreme Court served notice that it was going to be serious about applying the 4th Amendment to police behavior. The *exclusionary rule* would be used to keep illegally obtained evidence from being used in court. It said "get a warrant" if you're going to search someone's castle. The court was only dealing with federal officers in this case so nothing really big happened at that time. Then, in *Silverthorne* in 1920, it broadened the concept of exclusion of illegally obtained evidence with the *derivative evidence* concept which said that if the tree is poisoned, so is the fruit. Not only can the evidence obtained illegally not be used in the case at hand, it can't be used at all against this person—you not only have to give up on this case, but you can not open a new one against him using the same tainted evidence. But, like *Weeks,* this decision still only bound federal officers.

Gitlow, in 1925, didn't seem to have anything to do with search and seizure since it involved only freedom of speech. But it applied the due process clause of the 14th Amendment to the states and thus opened the door to taking the same approach with all of the first ten amendments, the Bill of Rights. On that basis police officers in all the states would in the future be bound to comply with these provisions, as interpreted by the various courts. But the states still didn't face up to this and even in *Cahan,* which for the first time saw the exclusionary rule applied at the state level, the California Supreme Court didn't make the decision out of anticipation that the federal Court would force them to under the 14th. Instead they did it because nothing else was working to control police violation of citizens' constitutional rights. This took place in 1955, forty-one years after *Weeks,* in one of the most professional and progressive departments in the country, and officers were still kicking down doors and bugging people's homes with no warrants simply because they knew the people were guilty, which indeed they were. But the courts said, in effect, "breaking the law to catch lawbreakers is no longer going to be tolerated in this state, so clean up your act."

In *Mapp,* six years later, the Supreme Court said that the states which hadn't already followed California's example on the exclusionary rule would have to from now on. Searches could be conducted legally under two basic sets of circumstances: with a *warrant* authorizing the search, and *incidental to an arrest.* If the court issues a warrant it specifies where the search is to be conducted and what is to be searched for. Prior to *Chimel,* in 1969, no such definition of where officers could search or what they could look for existed in searches made incidental to an arrest. When the Court reached its decision in *Chimel* these limits were set at an area within the reach of the arrestee, where he might be able to put hands on a weapon or evidence.

With these as the rules or guidelines, let's see how searches are legally conducted beginning with the search incidental to an arrest. Let's say you arrest someone, without a warrant, because you have knowledge that he's the person who committed a robbery. You don't want to wait for a warrant of arrest because he'll get away. You arrest him and search his person for a weapon, and you can search the area immediately around him to be sure there's no weapon he can reach or any place he might have quickly hidden evidence of the robbery when he realized he was going to be arrested. How, then, do you get the right to search the rest of the premises for evidence of the robbery? In one of two ways: You either get a *warrant,* signed by a judge, or you get the arrestee's *consent.* To get consent you simply ask if it's okay to look around. He may say "go ahead" and you're in business. But it often happens under consent searches that the search is challenged later on the ground that your "color of authority" (the fact that you're a police officer) created in his mind the feeling that he really had no choice. Thus, the surest way is to secure the premises and get a warrant. A fourth category of legal search, the *emergency search* (where you have reason to believe a person is in physical danger) is subject to the same general restrictions outlined above.

There's more to be concerned about to ensure you're on legal grounds and won't burn a good case by more enthusiasm than prudence (incidentally, don't be discouraged if this seems a little complicated because it *is!*). In order for what you find to be admissible, the search has to be conducted *reasonably.* This usually comes up when you find evidence of another crime, different from the one you're investigating. For example, if you arrest someone on a narcotics charge and find a color television set that you think is stolen and it proves to be stolen when you check the serial number, that is admissible to support a new felony charge. But if you arrest for stolen color television sets and happen to find narcotics in a dresser drawer, that is no good because it isn't reasonable that you'd look in a dresser drawer for a color television set. On the other hand, if you found the narcotics inside the television set, while you were looking for the serial number to check it against a stolen property list, that would *probably* be admissible to support the new charge of narcotics. ("Probably" is emphasized here because it's difficult to say how a court might rule on any given case and it might be difficult to prove that your suspect put the narcotics there rather than having unwittingly stolen them along with the television set.) As you've probably decided by now, the concept of reasonable cause in relation to search and seizure is one which generates a lot of academy and continuing in-service police training!

Confessions

It's easy to see how in *Brown,* in 1936, the Court would hold that the "rubber hose" confessions of the defendants were inadmissible. In *McNabb,* four years later, the court took cognizance of the psychological aspects of confession extraction although the reversal itself was not based on this constitutional ground. In *Escobedo* the decision was based on the fact that the defendant was denied right to counsel and because of this denial a confession that might not have otherwise been obtained from him was used to convict him. In *Miranda* the decision was much the same as *Escobedo,* but it was added that he should have been advised of his right to counsel before the custodial interrogation was conducted. The premise here clearly seems to be that as soon as a person is put into the intimidating situation where he is without counsel of attorney or friends, he is psychologically at enough of a disadvantage that he might confess without wanting to.

In terms of what all this means to life in the streets as a police officer, it's probably even more complex than search and seizure procedures. Obviously you don't want to deprive any suspect of his constitutional rights. If he asks for an attorney or wants to see his attorney who happens to be waiting at the desk to see him, you must avoid repeating the *Escobedo* mistake, but when do you advise him of his rights? Certainly you must do so before interrogating him in an effort to obtain an incriminating statement from him. Otherwise he might not be aware of his 5th Amendment rights and, even though he really wanted to get it off his chest, the fact that you were interrogating him, in custody, and he didn't avail himself of friendly counsel, would invalidate his confession. On the other hand, if he runs up to you on the street and says "I can't stand it any more, I shot her and I'm glad" you don't have to tell him to get a lawyer before he talks to you. He still has the right to make voluntary admission of guilt, but you don't have the right to elicit that self-incriminating statement from him until he has knowingly and intelligently waived his rights. That's why you advise him of his rights and ask him if he gives up those rights before you initiate the process leading to his self-incriminating statement.

There is yet another factor which might invalidate a confession and we haven't really addressed it here yet, although *Escobedo* might have been an example if the state supreme court had not reversed itself and decided to believe the officer. Promises, or hope of reward, will change a confession from voluntary to inadmissible in most courts' opinions. In the Escobedo case, the defendant contended that an officer spoke to him in Spanish and told him he could go home as soon as he made a statement blaming the other suspect. Escobedo's statement to that effect implicated him in the crime and was a self-incriminating statement, involuntarily given, because of hope of reward (his freedom) so the confession was inadmissible.

Like search and seizure, compliance with court requirements involving obtaining confessions (particularly as concerns the *Miranda* decision) is the subject of considerable discussion and training for law enforcement officers.

There's little doubt that the protections built into the Constitution and Bill of Rights by our founding fathers are to be complied with by law enforcement officers. The time required to learn what these protections are, and how to operate within them, is well spent by anyone in the field. Not only is it ethically mandatory, but it's also practical since nothing is more frustrating than to arrest a guilty person and then see him freed because of careless or too exuberant work on your part.

SUMMARY

The *4th Amendment* to the Constitution deals with the right of citizens to be secure from unreasonable *search and seizure*.

The *5th Amendment* deals with *self-incrimination* and *due process* of law.

The *6th Amendment* deals with an accused person's *right to counsel*.

The *14th Amendment* affords *equal rights* to all citizens and *forbids any state* the right to abridge these rights as provided by the Constitution or its Amendments.

Weeks v. *United States* established the *exclusionary rule* of evidence in federal cases, saying that any evidence obtained illegally was inadmissible in court, as violation of the 4th Amendment.

Silverthorne Lumber v. *United States* established the *derivative evidence* (or "fruit of the poisoned tree") concept under the exclusionary rule, saying that not only would illegally obtained evidence be barred from admission in federal cases, but that the evidence so obtained could be used in no way against the person (in this or any other case).

Gitlow v. *New York* made the provisions of the Bill of Rights applicable to state cases, as well as federal cases, under the provisions of the 14th Amendment.

Brown v. *Mississippi* ruled that confessions obtained by force were inadmissible as violations of the 5th Amendment.

McNabb v. *United States* established that delayed arraignment, for the purpose of extracting a confession through extended interrogation, was a violation of the 5th Amendment.

People v. *Cahan* extended 4th Amendment provisions to a state case, in the form of the exclusionary rule, for the first time.

Mapp v. *Ohio* made the exclusionary rule binding in all state cases by extending the 4th Amendment through the 14th.

Gideon v. *Wainright* guaranteed all indigent defendants, in all the states, the right to representation by counsel as guaranteed by the 6th Amendment, applied through the 14th.

Escobedo v. *Illinois* established that a defendant's right to counsel under the 6th Amendment can't be withheld until police have completed interrogation.

Miranda v. *Arizona* ruled that a defendant taken into custody and interrogated must first be advised of his constitutional rights and then make an intelligent and knowing waiver of these rights before self-incriminating statements may be taken from him.

Chimel v. *California* limited the area that can be searched, incidental to an arrest, to that area within which the arrestee could obtain a weapon or hide evidence of the crime for which he is being arrested.

In *searching* for evidence of a crime an officer must have a *warrant, consent* of the person involved, be *making an arrest,* or responding to an *emergency.*

Confessions, in order to be admissible, must be made *voluntarily,* without *coercion* through physical or emotional duress, without *promise* of hope of *reward,* and either with advice of *counsel* or after knowing and intelligent *waiver* of rights to counsel and to remain silent.

REVIEW QUESTIONS

Answers to these questions appear on page 385.

1. Beside each of the statements below write the number of the appropriate Amendment to the Constitution.
   _____ a. Extends provisions of Bill of Rights to all citizens in all state cases.
   _____ b. Protects you from having a confession extracted from you by unfair means.
   _____ c. Guarantees that even if you don't have money to hire a lawyer to defend you, one will be provided for you.
   _____ d. Means that no one can enter your house to search for anything without authority and reasonable cause.
2. Supreme Court decisions that evidence obtained illegally can't be used in courts of law have resulted in what "rule" of evidence? _____
3. "Fruit of the poisoned tree" is another name for a rule of law that is more formally called the rule of _____ .
4. The case which first applied the protections of the 4th Amendment to a state, rather than federal, case was _____ .
5. Was *Mapp* v. *Ohio* a *confession* or *search and seizure* case? _____

6. The case which assured that all indigents, in all states, would have counsel provided them was _____ .

7. The case which first applied a provision of the Bill of Rights to a state through application of the due process clause of the 14th Amendment was _____ .

8. Which case established, at the state level, that a person could not be denied counsel from his attorney until police had finished interrogating him? _____

9. The case which limited the area and purpose of searches conducted incidental to an arrest was _____ .

10. What case established that a person waiving his constitutional rights must do so with the knowledge of what these rights are and the awareness of what the consequences are? _____

11. On page 221 we listed four circumstances under which you can legally search a person or premises. See how many of them you can recall here before checking back. _____

12. Custodial interrogation relates to the validity of what type of evidence? _____

CHAPTER 9

POLICE AND THE COMMUNITY

OVERVIEW

Hardly anyone who seriously examines the societal problems of today questions the fact that the police have their hands full. Every paper or newscast contains evidence that crime is either the first or second most critical problem of the day, with the order depending mostly on which day it is. We also hear a lot about the need for a "marriage" of the goals of police and the community they serve and protect, but nobody, apparently, does an awful lot to bring this marriage about.

Actually, many people are trying, both as private citizens and as members of law enforcement agencies. Probably the main reason that there seems to be a lack of activity toward the goal is that a great many people don't understand what is needed to achieve it. The first thing necessary, then, is an understanding of why the commonality of objectives is needed. There's probably also a general lack of understanding of the attitudes and needs of both the police and the general community, and how to go about making them closer to the same.

In this chapter we will consider why there is the need for the goal, how police feel about themselves and the community, and how the community feels about police. We will also look at some ways people are trying to bring about better police-community relations.

WHY THE MARRIAGE IS NEEDED

The term "marriage" is used here because, like a marriage between two people, it's not just a simple matter of giving the community the kind of law enforcement it wants. A person, or a community, can get what is wanted relatively easily on a temporary basis, but what is needed for the continuing good of everyone involved requires a contribution by both parties. This simple concept is overlooked often enough in marriages and community service to cause both a high divorce rate and an unfortunately high failure rate in providing successful maintenance of peace in the community.

Why is there more to it than just giving the community the kind of police service it wants? Suppose, for example, that the community is *temporarily* (and this needs to be emphasized because most fears of anything unknown or not understood prove to be just that—temporary) extremely concerned over a particular type of social change that seems to be taking place too rapidly—long hair, for example. An easy and superficial solution might be to take a vote in the community and see how the citizens want it handled. Maybe 90 percent of the people in the city are afraid of long-haired men and want "something done about it." What then? Pass a local ordinance against it? Arrest the violators? Run them out of town or give them forced haircuts? Ridiculous? Maybe! If you're old enough to think back to the reaction of the "adult" public in general to the hair styles of the Beatles a few years ago, and can find a picture of them during that period, you'll see that their hair was about like that of the average policeman's ten years later.

If you want a more fact-of-life concept to wrestle with, consider how easy it is for most people fortunate enough to live in an orderly community to feel that "something really must be done" about the way people behave in a neighboring community that "really has a serious crime problem." Would it be all right if the police "went in there and knocked some sense into those people" for a while—just to get them straightened out and keep them from coming into another community and messing it up? Would it be only "too bad" if a few relatively innocent people got treated a little rough in the process as long as the overall result was for the good? Unfortunately, there's a little of this kind of fear-reaction in all of us.

This isn't a text on sociology nor is it our purpose to mount a crusade for social change. What we would like to do is make a case for the fact that, like it or not, there really is a problem and it really does have to be faced. There's a popular trend today among law enforcement administrators to want the barriers between the police community and the civilian community broken down, and this is what we're talking about in this chapter, to a large extent. But it can't be done simply by saying there is no such thing as a police community or that "police are just plain folks." Policemen are members of the general community as well as belonging to the special subgroup their profession places them in, and they have the same human weaknesses and needs as all citizens. But, unlike the rest of the community, police can't set aside, even for a day, the problems of the community. That fact alone sets them apart. The general community can afford to sometimes be only vaguely disturbed by the results of social and economic injustice, while it goes about performing its own immediate functions. Police can't. They live with it every minute of every day. This immediate and constant familiarity with the problem qualifies members of the police community to contribute special knowledge to the solution. At the same time it imposes on them an extra responsibility to do more than just give the community "what it wants" in law enforcement.

Since it has essentially hired the police to take care of this problem, the general community usually has one of two attitudes toward it: *apathy* or *reaction.* It either can't be bothered or it wants something done "right now." It thus becomes the professional responsibility of police to get the general community involved on a continuing basis so its attitude will be somewhere between these two extremes. The general community can never be as immediately concerned with the problem as police are and there's no need for it to be, but to the extent that it accepts solution of the problem as partly its own responsibility, the general community will increasingly receive the type of police protection and service it needs and deserves.

The statistics alone are probably enough to establish this. There are from 1.5 (in the smaller cities) to 2.9 (in the larger) policemen per 1,000 population. This is an average of about 500 inhabitants per sworn peace officer. Thus survival, let alone success, of protection and service to the community obviously

> ### Community Respect
>
> Community respect for law and those who enforce the law is a vital and indispensable element of public order. No police force can be large enough to maintain law and order on a continuing basis in the face of hostility, suspicion, or even apathy on the part of any substantial segment of its community.
>
> Community respect must rest upon confidence in the integrity, efficiency, understanding and impartiality of the police. It has long been recognized that integrity and efficiency require continuous training and review. We must now fully understand that the policeman on the beat is not fully equipped to perform his duties unless he is also carefully trained to deal with the broad complex of problems which spring from the mixed racial, ethnic, social and religious elements which make up the community he serves.
>
> Carefully prepared and executed programs for training police to cope with difficulties arising from intergroup tensions will make clear the fact that an understanding of group problems and aspirations is not only consistent with but essential to firm and effective law enforcement.
>
> The policeman on the beat is the citizen's major point of contact with the rule of law which is the basis of our society. (Robert F. Kennedy)

requires support of the citizenry at large. Police alone simply can't do the job demanded of them. This is especially true since "crook catching" is not the entire police function. Police are also traffic controllers, part-time lawyers, social workers, psychologists, teachers, and advisors on all sorts of things from the availability of government services to civil responsibility. Apart from the nonpolice functions the matter of crime alone would be more than police could handle without even such simple support from the community as reporting crimes when they happen. And, as already noted in this book and elsewhere, even this support is too often lacking in the general community.

HOW THE POLICE SEE THEIR ROLE

Before we go into this, let's admit that there's no way to speak for all police officers. Thus, anything said here has to be an estimate of average opinion. If there's an error, it will be on the altruistic side because there's no point in trying to reflect the views of those police officers who, for whatever reasons, have become cynical or disillusioned. Certainly no person contemplating a career in law enforcement would deliberately work toward reaching that state of mind. But, since there are job factors which, if one is unaware of them can build and cause concern, we'll talk a little about them as well.

To begin with, most police officers like their job. They gripe about a lot of things, but overall almost all of them find a degree of personal satisfaction that few other careers offer. One of the main reasons for this is the amount of responsibility they have. The organization they work in is paramilitary to a great degree and, while this concept may seem at odds with individual responsibility, it's really not. The policeman is by and large on his own in situations where what he decides to do has a profound effect on the lives of the people he serves, and that's responsibility in the true sense. The decision he makes—to arrest, refer, seek prosecution, use force—has to be made in a few moments or seconds and often under very difficult social circumstances. Unlike the other members of the criminal justice system he doesn't have time to consult his law books, ponder the meaning of decisions of wiser men as they affect his situation, and try to reach the fairest of all possible conclusions. Whatever use he makes of events that have gone before has to be based on whatever knowledge and conditioned reactions he takes with him into the situation as it happens in "real time" (to borrow a phrase from the computer people to describe an event that is happening now and has an immediate effect on all concerned).

There is another difficulty in the performance of the law enforcement aspects of the officer's job. This is the dilemma posed by policy on the one hand and practicality on the other. It's common knowledge that although policy almost always is to enforce all the laws (and, in fact, the officer is sworn to do that) this is never done. For one thing every officer sees more violations every day than he can possibly take time to enforce. For another, many technical violations of the law in no way pose a threat to the peace of the community or the well-being of its citizens and to enforce them would be counterproductive. So every officer is placed in the position of having to make his own judgments within the departmental policy in the full knowledge that he will be held strictly accountable for mistakes. That's no small challenge for a 21-year old—or a 45-year old for that matter!

Some of the decisions are dictated to a large extent by community standards and "normal" behavioral patterns, but the decision on whether to act, what kind of action to take, and the acceptance for the responsibility of those actions lies at the grass roots of the system: the patrol officer. As a quick example, three young men standing idly on a street corner in a residential area of an affluent city would probably be field-interrogated (as a matter of fact, even a car driving slowly through a city where affluent people reside might be stopped and the occupants interviewed). The same situation in the heart of the inner city might simply be noted mentally by an officer. There are at least two reasons for this: first, it's so common in the inner city as to be a part of the "normal" scene; second, a field interview would almost surely be regarded by the citizenry as harassment and be counterproductive in terms of keeping the peace. If the three young men break into a closed store before the officer gets back, he's made a mistake. It's obviously not simple, and this, of course, leads many officers to an overriding, if mild, "damned-if-you-do-damned-if-you-don't" attitude. They live with it, however, and most can handle it.

Because they accept this difficult role under these conditions and because they feel that they are doing a decent job of handling it, most police officers are a little hesitant about having the nonenforcement aspects of their job intentionally enlarged. They feel that their responsibility is handling acts of criminal behavior, without becoming extensively involved in treatment of the causes. So, while police top management is increasingly inclined to accept a new and broader police role in crime prevention, middle-management and street officers are inclined to feel they have enough to do in enforcing the laws. They also feel that this part of their job is the only source of the immediate satisfaction that comes from handling a situation that clearly has a beginning, a middle, and an end. Traffic control, peacekeeping (such as family disputes), and certainly the very long-range crime prevention aspects of the job have no such satisfaction-producing characteristics. Thus, most officers feel that the law enforcement role they play is the valuable part and the rest, though important, contains more frustrations than rewards. Increasing involvement with the nonenforcement aspects of the job is more the result of efforts of police program planners than a grass roots movement.

At the same time, patrol officers usually will admit that they like the increased direct contact with their "constituency" that comes with programs designed to recapture the more personal relationships that existed when beats were patrolled on foot. It is the degree and type of increased involvement that many police are ambivalent about. Having seen programs come and go in all phases of government and being charged with the continuing daily responsibility for keeping the peace on the streets of the community, most police officers want to know exactly what it is they'll be expected to do before they enthusiastically endorse any such changes. Of all the generalizations drawn about police, probably that which holds they are by nature somewhat conservative comes closest to being fair.

Limits of Authority

This subject must be looked at in two ways: the *formal limits* of authority as set up in the legal codes governing police agencies, and the *effective limits* established by the manner in which the police in any community carry out their jobs.

Under rule of law, the constitution and statutory law within the state and local government prescribe the authority of police. The power to arrest is set by law in the state. The authority for and manner of investigation is set primarily by case decisions in which the Supreme Court has ruled on individual application of statutory law under provisions of the Constitution. There is no lawful basis for exercise of police authority beyond the limits set in this way. When the police of any community attempt to act outside these limits of authority, even with the consent of the community, we develop situations like those discussed in the preceding chapter. These encourage disrespect for the law as well as for those who enforce it and bring about enforced behavior modification through court rulings.

While not actually opposed to the formal limits described above, effective limits of police authority can be broader, to the benefit of the community, if properly handled. For example, police routinely investigate suspicious behavior which proves to be innocent. If not carried off in a high-handed manner that breeds feelings of harrassment, no one is going to seriously challenge the fact that the police officer's expertise in such matters gives him probable cause for the interview. However, if he's arrogant or contemptuous of the citizens he interviews, even being right most of the time isn't going to allow him to continue using a valuable procedure that could benefit the community at large.

Another example of effective limits of authority beyond those formally set by law is the officer's perceived authority where none exists. When he responds to a landlord–tenant dis-

Field interrogation of a person doesn't necessarily mean he is suspect—just that his presence or appearance at a particular time and place is unusual enough to arouse an officer's curiosity.

pute or a family disturbance, his authority under law is extremely limited. Disturbance of the peace is about all he has to work with unless someone takes illegal action against another participant, and that is the very thing he's there to prevent. The same is true in any situation that is civil rather than criminal in nature, such as businessman-customer disputes, loud parties, even unruly crowds. In cases where no criminal violation has yet breeched the peace, the officer's role is simply to keep the peace by interjecting his presence to prevent escalation of a civil situation into a criminal one. When he does this he actually has no authority to order any specific behavior by the people involved. But if they perceive his authority as being greater than it is, his presence can have the necessary calming, peace-keeping effect. An important ingredient here is the general community acceptance of the police as a neutral, stablizing influence.

HOW THE COMMUNITY VIEWS POLICE

We've already said that if everything is going relatively calmly in the community, the police role is viewed with apathy, but if things are going badly, it is viewed with alarm because "something must be done." This is more than a defensive generalization, however, because there's a logical reason for it. If the streets are safe, the average citizen has a lot of other things to worry about; if they aren't he is entitled to be concerned. In between, he has a certain right to expect the police to take care of things. The only exception we're making is that when things get tough, the average citizen is going to have to do a few things he normally wouldn't have to be concerned with—like reporting crimes and suspicious incidents.

Apart from that, however, people do have some general attitudes toward police. Overall, it's a positive attitude. Certainly it varies with age groups, how parents speak of police, how police perform in a given community, and other such factors. The reason for the overall positive attitude is really as simple as it seems: most people are, and want to be, law abiding. They want to be able to earn a living and live in peace, and they see the police as a positive factor in their being able to do so. Even in communities where, for whatever reasons, this attitude is least positive the citizens believe police should be a protective force. Like any expectation, however, this one also carries a responsibility.

Living up to this responsibility is complicated by the fact that the general community's attitude toward police is usually ambivalent. While they have positive expectations of police they also have a subconscious distrust or fear of authority and certainly the police officer is the most conspicuous symbol of authority in any community. Most people frankly feel at least a little uncomfortable talking to a uniformed policeman. Even those with the most positive attitude toward police are subconsciously aware that the man with the badge has considerable potential power over their lives and they can't help but resent that. It's human to want to be in full control of your own life and anybody who threatens that ability is, somehow, set a little apart from you. Policemen if not consciously aware of this, at least sense it in their contacts with most citizens of the general community and this is a great factor in their tendency to seek the company of other police in private life. Whether this can ever be completely overcome is conjectural, but most police are able to have at least a few civilian friends with whom they can relax and be off guard. The hope for good relations lies in increased understanding and acceptance by the general community of the fact that police are not supermen and shouldn't be expected to be.

Strangely (but perhaps not) this superman expectation is strongest among those citizens who have the most positive attitude towards, and least contact with, police. It may not be strange to see this expectation for at least two reasons. First, their positive hopes and lack of real exposure tend to create an unreal, ivory-tower mystique about the power and role of police. They somehow expect police to take care of things involving "bad people" but be nice to "good people," including, of course, themselves. Any failure to meet these unrealistic criteria, such as issuance of a traffic citation or being too busy responding to an emergency to arrive promptly when called to investigate a day-old burglary, is viewed with disappointment. The second reason is that this positive expectation is similar to that in a parent–child relationship. Every parent realizes (or should) that he tends to judge his own family more harshly than someone else's. His hopes and expectations for his own, with whom he identifies most closely, create unreal behavior criteria which he doesn't impose on others. What may be viewed with a "boys-will-be-boys" attitude with regard to another youngster's behavior is at least a momentary disappointment when one's own son does it. This same human frailty causes those who support police to sometimes expect more of them than is reasonable. Conversely, the person who has had several direct experiences with police and found them to be both good and bad, weak and strong, fair and unfair, has a more realistic expectation. This apparent anomaly is the real basis for the concept that increased involvement of the law-abiding community with police, under nondemand circumstances (that is, those not involving a violation or a need for service) is widely felt to be important.

POLICE IN THE GHETTO

Up to now we've been speaking largely, if not exclusively, of police and citizen views of each other in terms of life in suburban or smaller communities and have not specifically addressed ourselves to the very special problems existing in the inner cities, often referred to as the hard core of the crime problem. Ghettoes have always been with us and historically have been inhabited by different ethnic groups. In the early part of this century and the latter part of the last, ghetto residents included many newly arrived immigrant groups—Irish, Italians, Jews, Poles, and others. As these groups became integrated into American society and experienced upward mobility, they moved out leaving the areas to other low-income groups. Today, ghetto residents include low-income blacks, Puerto Ricans, Mexican Americans, American Indians, and other minority group members. Tense relations have often existed between ghetto residents and police, and there are a number of reasons for this. Crowding is one factor as are other social factors related to poverty-level living conditions. These conditions in turn lead to ghettoes having the highest crime rates and ghetto residents being the leading victims of crime; thus, ghettoes have more police, investigation, crime control and prevention—in general, more contact between police and community.

Because the largest proportion of ghetto residents are blacks, most attention and studies focus on the relations between blacks and the police. When in this examination of police work we speak of black attitudes and police attitudes, we don't claim to present the feelings of all people in either group; we do, however, believe that the problems discussed are fairly representative of those faced by ghetto residents and police working in ghettoes.

The first fact to be established is that adult ghetto residents have a predominantly positive attitude toward police. While this may seem contrary to media accounts, study after study confirms that the overwhelming majority of black ghetto residents believe that police treat them either "very well' or "fairly well." Studies show that, among those complaining of dissatisfaction with the police, the most common improvements suggested were to increase the size of the police force and provide stricter law enforcement. This is not to say that many blacks in ghetto areas don't feel police use insulting language or search unreasonably and with unnecessary force; it only claims that the majority, and a substantial one in almost all major cities, do not regard the police as oppressors.

In any community the biggest adversary relationship exists between police and young men, who commit most of the crimes, get in most of the fights and riots, are the subject of most citizen complaints, and in general are the most frequent police customers. It is natural then that young men, as a group, have the lowest opinion of police officers, and this is particularly true in the ghettoes where twice as many blacks have this negative attitude as do others of the same age group in different neighborhoods.

An important fact to consider with regard to ghetto-dweller's positive attitude toward police is that it only includes

> ### A New Kind of Black Policeman
>
> Many reformists see the promotion of more blacks to command positions as an urgent necessity. Possibly because too few black policemen have been on the force long enough to gain the experience necessary for command, few cities have a large proportion of black supervisors. . . .
>
> Once black supervisors are in office, there is evidence that they are encouraging reformists' efforts—as, for that matter, are some white supervisors.
>
> Increasingly, they are putting their emphasis on training in human relations. Some are trying to devise strategies for putting the police into closer touch with the people they are supposed to protect. Boston's "Soul Patrol," New Orlean's "Urban Squad," and Detroit's "Mini-Stations" are examples of efforts to decentralize and personalize police work.
>
> Essentially the job of policemen involved in these efforts is to move into a neighborhood, get to know the people on a day-to-day basis, and secure their trust and cooperation.
>
> In Boston, New Orleans, and Detroit, such efforts seem to be having their effect. Crime in areas served by the special units is reportedly down and police-community rapport is up.
>
> But, while the "new" black policeman is winning friends among other blacks in their forties and older, and among the growing class of middle-income blacks, he is still viewed almost as a traitor among a broad segment of younger and lower-income blacks.
>
> "You join up and say to yourself, I'm going to try to help," said Larry Walker of Detroit, a 24-year-old black graduated from the Police Academy last November [1973]. "All of a sudden, the black group who you grew up with shut you right out. You no longer relate. You'd be surprised how you're not black anymore." [William K. Stevens, *New York Times* (August 11, 1974). Copyright 1974 by The New York Times Company. Reprinted by permission.]

the manner in which he's treated, not the effectiveness of the police effort. Citizens in these areas are about evenly divided on whether the police do a good job. As for the negative attitudes of young men, consider the only way police have of responding to the general community's demands for more police activity: increased patrol and increased interrogation of suspicious persons and incidents. And whom are they going to interrogate? The persons most likely to be involved in crimes—young males. So the cycle takes on the characteristics of a spiral.

In the ghetto black and white police alike believe the public doesn't give them the needed support to do the job demanded of them. They feel young people of the area not only don't respect them but actually view them as enemies. Failure to report crime, cited most often as evidence of lack of community support, is candidly admitted by adults, with fear of retribution by young hoodlums as the most frequently-given reason. Police also feel that if they are to be criticized for being ineffective they can't at the same time be criticized for trying. To the police a nearly 50 percent ratio of interviews turning out to involve solid suspects is very respectable; to the people making up the innocent 50 percent it seems like harassment. Similarly, finding weapons on 25 percent of those searched seems ample justification for the search to police who recognize that lives, including theirs, are threatened by those weapons; to the 75 percent who were clean it may well seem ample justification for a bad attitude toward police.

As if there weren't enough problems in providing effective police service in ghetto areas, it is common practice in most agencies which have such areas to assign new officers to them. The theory offered is that they're enthusiastic and, being young, best equipped physically to cope with the strenuous demands of such service. The wisdom of such reasoning should be measured against the desirability of having more seasoned officers in this most difficult and sensitive assignment.

COMMUNITY PROGRAMS

It should be apparent by now that the subject of relationships between police and the community is highly complex. Efforts at improving them are usually either aimed at increasing *communication* with, or *services* offered to, the community. Communication approaches, no matter what individual format they take (such as discussions, meetings, and the like are aimed at explaining the police to the public in an effort to win their support. Service expansion usually takes the form of advice and aid to community members such as taking up their cause before departments of the municipal government (including the police department, which obviously causes some conflict).

While the communication strategy is employed in both affluent and ghetto neighborhoods, it is more effective in the former. Before we take up the reasons for this and the alternatives employed, let's look at how communication programs are used to improve police–community relations.

Probably the most common attempt at communicating with the general community is the *neighborhood meeting.* This can range from informal get-togethers over coffee to more structured workshops aimed at extracting information on needs and expectations from the citizens and then, together, developing goals to which both parties are hopefully committed. An interesting case study occurred in one midwestern city which tried three separate workshops. The first was in a neighborhood with a high crime rate. The population was mixed; both affluent whites and lower-income blacks were well represented at the meeting which drew some 200 persons. Attendance was largely by adults who engaged in constructive conversation and planning resulting in the development of a new patrol format for police in the housing projects where blacks lived. Everyone felt the meeting was successful, and from the standpoint of communication, at least, it apparently was.

The second workshop in this city was held in a neighborhood of university students and young blacks. About one hundred attended, with the students dominating the conversation to complain about police handling of their antiwar demonstrations. The police contended they couldn't discuss it because it was currently before the courts and the blacks, tiring of all the arguing about problems not of concern to them, wanted to discuss the high crime rate. Shouting abounded and nothing was accomplished before the meeting broke up in confusion.

The third workshop was held in a racially-balanced neighborhood of affluent whites and blacks who enjoyed relative freedom from the disturbance of crime common to the other areas. A very small number turned out and the issues complained about were the chronic, but nonpolice issues such as animal control, refuse collection, and the like. Nothing was accomplished. Quite obviously workshops and other neighborhood meetings are not a panacea applicable to all neighborhoods.

Advisory councils also work well in some but not all communities. In some areas, notably Berkeley, California, and Spokane, Washington, they are mandated by local ordinance. Usually, however, they are less formally constituted and less likely to be viewed by police as distrusted, civilian review boards. The purpose of advisory councils is to help police formulate policies which are representative of the expectations of the community. To the extent that police in a given community view their council as truly representative and well-motivated, the desired result may be obtained. A collateral benefit to police with such a relationship is a forum for disseminating information on police problems and views into the community.

Community surveys are a means of determining needs and expectations that can be useful for communication and service. The communications aspect is provided simply by the fact that police are asking the community to give them information to help in policy formulation. The questions can be as open-ended as, "How can we improve our service to you?" or as specific as, "Do you believe police officers are respectful in their dealings with persons like yourself?" They can be conducted with a narrow, selected sample of the population, as in Baltimore where 200 persons who had called for service were queried on the quality and timeliness of the service provided them, or an extremely broad one, as in Nassau County, New York where over 300,000 families were asked about the area's law enforcement needs. The important thing is that the community is aware that the police are earnestly trying to make their service match the needs. Of course, it is then incumbent upon the police to show that they take seriously the information they gain by acting on it. This is where the service aspect is involved. There's also a collateral benefit for police administrators using this technique because they automatically get a measure of effectiveness that they can use to evaluate the performance of their officers. Unless the administrator has some idea of what is needed in the community he can only use the traditional and largely meaningless standards of arrests, citations issued, and the like.

School programs are quite common at all levels. St. Louis, Missouri, has a widely recognized Officer Friendly program, which takes officers into elementary classrooms. New Orleans has a junior high program featuring lectures on law, structure of the criminal justice system, and similar subjects; included are tours of police headquarters and courts. San Diego, California high school students meet in small groups with uniformed officers to discuss police organization, responsibilities, and authority. This program, which includes a "hot seat" question-and-answer session for the officers, is also presented in Spanish since the San Diego area has a large non-English-speaking population. A similar program in St. Louis operates at the junior high level under the contemporary title, "Rapping with the Fuzz."

In some communities *school resource officers* are assigned full time to junior high schools. They spend each day there, in uniform, filling a counselling, instructional, and law enforcement role. The latter aspect of the role is minimized and the officer serves mainly as a source of information to any class studying a subject where a law enforcement point of view is appropriate. He also confers with groups or individuals, at their request, on whatever subjects they choose. The idea is to provide a daily opportunity for contact with a representative of the law enforcement community who may present a different image from the stereotyped one existing in many young minds during the formative years. This program grew out of research in Cincinnati which indicated that 9th graders consistently had lower opinions of police than 7th graders and nothing was done to combat the growth of alienation. Statistics and subjective evaluation of the SRO programs developed in various states, notably Michigan, Arizona, and California, seem to indicate that this program functions well in that area.

Juvenile activities are conducted by many agencies in addition to their school programs. Salt Lake City has a public-supported athletic program for disadvantaged young people with police officers as coaches and officials in city-wide competition. New Orleans and Los Angeles operate "Send a Kid to Camp" programs, and police athletic leagues are common around the country.

Special *minority programs* range from Detroit's "Buzz the Fuzz" television program where citizens call in questions to be fielded by officers, to sophisticated bilingual programs designed to communicate with non-English-speaking minorities. San Diego, in a program of the latter type, teaches Spanish in its academy, identifies bilingual officers with special name tags, and publishes literature on departmental operation and complaint procedures in both English and Spanish. Other agencies maintain files on officers with bilingual capabilities to be called upon when the need arises. San Jose, California, broadcasts Spanish-language programs explaining the law, legal procedures, and the police function. Los Angeles grants points for bilinguality to compensate for employment deficiencies such as height requirements.

Reorganization of the patrol function is a means employed by an increasing number of police agencies to improve relationships with the community. Cincinnati uses a "Community Sector" plan similar to Los Angeles' "Basic Car Plan" where 24-hour responsibility for all police work in a fixed patrol area is given to a team of officers under the supervision of a senior officer. Teams not only provide police service for their city-within-a-city but organize community relations activities, including interarea athletic programs. The basic concept of such programs is to come as close as possible to the many social advantages of the old foot-patrol days without giving up the obvious economic advantages of motorized patrol. In Los Angeles the chief meets monthly with the team leaders; in Detroit patrol crews turn in monthly reports of main problems in their areas and submit suggested solutions which are reviewed promptly and acted upon by management.

As suggested earlier, communication programs are not as effective in ghetto areas as in the more affluent sectors. Because law enforcement is required to a greater degree in the ghetto and because this increase may lead to tense relations between police and the residents, communication efforts may not work as well as in other areas. Service efforts may be more successful in the long-run but only time will tell. One service effort tried in many areas is the *storefront operation.* In such operations a vacant store in a hard-core area is rented by police and set up as a sort of miniheadquarters or substation. The concept is to make police more available to the community, in somewhat the same way as reorganization of the patrol function, and thereby improve the service. Hopefully the police in the store-

Storefront operations aim at overcoming citizens' reluctance to contact police by setting up mini-headquarters which avoid the official atmosphere of the formal station.

front operation will identify with the problems of the people in their area, and vice versa. Success of such operations has been spotty. In cases where it is used mainly to explain police to the community, rather than increase the level of service and involvement, it has largely failed.

The internal problems of police assigned to storefront operations are similar to, but less intense than, those assigned to specialized units such as San Francisco's Police Community Relations Unit, in which it was found that the more successful officers are at their assignment, the more isolated they become from their fellow officers. In this unit officers work with problem population groups, young men and members of the street subculture, as their "clients." They do the normal things such as providing recreational programs, but also get into problems such as helping young men with arrest records get jobs. Their increasing effort at representation of their clientele in dealings with governmental agencies, principally the police, has been the source of success in their assignment and difficulty among their own ranks. Many other officers see this function as adversary to their own, and the thought of one officer helping file a complaint against another is difficult for most to accept. While the results of this program are debated, even after fifteen years of operation, if you consider a basic goal of the effort to be closer contact between some police officers and some members of the ghetto, it would have to be rated as considerably more effective than most communications efforts.

True improvements in relationships between police and the total community are much more likely to result from programs in which communication is a *tool,* rather than the ultimate goal, of the effort. Fortunately, the current thrust in police-community relations programs aims at a *partnership* with the community rather than simply increasing the community's understanding of the police position. Communication is an important part of such programs, but true involvement of all segments of the community is the overriding concept. While the results of the newer approach are far from conclusive, early indications are certainly encouraging.

SUMMARY

Cooperation of police and community is essential to effective establishment of a peaceful and orderly society. This cooperation involves increased understanding by both the police and the general community of the *needs and desires* of both and the *means available* to achieve the desired goals.

In general community members feel that it is the role of the police to take care of violations of law; police generally feel that it is impossible to solve the problems of antisocial behavior without increased cooperation and support from the general community.

The police officer has considerable authority to affect the lives of individuals and exercises this authority under difficult circumstances in terms of time and environmental conditions. He also has great responsibility for individual discretion in applying the law in a manner consistent with both policy and community needs.

While the satisfaction a policeman derives from his job is largely in the field of enforcement, nonenforcement duties make up an increasingly large percentage of his time. His limits of authority are *prescribed by law* but may be larger, in effect, because of the *perceived* authority in the minds of those he deals with.

The *community view* of the police is generally *positive.* Because of this the community sometimes has larger expectations of police than they are capable of delivering. The problem is compounded in the ghetto where older citizens desire more law enforcement and young males desire to be left alone. Police efforts to satisfy the desires of the older community are viewed as inadequate by the older citizens and as harassment by the younger.

Communication programs aimed at improving police-community relations include *neighborhood meetings;* participation in *advisory councils* to involve the community in police goal setting; *community surveys* to assess needs and desires of the community and provide measures of effectiveness for police operation; *school programs* to improve the police image in young people's minds; *school resource officers* to provide daily contact between police and students; *juvenile programs* such as athletic and camping activities; *minority programs,* including bilingual programs; and *reorganization of patrol functions* to increase daily involvement of the police in the community.

Service programs are aimed at improving police-community relations by increasing the level and type of service provided the community and include *reorganization of the patrol function,* which is a blend of both communication and service improvement; *storefront operations* to decentralize police-citizen contact; and *specialized units* which represent problem groups to both the community at large and governmental agencies.

REVIEW QUESTIONS

[Answers to these questions appear on page 385.]

1. *True or false?* The role of the police, rather than simply giving the community the kind of law enforcement it wants, is to determine what these desires are and provide the kind of law enforcement that is needed.
2. Which aspect of the policeman's job (enforcement or peacekeeping) provides the greater opportunity for him to see a clear beginning, middle and end to his work? _____
3. Do police officers feel generally that they should be held more responsible for dealing with the symptoms, or causes, of crime? _____
4. In dealing with a civil situation, such as a family dispute, is the officer's formal or effective authority used to obtain the needed result? _____
5. Is apathy toward police problems and needs more likely to exist in affluent or ghetto areas? Explain why in your own words. _____
6. What is the most common complaint about police among older residents of ghetto areas? _____
7. What is the most common complaint police have about citizens? _____
8. Label each of the following as either a communication or a service type of community program:
    _____ a. neighborhood meetings
    _____ b. advisory council
    _____ c. representation in governmental dealings
    _____ d. school programs

CHAPTER 10

PROFESSIONALISM AND ETHICS

OVERVIEW

For nearly two decades the subject of professionalism has never been far from the top of the list of topics discussed by police administrators, scholars, and critics. To scholars and critics the term has become something of a catchall phrase for police problems which in any way relate to job performance. To police it represents both a standard of behavior and a form of recognition which is highly desired. To all three groups it is a term directly related to the upgrading of American police.

    Achievement of professional status for the police segment of the criminal justice community has been frustrated partly by lack of a definition which would establish criteria agreeable to all. No single group addressing the subject has been able to come up with a set of criteria upon which they can agree, let alone one that would be acceptable to others. Lawyers and judges have always been considered "professional people," without the need for an express definition of requirements. But what is required for a policeman to be accorded a similar status? A university degree? Clarence Darrow only had one year of college, yet hardly anyone would question his skill in the practice of law. A state license, as required of professional engineers or accountants? Judges aren't required to have one. Or maybe just a standard of performance that would be acceptable to most people who desire to see peace maintained in the community by fair enforcement of its laws? Probably this latter approach is the only practical one and it's to this end that we'll address ourselves in this chapter. First we'll take our turn at trying to define professionalism, and then we'll examine how satisfying that definition might affect police and the community they serve.

TOWARD A PRACTICAL DEFINITION

Anyone attempting to define "professional behavior" is bound to come up with a wide variety of specifications to be met in the job being evaluated. The elements most frequently listed are, (in no particular order): *discretion* on the part of the individual as to how the task is done; *specialized knowledge* beyond that possessed by the general populace; an *extensive training period* or an *apprenticeship* during which on-the-job performance is monitored by persons currently performing the task on a professional basis; *high standards* of admission to professional status; *altruistic dedication* to the service ideal; an *ethics code* reflecting the service ideal and placing behavioral demands upon those adhering to it; *pride* of members in their calling; *public recognition* of the activity as having professional status or the necessary prestige; and, almost simplistically, *participation for livelihood* in the activity being considered (a further stipulation made here is that the activity is often engaged in by persons for reasons other than their livelihood).

If we can accept "professional behavior" as the general requirement to be met (rather than such prerequisites as a university degree or a state license), and consider those listed above to be reasonable, we have a practical basis for determining if police work should qualify as such. It's not necessary to formalize an evaluation process to the extent of rank-ordering or weighting the various criteria. There is, after all, no official body which sits in Olympian judgment on whether any field of endeavor should, with absolute finality, be called professional. It's not an academic consideration, however, because the subject receives much attention within the criminal justice community. It also deserves to be treated here because many readers have not yet decided upon the precise direction of their careers, and status accorded a particular job is a factor for some in making the choice. For others, personal satisfaction is more important and they are thus less concerned with formal recognition. In either case, an examination of the police officer's job in terms of how it relates to the generally recognized elements of professionalism will be beneficial.

Discretion is one of the elements about which there is least disagreement with regard to the police role. As mentioned earlier the police officer, in spite of belonging to a paramilitary organization governed by specific laws and policies, is expected to and does exercise a great deal of discretion in performing his job. Strangely, his is the role in the criminal justice system which one might normally think of as providing least opportunity for discretion; yet it often is the one where most discretion is exercised. The President's Commission on Law Enforcement and Administration of Justice in defining the police role in its 1967 report said, "That a policeman's duties compel him to exercise personal discretion many times every day is evident. Every policeman is an interpreter of the law . . . the manner in which he works is influenced by practical matters: the legal strength of the available evidence, the willingness of victims to press charges and of witnesses to testify, the temper of the community, the time and information at his disposal. Much is at stake in how the policeman exercises this discretion."

Even the courts, which exercise the most sweeping and direct control over police behavior through their case decisions, reluctantly act to formally limit the officer's discretionary powers because without his action the entire criminal justice process is virtually incapable of beginning. Beyond requiring his decision on whether to arrest or not for its initiation, much of the quality of the subsequent performance of the process depends on the nature of his decision to use or not to use various methods of detection or investigation. It may also be aborted by his decision to release rather than prosecute an arrested person. While not typical of how the average officer spends his entire working day, these examples indicate the quality of sophisticated judgments, all having a major impact on the lives of the persons involved, which he may have to make at any time and under the most immediate and difficult of circumstances.

Specialized knowledge is another area of an officer's job that should offer no grounds for disagreement. Yet it is an area where the attitudes of the general citizenry and the rest of the criminal justice system are somehow curiously reversed from what one might expect them to be. The average citizen probably feels that the policeman has much more knowledge than he actually does about certain things, principally the intricacies of the legal codes with which he's involved. Conversely, members of the legal profession who have spent several years formally studying the codes may feel that he has less knowledge of them than he in fact does. Precise knowledge of each provision of the legal codes is not required of the police officer and may even be counterproductive for the type of law enforcement decisions he has to make. But he does need and have a broad knowledge of both the letter and spirit of the criminal code. While his breadth and depth of knowledge can't successfully match point-for-point that of a skilled defense lawyer, it does set him distinctly apart from the average member of the general community.

Beyond the requirement of knowledge of law there is need for knowledge in other disciplines to a degree beyond that required of the normal citizen. Broad knowledge of psychology and sociology are important; so are a host of specific techniques and procedures useful only in performing the job of peace officer. And, if application skills are included in this corpus of knowledge, the gulf between the police officer and other citizens widens considerably.

Apprenticeship, in its strictest sense is not practiced in law enforcement. To the extent that the term implies learning through practical experience under skilled workers, however, all police agencies follow some form of apprenticeship. The academy situation is based on this type of instruction to some extent, and most agencies follow (some also precede) academy training with a probationary period. During this period experience is gained by riding with a veteran officer. After this he may or may not ride alone for a further period of close monitoring by experienced officers before he receives permanent status. In the largest sense this period of apprenticeship never really ends because the police officer is different from others whose journeyman status has been achieved through an apprenticeship program. Unlike a journeyman electrician, for example, who has only to show his card to a prospective employer to be accorded professional status without question as to why he is presently unemployed, an out-of-work police officer discharged from his last job for incompetence is extremely unlikely to be hired by another public agency. Even the protections of civil service employment usually offer no safeguard against termination for incompetence or malfeasance.

High standards for admission to professional status for police work don't formally exist yet. It's probably safe to estimate that when they are formally agreed upon these standards will be high, as evidenced by the current trend to greater emphasis on formal education.

Altruism and dedication to the service ideal seem to exist in virtually all officers at the time they enter the service. Most scholars and writers on the subject agree on this. They also agree that the frustrations which arise from the kinds and amount of services, as compared with the amount of crook-catching, do not greatly diminish the dedication. The fact that officers, in their disappointment and frustration with the amount required, still perform the myriad of services demanded of them, seems testimony to considerable dedication to the service ideal.

A *code of ethics,* advanced by the International Association of Chiefs of Police has existed for some years now. We'll talk more about it later in this chapter and when you read it, think of its tenets in terms of the demands it places upon those who must apply it in their job. While some critics claim the code doesn't place specific enough limitations on behavior, one may disagree on two grounds: first, it isn't necessary for such a code to define specific behavior under each possible circumstance (rather, a code of ethics should be an expression of ideals and values); and, second, an honest and conscientious effort to conform with the ideals expressed in this code, in the context of daily performance of the police officer's job in the streets, is likely to result in behavior that will satisfy any reasonable person with practical expectations.

We are not taking the superficial position here that police each day read the code of ethics and dedicate themselves anew to it. That wouldn't be a reasonable expectation any more than it would be for a doctor. What all citizens can hope for, however, is that a constantly increasing percentage of police will perform to a level somewhere near the ideals expressed in the code. It would seem that anyone who does perform to the level demanded by these ideals would be entitled to whatever respect and dignity is accorded a person designated as a professional.

Pride of membership in their calling isn't seriously questioned with regard to police. Even critics concede that a high percentage of police officers not only like their work but are proud of it. It seems, however, that while pride is certainly a desirable and laudable attribute, it is not a stringent means of distinguishing one activity from another in terms of quality.

Pride is, afterall, largely a personal thing and should exist in every person, regardless of his calling.

Public recognition of police work as having professional status is probably not yet a fact. The word *probably* should be stressed because there is a strong likelihood that most of the public doesn't know, or care, if any group of workers becomes adjudged professional. Most people, if asked to list the professions would probably include medicine, law and teaching. If the interviewer paused, as if expecting more, a person might venture a guess that perhaps theology would also qualify. Further pause by the interviewer might elicit a response including certified public accountants. If pressed to still further expand the list the average citizen would probably either assume the interviewer wanted to include occupations such as ballplayers or wonder, aloud, who cared. In either of these two states of mind the person would quite likely be willing to accord professional status to police officers or any other group wanting similar recognition. The purpose here is not to be facetious but to suggest that public recognition may be too weak a criterion for serious determination of whether a particular career activity qualifies for professional status.

Participation for livelihood in an activity often engaged in by amateurs is the broadest of all the qualifications used to define professionalism. By this, of course, such groups as athletes and tradesmen become designated as professionals. Strangely, police would be excluded by this broad method of qualification simply because there are virtually no amateur police. Probably most people would draw a professional-amateur distinction between police forces employed by governmental bodies and those private or merchant police who perform guard and private patrol services. But even this distinction is not satisfactory under the livelihood standard because the private forces are, indeed, engaged in a full-time career for pay. So the definition that would seem to offer the easiest route to professional recognition actually offers the most resistance of any in the case of police.

At this point it would seem that the case for police recognition as a professional body rests on the most stringent of the qualifying elements: discretion in matters of great importance and effect on the lives of those involved; specialized knowledge beyond that of the general populace; dedication to performance in accord with the service ideal; an ethics code which members swear to strive toward; and, hopefully, increasingly high standards of performance. The "easier" qualifying elements—pride, public recognition, and participation for livelihood—may or may not be met, depending upon the point of view of the individual making the assessment. There is, however, one qualifying element we haven't examined individually: training. Unfortunately there has been a great degree of polarity in the quantity and quality of training provided police agencies. Fortunately, there is a very strong trend constantly increasing both the amount and quality as we'll explore in the next chapter. In 1965 a survey by the International Association of Chiefs of Police determined that less than 15 percent of agencies studies provided immediate training for recruits and that about half provided it as soon as possible, within the first year. At about this time the need for increased training was becoming widely recognized and the federal Law Enforcement Assistance Act in 1966 began to make available millions of dollars for this purpose. Most agencies now demand or provide greatly increased preparatory training on a continuing basis and subsidize job-related education for officers in public schools and colleges.

In summary then, it would seem fair to say that in terms of the requirements of the job, police work clearly qualifies as a profession, but the training requirement may not yet be met. If one accepts performance in a professional manner as the main criterion, then professionalism becomes the individual concern it really should be, even for those universally-recognized activities of medicine and law. Thus an officer whose career began at a point in time when formal training was not as highly valued as it is today or will be in the future is not to be denied recognition as a professional on this basis alone. Rather his status will be judged on the more realistic basis of his performance which is, of course, the product of all his training (formal and experience-derived) and his individual orientation toward his job. As a matter of fact, this last consideration, his individual orientation toward his job, will either multiply or nullify the effect of any amount of training he is given. So, we will examine some of the factors other than training, that affect an officer's ultimate ability to perform in a professional manner.

ROLE CONFLICTS FOR POLICE

The three universally-accepted roles played by police are: the *peacekeeping,* or public safety role in which he protects the rights and lives of citizens; *law enforcement,* or crime fighting, which is the most common image of real police work for both

Service aspects of the police role occupy the vast majority of the officer's time. First aid is a typical example of such activity.

citizens and police; and *community service,* which includes social service functions ranging from emergency first aid treatment through counselling indigent or ill persons to rescuing pets. Depending on which of these roles he is fulfilling, an entirely different set of behaviors and standards of performance is rightfully expected of the police officer.

Inevitably these three demands create a conflict within the individual officer. His ability to manage this conflict has a lot to do with the impression he creates of professional, or unprofessional, conduct. Take the seemingly straightforward matter of issuing a traffic citation, for example. Although a violation of law is involved, this could hardly be considered a crime-fighting or crook-catching activity. Yet it may be. An officer is aware that he is statistically five times as likely to be killed during a traffic stop as during a civil disorder. And although not tabulated, the number of arrests (for crimes other than drunk driving) resulting from "routine" traffic stops is very large. Still the vast majority of citizens, when stopped for a traffic violation, rightfully expect to be treated in a manner more in keeping with the community service behavioral mode than that for law enforcement.

As noted earlier, even more role conflict for the policeman is due to the fact that when he first contemplated his career he saw it as primarily law enforcement. He basically wanted to catch crooks, and keep the peace, in that order. His commitment to the service ideal was an altruistic one and, if he actually thought about the activities that would be required to dispatch that commitment (which is doubtful), he accepted them rather than enthusiastically looked forward to them. More probably he anticipated that the best part of community service would really consist of catching criminals to make the streets safe. Then he found early in his career that while this could be considered a form of community service it certainly wasn't going to be the most frequent form. Somewhere between 10 and 30 percent of his time was going to be spent in this "real police work" and the balance was going to be spent in nonenforcement duties, with the largest percentage by far involving neither enforcement nor peace-keeping. Thus he encountered the critical crossroads of his individual orientation toward his career: either adopt the true professional's ability to perform well all aspects of the job or become preoccupied with those which give the most personal satisfaction. While the choice isn't a conscious or exclusive one, every police officer makes it according to his own ability and personality. The degree to which he follows one path or the other is a large measure of his professionalism.

THE POLICE PERSONALITY

The personality which the recruit brings to police service is already largely formed by his experiences in childhood and early manhood. It will, of course, also be shaped by his experiences in service, but the potentials which control how this shaping will occur are already built-in. By examining the way in which most police recruit's personalities have developed by the time they begin their careers we may be able to anticipate how they will further develop in normal police experience.

Many psychological studies have been conducted of police officers and the results, while differing slightly in specific conclusions, do present some common characteristics which can be useful to us here. Police are found to have high intelligence and superior personality adjustment in general, with assertive, aggressive tendencies which lead them to be willing to take risks and act on their impulses. They are competitive, with high levels of physical energy to the point of being restless and disinterested in routine work. Similarly they favor participation in sports rather than watching them, like fast cars, and seek stimulation from their environment. They tend to be less introspective and more suspicious (less naive) than average. They are ambivalent toward authority, taking pride in their position but preferring to be left alone in their own territory without intervention from supervisors.

On patrol, the tendency toward suspicion and the need for stimulus from his environment are a great aid to the policeman. Patrol officers have natural outlets for these needs because one of their main tasks is observation of unusual conditions in the area and identification of those unusual conditions which may be indicators of crime. Patrol can be boring but an officer can keep himself profitably occupied by constantly looking at and listening to the environment as he drives along. To the extent that he correctly evaluates these observations against his knowledge of what is normal for the area and the implications of any abnormality, he both avoids boredom and performs his job well. Detective work, of course, offers excellent outlets for these personality characteristics later in an officer's career.

The tendency to impulsiveness and assertive, aggressive behavior should develop, along with the lack of introspective tendencies, into the decisive personality so important to a police officer.

Intelligence and personality adjustment are, of course, important in any career. Psychologists tell us that our identity must be secure if we are to be considered mature human beings. By this they mean that our feelings about ourselves (our own evaluation of our desires, values, goals, worth, and so on) must match the feelings about us that we perceive in others around us (our parents, peers, those we come in contact with at work). They say we need to be able to express ourselves in our work and have this expression approved by others, and that if we can do this we'll be well-adjusted and if we can't we will develop anxieties. The importance to the police recruit of having a well-adjusted personality at the time he enters service would seem then to be very great since there will be so many immediate problems on the job which will deny him positive reinforcement of his feelings about himself.

JOB-RELATED PROBLEMS

One of the special problems of being a policeman is the age of the average recruit when he enters service. Even though he has a well-adjusted personality, there is considerable identity development yet to occur. The cliche is that, the concrete isn't quite hard. He is full of drive, idealism, and a desire to live up to his ideals but is still somewhat unsure of the processes required to achieve them. In this situation he requires a model, for reference, and this model comes from his peers and superiors (principally his sergeant and training officer) in his initial assignment. If he is fortunate enough to get good models his development will be easier; if not, he can become confused by the apparent difference between his idealistic self-model and that provided him by others. While a degree of this same problem exists for the new employee in any job, few young men are placed in such responsible roles at the age of the beginning police officer. The need for immediate, successful performance is probably felt more acutely in the beginning policeman for this reason.

The role conflict mentioned previously is another problem more acute for the young police officer than his civilian counterpart. While striving to meet his self-imposed standards, he finds that to perform well in one area of his job can mean compromising part of his performance ideal in another. The result can be confusion and deterioration of self-discipline through accelerated development of his cynical tendencies at the expense of his dedication to the service ideal. While the vast majority of recruits don't support the concept that treating the symptoms of crime is more important than trying to treat the causes, frustration during the formative period of their career can drive them toward the relative simplicity of this attitude.

The possibility of boredom on patrol duty can be a problem for the action-oriented, restless officer. His need to see results from his activity can lead to a tendency to overrate the seriousness of an offense such as a traffic violation or minor misdemeanor, in order to subconciously promote the feeling that there's value to his being on duty. Officers have been known to write technically-allowable tickets for such innocent violations as a cracked windshield simply because "nothing much has been happening" for a few hours. Failure to control such impulses no matter how human they may be is not only unprofessional but impractical because of the damage it does to police-community relations (especially in high-crime, low-income areas).

Lack of interest in paperwork details can lead to another form of unprofessional behavior. In contrast with the overrating described above, a situation will sometimes be underrated by an officer who simply doesn't want to get involved with all the paperwork it entails. This happens most frequently near the end of a shift. Rather than stay over long enough to run a breathalyzer test, for example, an officer may let a drunk driver off with only a warning, or he may put off responding to a burglary report call (one where there is clearly no possibility of doing any more than taking a report on an incident several days old) until his shift is over so the next officer will have to handle it. While understandable in light of the personality characteristics specified, such behavior is obviously undesirable.

The personality traits we've described would seem most likely to apply to an individualistic person: assertive, aggressive, action-oriented, and so on, and indeed they do, creating still another conflict for the policeman. The organization in which he works is paramilitary and authoritarian. He wears a uniform and his superiors have military titles. He is expected to, and must, perform as a member of a team, submissive to and respectful of, authority. Yet his nature, including his desire to have sole responsibility for law enforcement in his territory, puts him inherently at odds with this situation. In addition many characteristics of the job itself would seem to demand individualistic behavior: the need for quick decisions; actions which are initiated because of his own intimate knowledge of the territory; even an increasing trend in management to enhance the role of the beat officer through decentralization of authority. All these demands serve to feed this conflict.

On the surface it might seem that the patrol officer's proprietary claim to his territory is threatened both by supervision and by the well-known tendency of other officers to flock to the scene of a "good" call—one with action potential. Actually, this isn't so. The arrival of other officers is clearly understood as back-up and the officer to whom the call is assigned is unquestionably in charge (if anything, his ego position is enhanced, rather than threatened, by the presence of the "troops" who are implicitly under his command). In most agencies even a supervisor arriving at the scene does not take command merely by his presence. This organizational anomaly gives practical testimony to both the need and ability of police officers to function as individuals in a situation which basically demands sublimation of individuality. The ability of the individual officer to cope with such a situation is another factor in determining the amount of professionalism he will be able to achieve in his job.

Protection of the established social order is a problem faced by most police officers at two levels: management and personal bias. An officer may be directed to provide special patrol for financial, social, or political elements of the community and thus be subjected to management bias. His personal bias may lead him to treat an affluent person with greater respect than an indigent one; a middle-aged person with more courtesy than a young one; or a member of one racial group differently from another. No amount of proficiency in the crime-fighting or peace-keeping aspects of his job can compensate, in terms of professional behavior, for such failure to perform the service aspect evenly. Nor can such failure be justified on the basis of giving a community the kind of law enforcement the majority of its citizens wants or demands; in fact, just the opposite is true since ability to perform the service aspect well in spite of any external pressures is one of the more realistic measures of professional behavior.

Dealing with the temptations of "goodies" which many people think simply go with the job, is a problem every policeman faces early and throughout his career. Gratuities from either genuinely grateful citizens or those consciously or subconsciously seeking favor are one of the oldest forms of this problem. In some cities they are, unfortunately, still considered normal and acceptable. No amount of moral lecturing on this point is as sobering as the realization that almost every cop who ever went to jail for being on the take will tell you it started with a cup of coffee, then a bottle of booze at Christmas, and so on inch by inch, until finally there seemed no difference between what was already being done and accepting money. While it might seem that the line could be easily drawn, try to evaluate honestly the simple situation in which you might have to decide whether or not to cite a driver for a minor traffic violation. Would you have any inclination to treat differently a person from whom you'd accepted even a small gratuity, say a daily cup of coffee? Most people would honestly answer "yes." If they also have to admit that they followed that inclination, it should be easy to understand why officers are well-advised to make it easy for themselves and just avoid any form of gratuity, no matter how innocently offered or well intended.

Integrity Training

"Hearing the cops coming, the burglar drops the sack of stolen jewelry and flees. Seconds later, two uniformed patrolmen discover the loot left behind. "Holy Christ!" exclaims one mustachioed cop bending over the bag. "Look at this."

(Freeze.)

Sergeant Andy Danschisch of the New York City police department's internal affairs division suddenly stops the video-taped drama and looks out at his "Integrity Training" class of 38 police academy students. "What kind of situation is this?" he asks. "Very tempting," offers one student. The class laughs. Danschisch is not amused. The brand-new mandatory 10-hour course uses films and actual case histories to prepare the future cops for the ethical pressures they will face. Instructors like Danschisch take the program very seriously. The video tape moves again. "I'm sure this guy's insured," the rogue cop says of the jewel robbery victim. Danschisch interrupts: "A typical rationale. Pretty soon somebody says to you in these situations, 'Don't worry about it.' That's when you *should* worry."

During a break the students and instructors mingle. "How are you going to change something that has been going on for so many years?" asks a recruit. "Maybe the street just crumbles you," says another. Detective Lynn Cutler replies: "When you help people day in and day out and don't get the thanks you think you deserve, it's rough. I know that. But your job is to be a professional. We didn't say it was easy." [*Time* (May 6, 1974). Reprinted by permission from TIME, The Weekly Newsmagazine; Copyright Time Inc.]

Special privileges, such as driving in violation of traffic laws when not responding to an emergency call or parking illegally, are taken far too often by officers, even those who zealously strive for professional behavior in other aspects of their job. This isn't a federal matter, obviously, and driving ten or fifteen miles beyond the speed limit responding to a citizen's call which, though important, isn't urgent enough for red lights and siren, may seem justified, especially if traffic is light, streets broad, and so on. But another citizen, who sees it happening and who may have been cited for the same or perhaps an even lesser violation, really can't be blamed for not understanding.

A final form of temptation, and for many the most difficult

to resist, is the sexual attraction many young women feel toward policemen. There's no way to offer effective advice or admonition on this subject beyond pointing out that the problem of objectively treating a traffic offender who has given you a cup of coffee may be considerably simpler than dealing evenly with someone whose favors have been more personal. There also may be a cooling effect to be gained from the realization that the attraction is in reality almost entirely nonpersonal; it is the authority and its implicit power that are attractive and may overcome what would otherwise be a complete lack of interest.

A final problem for police officers to overcome is internal resistance of the system. While resistance to change exists in any profession (consider the legal and medical professions if an example is needed) the problem here is that police work needs the changes most likely to come through the young initiates in order to achieve the status it desires. Unfortunately, the system conservatism increases the likelihood of young idealists becoming discouraged and leaving the service before the full impact of their dedication is realized. Increasing numbers of young professionals are staying with the service, however, and as they do the internal resistance of the system decreases geometrically, making it more receptive to the needed change.

LAW ENFORCEMENT CODE OF ETHICS

As we've already said, a code of ethics is not obliged to spell out specific behavior to be exhibited under all possible circumstances. Rather it should describe exemplary behaviors that reflect attitudes which will make the desired behavior probable in all circumstances. Moreover, it is important that these attitudes give both moral and practical guidance to those who adopt them. This is not to say that morality is only a matter of practicality, because this would deny the existence of morality. But the fact is that a code of ethics is not divine; it is designed by men in the hope of guiding the actions of other men. If those who must be guided do not perceive some relationship between a stated principle and their need to live life in its real context, the morality of the principle becomes obscured and vaguely distrusted. At the very best it is "accepted, but not understood," which means it is paid lip service, but not followed.

The Law Enforcement Code of Ethics, while based on high moral principles, is easily placed in a practical frame of reference for application to the task of daily living as a peace officer.

For those who have not read it (and for those who have neither read nor thought of it recently) we offer it now, annotated with our concept of its meaning in terms of professional police performance. The Code has four sections: duty definition; standards of performance in personal life; standards of performance in official life; and, the oath of commitment to these professional standards. We'll take each section in order.

> *As a Law Enforcement Officer, my fundamental duty is to serve mankind; to safeguard lives and property; to protect the innocent against deception, the weak against oppression or intimidation, and the peaceful against violence or disorder; and to respect the Constitutional rights of all men to liberty, equality and justice.*

What we expect in the way of professional behavior depends in large upon our own perception of the role being fulfilled. A leader of a group, for example, might highly value courage and loyalty as professional attributes, while a customer might place courtesy and honesty higher on the scale. Thus, definition of the role is a logical beginning point for a code of professional ethics.

The first phrase ends with the words "serve mankind" and thus establishes the service ideal for law enforcement officers as a "fundamental duty." The balance of this first section of the code establishes the peace-keeping aspects of the role, using such words as "safeguard," "protect," and "peaceful." There is no direct reference to law enforcement as crime fighting, only the implication that there must be laws designed to "protect the innocent against deception" and so on, and that these must accordingly be enforced to achieve that protection.

Reading the code carefully one will find that nowhere does it impose a duty to risk life and limb in pursuit of a suspect at dangerously high speeds through city streets or serve as target for psychopaths who take up a weapon to avenge the wrongs they perceive as having been inflicted upon them by society. These and countless other assumed obligations derive from individual interpretation of the specific obligation to "serve mankind" and exemplary behaviors such as "protect the innocent, weak and peaceful . . . against deception, violence and disorder."

Perhaps the most stringent obligation defined in this section is that the service and protection demanded must be performed while respecting "the Constitutional rights of all men."

Certainly it would be much simpler to provide the protection and service, with even greater proficiency, if the citizens being served would give up the rest of their personal liberties (some sacrifice of personal liberty is required simply to have order under a lawful government). Of course, as the founders of our government were wise enough to realize, humans are too imperfect to be able to guarantee the quality of the end, and it must therefore never be used to justify the means. This stipulation of the conditions under which the task is to be performed thus becomes extremely important not only to professional standards but to maintenance of the quality of life we treasure as citizens.

> *I will keep my private life unsullied as an example to all; maintain courageous calm in the face of danger, scorn, or ridicule; develop self-restraint; and be constantly mindful of the welfare of others. Honest in thought and deed in both my personal and official life, I will be exemplary in obeying the laws of the land and the regulations of my department. Whatever I see or hear of a confidential nature or that is confided to me in my official capacity will be kept ever secret unless revelation is necessary in the performance of my duty.*

The unfortunate obligation to forego the right to privacy is one which must be accepted by those who aspire to govern others. Government must serve as an example, not merely provide rules, for the governed to live by. Thus the code must demand both an unsullied personal life and the most scrupulous honesty and obedience to law.

Courage and calm demeanor are concepts more easily dealt with around the campfire than in the field, yet it is only there that they are of real value. So, in order to have an ethic of practical as well as moral value, courage has to be placed in the performance context of danger, and calm in that of scorn and ridicule. Certainly this portion of the code is tested practically every day by officers who must deal with persons openly contemptuous of the institutions they represent. Self-restraint, far beyond that required of the normal citizen who can afford the luxury of self-indulgence occasionally, is required under these conditions.

The need to respect the confidentiality of information gained through one's job as a police officer is sometimes difficult to reconcile with the fact that others may be privy to the same information. It may even be covered in the public news media. However, because knowledge that a police officer has may be damaging to another person, he shouldn't repeat it unless required to do so in the performance of his job. Even media coverage of an event of which he has knowledge doesn't grant him license to tell everything he knows about it, from either a moral or practical point of view. For one thing, he may disclose additional knowledge beyond that already revealed which could wrong the person involved, weaken or destroy the state's case, or both. Another, more moralistic consideration is that most people tend to have some reservations about the absolute validity of what they read in public print. What is heard from "a police officer involved in the case," however, is largely taken by the public as gospel (especially if it is damaging to another person). This is true whether or not the information is accurate or even firsthand. This places a responsibility on every police officer and is properly included in the Code of Ethics of an organization with professional aspirations. Aside from the obvious moral standpoint there is the practical consideration that while most people are quite willing to listen to gossip, they also lose respect for those who purvey it.

I will never act officiously or permit personal feelings, prejudices, animosities or friendships to influence my decisions. With no compromise for crime and with relentless prosecution of criminals, I will enforce the law courteously and appropriately without fear or favor, malice or ill will, never employing unnecessary force or violence and never accepting gratuities.

This is the first section of the Code to solidly address the law enforcement aspects of the police role in terms of crime fighting. Appropriately, it does so in the context of even performance, advocating self-restraint from indulgence of personal bias in favor of or against individuals. It begins with a denunciation of officious behavior which technically is "volunteering services where neither asked for nor needed; meddlesome." Police presence is often interjected where not asked for, of course, if it is needed. However, use of the inherent authority of the police position to force one's presence or views into a nonpolice situation is a corruption of that authority. This perversion of power will rightfully not be tolerated by any citizen with enough courage to stand up to the offender.

The balance of the first phrase of this section deals directly with the problem of letting personal feelings enter into the decision-making process. One form of this is the "contempt of cop" arrest where a person who has committed a technical violation of law would have gotten off with a warning had he not failed to maintain a sufficiently low profile. Instead, he smarted off to an officer who, unfortunately for the person with the problem mouth, lacked sufficient professionalism to make his decision evenly, regardless of his personal feelings. Such action is a human failing and one which is legal, but unfortunately it's neither morally nor practically defensible. The practical risk is that since the real reason for the arrest is clearly understood by all who are either involved in or witness the incident, both community cooperation and respect for the force suffer with each incident. The moral injustice is that by assuming the punitive role (which is what the officer does no matter how he might try to defend his action on the basis that his arrest was technically valid) he has both lowered himself and inflicted considerable suffering (including an arrest record which can never be entirely gotten rid of) on someone for an act on which even the arresting officer would agree doesn't warrant it.

Another form of failure to live up to this provision of the Code is giving preferential treatment to friends. Admittedly this is a difficult problem to cope with and one that many policemen give as a reason for having few or no nonpolice friends. Anticipated favors by civilian friends are by no means the extent of this problem, however. Nowhere in the Code does it say that it's okay to let your decision be influenced by your friendship with a brother officer. Yet such influenced decisions are rendered daily in countless agencies throughout the country. Many agencies even have written policy that extends this "brotherhood of the badge" protection to officers, including those of another agency. Typically this makes them immune to citation for traffic violation under all but specified circumstances which usually include drunk driving or any misdemeanor or felony violation. Some feel this policy is justified and no more than the equivalent of the professional discount extended to members of their professions by doctors and lawyers, for example. As awkward as it may be to take a moralistic stand against a practice so widespread, there is a rather compelling logical argument against it: namely, the professional discount offered by doctors and lawyers is a willing donation of their personal services while the "discount" extended by police officers under the "brotherhood of the badge" concept is not really theirs to give; it's a gift of a part of the public trust deposited with them. This is particularly hard to justify in light of the "exemplary behavior" provisions of the second section of the Code and the "public trust" provision of the section which follows this one. While it would be unrealistic to believe that this double standard will disappear in the near or even forseeable future, it is equally naive to believe that it and the Law Enforcement Code of Ethics can coexist in a profession free of hypocrisy. While established policy to the contrary would probably be largely ignored initially, lack of such policy certainly isn't going to eliminate a practice which stands as a stumbling block to professionalism.

The phrase "no compromise for crime" does not imply that every law will be enforced to the letter; the behavior imposed on those subscribing to the Code is much more difficult to achieve than that. What it means is that an individual officer will act intelligently and make every effort possible in enforcing the spirit of the law. Included in this phrase is the requirement to enforce the law courteously. Occasional lack of courtesy may be understandable in a young officer who lacks the experience required to handle a situation with tact and wisdom and compensates for this by assuming a brusque manner. As he gains experience, however, he should come to realize that few of the people he deals with each day are criminals, and they thus have every right to resent being treated as if the officer believes they're guilty of some serious offense. As a matter of fact, although to some the term *criminal* mistakenly implies a sort of subhuman being unworthy of consideration, nothing except ego-release is gained by the officer who treats those whom he knows to be guilty of a crime with less than human dignity. Again, this is admittedly difficult for an officer in cases where he knows with certainty that the arrestee has committed a foul and reprehensible offense, but such instances are not nearly as common as the examples of errant behavior by arresting officers would lead an observer to believe. In instances where a person arrested for a minor misdemeanor is treated as though he were a mass murderer, it is almost always simply a case of the officer venting his frustrated virility and far from professional behavior.

The admonition on use of force does not preclude using necessary force. When force is required, as much as is needed should be delivered as quickly and effectively as possible. Routine use of force, however, is not acceptable. Not only is this a professional and moral requirement, but it can be an extremely practical one in terms of keeping a case in court long enough to get a conviction if one is deserved. Any suggestion of use of force would very probably negate the admissibility of a confession, for example.

The wording of the provision on gratuities is interesting in light of our previous discussion on the point. Note that it doesn't say, *"sometimes* accepting gratuities" or "accepting gratuities *if they are honestly and sincerely offered,"* or any such thing. It says, *"never* accepting gratuities." As we said before, this is not only the simplest but also the most effective way to avoid a potential situation which can lead through a series of small, easily taken steps to the acceptance of bribes, a criminal offense.

> *I recognize the badge of my office as a symbol of public faith, and I accept it as a public trust to be held so long as I am true to the ethics of the police service. I will constantly strive to achieve these objectives and ideals, dedicating myself before God to my chosen profession . . . law enforcement.*

This section of the Code establishes the officer's acceptance of his role as a public trust which he must honor. His promise is not an unrealistic pledge of perfect performance, but rather is the best that can be asked of humans: constant effort to achieve the goals and ideals of, and dedication to, his profession.

SUMMARY

By most definitions a *profession* is an occupation which requires the person performing it to: exercise *discretion* in method of performance; possess *specialized knowledge* necessary to perform the task; go through a period of *training* and/or *apprenticeship;* meet *high standards* of admission; be altruistically *dedicated to the service ideal;* take *pride* in his calling; and *participate for livelihood* in an activity often engaged in by amateurs. In addition it must have *public recognition* as a professional calling and a *code of ethics.*

It is felt that in general the job of the police officer meets the requirements for professional standing although his training may not. The ultimate criterion is believed to be performance rather than any combination of individual standards no matter how representative they may be of the likelihood of professional ability.

Role conflicts are generated for police officers by the differing requirements for the *peace keeping, law enforcement* and *community service* functions of their job. The ability of the officer to manage these conflicts affects his success in achieving professional performance in his job.

The officer's personality also determines his behavior. Most policemen have well-adjusted, assertive, aggressive personalities. They are action-oriented with high energy levels, more suspicious than average, and ambivalent toward authority.

Special problems of being a policeman include the need to *complete one's identity formation* under circumstances of great responsibility; the *role conflict* generated by the nature of the job; possible *boredom with patrol* which can lead to overrating offenses; *lack of interest in paperwork* which can lead to underrating offenses; the need to fit a basically *individualistic personality* into a situation demanding sublimation of self; possible need to resist *protection of established order* demanded by either the community, management or one's own biases; the need to resist the temptations of *gratuities, special privileges,* and the *sexual attraction* often felt by young women for policemen; and the *internal resistance* to change inherent within the system itself.

The Law Enforcement Code of Ethics *defines the role* of the officer, sets standards for his *personal* and *professional* lives, and demands *commitment and continuing effort* toward achievement of the goals of the profession.

REVIEW QUESTIONS

Answers to these questions appear on page 385.

1. Label each of the following aspects of the policeman's job as either predominantly *positive* or *negative* with regard to achieving professional status.
   _____ a. Discretion
   _____ b. Specialized knowledge
   _____ c. Training
   _____ d. High standards for status recognition
   _____ e. Altruistic dedication to the service ideal
   _____ f. Code of Ethics
2. Most of the conflict caused by the officer's three roles comes from the fact that he would really prefer to spend more time performing (which role?) _____ duties.

REVIEW QUESTIONS 269

3. With reference to the preceding question, which two roles does the policeman spend most of his time fulfilling? _____

4. *True or false?* The average police recruit brings with him a considerable degree of intelligence and tendency to introspection.

5. The average police recruit's tendencies to seek stimulation in his environment and be more suspicious than average can serve him in good stead in performing what part of his function during his initial assignment? _____

6. The tendencies he often has toward assertive, aggressive behavior and impulsiveness can serve the officer well if they develop into what desirable characteristic? _____

7. During periods of low activity on some patrol shifts the need for action in the officer can lead to what form of unprofessional behavior? _____

8. His natural aversion to detail work can lead to another form of unprofessional behavior by the patrol officer. What is it? _____

9. Of the three forms of temptations described as dangerous for the police officer, which is:
   a. most likely to lead ultimately to serious conflict of interest and possibly dismissal and criminal charges? _____
   b. most likely to irritate citizens? _____

10. Which of the following practices are in *conflict* with the Law Enforcement Code of Ethics?
    a. crime-fighting aspects of law enforcement
    b. discussion of confidential aspects of a case once it has been decided by the jury
    c. revealing confidential information at the request of the district attorney or judge
    d. not issuing a traffic citation to an off-duty police officer for illegally parking his car.
    e. use of force to subdue a violent suspect

PART 5

Trends in Law Enforcement and Criminal Justice

CHAPTER 11

SELECTION, EDUCATION, AND TRAINING

OVERVIEW

Just about everyone recognizes that the constantly growing need for more effective law enforcement and improved criminal justice isn't going to be met by a simple application of federal funds. It's going to take organizational, philosophical, and technological change in every element of the criminal justice system, and that takes time even more than it takes money. Time is required for the best minds available to figure out what changes are needed; more time to try the changes out to see if they work; and, finally, still more time to get them implemented on a system-wide basis.

In the interim it's easy to become frustrated with apparent lack of progress while the increased need is all too apparent. Instances of failure of the present system can be seen several times each day if we but read the paper or listen to the news. Countless other instances go unnoticed each day simply because there's a limit to what can be uncovered and reported. So it's important that, rather than becoming disillusioned and cynical, we actively seek out signs of progress and take encouragement from them. Fortunately they do exist.

Most of the progress seems to exist in the law enforcement segment of the criminal justice system, which is only natural because that segment is more visible than any other. It's also the first step in the process in almost all cases, so change there can be more immediately effective on the entire system, which has led to more efforts being made there.

We've already examined one such sign: the desire of police to upgrade their calling to professional status. In this chapter we'll examine another: the increasing emphasis on improved selection, education, and training of law enforcement personnel. In Chapters 12 and 13 we'll discuss the increasingly important role of women and minority groups in law enforcement, some of the more important organizational and philosophical developments in police agencies, and recent technological developments in the police field.

THE SELECTION PROCESS

Selection of more qualified recruits for police agencies offers one of the best hopes for the continued upgrading of the service, but simultaneously presents a perplexing management problem. With between 80 and 90 percent of the average police budget going for personnel it's obvious that higher quality performance by an agency's officers is the single best opportunity for improvement in cost-effectiveness of its operation. At the same time most agencies are about 10 percent understaffed so there's also an obvious need to actively recruit more personnel. The dilemma then becomes that of needing both more and better qualified personnel. This classically difficult problem is being attacked through several positive programs. Traditionally, police agencies have used a weeding-out approach in which numerous "likely" candidates were selected and then simply let go if their performance in the field or training wasn't up to expectations. This approach may never be entirely abandoned because a continuing monitoring of performance helps to ensure that standards of professional service are met. However, casual use of this approach breeds inefficiency because it costs money to hire and train personnel. Having a very high percentage fail not only wastes the time of both recruits and agencies but dilutes the police effort during the time ineffective officers are on the streets. It also reduces morale, increases discipline and turnover problems, and destroys public confidence in the police.

The problem is one of avoiding the introduction of marginally qualified applicants into the system. Lack of definition of what "likely" means, in terms of probability of success, is the root of the problem. In the past this determination has been made almost entirely subjectively by a senior officer or administrator who simply relied on his experience and intuition. Screening consisted at most of an interview and a cursory background check. The danger of such an approach is inversely proportionate to the skill of the person making the evaluation; the alternative is some more formalized system placing emphasis on higher educational standards, more effective preemployment testing, and more thorough background investigations.

Educational Standards

Raising educational standards is a traditional approach taken by management when the quality of its applicants appears to be unsatisfactory. Unfortunately this approach can be applied too casually, especially by administrators without college experience. Simple reliance on the physical evidence of college—the diploma—will not necessarily provide candidates who meet the requirements of any employer, least of all police. Fortunately, most police administrators realize this and look upon the degree mainly as a possible indication of motivation, intelligence, and self-discipline.

The case for higher educational standards in police selection doesn't rest entirely upon these points, however. Statistically, some 60 percent of high school graduates go on to college, and the percentage is constantly increasing. The general citizenry is better-educated than ever before, so it is reasonable that police should be, too. The traditional high school requirement (still predominant, but decreasingly so) for entry into police service places the policeman at a lower educational level than most of those he serves. This is undesirable from both professional and practical points of view. For example, the issue of wages can't help but be affected adversely by a negative disparity in education between police and the general community. So there is practical as well as theoretical support for increasing educational requirements and programs for police. At present the trend is more formative than widespread, but it very likely will continue to develop, especially since agencies in various parts of the country are reporting a positive correlation between higher educational standards and officer performance.

Preemployment Screening

Another trend contributing to improvement of the selection process is increased use of testing. In general, testing is used to make objective determinations of subjective qualities. The process, in its simplest description, is to first determine which qualities are most important in a police officer and then develop or select tests which measure these qualities. The only problem with this simple concept is establishing reliability. Development of a profile on the ideal police officer is no simple task in itself. Exhaustive analysis is needed on both desired behavior (under an enormously varying set of performance conditions) and personal characteristics likely to produce that behavior. To specify the behavior, someone has to sit down and describe in complete detail exactly how a "good cop" should perform under all possible conditions. This takes more precise specification than "A good officer must show self-restraint in the face of adversity." It means saying, for example, that, "The officer must not react with physical force (or verbal abuse) when subjected to verbal abuse by antagonists." This type of specificity is required for the entire range of possibilities of police performance. Once this has been done and the specified behaviors are acceptable to a majority of those concerned with what police behavior should be, there remains only to find a valid test instrument.

Again, the ultimate test is actual performance in the field; but we're talking here about some way to predict what that performance will be. This means we're dealing primarily with paper-and-pencil tests which must be designed to provide us a profile on the applicant to compare with the one set up for the ideal officer. The process of validation, or establishment of reliability, of the test instrument means putting people through the testing procedure and estimating the likelihood of their success. Their performance in the field is then evaluated and compared with that predicted by the test. If there is a high degree of correlation the test is considered valid and predictive; if not, a new test or revisions of the existing one are required.

The Chicago police department has done experimental work with a control group of some 500 officers who were tested and then rated by supervisors over a period of time on the basis of technical performance and other criteria, such as citizen complaints. Not enough cities have conducted such validation procedures yet to say that predictive tests are totally effective; but in Chicago it was felt that enough correlation existed for their own departmental purposes. If a universally validated testing procedure can be found to successfully and consistently predict officer performance, a major step will have been taken toward improving the selection process. The complexity of the conditions under which police officers must perform and the infinitely variable nature of the human psyche are such that the best tests will probably always be only indicators, rather than assurances. They will ultimately be considerably more reliable than intuition alone, however.

Another form of testing, which combines some of the best elements of the paper-and-pencil test and the subjective evaluation by an experienced policeman, is the psychiatric or psychological evaluation. Many agencies have been using a staff psychologist or an outside professional person to interview candidates who have passed written and oral examinations. The approach is basically similar to the paper-and-pencil test in that the interviewer compares the profile of the candidate with one he has established as a standard. The difference is that instead of validating a fixed set of questions to be used as indicators of traits, the psychologist or psychiatrist relies on his professional expertise to make a largely subjective evaluation of the candidate. The interviews are usually unstructured, with interviewer and applicant discussing a wide variety of topics for an hour or so. Results, of course, are kept in strict confidence, normal in patient-doctor relationships, and reports furnished the agency bear only on the estimated suitability of the candidate for the position sought.

The main advantage of this approach is the flexibility it provides through the ability of the questioner to adapt himself to situations which develop in the process of the interview. A questionnaire, of course, can't do this, and to the extent that it has not been thoroughly conceived or sufficiently validated, it will be inferior to the human questioner. On the other hand, the lack of a formal validation procedure in the interview format forces reliance on the ability of the interviewer to ask the right questions and correctly interpret the answers. In the final analysis the validation process takes place in the same way for either method of testing: by correlating predicted results with actual results. The choice of which method is thus less important than the choice of which tests to use or which people to do the interviewing. The most important thing is that some effort be made to introduce into the system only those officers who appear to have the highest potential for success, rather than using the academies and the streets as winnowing devices for candidates selected primarily on the basis of their willingness or desire to serve.

The trend to testing and psychological screening should lead to great improvement in the selection process. However, the need for validation must be emphasized and, fortunately, this need is recognized by police administrators. If unvalidated "off-the-shelf" tests were used the result could be an artificial narrowing of the manpower pool and an unfair exclusion from service of individuals possibly quite well suited to it. The way it is developing at present gives positive indications that testing is going to be an increasingly realistic measuring device for police service, matching or even exceeding in most cases that used in business and industry.

Background Investigation

This procedure has traditionally been used to screen out those unfit for police service. That there is a developing new trend in such investigations is evidenced by the statement of purpose in California's Commission on Peace Officer Standards and Training (POST) administrative manual. The manual expresses both the traditional and newer philosophies of such investigations: "The purpose of the personal history investigation is to find examples of any character traits in the applicant's life which might *prevent* his becoming a successful police officer. The investigation will also examine the applicant's past work performance and his impact on other people to determine whether or not he has those *affirmative* characteristics which are desirable in a peace officer."

Among the negative sources checked are:

1. State departments of motor vehicles, division of drivers' licenses (to determine the applicant's driving record)
2. State bureaus of vital statistics or county records (to verify birth and age records)
3. Police files in all jurisdictions where the applicant has lived or worked (to determine if any record exists)
4. Criminal records of the state bureau of investigation and identification (to determine if any record exists)
5. Federal Bureau of Investigation records (to determine if any record exists)

Sources of either positive or negative information checked include:

1. High school and all higher educational institutions attended by the applicant (to determine the educational achievements, character and career potential of the applicant)
2. Previous employers (to determine the quality of the applicant's work record)
3. References supplied by the applicant and others, if any (to determine the applicant's character and career potential)
4. Neighbors in present and prior neighborhoods where the applicant has resided (to determine his reputation as a good neighbor and citizen)
5. Credit records (to determine his credit standing with banks, department stores, and other commercial establishments that would tend to give a clear record of the applicant's reliability)
6. Military records (to determine the quality of the applicant's service)

Polygraph examinations are used in many departments to screen applicants for police service.

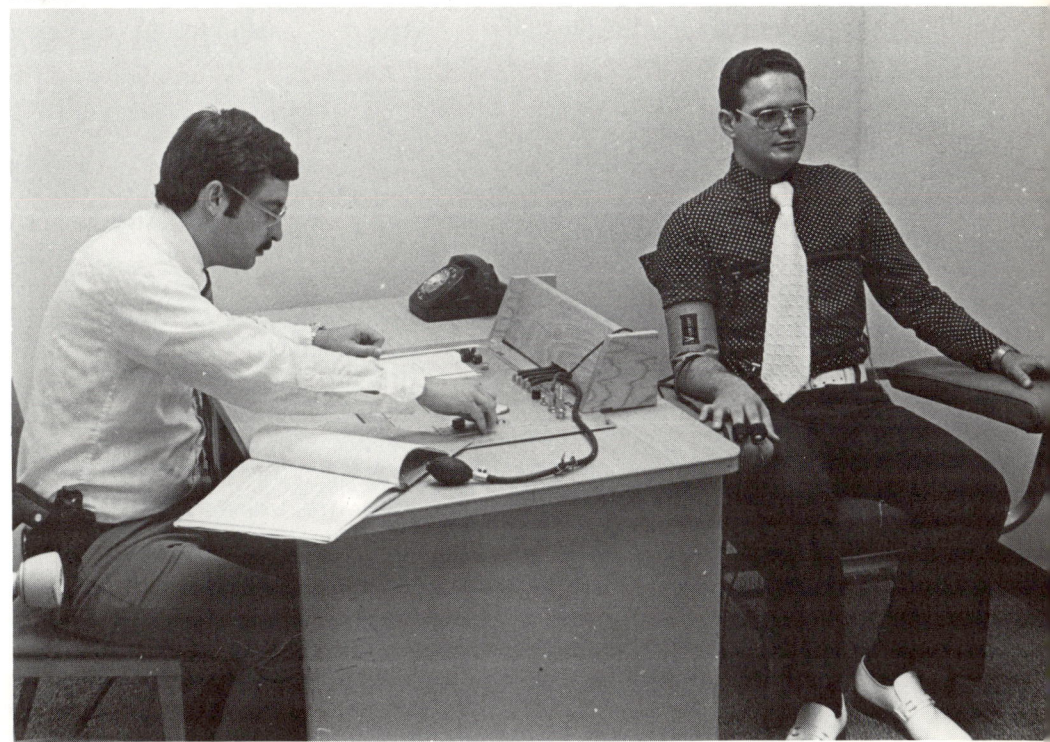

The results of these investigations are formalized in writing and given to the personnel administrator for evaluation to determine the career potential of the applicant. They're also used in most cases as a source of questions during the psychiatric or psychological screening, and polygraph examinations in agencies which employ this method of screening. Polygraphs have long been used as "lie detectors" on witnesses or suspects in criminal actions and are being used increasingly in preemployment screening of police applicants. Like the psychiatric screening, the use of the polygraph or any other sensing device which detects changes in bodily functions such as heart rate or blood pressure is successful in direct proportion to the professional capacity of the machine's operator. The peaks can be detected with great accuracy and dependability but interpretation, in context with the questions asked and other factors, requires considerable skill. Many agencies use the polygraph following the results of the background investigations and ask questions on statements made in the application or background investigation and such areas as general loyalty and honesty, use of narcotics, and so on. The test itself is used mainly as a basis for directing in-depth questions in a subsequent interview to determine (subjectively) the real reason for any physiological changes noted.

RECRUITMENT

The need to broaden the pool of applicants and at the same time raise standards has led to increased recruitment activity and innovative techniques in many agencies. The value of recruitment has long been recognized, but the emphasis on innovation is more recent and due largely to the demands for higher quality applicants. Recruitment efforts have been aided by removal of artificial barriers and a substitution of more realistic standards for selection. For years police employment standards have been arbitrarily set at superficial ideals or norms. For example, 20/20 eyesight was "the best" and since police obviously needed good eyesight, the standard was simply set at the top. Why policemen couldn't wear eyeglasses probably was more closely tied to someone's preconceived image of masculinity than the sometimes-offered explanation that injury might result during hand-to-hand combat. Hearing is another example. Since policemen must be able to hear, the acceptable level stayed for years as "no hearing loss." And so on it went

How Strong Should Arm of the Law Be?

Can a near-sighted, 4-foot-9 police officer apprehend a burly fugitive?

Is a bone-crushing handgrip a prerequisite to success on the force?

Should a woman officer be able to scale a 6-foot wall or lift a 125-pound sack waist high?

These are but some of the questions that have emerged during an 18-month court battle here over what standards should be applied to prospective members of the San Francisco police department. . . .

Past written and physical tests were found to be discriminatory by the judge and the commission was ordered to devise new ones.

A new written test was administered Oct. 5 to 981 Anglo applicants, 328 blacks, 203 Spanish-Americans, 65 Filipinos, 14 American Indians and 49 other nonwhites.

A new physical test was also prepared, apparently somewhat less rigorous than previous tests.

For example:

—Instead of carrying a 150-lb. sack of sand up three flights of stairs, applicants would have to hoist a 125-lb. sack to the top of a waist-high table.

—Instead of running 220 yards in 32 seconds, they would have to run a mile in 25-yard increments in an as yet undetermined time.

—Instead of vaulting a 4-foot wall, they would have to pull themselves over a 6-foot wall.

—Instead of lifting 50-pound dumbbells five times with each arm, applicants would use special pulling and gripping devices to measure the strength of arms, shoulders and hands.

. . . [O]fficials express concern with the court-imposed changes in police standards, noting for example that although 30% of the applicants formerly had passed written exams, as many as 80% may have passed the latest one; that the new physical test is clearly less demanding than previous tests; and that changes in some physical requirements—applicants now may pass with 20/100 vision where in the past 20/30 was required—may produce less qualified officers.

Height requirements, once 5 feet 7 inches, have been abolished under new standards. Among the recent group of applicants are two who stand but 4 foot 9. The average height of the 415 women applicants was 5 foot 3. [Philip Hager, *Los Angeles Times* (Oct. 30, 1974). Copyright, 1974, Los Angeles Times. Reprinted by permission.]

with height, weight, and all standards including age set more according to traditional levels of excellence than demands of the job. The same approach described for profile development is useful in setting realistic standards in all areas. Rather than arbitrarily lowering all standards on the same superficial basis used to set them in the first place, extensive examinations are now being made to determine what the standards really need to be and then to be setting accordingly.

When such an approach is taken it naturally results that *compensating factors* are discovered which will effectively achieve the goal originally desired. For example, a height-weight requirement may have been arbitrarily set originally in an effort to assure that those who were accepted would be able to "take care of themselves." However, strength could be made a compensating factor which would allow an individual who is a bit shy in height or weight to be employed. In the course of establishing such compensating factors it sometimes develops that the wrong selection factors were used in the first place; in other cases there may be multiple reasons for selecting a standard and it will have to stand, with modification to allow application of the compensating factor. Using the height-weight relationship as a continuing example, there could be minimum and maximum limits related to health (and thus even budgetary) considerations, ability to get in and out of a police car (or see over the dashboard!), and so on. The specific instances cited here have no significance beyond pointing out that there is now a trend which will allow many people who otherwise would have been excluded from police service to enter into it. Qualities such as moral character, intelligence, and mental or physical health will of course not be compensated for and will continue as absolute standards. In agencies using compensating factors, they are not applied until an applicant has met the requirements to which no exception can be made. Continued expansion of this trend represents a professional approach to selection and should have many long-range benefits to the service and the community.

Residency requirements, where they still exist, make it mandatory that police live in the community for which they work. At least in preemployment situations such requirements are virtually indefensible and rapidly disappearing. The legality of preemployment residency requirements is in doubt under the 14th Amendment. In the case of *Carter* v. *Gallagher,* in Minnesota (1971) the state supreme court ruled against a residency requirement for veteran's preference in hiring for government jobs, citing the equal protection clause of the 14th. Doing away with the preemployment residency requirements developed as a trend as much from practical considerations as moral or legal. They simply reduced the size of the labor pool too much. Free from this restriction, even such relatively small agencies as Overland Park, Kansas, and Lakewood, Colorado, have recruited on a national scale. Usually it's the larger agencies which try nationwide recruiting programs for the obvious reasons of greater need for personnel and better ability to finance the operation. Agencies using the technique sometimes send teams around the country, testing and taking applications on the spot, and sometimes do it by mail. In the mail operation applicants whose qualifications seem acceptable are tested by a local school administrator (or some such person) who gives them the test specified and mails the answer sheets to the agency for evaluation.

The trend toward eliminating the residency requirement is not nearly as evident once a person has accepted employment; in fact a countertrend is indicated because of the growing movement to increase involvement between police and the community. By living in the city he serves, a policeman has more likelihood of becoming involved in citizen activities such as school associations, scouting, service clubs, and so on. Some genuine problems exist in cases where a city may not offer housing equivalent to that which an applicant already owns in another community or can afford to buy; such situations can impose an unfair economic hardship or force a person to live in housing unacceptable to him. For these reasons, as well as the uncertain legality, even postemployment residency requirements are not universally enforced without consideration to individual cases.

College recruiting is a natural result of the trend to higher educational standards. Some agencies rely solely on personal contact with local colleges for their recruiting effort. Classes taught by a member of the police department are a recruiting medium as well as a community relations aid. Job opportunities are sometimes listed with the employment offices of schools in the same manner as opportunities in the private sector. Only a few of the largest agencies, such as the FBI, actively recruit on campuses through personal interviews. Student worker programs are gaining acceptance in many colleges. Normally students must be between age 17 and 25 and carry a minimum of twelve college units in a field related to the work of the agency. They work part time during the school year and usually work full time during vacation. Agencies using such programs report a very high percentage of participants ultimately joining the force on a career basis. Because of this, entry requirements for the programs are usually very similar to those for joining the department through normal channels. Exceptions are made for factors which are normally expected to change during the period of participation, such as size and educational achievement. These programs come as close to a traditional apprenticeship program as is practical for police work.

Because these programs offer practical experience and an outstanding opportunity for the agency and the applicant to get to know each other, they are generally well-received by both parties. The work performed is as close to the ultimate career role as possible, although the student must be unarmed and not placed in physical danger. Assignments in radio communications, report taking, subpoena service and similar areas which require more-than-average knowledge but less-than average risk, are commonly used.

An interesting sidelight to college recruitment is that the relatively small percentage of agencies that have adopted the requirement of a four-year degree for entrance seem to experience less difficulty in recruiting college people. The reason may be that college people tend to shy away from jobs which don't nominally require a degree. This could be partly because they have put out four years of relatively hard effort and feel their job should be a reward for that effort, and partly because of the lack of wide recognition of police work as a profession. In either event the trend to seeking and actively recruiting college graduates will probably be both accelerated and made easier by the raising of educational requirements for entry. It will probably be accelerated still further as the possibility of lateral entry into service (rather than the normal bottom-rung entry) increases. Pay is not as big a problem as it once was in attracting the college graduate to a career in law enforcement. The salary gap between industry and government service is not nearly as wide as it used to be and in some cases has even swung the other way.

Involvement of the entire department in recruitment is producing results for many agencies in two ways. First, and of primary importance, is the fact that higher quality recruits are being obtained. A second benefit is that with more recruiters active than there would be if only a specified person or team were assigned, the task and the number of recruits is higher.

The program usually provides some incentive, such as a cash reward or extra time off with pay, for furnishing a successful candidate. Departments in such diverse geographical areas as Baltimore, Dallas, and Kansas City have tried these incentive programs with good results. While there aren't enough such programs to qualify as a definite trend, the rationale offered for their success suggests that a trend may develop. Specifically, success seems to stem from a strong, vested interest felt by recruiters (if their orientation is toward professionalism), resulting in enthusiastic and more selective recruiting. There is also a correlation between successful programs and the amount and type of incentive offered (examples: $75; five days off with pay). While one would like to think that a significant incentive merely fans the flames of idealism or crystallizes the seeds of dedication for the recruiter, even if the bonus is viewed simply as a bounty, the programs do seem to be working both quantitatively and qualitatively.

EDUCATION AND TRAINING

After careful selection of recruits, education in the various disciplines related to the police role and training in the skills of the job are the logical next step. No one has yet been able to list knowledges which absolutely do or do not apply to the police function. It's generally agreed that there is need for some knowledge of the physical and social sciences, behavioral sciences, mathematics, English and other liberal arts. Not all of these, as taught in their normal disciplinary contexts, would qualify as necessary skills for police work, but some knowledge of each can be helpful to the officer. The more immediate need lies in the area of improved training since, obviously, persons exercising police authority need to know how to perform their daily tasks proficiently. Beyond this is the vast body of "nice-to-know" information—practical but incidental—which will help them perform their jobs more humanely, more wisely, even more professionally if you like, but the "need-to-know" must come first. Ultimately there may be no difference between these two types of information since a case can be made for having everything that contributes to the best possible performance of the job considered part of the need-to-know body of knowledge. But at the moment a useful distinction can be drawn between the two types of knowledge, and the main emphasis must be placed on development of officers who meet the requirements most critically needed. As we examine the state of the art in *academy* (a term used here to distinguish and identify any form of preservice training restricted to persons who have accepted employment as a peace officer), *field, inservice* and *career development* training we'll deal with both the immediate and long-range educational trends.

Academy Training

The clearest trend in preservice training is that of *state-mandated standards.* In a decade we've gone from a condition where no states had minimum standards to one where over two-thirds have some sort of official body set up to govern training police. The most frequent (but not universal) requirement is for a minimum of 400 hours basic training. Few states require that this training be completed before the recruit is considered a police officer, but most require completion within the first year to eighteen months of employment. An unfavorable comparison is sometimes drawn between police training in America and Europe on this basis. In Germany, for example,

Academy training provides the most concentrated form of police preservice training.

a recruit must have two years of training before any police authority is exercised. Some agencies in America require as much as a half year of training, but these are very few and recruit-officers supplement their academy training with field training prior to receiving permanent status. How soon, if ever, the time requirement in this country will reach European proportions is conjectural, as is the need or practicality of such extensive basic training. Certainly, however, there is a trend to longer and more thorough training in American police agencies and this is desirable.

An outgrowth of state-mandated standards is the *certification* of officers who complete the training. Not all states have followed Texas' lead in making it a misdemeanor to appoint, retain, or accept employment as a peace officer without satisfying the state's training requirements, but many others do certify officers who complete the mandated basic training. Some, such as Michigan, California, and Oregon, have the power to revoke certification which certainly supports professional status. Some states have reciprocal agreements which provide for recognition of training performed in another state. This is a desirable situation, particularly from the standpoint of lateral transfer between agencies, but one not likely to become too widespread until more uniform minimum standards exist among the various states.

Another positive effort, which is not yet widespread enough to be called a trend, is that aimed at identifying training needs for police work. Early standards of training content and time were based largely on traditional classroom efforts in the then few academies and colleges teaching people to be police officers. The result was a set of relatively loose standards prescribing only a specified number of hours of instruction in various disciplines. Today instructional technology begins with careful specification of behavioral objectives derived from analysis of the task and the conditions under which it must be performed. The objectives to be achieved by training are then stated in terms of the observable, measurable behavior to be exhibited by the learner at the end of his training. All proposed goals of training are forced through this filter and some are kept, some changed, and some discarded. Those which survive represent the body of knowledge which is needed by the police officer, stated in terms of what he must be able to do with that knowledge and the conditions under which he must perform.

Not all the knowledge required by a policeman is yet specified in this way, but progress has been made in projects such as Los Angeles' MILE program. The ultimate goal will not be reached until the behaviors are not only specified but validated in the manner described earlier for test instruments. When this goal is reached it will be possible to put together a realistic curriculum in terms of content and time and know exactly how to tell if training has been successful. In the interim, most nontechnical aspects of police work continue to be learned as general rather than specific disciplines (a policeman takes the same psychology course as a predental student, rather than a "Psychology for Police Officers" course). Much of the specific nature of each discipline is taught during procedural training. For example, covering how to "sell" a traffic ticket involves teaching some elements of psychology. If all the tasks a policeman has to perform were analyzed properly, however, the content for a specific discipline of psychology for police officers would be identified and could be taught at one time in a more efficient manner. Since this state of instructional technology hasn't yet been fully achieved in police training, and since it is generally recognized that police do need some knowledge beyond the strictly technical aspects of their job, there is a growing trend to support general college training in many "nonpolice" fields of study. This is evidenced by the fact that LEEP (Law Enforcement Education Program) participation is

Advanced instructional technology, such as these multi-media carrels, is employed in larger academies.

subsidized in close to a thousand colleges and not just in the approximately four hundred which have degree programs in directly related law enforcement areas. This trend will probably continue until such time as more precise training and educational curricula are defined for law enforcement.

One of the most promising trends in police training is that to higher quality instruction made possible in large part by the adoption of instructional techniques based on behavioral objectives. Once the precise nature of the content to be taught is known (including why it is to be taught and how it is to be demonstrated) more effective decisions can be made as to methods and media to be used in developing each specified behavior. Media such as closed circuit television, video and audio tapes, programmed texts, and computer-assisted instruction are now being used in academy training where appropriate. Methods are no longer restricted to lecturing but now feature extensive student involvement at all stages. Provisions are increasingly being made for different learning rates among individuals rather than facing the traditional choices of leaving behind the slower learner or boring the faster one. In at least one academy it is possible for a recruit-officer to challenge a particular course if he feels his existing background has sufficiently prepared him to pass the final examination without further instruction. The validity of this approach, and the degree to which it might spread, depends entirely on the comprehensiveness and validity of the test instrument. If the test is inadequate, a superficial knowledge of the subject could result in a successful challenge but substandard performance on the job.

The trend to higher quality instruction of recruits is supported by a similar movement toward increased training and certification of instructors. This trend has a considerable way to go since many instructors with little or no training in the art or science of teaching are selected simply on the basis of subject matter expertise. Since subject matter expertise changes with conditions on the street, some agencies rotate instructors through academy and operational assignments. Even this effort, however, fails to compensate for (and in fact may aggravate) instructional weakness caused by lack of teaching skill. Some agencies are trying to combat this problem by using teams consisting of subject matter experts and civilian teachers skilled in instructional techniques.

In addition to the curriculum changes developing from instructional analysis, there is a strong trend to a *criminal justice system approach* in preservice training. This philosophy stresses the interdependency of all elements of the criminal justice system and attempts to improve understanding and communication throughout the system to increase effectiveness of all parts and the system as a whole. There are now regional criminal justice training centers which train not only police recruits but correctional and other system personnel. Several such centers serve different regions of the country and offer different types of programs. In Modesto, California, for example, the regional center provides eight different counties preservice and inservice training in the judicial and corrections phases of the criminal justice system as well as police. In the state of Florida, Dade County police recruits and Department of Rehabilitation and Corrections employees are trained in the Southeast Florida Institute of Criminal Justice. In addition to the regional training centers, many individual agencies are adapting some form of this approach to all or part of their training efforts. Some just offer a course in other elements of the criminal justice system, while some go so far as to schedule cross-training programs in which they exchange members with other agencies.

A variation of the regional training center is the cooperative training center. Typically such centers are financed and maintained jointly by several agencies to provide a higher level of training than they could provide individually. Some of these centers are run through local colleges which also offer classroom law enforcement training to preservice students but limit academy training to those who have been hired as peace officers. By pooling their financial and instructional resources, cooperating agencies are usually able to offer training that exceeds the mandated minimum and matches local needs nicely. Still another approach is for smaller agencies to contract with a nearby large agency for all or part of their curriculum. Most contract for less than the full package because they feel the need of the officer's services more acutely than the large agency. Not many small agencies, for example, feel they can afford to hire a man to fill a vacancy on their fifty-man department and then wait six months for his services. So they arrange for ten weeks training at a large agency nearby which has a full-time, year-round academy. The trend to centralized training of police is perhaps clouded by the many forms it is taking, but it is clear and strong if the overall movement is studied. The result will probably be more and better training for recruits with a growth of the criminal justice system approach as opposed to the individual agency orientation.

Growth of centralized training will also support another trend which might otherwise be stunted by lack of funding or in-house capability. This is *remedial instruction* where the need is identified during academy training. In earlier times recruits who were found deficient were simply washed out; in fact it was an aim of the academy to further refine the group which survived the selection process. This not only wastes the time invested in the recruit up to the point of deficiency identification but also leads to sloppy recruiting and selecting practices. Beyond that, many people are eliminated from service who, with a little remedial effort, could become effective officers. There is no way that everyone entering academy training can be assured of success; this would make the remedial investment much too high. But with larger training staffs it can become possible to save many whose deficiency is due to personal problems, communication weakness, or simply low achievement in some of the technical skills. These technical weaknesses can't be in areas where quick, high-quality decisions must be made in critically important areas (such as the decision on whether to shoot). But, in subject areas where additional effort on the recruit's part can bring him up to an acceptable level of performance for real-life functioning (such as points of law or report writing), the ability of the academy to offer remedial help can be important.

Similarly, the basic skills of reading, writing, and oral communication may have been neglected during the recruit's early schooling. A relatively small investment in remedial work now, at a time when motivation is high in the learner, can return great dividends in the candidate who is otherwise well qualified for police service. The academy experience is also usually stringent enough for a young officer without the strain of personal problems brought on by financial affairs or family relationships. Counselling, whether by staff specialists or outside professionals on a contract basis, is now used by some academies to try to provide enough relief to allow the recruit to function to the best of his ability. All of these extra services are more likely to be possible in the large centralized academies than in smaller training facilities maintained by individual agencies.

Field Training

Field training is that learning experience which follows academy training and precedes assumption of full police responsibility by the officer. In some cases field training is structured as an extension of the academy experience, but more often it's a probationary period during which the supervisor and training officer do their best to guide the new officer in right paths. Nine out of ten officers will agree that this period is the most important in their careers. Not only does the young officer's identity form mostly during this period (emphasizing the importance of his having training officers and supervisors whose identity is secure) but it is here that the instruction of the academy takes on real meaning. Many concepts which have been accepted and understood in lectures and role-playing take on harsh reality only in their actual context. The family dispute, for example, can be discussed for hours in terms of its danger to the policeman, but only experience can provide the gut realization of that danger and the awareness necessary to survival and proper handling of such a call. The same is true of traffic stops, but here actual experience can work to the detriment of academy training since there are so many "routine" stops that there is a tendency for awareness to be relaxed rather than heightened as experience is gained. Again the importance of the experienced training officer in field training is stressed. Aside from the dangerous aspects of the job, even such common experiences as taking a burglary report are vastly different in real life than in the academy context, and field training is where the real skill is developed.

The presidential commissions which have studied crime and police during the last decade have recommended field training terms of four months, with frequent counselling sessions by training officer and supervisor, immediately following completion of the basic training. They also recommend two weeks formal training at the end of the first six-month and one-year periods of employment. Not all agencies are adopting these recommendations yet, but in some of the larger academies field training is integrated with the academy experience. Recruits will spend weekends riding as the second or third man in a patrol car observing and putting into context their classroom learning. Sometimes there will be a week or two-week hiatus in the academy experience during which recruits are assigned to full-time field duty to apply what they've learned and to prepare themselves for future learning. Assignments are carefully controlled so the new officer doesn't get in over his head or have to deal with situations too dangerous for his level of training.

In some academies the field training is structured to provide confrontations with carefully selected citizen groups. Or, the recruit may spend from a day to several weeks living and working in the community as a private citizen and/or employee of a government agency other than police. In such programs he gains first-hand experience in the frustrations of government service and seeking service from governmental agencies. Agencies using this type of awareness-developing field training experience a remarkable lack of citizen complaints against officers who have taken part in it. Perhaps the ultimate (so far, at least) program of this type is the one mentioned earlier where officers take part in such activities as a love-in, picketing a movie theater, living several days on skid row and even being booked into jail in neighboring cities where their identity is unknown to their jailors. Among the many things participants claim to have learned from such experience is that there are ways of communicating other than through the spoken or written word. For example, they find that officers often convey contempt and hostility without conscious act or deed, and they learn first-hand how this attitude-betrayal affects citizens. Their self-image as police officers is bound to be partly shaped by such an experience of true helplessness and futility in the police-citizen relationship. Such realization can never be gained from textbooks or lectures.

Far less dramatic, but more common, are informal field training experiences such as rotation through the various shifts and patrol districts during the initial months of service following basic training. Such a program aims at providing the new officer a condensed exposure to the various geographical, chronological, and demographic aspects of the agency's work. He also becomes quickly aware of the various styles of supervision used by different watch commanders and sergeants and, in general, broadens his base of experience in a short time. During this period rating and evaluation conferences with his supervisor and training officer apprise him of his progress, shortcomings and ways to overcome them, and give him an opportunity to criticize the training he has been given. This feedback aspect is important for improving the quality of training for future recruits, and any new officer who feels reluctant to appear critical of the system should remember that the officers who follow him through that system will one day have to back him up, possibly in a situation where his life is at stake.

Most academies feature in their training plan a number of "field problems" which attempt to provide an approximation of field experience. While these have value, they can sometimes be less beneficial to the participant than the spectators because of their generally failure-oriented nature. The recruit is often allowed to fumble his way through a situation, to the glee of his peers, and then is criticized orally in the hope that he and the others will learn from this woeful experience. More enlightened use can be made of such experience when the recruit is prepared to succeed (through prior instruction) rather than fail. Problems are then made progressively more complex to prepare learners for the unpredictable situations to be encountered in both the structured and random experiences of their live field training.

Inservice Training

The purpose of inservice training is to continually update the skills and improve the knowledge of the existing police force. One of the problems inservice training has to cope with is the broad range of skills required of police, any one of which can deteriorate with infrequent application. Identifying need here is more difficult than for recruit training where it may safely be assumed that virtually all skills are lacking. With inservice training the only accurate indicator of a need for training is inadequate performance in a particular facet of operation. Beyond this there is the continuing development of new techniques to meet changing needs (for example, riot control), the annual revision of laws, and, of course, continuing weapons practice.

Nearly half of the states now have made some recognition of the need for increased inservice training, but only about a fourth have established minimum requirements and only a handful have actually mandated compliance with these standards. The most common standard is forty hours per year, which matches the recommendation of the president's commission, but some agencies require more (for example, sixty-four in Dade County, Florida, and eighty in New York City).

There is a trend to decentralization of inservice training, providing it at the point of need, most often during the roll-call period as described earlier. For some time there has been general dissatisfaction with the quality and effectiveness of roll-call training. This has been due largely to the inability of instructors who were, in fact, sergeants untrained in instructional techniques. The trend currently is to overcome this inadequacy by increased use of audio-visual programs such as those furnished by state and federal agencies and associations such as the International Association of Chiefs of Police. Slide-tape programs are often favored because the oral presentation in presented professionally and the visual may be customized by substituting slides of local persons or places as appropriate. Many agencies now have videotape recorders and playback units and can prepare custom materials in-house, or use stock tapes available through larger central agencies. Cassette audio tapes are used fairly extensively for language and remedial instruction. Some agencies even issue cassettes to officers for their use on the way to and from work. A few agencies in larger metropolitan areas have home-study programs in both technical subjects and career development courses on management skills.

Another problem with roll-call training is that some subjects require a larger block of time than is available in the period just prior to or following the shift. One solution to problems of this type is the training day where an entire shift is spent on training, with the required time obtained by juggling days off.

Career Development

Whereas inservice training aims at updating existing skills in police officers, career development efforts are aimed at creating a pool of trained personnel from which promotions may be made. The skills developed are not so much technical in nature as managerial. There is a minor trend developing toward requiring training of this type prior to promotion to sergeant but, though nearly half of the states have established recommended minimum curricula, very few have mandated training. The state of New York, for example, mandates seventy hours of supervisory training but doesn't specify that it take place prior to promotion. The city of New York, however, makes the training a requirement for promotion as do a few other larger cities around the country. The length of courses varies considerably, with one and two-week courses most common. Some run as high as three weeks and New York's runs over six.

Generalization, rather than specialization, of knowledge is the rule as a person progresses up the supervisory ladder. To build their pool some agencies use a planned rotation schedule as a means of developing this broad knowledge base. Often an officer who is interested in promotion (not all are, and acceptance of this is something of a new concept in itself) will actively seek diverse assignments on his own to generalize his background. Many administrators are of the opinion that such a tendency in an officer is a favorable factor in deciding on promotions. Most agencies now provide some form of educational incentive such as pay differentials and cost subsidy. In addition, participation in an educational program is usually made easier by arrangement of shiftchange dates to accomodate semester or quarter schedules. Often local colleges provide duplicate programs in police science areas during daylight and evening hours so any officers interested in attending can do so.

College Programs. Some agencies using career development programs develop them in cooperation with local colleges which design special curricula to provide both college credit and direct vocational training for participants. Personnel from participating agencies are often used as full or part-time instructors in the program which both improves acceptance by students and broadens the experience of those providing the instruction. Other agencies have programs where officers enroll in conventional college courses, which have application to police management, and subsidize their participation to the extent of tuition and/or books and expenses. Books paid for under the program are often added to the department library upon completion of the course for use as reference texts by any who have need of them. Business and industry often make their management seminars available to law enforcement personnel, as do colleges and universities in all parts of the country.

Internships. Sometimes an agency will arrange internship programs with other agencies having similar problems and needs. Under such programs personnel (usually at command level) are temporarily exchanged and a cross-pollenization of ideas and approaches occurs. Exchanges can be arranged laterally, as between police agencies in various geographical areas, or vertically within the criminal justice system, as between a police department and a correctional institution or prosecutor's office.

Trial Assignments. To evaluate their management-candidate pool (or to build it) trial assignment to a higher level job is sometimes arranged. This approach provides on-the-job experience without the possible onus of failure since it is known in advance that the assignment is temporary. It also gives the administrator a chance to avoid the "Peter Principle" (named for its propounder, Dr. Lawrence J. Peter) which holds, roughly, that arbitrary promotion of persons who excel at one job leads to their continued promotion until they reach a level at which they no longer excel and are thus ineligible for further promotion. The ultimate result of such a phenomenon would be that all promotional positions would be held by incompetents and all persons below them in the organization would be frustrated by the lack of vacancies above them. Promoting only those who desire and can handle management positions, as opposed to technical roles, seems to be a reasonable alternative to this dilemma.

Lateral Entry. A concept held important to improvement of the service through increased professionalism, lateral entry is becoming more common in command positions than at other levels. It's not unusual today to find the positions of chief, deputy chief, and captain open for competitive examination rather than being limited to members of the department. This is due to a genuine desire to get the best persons available and recognition of the fact that in many agencies the job of building a pool of promotable candidates has been neglected too long. Conversely, those agencies which have been active in career development have often built a surplus of good candidates who take advantage of the opportunity to accelerate their career progress by changing agencies. Fortunately, the agencies which have developed the surplus pools are the better, and often larger, agencies so they can more easily survive the loss of good managerial personnel. At the same time the recipient agency gets instant upgrading of its staff, and improvement of the service as a whole is accelerated.

With all the improvements being made in selection and training of recruits and supervisors, weak middle management has remained the single large stumbling block to real progress in development of improved police forces. Lieutenants to a lesser degree, and captains to a greater, in too many weaker agencies are anachronistic holdovers from the era when promotions were made on the basis of technical skill rather than managerial ability or (worse and more often) simply on the basis of seniority. The result of this was to create a layer of insulation against innovation, fear of adjustment in policy, and resentment of young officers who were seen as a threat because of their aggressiveness and ability. The increase of training and education at entry level (with a corresponding lack of training at the command level) aggravated, rather than helped, this problem. Similarly, the frustration experienced by young officers because of extreme conservatism at higher levels caused some to leave the service before their best contribution could be made. Fortunately, many of the trends in career development offer hope for relief of this situation in the near future, and the persons now reaching command positions are younger, better educated, and more secure and interested in needed change than ever before.

SUMMARY

The selection process for obtaining police recruits is being upgraded by *raising educational standards,* increasing the use of *preemployment testing procedures,* and more thorough *background investigation.*

Tests used to screen applicants must be validated to insure that they measure the appropriate skills, knowledges, and attitudes indicative of probable success as a police officer. *Psychological screening,* another developing method, is subject to the same requirements.

Recruiting is being used more extensively and is aided by removal of artificial barriers to employment and the substitution of realistic requirements in terms of job performance. *Compensating factors* are considered where certain inabilities to meet standards are found.

Residency requirements are no longer common for preemployment but are increasing as a requisite for continued employment after selection.

College recruiting efforts are more common now as the trend to higher educational standards in the selection process develops. Different types of efforts include *student worker programs,* use of *recruiting teams,* and placement of police personnel on teaching staffs of colleges.

Department-wide participation in recruiting, featuring incentive programs for nomination of a successful candidate, is resulting in more and better-qualified applicants.

Training, as a concept, now includes nontechnical knowledge areas as well as the skills required for daily proficiency of officers. Training continues throughout the officer's career, beginning with *academy training* and progressing through *field training, inservice training* and *career development programs.*

State-mandated standards now affect police training in some two-thirds of the country. Four hundred hours is the most common recommendation for basic training and, although not all states recommending it make it mandatory, many agencies exceed this minimum by as much as 150 percent. Several states certify officers who have completed basic training, and some have power to revoke certification.

Training needs are being identified for police by advanced techniques of instructional technology including specification of the behavior to be exhibited in terms that allow its measurement for performance evaluation. Nontechnical training needs, still taught in conventional classes, can eventually be structured into special courses for police by continued application of these techniques. Higher quality of instruction in technical aspects of the job is presently being realized through use of more effective methods and media based on this type of analysis.

A *criminal justice system* approach is being used increasingly to stress the interdependency of all agencies and the value of increased cooperation and communication between them. *Criminal Justice Training Centers* are being developed across the country to train not only police but other members of the system.

Cooperative training centers are being established by joint action of several smaller agencies which can't afford to maintain a full-time training effort of their own. Other small agencies contract for training at academies maintained by large departments.

Remedial instruction in basic educational skills and technical areas is now available at some academies to avoid terminating recruits who are unable to keep up with regular training. Counselling is also provided to deal with financial and personal problems which are interfering with academy work.

Field training takes place following and/or during the academy training experience to give recruits a chance to apply what they learn in classes and have their actual performance criticized by experienced officers. A form of awareness-development training is practiced in many agencies to provide officers with experience in interpersonal relationships required in service.

Inservice training takes place continually to build new skills and polish old ones in all officers. Decentralization is commonly practiced in inservice training with roll-call sessions being the most common. Training days are sometimes used to allow all-day training in subjects which can't be properly covered in the short roll-call sessions.

Career development programs are used to develop pools of personnel from which promotions to supervisory and management positions can be filled. Planned rotation is one way of building the broad base of generalized knowledge required for managerial duty. College work, sometimes with credit toward a degree being granted for courses designed primarily to meet the vocational needs of police officers, is used as a career development method, as are seminars offered by business concerns and associations. Internship programs provide for the temporary exchange of personnel with other police agencies or between police and other agencies within the criminal justice system. Trial assignments are sometimes used to give the trainee on-the-job experience and allow the administrator to evaluate his potential prior to promotion. Lateral entry into management positions in another police agency provides a means of upgrading the service as a whole and accelerating the career development of persons ready for promotion prior to existence of a vacancy in their own department.

REVIEW QUESTIONS

Answers to these questions appear on page 386.

1. Which of the three selection processes (testing, psychological screening, background investigation):
   a. depends most on the special ability of the person using it? _____
   b. is most objective? _____
   c. evaluates real-life performance best? _____

2. What recruitment technique most closely approximates an apprenticeship program for police work? _____

3. High quality recruits are obtained in department-wide recruitment programs for what reason? _____

4. What is the most common minimum recommendation for hours of basic training? _____

5. Which type of training (academy, field, inservice, career development):
   a. is most likely to involve taking conventional classes in local colleges? _____
   b. offers the best chance for a young officer to "get his feet wet?" _____
   c. is most likely to review prior training? _____
   d. is widely used to develop basic police skills? _____

6. Of the two types of training centers (cooperative, criminal justice):
   a. which is more likely to be used by large, as well as small, agencies? _____
   b. which is more likely to train only police officers? _____

7. What is the basic difference between an *internship* and a *trial assignment*? _____

CHAPTER 12

MINORITIES AND WOMEN IN LAW ENFORCEMENT

OVERVIEW

If the simultaneous need for more and better police recruits from among the pool available poses a dilemma to the police administrator, an even tougher one must be posed by the problems of sexual and racial balance. It is now against the law for a police department to discriminate in hiring practices on the basis of sex or race. Yet only 2 percent of the nation's force is female and only 4 percent either black, Latin, or Asian. No simple formula exists for the police administrator who wants to change this situation and, in fact, not all agree that it needs changing. But none would deny that there is a movement under way toward increasing both the numerical representation and role of underrepresented groups. In this chapter we'll look at the reasons for the trend, the benefits it is hoped will result, the problems involved in effecting the changes, and some of the results being obtained by those agencies trying to effect them.

THE ROLE OF THE MINORITY OFFICER

The need for more and better law enforcement personnel plus the need for greater police-community rapport would seem to

Even though racial or ethnic minorities make up 14 percent of our population, only 4 percent of the nation's police force are from minority groups.

make the need for more minority police obvious in communities with significant minority populations. But, with some 14 percent of the nation's population belonging to a racial or ethnic minority and only 4 percent of the nation's police being drawn from this same group, it is obvious that parity hasn't yet been achieved. There is a considerable effort being made to achieve proportionate racial composition within police departments serving communities with significant minority membership in the general citizenry. The principal hoped-for benefit to the departments in such cases is increased respect and identification from the community. If the minority officer also lives in the community, his insights into community attitudes and feelings can be very important.

The desirability of having minority members in the police force is based on both moral and practical points. Morally, there is the principle that the police are the people, as pointed out by the National Advisory Commission on Criminal Justice Standards and Goals. Practically, as the President's Commission on Law Enforcement and Administration of Justice reminded, "to police a minority community with only white police officers can be misinterpreted as an attempt to maintain an unpopular status quo rather than to maintain the civil peace. Clearly the image of an army of occupation is one that the police must avoid." The Commission went on to point out that minority officers, by their presence in the force, can reduce prejudicial stereotyped images held by their fellow (but majority) officers and, through their familiarity with the culture of the minority community, are better able to police it. In cases where a foreign language is involved the benefits of bilinguality on the part of the minority officer are obvious. In any event there is likely to be less resentment overall on the part of the minority community than if the entire police force were made up of majority personnel.

Legal Considerations

Although the ideal of minority representation on the police force in direct proportion to the number of the minority in the community is simple, it is often more easily endorsed than achieved. Most agencies are now under an *affirmative action program* (those with over twenty-five employees or receiving over $25,000 in LEAA grants are required to have such a program) which hopes to ensure equal opportunity by demanding physical evidence of such opportunity. The evidence consists mainly of a formal policy of abstaining from allowing race to be a consideration in the selection process for personnel. There is sometimes a requirement that sincere effort to enforce the policy be demonstrated, and in cases where flagrant violation of the concept is suspected an audit may be required. In such cases past applications may have to be opened to inspection and justification given for instances where minority members have not been hired.

In some cases minority underrepresentation is due to failure of minority applicants to meet the standards of selection. Traditionally minorities are disadvantaged both culturally and educationally and, with the increasing emphasis on raised standards of entrance, the failure rate of educationally-disadvantaged persons is bound to increase. An administrator can argue with sincerity that to admit employees with substandard qualifications weakens the force. This dilutes the ability of the agency to provide the service which the community is entitled to receive. This does not allow cultural bias to be used as a selection factor, however, and courts have demonstrated amply that they won't tolerate such a course. In many cases the courts have gone as far as designing programs for cities to force preferential hiring of minority members in an attempt to rectify situations brought on by past employment practices.

The 1971 case of *Carter* v. *Gallagher,* involving the Minneapolis fire department, was one such instance. After finding that some of the selection criteria were not demonstrably job-related, but rather were discriminatory, the court ordered the city to hire one minority person for every three whites until a total of twenty minority-group persons were hired. In the court's opinion this would bring the racial balance of the department to approximate parity with that of the general community. In the same year, as the result of the case of *Allen* v. *Mobile,* the city of Mobile, Alabama, was ordered to consult with leaders of the black community to develop a recruiting program aimed at increasing employment of black officers. Interestingly, the case itself didn't even involve selection practices but dealt with discrimination in assignment and promotion policies.

Because of the court's demonstrated willingness to formulate policy, and also because of the desirability of the possible results of increased minority representation on the force, most police administrators in cities with minority populations actively recruit from among those populations. With few exceptions, however, standards for selection remain the same for both majority and minority personnel. The hoped-for result of these two policies is the avoidance of court-ordered policies of preferential hiring practices coupled with an artificial lowering of standards that would be harmful to both agencies and communities.

PROGRAMS FOR INCREASING MINORITY REPRESENTATION

Given the set of problems it is easy to see that successful solution will require innovation of approach and dedication of application. In the larger cities it is often possible to recruit larger numbers of minority applicants than are actively needed in order to allow for the experienced higher-than-average attrition rate because of educational disadvantage. This approach comes with a built-in problem of its own, however, since processing large numbers of applications means long delays in many cases. When such delays become extended and no communication is maintained with the applicant pool, an attitude sometimes develops that the recruitment was merely tokenism and further recruitment from the minority pool in that community is hampered. Cities with such problems are gradually overcoming them by increased attention to applicants on waiting lists; such effort, however, is not natural for government service personnel functions and can slip a little from time to time.

The ideal program, which isn't being used yet to our knowledge, would be one where highly-qualified persons among the minority community were identified and actively recruited for police service the same way outstanding engineering graduates are recruited by industry. Short of this ideal, some positive programs are underway to make more effective use of the pool that is attracted by both new and conventional methods.

One of the more promising programs to come out of the increased effort to hire minority personnel is the reevaluation of entrance requirements. While it is recognized that standards can't be lowered arbitrarily, the need for analysis of each requirement in terms of its relation to actual job requirements (as described in the preceding chapter) has been emphasized by the inability of many minority applicants to meet traditional standards such as height. While the possible artificiality of such standards may have been recognized for years, they were often tolerated because the need for revising them was not urgently felt. The need to hire minority group persons who, because of an inability to avail themselves of proper medical care and diet, are effectively screened out by stringent physical standards, focused new attention on these standards and realistic revision is becoming more common. Increased use of compensating factors has also been used in seeking additional minority personnel. Allowing excellence in one requirement to compensate for a minor deficiency in another is used, as described earlier, in all recruiting but is especially helpful in the case of minority applicants. Typically, educational achievement is used to compensate for minor physical shortcomings, but many forms of compensation are worked out by different agencies to match the real need as they see it. An agency with a large Puerto Rican segment in its population, for example, might well consider bilinguality more than compensatory for a deficiency of an inch or two in height or a less-than-perfect set of teeth. In another community, having been born and raised in the area and demonstrated leadership abilities might combine to make up for a certain amount of visual weakness, and so on.

Among the special recruitment efforts employed are use of minority personnel from within the agency as recruiters and use of minority community leaders and civic organizations as recruiting agencies. Advertising and publicity campaigns are also set up in both the general and minority media if the need is large enough to justify the expense. One of the most effective and critically important types of program aiding recruitment of minorities is not even aimed primarily at that goal. Communications programs, described earlier as aimed at increasing the commonality of police and community goals, can do more good (if the program works) than any straight recruiting program because they overcome the distrust of police existing in so many minority communities. The most effective minority police officers are those who grew up in and intimately know the community. Their ability to relate directly to the needs of situations as they arise can't really be duplicated by anyone from outside the community, regardless of skin coloration. Police recruits must be drawn largely from the pool of young men in any community, the group which has been shown to be the most antagonistic to police. While the individuals involved will seldom be the same, even those young men with propolice tendencies are subject to some amount of peer pressure from their contemporaries, and this must be overcome before direct recruitment programs can achieve maximum effectiveness. To the extent that communications programs are successful in the community at large, the job of recruitment becomes much easier and more likely to produce successful results.

PROBLEMS OF THE MINORITY OFFICER

The most obvious and anticipated problem the minority officer may face upon entering police service is discrimination. This is a problem with which he is familiar, but the frustrations can be a little more severe in the context of a career. Some (fortunately, not too many) agencies have been found to maintain policies limiting minority officers' advancement and assignment. The President's Crime Commission found in 1967 that some agencies even restricted black officers' authority to arrest while limiting their assignment to minority neighborhoods and precluding their partnership arrangements with other black officers. Such policies have largely, if not entirely, been abolished by now (since they are illegal), but it is unrealistic to assume that police, as a group, are any less likely to retain old prejudices than the citizen at large. In point of fact, a police officer who works constantly in situations where members of one race make up the bulk of his problems will probably be

> ### Blacks on the Force
>
> Black policemen are sometimes reported to have a restraining influence on white colleagues who might otherwise tend to act in a cavalier, racist manner, as is indicated by the remark of an 18-year-old black youth in the South Bronx: "It used to be bad the way those white cops used to rough us up. Now, usually you see a black cop and a white cop in a car, or two black cops, so they think twice about cracking heads. They talk to you like they're supposed to talk to you."
>
> Finally, there is the effect that growing numbers of black companions has upon the black policeman himself. Once it was commonly understood that a black policeman was not to arrest a white person. A little later, blacks were typically used as "fingermen" in black neighborhoods, identifying suspects who would then be arrested by whites. "It made you feel like a Judas among your own people," said one black.
>
> Now, the black is mostly a full-fledged policeman in his own right, and he can bring his own perceptions more easily to bear on the job.
>
> However, many observers believe that his simple presence is unlikely to make much of a dent in either the crime rate or community unless certain other conditions apply as well.
>
> One is that the black policemen must have a genuine identification with the community and resist turning into the middle-class carpetbaggers that many white policemen are accused of having become. In this regard, there is agitation in some communities for requiring the policeman to live in the neighborhood he patrols, so that he can be held directly accountable to the populace.
>
> Further, say the reformists, such men . . . will be fighting a losing battle unless supervisors share their goals and encourage their efforts. [William K. Stevens, *New York Times* (August 11, 1974). Copyright 1974 by The New York Times Company. Reprinted by permission.]

more apt to develop racial bias than the average citizen. The minority officer, if he is able, has an excellent opportunity to make a significant contribution to the elimination of stereotypical images held by his fellow officers.

In addition to the problems of discrimination and being a minority within a minority, the minority officer faces problems that are uniquely his. Often a segment of his own ethnic group will consider him a traitor—an Uncle Tom or a Tio Taco at best—and considerably worse at worst. Some of the young, non-law-abiding males who resent police in general may have a special hatred for someone they consider one of their own who goes into law enforcement. Despite the fact that the officer may never consider himself part of their group, their attitude alone makes him part of their problem.

Most adults in the minority community, of course, don't regard him as a sellout since they favor stronger law enforcement and the minority officer offers them the added hope that someone in the police force may be able to actually identify with their needs. This position offers him still another chance to function uniquely. Although minority officers take just as stark a view of the crime picture in the ghetto as other officers, they don't have the same tendency to associate that crime with racial characteristics. This allows them to maintain a better perspective of their peace-keeping role both from their own point of view and the community's. The minority officer's identity thus may be more secure since his image of himself more closely matches that reflected back to him by the community he serves. If he is fortunate this security will carry him through the conflict of identity that arises from the negative reflection of his image as it comes back from the segment of the community that regards him as a sellout. If he's not lucky, the latter conflict can eventually embitter and defeat him.

THE NEED FOR FEMALE PERSONNEL

If racial minorities can be considered underrepresented in law enforcement on the basis of their percentage of the total population, a ratio of 4 percent vs. 14 percent, women, with 2 percent in police work and 51 percent of the total population, are represented only on a miniscule basis. While this may seem a superficial observation (and largely it is) there is more substance to it than might be apparent at first reading. The role of women in police work is much more severely limited in the United States than in many other countries. In Israel, for example, 90 percent of traffic police are women and some consider Israeli traffic police the best in the world (they have been invited to train equivalent functions in such countries as Great Britain, Japan, and France). In contrast with our meter maids, Israeli traffic policewomen perform intersection control duties and issue citations for moving violations as well.

The trend to increased numbers of women in American law enforcement is so new, in terms of noticeable movement, that no definitive statements can be made as to how it will ultimately shape up. We can, however, look at the history of it and the benefits claimed to be available and then logically estimate the chances of change. Women began to be involved in police work as early as 1845 when two matrons were hired to process female prisoners in The Tombs prison in New York. They were used only in such capacities until 1893 when, in Chicago, a police widow was appointed to the detective bureau to work with the courts and other detectives in cases involving women and children. Shortly after the turn of the century a woman in Portland, Oregon was given official police status and headed a corps of volunteers to look after the moral well-being of young girls and women attending an exposition being held in that city. During this first decade of the century, enforced prostitution burgeoned in America's cities and public concern grew to the point that Los Angeles, in 1910, appointed the first American policewoman. More than a dozen cities followed this lead in the next few years, with assignment of policewomen to handle all cases involving women and children. The role of women in police work was thus pretty clearly set for several decades to come. Many departments set up Women's Bureaus, staffed and supervised by women, to handle all such cases; all policewomen were assigned to these bureaus when they existed. Women's Bureaus still exist today, and the traditional role of women in police work hasn't changed. But today, all women's roles in society are subject to immense pressure for change and that of the policewoman is in no way exempt. Experimental programs are underway in almost every major city and women are being used in virtually every police role. Results are too far from conclusive at this time to report meaningfully but some of the claimed benefits are interesting to examine.

In the first place, in times when recruitment needs are at a high for police agencies, the size of the available pool can be increased dramatically by including women in it. Over half of the people in the country are women, and the 2 percent of the police force comprised of women hardly begins to tap the source. Combining the need for more minority officers with the general recruitment need, the advantage is even greater since the percentage of women is even larger in the minority populace. Whether such utilization of personnel would require restructuring police assignments (to exclude women from potentially dangerous assignments) is as yet uncertain. Even if such restructuring is required, however, there are other factors such as the increased possibility that civilians should be used more extensively which support the desirability of such a move.

Interestingly most women in police officer positions have college educations since this has become almost a traditional entrance requirement for them. The theory advanced to support this requirement has been based on the small number of openings: "Since we have so few openings we may as well have the best." The lateral entry ratio among women is considerably higher than for men since very few enter at the traditional patrol level but start in such positions as juvenile officer. Many others, however, serve in secretarial positions after receiving considerable training as police officers. In the vast majority of such cases the assignments are those the officer sought when she joined the force and mandatory reassignment would not be welcomed. To restrict newly-hired female officers, who may be otherwise qualified for broader assignment, to clerical roles, however, could be wasteful at a time when personnel needs are greater than ever before. It is also probably true that more women will be attracted to police service as broader, more challenging roles become available to them. Certainly the ever increasing waiting lists of female applicants in many agencies would tend to support this theory. Many current programs in federal and municpal agencies in all parts of the country are developing data bases that will soon clarify the validity of this claimed benefit.

The image of the police force is most certainly undergoing change with the increased use of women in all functions. One of the complaints offered by male officers as a reason for not wanting to see more women officers is their lack of aggressiveness. In the many functions of police where nonaggressiveness is indicated as the best way of handling the situation (the service functions generally fall into this category and, as is widely known, make up the majority of police work), such a quality would actually be an asset to the officer rather than a liability. A police officer, however, must be prepared to handle either a service function or an enforcement function at any given moment, so lack of aggressiveness must be examined in terms of its desirability for the total police function rather than one part of it, no matter how statistically dominant that one part may be. There is a case to be made for women in what would normally be considered situations where aggressiveness would be an asset and we'll get to that shortly. On the point of image, however, there can be little doubt that the traditional, paramilitary image of police at times works to the detriment

> ### Why Women Join
>
> Why are so many women eagerly taking on the dangerous, tedious and largely thankless responsibilities of law enforcement?
>
> One reason: Boring as walking a beat can be, many women find that it is more interesting than traditional women's jobs —office work or teaching, for instance.
>
> Miami Officer Sharon Koehler, a former legal secretary, joined the force to find something "more challenging" than clerical work.
>
> In Atlanta, a former social worker says she joined the force because she enjoys working with people. She explains:
>
> "I realized long ago police work involved helping people. It's a dangerous job, walking around with a uniform on, but I feel good when I go home knowing I've done some good that day."
>
> Another reason for women's invasion of police work is that the pay is considered good for high-school graduates—the standard educational requirement for police recruits.
>
> Still another reason: Women officers are breaking out of the specialized niches where they traditionally have been assigned by police departments. ["No Longer Men or Women —Just Police Officers." Copyright *U.S. News & World Report* (Aug. 19, 1974).]

of the operation, and there can be no doubt that the presence of women in the operating force softens this image. Whether the overall effect of this lowered image is good or bad, from the police administrator's point of view, depends largely on the style of policing he wants for his department. In the future it will depend more on the results obtained in current programs which are gathering, among other things, evidence on the need and desirability of the high profile for police. It is claimed that some departments which are enlarging the role of women officers are experiencing fewer citizen complaints against officers. To the extent that this reduction consists of fewer complaints of brutality or rudeness, this is of course a desirable change. To be really meaningful the comparison must be made not with complaints as a raw figure, but complaints which are substantiated by investigation. Many complaints come from people who are simply troublemakers and achieve a certain amount of personal satisfaction and even status among their peers from "standing up to the man" and making trouble for him. The same satisfaction isn't gained from complaining against a female officer, and this factor has to be taken into account when evaluating a statistical drop in complaints.

A case in point for image alteration working to the benefit of law enforcement in general is the handling of rape victims. Rightly or wrongly a great many female rape victims (there are both kinds) simply don't report the crime because they lack confidence in the treatment they'll receive at the hands of a male police force. Even if a woman is available at the station to take the report the feeling is not as much improved unless the woman is seen as having authority which can be brought to bear in the victim's behalf. If the image of the female police officer is simply that of report-taker, her service is viewed as a token one and the image of the total force remains one of moderate helpfulness at best and distrust at worst.

Use of women officers increases the crime-fighting ability of an agency in many ways. In surveillance, for example, suspects are notoriously aware of tall men because of hiring standards over the years. Use of a woman, even a tall one, avoids this problem and increases effectiveness dramatically. When a male and female officer pair up for surveillance the result is even more effective since the thought of a "police couple" seems not to occur to most suspects. With the large rise of female offenders in recent years, another benefit accrues from increased use of policewomen in the field. In the first place, if physical handling of the suspect is required a policewoman is less likely to feel any hesitancy at doing the job. In the second, the female suspect is less likely to think she can get away with anything because of her sex if the arresting officer is another woman. Searching suspects at the scene, particularly in cases such as drug arrests where evidence is easily hidden or disposed of, is much more effectively done by a policewoman and is less likely to arouse the sympathy of onlookers to the detriment of the situation. Women are also able to get information from suspects, witnesses, and victims in many cases (particularly offenses involving sex or juveniles) than men because of the stereotyped image of a woman as being more sensitive and understanding than a man.

It is often claimed that women have a tendency to defuse violent situations, and instances where they have been involved in potentially violent situations tend to support the claim, although again there are far too few cases for statistical significance. The theories as to why this may be true are interesting. One holds that the average male officer, because he knows he is expected to be able to handle violence, enters a potentially violent situation prepared to handle it. Every movement and expression betrays the fact that he anticipates violence and can handle it. The citizen, even if he was not predisposed to violence, is aware of the policeman's behavior and perceives it as a challenge to be met if possible. Women, according to this theory, are not under the same pressure as men to "handle" violent situations and thus approach them differently, with a lower profile less likely to trigger latent violence in the citizen. Another interesting theory advanced by a female officer is that the presence of an armed woman creates a momentary confusion in the mind of the citizen who must plan how he is going to handle this unforeseen situation. As he evaluates the possibilities it probably occurs to him that while a male police officer might try to subdue him with physical strength, this woman might well resort to use of her weapon since she lacks the strength to overcome him. The combination of possibilities provides the female officer an advantage in terms of time and attention, both to her benefit.

The psychology of many police-citizen confrontations is also decidedly in favor of the female officer. For most young men in the subculture of the street, the uniformed cop is fair game, a challenge to his evolving manhood which can be bolstered by the simple act of attacking the authority figure. A certain amount of peer-group prestige goes with the attack on the officer, even if it fails. Conversely, an attack upon a woman, even though she may be a policewoman, carries with it the stigma of cowardice. There is no reward, even if the attack is successful, and certain contempt if it fails. Thus we find the female officer protected by her own vulnerability in cases of this type.

It should be pointed out that this is one particular kind of case in point and certainly not the only type of danger police officers, male or female, face in performance of their jobs. In two dangerous police situations, family disputes and traffic citation issuance, it is difficult to imagine how an officer's femininity could protect her. In the family dispute, her naturally lower profile could be helpful in cooling off heated discussions, but that's not where the danger to the officer lies. The danger comes when the disputants jointly turn on the authority figure as the real cause of all their problems. Here it seems unlikely that the sex of the outside party would be a controlling factor in safety; the male in such actions is certainly not loathe to do physical harm to his wife so it seems unlikely that he would refrain from transferring blame to an outside female. In the traffic citation situation the danger to the officer is not so much a matter of premeditation on the part of the offender as it is reaction to the realization that he is trapped and likely to be caught. The person likely to do harm to the officer is usually either alone or in the company of others equally afraid of exposure, so there is no potential loss of peer status to constrain him. The danger would thus seem to be as great for a female officer as a male in similar situations. Again it is not aggressiveness that causes the male officer to get hurt in these cases, but his carelessness coupled with the bad fortune to have stopped someone who has more to lose than the price of a traffic ticket.

Improved service quality is claimed on behalf of some agencies using women in new, broader roles. It is widely known that most male officers prefer the law enforcement aspects of the job but are heavily occupied with the service aspects most of the time. Studies indicate that a higher percentage of women entering service (also a higher percentage of minority officers, interestingly) do so because they want to serve or help people. This is, of course, more in line with the traditional role of women in law enforcement, and whether it is performed in a juvenile hearing room or a patrol car is perhaps less important than the fact that it is efficient utilization of personnel.

A final benefit of the trend, and one which is visibly being achieved, is that standards and policies are being reevaluated in terms of job requirements. As discussed in earlier chapters, standards and requirements are indeed being increasingly set and validated in terms of what is actually demanded by the job rather than some artificial plateau of excellence that conforms to an image. For example, if it develops that a 5'4" woman with proper physical defense training can handle a certain situation, why must a man be at least 5'7" to qualify for the position that normally handles this type of situation? Shouldn't he be given the same training and be allowed to enter at the same height? As pointed out earlier, there may be other factors which bear on a particular requirement such as height, but the important concept here is that the arbitrary and sometimes artificial barriers to employment as a peace officer are being examined more carefully than ever before to see if they still have relevance. This is a healthy situation for any job, particularly one as important as that of police officer.

Legal Considerations

With few exceptions, women have not been active in pursuing the cause of employment as police officers through the courts. The outstanding piece of legislation on the matter is the still unratified Constitutional Amendment, passed by the Senate in 1972, known popularly as the "Equal Rights Amendment." If ratified by three-fourths of the states within seven years it will provide that "Equality of rights under the law shall not be denied or abridged by the United States or by any state on account of sex." What its actual impact on police departments will be is still conjectural, but we can examine the trends in the courts during recent years for an indication.

The 14th Amendment, which guarantees equal protection and due process for all citizens, is the basis for many decisions in the Supreme and lower courts affecting the status of women in law enforcement. In 1971 the Supreme Court, in *Reed* v. *Reed,* ruled against an Idaho statute giving preferred status to males over females of the same relationship as executors of estates. Because the statute involved an obvious sex bias, the court overturned it without facing, as civil libertarians and womens' rights groups had hoped, issues already established for racial discrimination cases. These issues would have placed on the state the burden of showing compelling interest of the state to justify depriving a class of people a fundamental right. Designation of sex discrimination as a suspect classification was also not faced in *Reed* although it had been in Connecticut in 1968 when in *Robinson* v. *York* a state law imposing longer sentences on women than men for similar offenses was struck down. A "suspect classification" is similar to the compelling interest test in that a heavy burden is placed on a state to justify discrimination on the basis of that classification or quality in a person.

In 1971 the California Supreme Court declared sex a suspect classification in ruling on the case of *Sail'er Inn* v. *Kirby.* The wording of the court in its ruling is more interesting than the case itself:

> Sex, like race and lineage, is an immutable trait, a status into which the class members are locked by the accident of birth. What differentiates sex from non-suspect statuses such as intelligence or physical disability and aligns it with the recognized suspect classification is that the characteristic frequently bears *no relation to ability to perform* or contribute to society. The result is that the whole class is relegated to an inferior legal status without regard to the capabilities or characteristics of its individual member.

The italics were added to emphasize the fact that the Constitution allows states to set up requirements for law enforcement officers if they can show that the qualifications are *reasonably related* to the work performed. The decision of the court went on to state: "Laws which disable women from full participation in the political, business and economic arenas are often characterized as 'protective' and beneficial. Those same laws applied to racial or ethnic minorities would readily be recognized as invidious and impermissible. The *pedestal* upon which women have been placed has all too often, upon closer inspection, been revealed as a cage. We conclude that the sexual classifications are properly treated as suspect, particularly when those classifications are made with respect to a fundamental interest such as employment." The italics here refer to the commonly advanced premise that women should be protected from the dangerous aspects of police work. Without addressing the philosophical issues raised by this point, the quotation from the California court is offered for consideration because of the high likelihood that it will be the basis for much future litigation.

Another prominent legal consideration is the stand of the Law Enforcement Assistance Administration. As mentioned earlier, agencies receiving LEAA funds (and most do) are required to have affirmative action programs on minority employment. They are also enjoined by LEAA from discriminating against women on the basis of sex. In 1971 LEAA decided that *Reed* had settled the issue of whether the 14th Amendment applied to sex discrimination and prohibited such discrimination by recipients of LEAA funds. LEAA has also ruled against height and weight requirements unless they are shown to be essential to job performance.

The Civil Rights Act of 1964 prohibits discrimination on the basis of sex under its Title VII provisions. The basic tenet of Title VII is that all jobs must be open to all people, including women, unless it can be proved that sex is a "bona fide occupational qualification reasonably necessary to the normal operation of particular business or enterprise." Beyond body searches, it seems to be very difficult to build a case for excluding women from any police role under Title VII. Separate divisions for women, special hiring procedures, tests, quotas, lines of progression through the ranks, and advertising jobs under male or female headings are prohibited by Title VII provisions of the Civil Rights Act. The bona fide occupational qualification even excludes dangerous assignments as an exemption. That is, concern for the safety of a woman on the job is not a valid reason for refusing employment; concern for other workers on the job or the public to be served by her might qualify if it can be proved that she personally, not she "as a woman," is incapable of handling the job safely or adequately. This, in fact, is the thrust of all legal action involving women: they must be considered as individuals, rather than members of a class. Such consideration has been guaranteed all women, except those interested in a law enforcement career, since 1964; since 1972 the provisions of the Act have been extended by an act of Congress to cover not only private employers but state and local agencies as well. It is this broadening of the applicability of the Civil Rights Act that has really made possible the many programs now being evaluated in cities across the country.

NEW ROLES FOR POLICEWOMEN

Probably no single instance demonstrates the changing potential for women in law enforcement as much as the case of Gertrude Schimmel of the New York Police Department. Following a lawsuit by her fellow policewoman Felicia Shpritzer to overturn departmental policy which effectively prevented women from taking competitive promotional examinations, Officer Schimmel took the sergeant's examination in 1964 to become one of the first two female sergeants on the force. Both women became lieutenants in 1967 and Lt. Schimmel subsequently rose to captain in 1971 and deputy inspector in 1972. Today there are many women in supervisory ranks across the country and some are supervising line functions staffed by men and women alike. Police departments are still, however, 98 percent staffed by male officers and likely to remain predominantly so for many years to come.

Departments of all sizes are currently expanding the role of female officers in their forces. One of the easiest transitions for women is into criminal investigation. The change in work assignment is frequently not too different from their traditional roles in juvenile work, and their greater invisibility in surveillance work, as outlined earlier, is an asset. Although women aren't used in detective work nearly as widely in America as they are in Germany, Israel and England, cities such as New York, Miami, and Washington, D.C., have female investigators working assignments from homicide investigation through pickpocket details to undercover narcotics and vice work.

The transfer to administrative duties is also an easy one for women who have been accustomed to working inside assignments in their more traditional role. Women hold teaching positions in Los Angeles and Washington academies and fill key posts in personnel and other service functions such as community relations. Planning and research positions are being filled by women in many departments and in at least one major department, Dallas, a woman officer performs a key function in internal affairs investigations.

In Philadelphia most female officers not in youth work are assigned to the Civil Disturbance Unit, an unusual unit made up of both male and female officers and assigned crowd control at demonstrations, strikes, and similar disturbances. Women are used extensively, but not exclusively, in handling the female and juvenile constituents of the crowds. Interestingly, this unit was under the supervision of a female sergeant for several years. The Peoria, Illinois department has no special unit for civil disturbances but does use female officers frequently in a similar manner.

Women are used almost exclusively in radio dispatch positions in many cities although they are often not sworn personnel. Crime analysis functions in laboratory and field positions are being assigned to women, usually sworn officers, as are many other technical services. Few cities use women in traffic work to the extent that they are used in Europe and Israel, but in Dallas and Los Angeles nonsworn but uniformed women are performing intersection control duties. In Washington, D.C., policewomen perform both intersection and moving traffic control duties. Nationwide, however, the greatest interest in the expanding role of women is focused on the several major cities conducting experimental programs with female officers in the patrol function.

Women on Patrol

While many small departments have used women officers on patrol, virtually without notice, the cities which are getting the most attention currently are relatively large ones, the smallest being Peoria, Illinois, with 127,000 population and the largest New York City; in between are cities such as Washington, D.C. and Miami. An examination of the programs in terms of selection criteria, training, nature of assignments, and evaluation of results as seen through the eyes of participants, administrators, male officers, the public, and outside evaluators shows many interesting similarities and equally interesting differences of opinion.

Women in these programs were volunteers and transfers from the existing force of policewomen and women recruited specifically for the program. Women recruits were given a height concession except in Washington where the chief, consistent with his policy of equality of opportunity and interchangeability of officers regardless of sex, held to a 5'7" minimum height—the same as for male officers in that department. The training given female officers was the same as males, ranging from six to twenty-four weeks followed by a period of field training with experienced officers acting as training supervisors.

Assignments were to both foot and motorized patrols and in districts ranging from low to high crime rates. No department had a policy supporting screening of dangerous calls, although some officers felt that there was an occasional reluctance on the part of dispatchers to send female officers on dangerous calls. In any event screening was more the exception than the rule. Women were assigned to work alone or in combination with a male officer in all cities. New York allowed two women to be assigned as partners on a permanent basis but restricted male-female partnerships to a temporary basis to avoid possible criticism from the public or families of participants. Only in Washington were women allowed to work the morning (midnight) watch.

In evaluating the performance of the women on patrol, administrators in the four departments were uniformly positive. Some doubt was expressed in all but one department about the ability of women to handle the aspects of patrol where physical strength was required. Interestingly, the only department where this was not expressed as a concern was Washington, which did not lower its height requirement. Washington was also the only department to experience noteworthy attrition during the trial program, but this loss of personnel resulted entirely from among the twenty-seven women transferred from existing jobs to patrol; the eighty women hired specifically for patrol remained throughout the program. The performance of the women was rated as good in all departments, with Washington noting that the newly-hired officers performed better than those transferred without requesting it. Most administrators felt that the supervisors had experienced some difficulty turning down requests of the women officers for extra time off and other special considerations. Two of the departments commented that not only did the women seem to handle the service aspects of the job more willingly than men but did outstanding work on reports, not only from the writing standpoint but also the investigative. The Peoria department found that while the female officers sometimes backed off on potentially dangerous situations, leaving the handling of them to their male counterparts, they found alternative ways of handling such situations that minimized the potential for violence where their lack of physical strength could have placed them at a disadvantage. How easily these same techniques might be adapted by males lacking the protection sometimes conceded to femininity is not clearly known yet. Administrators felt that women officers had functioned particularly well in crowd control and accident investigation work and had overcome some of the initial resistance on the part of male officers by their willingness to handle jobs distasteful to men such as the service aspects.

In general, supervisors expressed less enthusiasm for the programs than administrators. The most frequent complaints were the special consideration sought by some women and found difficult to handle by male supervisors. Female supervisors in Washington felt that the male supervisors would benefit from special training in handling women employees. They also felt the female officers would benefit from continued and expanded self-defense training. This corresponds to the second most frequent complaint expressed by male supervisors: that the female officers' lack of physical strength limited their ability to handle some phases of patrol work and was sometimes a hazard to their male partners. Part of this concern came from an initial tendency of male officers to be overprotective of females, overresponding to back-up calls, and in general lacking confidence in them. Supervisors in one department also felt that women contributed to this by calling for help sooner than might have been necessary in many cases.

Supervisors also generally complained of female officers' lack of aggressiveness, although some admitted that this was common for new male officers as well and might be due more to inexperience than any inherent quality of personality. On the positive side women were commended for such performance as better driving records, fewer citizen complaints, better reports, and willingness to handle the service aspects of the job. An interesting sidelight to the noted good performance of female officers in handling family disputes in one agency was that this success was not experienced in Latin homes where the woman as an authority figure was more resented than in black or white homes.

Male officers in participating departments were almost uniformly negative about the value of women on patrol. The most frequently mentioned concern was the lack of physical strength and aggressiveness of the female officers. The men felt that the women lacked initiative and, when partners, generated enough concern in the minds of the male officers that they sometimes hesitated to enter situations that might call for two full-strength officers. They felt that the lack of authoritative manner common to female officers diminished the public's respect and that the women sometimes weren't taken seriously by the public. One agency's male officers reported that when they dealt with citizens as part of a male-female team the citizens would invariably direct their remarks to the male officer, virtually ignoring the female. They also reported that some citizens seemed to actively resent the female officers.

The male officers in all four cities felt that uniformed women were an asset in some situations but felt that their participation in patrol was not appropriate. The assignments most often mentioned as being appropriate for women were calls involving women or juveniles, family disputes, traffic and accident investigation, and report taking. To summarize, most men seemed to agree that the women did better than they had expected but that they could be expected to perform satisfactorily on patrol in no more than 80 to 90 percent of situations and they preferred a male partner on whom they could rely in all cases.

Female police officers who took part in these programs took

a different view of the results. They felt that they had overcome the initial resentment of the male officers (although most admitted they realized most men would still rather have a male partner) and could do as good as, or better than, men in 80 to 90 percent of the patrol officer's job. Many also stated that they would prefer to have a male partner than a female but felt that the presence of women in patrol brought a new, more progressive approach to law enforcement. The basis for this feeling was the success that had been experienced in defusing violent situations rather than developing confrontations and in securing cooperation as a source of conflict resolution rather than fear of force. Although they recognized their limitations due to inferior physical strength, most women felt the negative effect of this shortcoming was exaggerated and could be overcome with more and better physical training. They did not as a whole feel that their physical shortcomings generated apprehension to the extent of debilitation. The lack of authoritative demeanor, which was generally recognized, was seen as contributory to the new approach mentioned above, rather than the handicap it was considered by the male officers. This psychological approach was felt to have been particularly helpful in handling family disputes except in the Latin homes where their sex was a definite handicap.

Most women officers felt that any screening of calls which may have existed initially diminished rapidly as they became accepted by the men in the department. Interestingly, the women in one department felt that the male supervisors should learn how to handle women workers more firmly and not give in to requests for special consideration on such matters as time off or assignments.

Performance Evaluation

Only one formal public-opinion sampling has been made in these cities to our knowledge, but it and the attitudes informally gathered seem to range from neutral to favorable. It seems reasonable to believe that a public concerned with rising crime rates is inclined to take a wait-and-see attitude on any innovative approach that might possibly help.

Two cities, New York and Washington, have used outside evaluators of their programs. Neither produced results significantly different from the subjective attitudinal reports cited above. In fact, both reports were more attitudinal than objective except for the statistical fact that women on male-female teams generated fewer self-initiated actions than all-male teams or lone male officers. Evaluation of performance of police units in general, and individuals in particular, remains one of the most inadequate areas in the field. The problem is that objectives have seldom been set in terms of performance expected so there is no way of telling whether that performance has taken place or not. Traditional measurement devices such as arrest rates are of little use and simply asking a supervisor or associate to evaluate performance, while still the most common form of evaluation in both public and private service, is so subject to personal bias as to be almost meaningless. Evaluation of the effectiveness of women on patrol is done on a no less subjective basis, and the future of programs will thus remain subject to the push and pull of administrative whim and social pressure. There is a slight movement underway to build objective evaluation systems for women-on-patrol programs. If a model were developed it could provide for evaluation of performance in general which would be worth a great deal to both the public and law enforcement administration.

PROBLEMS OF THE FEMALE OFFICER

The problems of a woman going into law enforcement should by now be fairly obvious. They depend largely on the role she seeks for herself. If she is content with the traditional role, her way will be much easier than if she seeks full equal assignments such as patrol duty. In addition to the selection barriers of higher education and physical standards that are difficult to meet, the attitudinal encounters she will face will challenge her self-image. Her fellow female officers, if they don't share her desire for full equality are likely to resent her. If they wish to preserve the traditional role, with its benefits to them if salary is equal but assignments are not, they may fear that her success will lead to a unisex system that may require them to be rotated into field work.

Her male peers are likely to be a continuing source of frustration although, if she is able to prove herself and gain their acceptance, they can be a source of great personal fulfillment. The attitudes of her male coworkers are in any event likely to be better than that of their wives, at least unless and until the wives have the program adequately explained to them. Some agencies using female officers on patrol offer the choice of rejecting a female partner to any male officer who feels it will cause problems at home. Experience so far has indicated, however, that if the wives are properly prepared for the program, few problems do in fact result. If the agency chooses to not assign permanent male-female partnerships, a further problem results from the fact that the partnerships are not in effect long enough for mutual trust and confidence to develop and the normal male resistance never really disappears.

If, in spite of all these potential problems, a woman chooses a career in law enforcement, it is hard to imagine a time during which a greater opportunity existed for witnessing and being a part of change. And even if the changes don't develop to the extent that it seems they surely will, the opportunity for service is certain to remain and almost certain to grow.

SUMMARY

While ethnic and racial minorities comprise 14 percent of the nation's population, only 4 percent of the nation's police are minority group members. There is now considerable effort being made to achieve proportionate racial composition within police departments serving communities with significant minority membership in their population.

Representative participation of minority races in a police department aims at increasing the respect of the community and identification of its goals with police goals. If the minority officers also live in the community they can provide valuable insights into its attitudes and feelings.

Affirmative action programs, plans to achieve equal opportunity for employment of minority race members, are required of all law enforcement agencies receiving grants under LEAA. It is not required that standards be lowered to increase representation of any under-represented group, but selection criteria must be shown to be job-related rather than discriminatory. If selection criteria prove to be discriminatory, the courts may design programs for the offending cities to build minority representation to specified levels by specified dates.

Programs being used in cities with significant minority populations include *over-recruitment* to allow for the higher-than-normal attrition rate experienced in the minority applicant pool due to the cultural and educational disadvantages among such groups; *use of minority personnel* from within the department as recruiters; *reevaluation of standards* to ensure that they are job related and not arbitrary; use of *compensating factors* in evaluating applicants; *involvement of community leaders* in recruitment; and *coordination* of recruitment and community relations programs to overcome inherent distrust of police.

Problems of minority officers include general discrimination and prejudice within the force; possible limited advancement opportunity (illegal and rapidly disappearing); and resentment from among some members of the minority community.

The traditional role of women in law enforcement derives from their beginnings in programs designed to protect women and children from the evils of contemporary society.

Claimed benefits of expanding use of women in law enforcement are: a *larger pool* for recruitment of new personnel; a less-aggressive *image* for the police force; increased ability to *defuse violent situations;* increased performance quality in the *service functions;* and *reevaluation of standards* to assure job-relatedness.

Legal status of women in law enforcement will probably be clarified greatly when the *Equal Rights Amendment* becomes ratified and the means of its implementation are established. Until then the *14th Amendment* remains the principal legal grounds for cases in which women's rights are involved. Extending a Supreme Court decision which didn't actually address the issues of *compelling interest* of the states, *fundamental rights* of women as a class, or *suspect classification* status for sex as a selection factor for personnel, a California case in 1971 declared sex a suspect classification, holding that it frequently bears no relation to ability to perform the job. Further limitation of participation of women in the full range of police responsibility must now be based on demonstrated inability of women as a class to successfully perform those duties.

LEAA requires affirmative action programs for women on the same basis as it does for minority group members. Title VII of the 1964 Civil Rights Act demands that all jobs be open to women unless it can be proved that sex is a bona fide occupational qualification reasonably necessary to the normal operation of the agency.

Women are now filling many roles other than the traditional ones, especially in foreign countries but also increasingly in America. The new roles are principally in the areas of administrative duties, investigative units, technical services, and disturbance control.

Programs evaluating *women on patrol* are taking place in many major cities. Preliminary results indicate that administrators are supportive of the programs and their results, supervisors are less enthusiastic, and male officers largely opposed to them. Women who have participated strongly believe they have performed well and are capable of handling all assignments equally as well or better than men, with the exception of those in which physical strength is a significant factor. Women also feel that they bring a new approach to law enforcement and that the alternative solutions they are forced to seek, because of their lack of physical strength, may indicate that traditional methods of force and threat of counterviolence may not be the best solution to confrontations between police and citizens where violence is likely to result.

Male officers in experimental programs generally feel that women do a better job than they had anticipated but still prefer to have male partners in whom they can have confidence to furnish assistance when necessary. Supervisors feel that many women take advantage of their sex to seek special consideration for time off and assignment and that the male officers are inclined to overprotect female officers thus weakening normal deployment capabilities of the force.

REVIEW QUESTIONS

Answers to these questions appear on page 386.

1. Which is more restrictive of the normal operation of a police department, an *affirmative action program* or a *court-designed program* for assuring racial balance in the department? _____
2. Which of the following operational procedures, common to police departments in communities with significant minority populations, are due to the higher-than-normal disqualification rate experienced among minority group applicants? (Circle as many as are correct.)
   a. over-recruitment among the minority group
   b. use of minority-group personnel as recruiters
   c. reevaluation of standards for selection
   d. use of compensating factors in selection
   e. involvement of community leaders in recruitment
   f. coordination of recruiting and communication programs
3. Which group, *racial minority* or *women,* is more underrepresented in law enforcement in terms of its percentage of the total population? _____
4. *True or False?* The traditional role of women in law en-

forcement has been largely limited to working with women and juveniles or clerical positions.

5. Which of the following benefits claimed for increased use of women in law enforcement are also true of increased use of racial minority personnel? (Circle as many as are correct.)
   a. larger recruitment pool
   b. less aggressive image for police
   c. special effectiveness in defusing violent situations
   d. increased quality of performance in the service functions of police work
   e. reevaluation of standards to assure job-relatedness

6. Which proposed Constitutional amendment and which existing Amendment have the most direct bearing on employment of women in law enforcement? _____

7. Is the suspect classification status of sex as an employment criterion more directly due to the Court's decision in Reed V. Reed, or Sail'er Inn v. Kirby? _____

8. Is the increased use of women on patrol more directly due to the impact of LEAA's Affirmative Action requirement or Title VII of the 1964 Civil Rights Act? _____

9. In handling a direct confrontation with a group containing young males, which offers more protection for the female officer: the fact that she is armed, or the likelihood of peer group disapproval of an attack against a woman? _____

10. What shortcoming of female officers was most consistently cited in different groups' evaluations of women-on-patrol programs? _____

11. Women who participated in the programs mentioned in the preceding question felt that the shortcoming cited actually may have resulted in a benefit to police practices. What is it? _____

CHAPTER 13

OPERATIONAL AND PHILOSOPHICAL DEVELOPMENTS

OVERVIEW

The results of the first decade of America's "war on crime" can hardly be viewed as encouraging. Advances on some fronts are more than overbalanced by losses on most as crime continues to spiral upward and every element of the criminal justice system reports inundation. This occurred during a period when the federal government poured billions of dollars into local law enforcement agencies hoping to stem the onslaught of the antisocial subculture. The conclusion can only be that increased application of old methods simply isn't going to get the job done.

Innovation, largely uncoordinated and either ignored or resisted during the better part of the first decade of federal application of funds, is finally beginning to take on a recognizable shape. Philosophical changes are always slow to be accepted and even slower to evolve into actual operational and organizational developments. But both institutions and procedures have been challenged so strongly while we have been losing the war against crime that even the most conservative elements of the system are now not only willing but almost anxious to accept changes which bring with them any promise of success.

Virtually everyone seriously involved with law enforcement and criminal justice today recognizes the fact that traditional methods and traditional efforts are insufficient to cope with the crime problem, and new ideas are being tried in every agency of the system from street policing to rehabilitation of convicted offenders. Overall, most of these new ideas can be put into one of three categories: those that seek solution through *increased citizen involvement* with some element of the criminal justice system; and those that deal with some form of *redeployment* of, or *technological augmentation* of, police forces. In this chapter we'll look at programs in each of these categories.

CITIZEN INVOLVEMENT IN THE CRIMINAL JUSTICE SYSTEM

The one thing that most observers of the criminal justice system agree upon is the need for greater involvement of all members of the community in dealing with crime. Clarence Kelley, director of the FBI has said, "We cannot rely solely on the law enforcement officer or the criminal justice system. The police officer can do little to alleviate isolated poverty in a land of wealth; he cannot insure the integrity of businessmen bent on defrauding the public; nor can he strengthen the unity of families shattered by indifference. These and myriad other problems must be solved by all of society."

A former head of the LEAA agrees: "The criminal justice system alone cannot solve this problem. Unless we do substantially more as a society we will have a continuous, insoluble problem . . . we have to bring people into the criminal justice system." Administrators and planners at all levels of the system are taking action to accomodate this need. The "Citizen's Initiative," for example, was started in 1974 by the Office of National Priority Programs (under LEAA) to provide funds for projects for citizens who are victims, jurors, or witnesses relative to criminal actions. The basic thrust of the program's activities is to promote positive interaction of citizens with the system by increasing the awareness of the mutual needs and interests of police, courts, corrections, and the general citizenry. While the members of the system have long recognized this interdependency, citizens have been somewhat insensitive to the reliance of police on them (for reporting of crimes, for example) to initiate the operation of the system. Similarly the dependence of courts on citizens as jurors and witnesses and the corrections segment for the success of rehabilitation efforts have been generally unattended by citizens and communities. The program seeks, on a national basis, ideas, methods, and approaches to use as model projects. Many completely innovative projects have been initiated through this program which, if validated, will be replicated on a national basis.

Police agencies in all parts of the country (particularly in high crime areas) are aiming major efforts at community involvement and awareness of police needs, procedures, and limits of authority. In New Orleans, for example, the uncontrolled crime rate in a housing project prompted initiation of an Urban Squad which met regularly with a committee of project residents to determine better ways of combating the problem. The resulting increased foot patrol and thorough investigation of all reported crimes increased citizens' willingness to report crimes and resulted in a drop in the crime rate to the lowest in the city. The program has been expanded into other housing projects and citizens are reportedly now willing to move back into these areas which, by their increased abandonment, were becoming virtual cesspools of crime. In Indianapolis, citizens' involvement in projects designed to increase attendance in schools, improve street lighting, and active participation in all elements of the criminal justice system resulted in a two-year crime drop. Over 500 cities have now adopted similar plans with an increase in cooperative programs and are developing supportive measures such as universal emergency police telephone numbers and pay telephones on which the operator can be reached without use of a coin. There is promise for at least greater citizen responsiveness to the police need for more effective reporting of crimes and thus a better chance for initiation of the criminal justice process.

COORDINATION OF THE CRIMINAL JUSTICE EFFORT

In 1967 New York City established the nation's first Criminal Justice Coordinating Council. Chaired by the mayor, this 75-member committee included representatives of city government, federal programs, community organizations, labor unions, and all agencies of the criminal justice system. This was in response to the need recognized by the President's Crime Commission for state and major city coordinating agencies to plan and implement new methods of crime prevention and control. One of the most important goals of such cooperative effort is an increase in both speed and certainty of justice. The aim is to do this by promoting understanding and cooperation among the various elements of the criminal justice system so that correctional institutions, for example, are not so unnecessarily burdened with persons who can't really benefit from rehabilitation that they have no means of treating those who can, or that police officers who must testify at criminal trial may be summoned by telephone shortly before they are needed rather than spending a whole day, away from their job, waiting outside a courtroom.

Coordinating councils, which now exist in most major cities, are by no means the only way of achieving the desired coordination and cooperation among agencies of the system. Direct liaison between police and courts is becoming more common and, since understanding is an important prerequisite, the knowledge gained of other agencies' operation and problems in programs such as the Criminal Justice Training Centers in Florida and California is extremely valuable. So is the cross-training many agencies arrange on a direct basis between themselves as, for example, when members of a prosecutor's staff ride with police officers or police administrators work in the courts for a period of time. Hopefully all these efforts will lead to a community of goals and effort that will result in operating efficiencies between and within agencies.

The Role of the Federal Government

Obviously few, if any, cities in America can afford the dollar expenditures required to develop and validate the innovative programs being conducted today. Million dollar projects are not uncommon and $100-200,000 programs are ordinary in the search for new and better methods. The big application of federal funds to these projects began with the 1968 Omnibus Crime Control and Safe Streets Act. Recognizing that the immediate problem was essentially a local one, Congress provided that it be dealt with at a local level. It set up the Law Enforcement Assistance Administration in the Department of Justice to evaluate proposals and disburse funds for developmental projects in the various states. In most cases the funds are granted to the state in the form of a "bloc" grant.

As shown in Figure 13-1 each state is required to have a State Planning Agency which functions as a reviewing authority and disburses funds to the various agencies actually conducting the programs. This organization provides control at the local level as much as possible. The organization shown here is that of California and provides for still more local control through the twenty-one regions into which the state is divided. The role of the federal government is not limited, however, to that of doting parent, sending money from home upon receipt of letters of request. For one thing, LEAA has assumed responsibility for replication of successful projects. If a particular project works well in one area, the National Institute for Law Enforcement and Criminal Justice (one of three major subdivisions of LEAA) will select other communities which have similar needs and provide financial assistance, training for personnel to be involved, handbooks and other necessary materials, and evaluation services. The purpose of this effort is to assure that advances in methods and technology don't become lost in some archive and fail to benefit the largest possible segment of the country. The Institute also selects appropriate communities for testing new concepts. While this may seem contrary to the principles of states' rights and local control, it was built directly into the original design of LEAA and provides still another means of assuring that all potentially helpful concepts are evaluated, regardless of where they are initiated. There are so many of these programs in progress now and so many more being considered everyday that it is impossible to hope to cover them all, but examining some of the more typical ones will give an idea of the type of problem that has been identified in various areas of the system and the solutions being sought.

THE COURTS

Certainly the judicial process is fraught with problems and probably the worst of these, congestion, will get worse as police improve their ability to apprehend criminals. Law enforcement administrators nearly all agree that a mandatory sentence of a year handed out within weeks of arrest is a far more likely deterrent to the rise in violent crime then the longer, uncertain terms which may take up to two years to be handed down. Many projects under study now are aimed at improving both the speed of the judicial process and the quality of sentencing. In one current program comprehensive, integrated information systems are being sought to provide prosecutors and judges with comparative information on reasons for acquitals and why certain cases go to jury trials and others to nonjury court trials; reasons for dismissals to preliminary hearings; effects of scheduling practices; and other simple inefficiencies in present court practices.

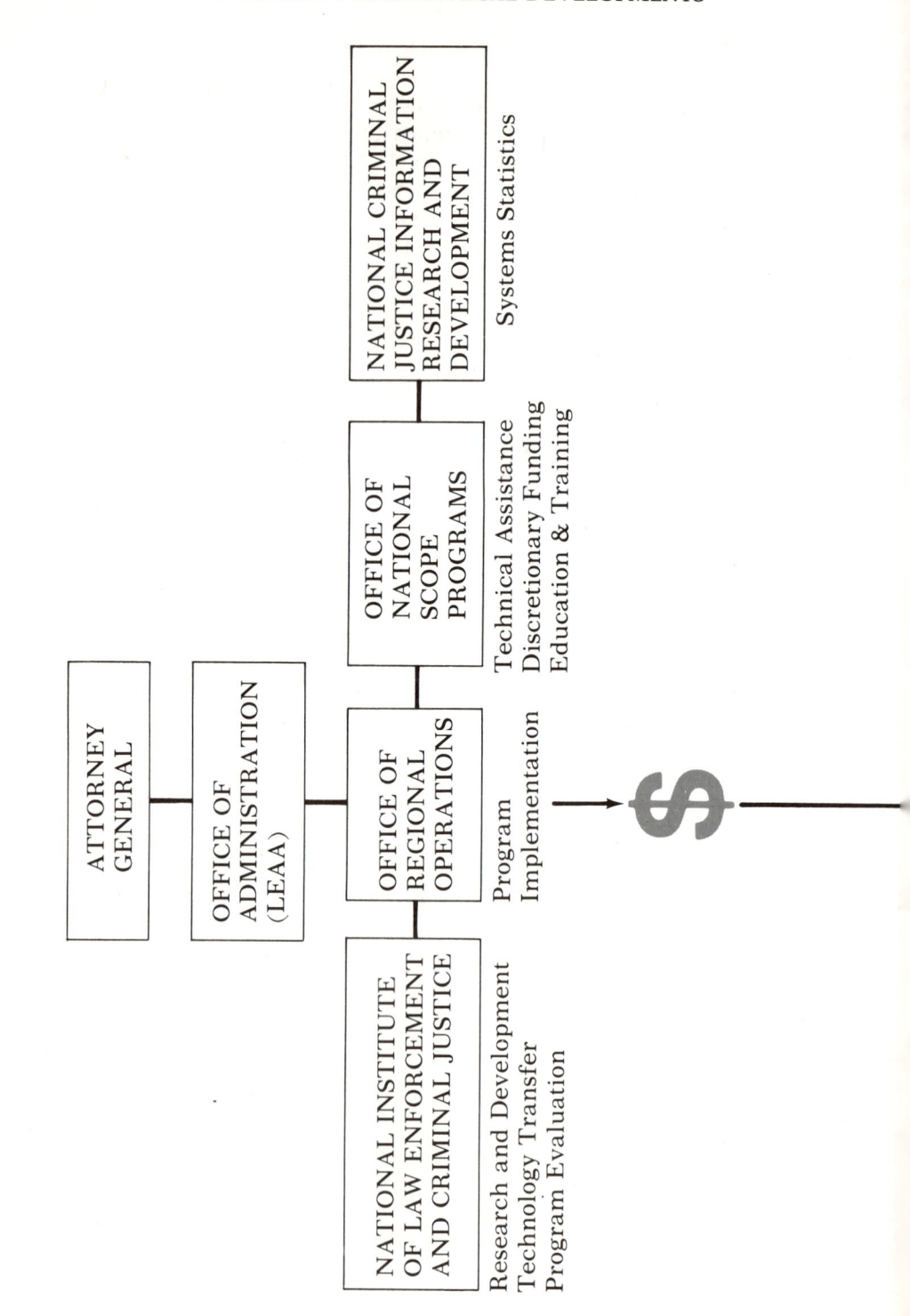

334 OPERATIONAL AND PHILOSOPHICAL DEVELOPMENTS

ATTORNEY GENERAL

OFFICE OF ADMINISTRATION (LEAA)

OFFICE OF NATIONAL SCOPE PROGRAMS
- Technical Assistance
- Discretionary Funding
- Education & Training

NATIONAL CRIMINAL JUSTICE INFORMATION RESEARCH AND DEVELOPMENT
- Systems Statistics

OFFICE OF REGIONAL OPERATIONS
- Program Implementation

NATIONAL INSTITUTE OF LAW ENFORCEMENT AND CRIMINAL JUSTICE
- Research and Development
- Technology Transfer
- Program Evaluation

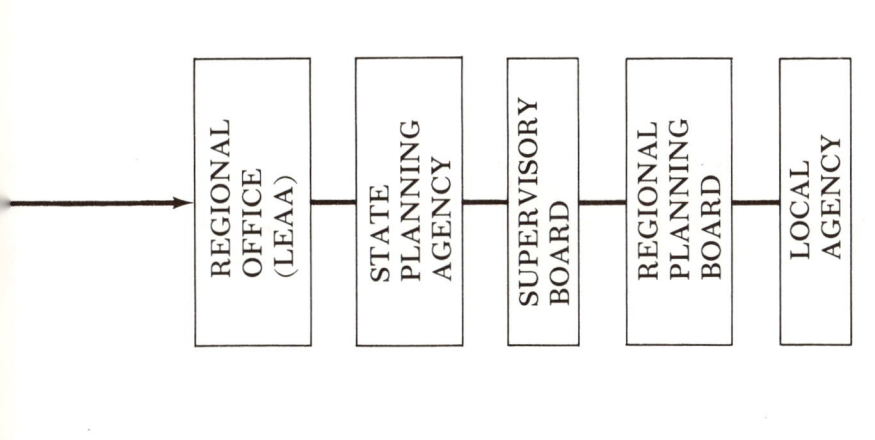

REGIONAL OFFICE (LEAA) → STATE PLANNING AGENCY → SUPERVISORY BOARD → REGIONAL PLANNING BOARD → LOCAL AGENCY

Figure 13.1. FEDERAL FUND DISTRIBUTION AND ORGANIZATIONAL STRUCTURE LAW ENFORCEMENT ASSISTANCE ADMINISTRATION (LEAA)

Use of videotape is being studied along with programs to see if the trial process can be expedited by more efficient use of jurors, witnesses, and counsel through prerecording portions of the trial. Programs are also being developed to increase the training level of administrative and paraprofessional personnel in the courts. Part of the delay in arraignments (presently from two to four weeks on a national average) is due to the practice of processing felony offenders through both municipal and superior courts and alternative systems are being evaluated. If successful, such programs would provide relief not only for the courts but custodial institutions as well. Projects are also under way to evaluate automated systems in large trial courts and improved calendaring procedures.

Community relations between courts and citizens, as well as other elements of the criminal justice community, are also in need of improvement, as are the security of court personnel and records. Court proceedings have increasingly been disrupted by outbreaks of violence resulting in injury and even death to judges and other court personnel. The programs being developed face the double problem of meeting the needs of those in jeopardy while still complying with the constitutional guarantees of fair, expeditious public trial. Improved diversionary programs for alcoholics whose behavior has not manifested itself in problems more serious than public drunkeness (that is, not in drunk driving or more serious criminal offenses) is an increasingly recognized need. In Washington D.C., for example, the classic case of six drunkards being processed through the "revolving door" of the system *1,400 times* at a cost to taxpayers of $600,000 points dramatically to the need for review of our attitude toward the true nature of this widespread problem. Criminal sanctions are obviously ineffective in combating it and programs similar to the decriminalized British approach are moving forward in America. Similar approaches are being taken to drug addiction and, if successful, will not only result in great reductions in court caseloads but also possibly reduce criminal offenses committed by addicts to support their habits.

Inequitable bail practices are being reviewed to avoid possible discrimination against poor persons who must now await trial in jail because they are unable to post bail. Studies seem to indicate that those who lack funds but are able to pass a critical review of their history do not show disproportionate failure-to-appear rates when released on their own recognizance. If successful, such expansion of O.R. release programs could have far-reaching affects on the economy of the community through decreased loss of wages and lowered custodial costs.

Typical of programs designed to make the courts more responsive to citizen needs is one in Milwaukee, which has a telephone alert system to obviate the need for witnesses and victims to wait in court for their appearances. The program also provides financial, medical, and legal counselling for victims. Similar programs are being tried in other cities, sometimes including counselling victims on proper use of small claims courts and their rights in them.

While the $200 million estimated annual cost of jurors is not a staggering amount by today's big-number expenditures, programs under study aim at reducing that by 25 percent through better management. Other improvements being attempted in this area include a better call system to avoid the sometimes prolonged wait jurors experience while lawyers and judges discuss procedures in chamber.

A final consideration in this review of court innovation is the matter of sentence disparity. It has long been recognized that the nature of the sentence in any given action depends almost entirely upon the accident of which judge is issuing the sentence. In some cases it comes down in fact to a matter of whimsy as when, following President Gerald Ford's controversial pardon of former President Nixon at least one judge dismissed charges against all who came before him one day on the basis that "if the President can do it, so can I." Fortunately, such instances are rare, but inequitable sentencing is not; it is rather the rule and measures are being developed in some court jurisdictions to correct this flaw. One such program, the *sentencing council,* is already in use in several U.S. cities. The council consists of several judges meeting periodically to review and discuss possible sentences in cases before them. The judge in each case retains the ultimate responsibility for the sentence, but he does avail himself of the experiences and attitudes of his colleagues who also advance their reasons for their position in each case. Hopefully this device will have not only a leveling effect on sentencing practices but may also evolve standards for widespread use. The other measure being used in some states is *appellate review.* In this procedure sentences within a jurisdiction are automatically reviewed by an appellate court. In submitting his sentencing decision for appellate review, the presiding judge also submits his rationale in support of that sentence, much in the same manner as the judges participating in sentencing councils. While the reviewing body may be smaller in appellate review than in a sentencing council, the net result aimed for—elimination of inequitable sentencing—should be about the same.

THE PROSECUTOR'S OFFICE

While actually an agency of the judicial portion of the criminal justice system, the prosecutor's office functions in what must be at times an uneasy role between the courts and the police. The sometimes investigative (as in preparing cases for a grand jury hearing), sometimes prosecutory (during court trials) and sometimes judicial (the net effect of his ability to terminate the process by failing to issue a complaint or by plea bargaining) natures of the prosecutor's role provide him with several distinctly different interfaces to serve. The projects developing data systems on an integrated basis, as outlined above, are aimed at helping the prosecutor perform his difficult role.

A large program to develop the investigative role of the office of prosecutor in the area of white-collar crime is under way. This particular part of the crime problem has long been neglected and has cost taxpayers uncounted millions of dollars each year. Citizen involvement is also provided for in this program which includes a restitution plan allowing the offender to make compensation to the victim. Rather than serving a prison sentence with resultant loss of his earning potential, the convicted party may serve time in a kind of halfway-house, a "Restitution Shelter," and maintain normal employment while restitution is being made.

Another type of project involving the prosecutor's office is the citizen awareness program similar to the one in Milwaukee described above. In addition to furnishing legal counselling to victims in this type of project, the prosecutor may maintain an emergency protection unit to guard against intimidation of witnesses and victims who may fear retaliation if they participate in trials.

One of the most sensitive current issues involving the office of the prosecutor is that of plea bargaining, as described in an earlier chapter. With 80 to 95 percent of felony criminal cases in America being disposed of via a negotiated guilty plea, the importance of quality performance in this critical area of justice is apparent. It has been estimated that a 5 percent increase in not-guilty pleas would paralyze the court system. Since sentences are usually shorter when negotiated prior to trial, increased trial volume would probably paralyze the correctional system as well. The cost to taxpayers is also obviously less with bargained-for sentencing and the cause of speeding justice is advanced. The danger feared most by some observers, however, is conversion to a system which pre-supposes *guilt* rather than innocence as is our traditional basis for trial. Plea bargaining presupposes guilt and the adversary process, which could dispose that presupposition, is by-passed by acceptance of the negotiated plea by the defendant. Perhaps an even greater potential danger is that a growing work load could lead to acceptance of lower quality personnel or performance, and this is an area which is receiving attention. To a large extent the public defender's and prosecutor's offices serve as training grounds for young lawyers fresh from university and on their way to private practice as defense counsels. The need for additional training for both prosecutors and public defenders has been recognized and programs are being developed. Needed definition of performance and skill requirements for both offices (and judges for that matter) has been the subject of many projects, notably STAR (Systems Training Analysis of Requirements). When these program results are validated, more specific on-the-job training programs for all levels of professional personnel will undoubtedly develop.

JUVENILE PROGRAMS

With almost half of the serious crime in America committed by juveniles and the rate of increase growing faster than for adults, innovative procedures are obviously needed in this field. Over a million juveniles are processed through the criminal justice system annually and not many are there for stealing hubcaps. There are as many homicides and other crimes of violence in juvenile court as in adult. At the same time the basic premise of the juvenile justice system, protection and rehabilitation of minors, can't be forgotten. A Juvenile Justice Division was formed in 1974, under the Office of National Priority Programs, to coordinate on a national basis the many programs funded by federal grants. Juvenile problems cover the whole range of possibilities within the criminal justice system, but the most promising area for attacking the general problem is the diversionary program. If the agency is selected properly for the youngster, a program may possibly be designed for him that will not only keep him from entering the judicial segment of the system but reduce the chances of his reentering the system at all. Diversionary programs appear to be working although they are unevenly applied. That is, the range of referrals to diversionary agencies varies as much as 300 percent depending on the agency bringing the juvenile into the process. Agencies with high percentages of diversion experience 40 percent less recidivism than their counterparts that channel most young offenders into the judicial segment. One of the reasons agencies with low diversion ratios give is lack of knowledge of available sources. The national coordinative efforts of the Juvenile Justice Division are aimed at directly affecting this inadequacy by functioning as a clearinghouse for such information.

Beyond diversionary programs, most of the preventive work among juveniles is aimed at reaching potential drug users in time to prevent their involvement with drug abuse. The goal is to divert youngsters who become initially involved and also to reach those who may, because of peer association or other reasons, be headed for experimentation with illicit drugs. These programs are the most numerous and heavily funded of all juvenile justice efforts.

CORRECTIONS

Recidivism has to be the root problem of greatest concern to corrections administrators. No matter how well other aspects of their role are performed, a high percentage of returning customers is considered a sign of failure. This may not be entirely fair. Some factors of life on the street, which may be responsible for an individual failing to make it on the outside are, after all, beyond the control of the system. But, in large part, correctional institutions are known to be more custodial than rehabilitative. Lack of effective rehabilitative programs remains the major problem for corrections, and all innovations proposed must be judged in terms of how they contribute to its solution. One of the main efforts being mounted is to match inmates' characteristics with the different types of programs available or proposed—in other words, identifying inmates who are more likely to require protective custody or who may be able to succeed in noncustodial programs. Special problems exist in noncustodial programs such as work furlough. Problems also exist in the cases of nonsentenced misdemeanents who are often not in custody long enough for full-fledged programs and, in fact, whose constitutional rights may be abridged by forced participation in a program of rehabilitation while not under sentence. But the idle time for such offenders, especially first-timers, greatly increases the likelihood of their becoming recidivists because of the "instruction" they get from cellmates on how to do better next time. Programs are now being evaluated for separate handling of unsentenced, nonrecidivist offenders to avoid their being contaminated by exposure to the recidivist syndrome.

A similar isolative program, but for opposite reasons, seeks to develop procedures for separate handling of narcotics addicts. The goal is both rehabilitative for the addicted offender and protective for the noncontaminated inmates in the same institution. The cost of such programs, plus the specialized nature of the treatment required for behavior modification in narcotics cases, has lead to a tendency away from treatment in the normal custodial institution. Instead, specialized hospital facilities and halfway houses are favored.

Other common programs in corrections are rehabilitation training for local correctional officers and coordination of probation and parole services. The problem in the training of correctional officers is that their instruction is almost exclusively in custodial duties. To correct this imbalance, inservice training programs are offered in rehabilitative methods, techniques, and philosophies. Coordination of parole and probation services aims at attaining economies by combining systems with common interests, goods, general functions, and clientele.

Conciliation and mediation programs have been developed to help prevent reoccurrence of riots such as the four-day uprising at Attica Prison in New York in 1971. Forty-one inmates and guards lost their lives in that tragedy, prompting extension of community relations counselling programs into prisons to help ease racial tensions. These and other programs hope to turn around the generally conceded failure of the correctional part of our criminal justice system. While changing human behavior has never been the most rewarding of efforts, considerably more progress now appears to be possible through application of new concepts and techniques than was ever before contemplated.

CHANGES IN THE POLICE ROLE

As we mentioned earlier, more innovation at a practical level has taken place in the police segment of the criminal justice system than any other. This is partly due to their greater visibility and partly to the realization that the critical initiation of the whole process lies with the police. It has been said, with considerable justification, that the overwhelming portion of justice in our system is dispensed by police rather than the courts. With almost total discretion and virtually no review of decisions not to arrest, police are social workers and judges more than they are dispassionate enforcers of unfeeling codes. And this is the thrust of the "change" in the police role: a *recognition* of the true nature of their work rather than an actual change in that nature. The role itself has always been about the same and, in fact, with increasing crime rates in recent years there is probably more law enforcement involved in the job than ever before. But now the increased awareness of and attention to the service aspect has created an increase in training and organization to better handle that aspect. Although police officers consider themselves too busy with the symptoms of crime to be also charged with responsibility for treating the causes of crime, this is a responsibility they really can't avoid.

A typical example of this unavoidable responsibility is handling the family dispute. Certainly police can't treat all the causes of family crisis, such as poverty, but they are directly involved in another equally important cause, social injustice. How they handle a dispute has a great effect on whether it will escalate into a need for law enforcement rather than service. Obviously police are not alone in this responsibility, but their role is critical and must be performed under the most difficult conditions with active and latent antagonism and resentment from those they must serve. Recognition of the critical importance of the police role in such situations and the general lack of training in handling them has led to the development of special training in crisis intervention. The first program of this type was undertaken in New York City where a Family Crisis Intervention Unit was developed in one precinct. The remarkable success of the experiment included a record of 1,400 interventions in a patrol area of 85,000 persons with *no injuries* to police officers involved despite the increased exposure of officers to a situation which at that time accounted for some 40 percent of lost-time injuries and 22 percent of police fatalities. It is not known how many homicides within the family were prevented, but studies in New York have indicated that 35 percent of homicides result from quarrels among family or friends. The success of the New York experiment has led many other cities to develop similar programs which now have high priority in LEAA sponsorship. It should be noted that in these

Cops and Couples

The prowl car radio barked a familiar call: "Domestic trouble." Two young Chicago cops arrived at a South Side apartment to find an elderly couple screaming and clawing at each other on the floor. As the officers struggled vainly to separate the thrashing pair, their beat sergeant arrived. He ordered his men to stand back, then calmly persuaded the couple to unhand each other. The sergeant patiently explained that the police did not want to arrest anyone and that if the pair promised to calm down, the officers would depart. Both the husband and wife conceded that they wanted no trouble and agreed to behave.

As the three cops were descending the stairs, the sergeant smiled. "You don't have to slug it out with them," he told his juniors. "All it takes is a little psychology. . . ." At that moment, the sergeant was interrupted by the roar of a shotgun blast reverberating down the stairwell. Even as the officers were leaving, the old man had walked into his bedroom, assembled a shotgun and fired both barrels into his wife's chest. . . .

According to the FBI, 30 policemen were killed last year breaking up personal disturbances, more than in any other area of law enforcement. . . . One-quarter of all assaults on police in Chicago occur during domestic disputes. In Boston, these calls average 45 a day; in Atlanta, 60 percent of all calls during the overnight "morning watch" involve family trouble. Police nationwide agree that such calls follow an easily traceable pattern. They are most commonly caused by hard drinking; they most commonly result in a husband's beating a wife; they most commonly occur on Saturday nights and paydays and are especially frequent in hot weather. But even knowing all this, no police department anywhere has yet been able to devise a satisfactory technique to cope with the problem. [*Newsweek*, (July 8, 1974). Copyright Newsweek, Inc. 1974, reprinted by permission.]

programs the officers are not relieved of their normal patrol duties. This not only maintains reasonable costs but increases overall effectiveness of all police operations through greater identification, among community members, of police with a service role rather than a strictly enforcement role. Community acceptance of these programs has been positive.

Crime prevention in general is the overriding concept of

the newly developing police role. Programs take many forms ranging from treatment of the conditions that lead to crime to the "site hardening" programs which aim at making commission of crime more difficult. While the latter group of programs may not be the most effective in the long range, they are expeditious during times such as these when the system as a whole is so overburdened. Many cities are currently using neighborhood security and property identification programs to increase reporting of crimes and to discourage burglaries. Neighborhood watch programs typically contact citizens in the community and urge them to call police when any suspicious incident is observed. Citizens who call in are not contacted directly by officers responding to the scene of the incident in order to preserve the anonymity of the reporting party. If additional information is needed by the officer, telephone contact is made. This effectively overcomes one of the reasonable fears, that of retribution, in the minds of most citizens who avoid involvement. Response to these programs has been considerable particularly in those agencies which follow up by advising reporting citizens of the outcome of the call. The feeling of involvement on the part of the citizen is greatly enhanced by the knowledge that some action resulted from his effort—particularly if that action is an arrest.

In neighborhood security programs citizens are of course not allowed to take enforcement upon themselves. But an experimental program in Harlem did go considerably beyond the scope of typical reporting programs. This 1968 program formed a community patrol corps that consisted of young men from the community who performed escort duties for women afraid to walk home at night and other service functions such as assisting drunks and breaking up fights. They also filled a reporting function for police. There were problems to be expected in such an experiment (lack of training and discipline, typically), and citizen patrol groups as a whole are uncomfortably close in concept to vigilantes. But the experiment was evaluated favorably by most community members and some officers involved. In any event, it serves to illustrate the range of possibilities being explored by police in their crime-preventive efforts. It also probably represents one extreme end of the scale of citizen involvement in law enforcement.

In identification programs, the agency furnishes electric engravers to citizens to mark their property with some identifying number (such as a driver's license). Serial numbers may also be recorded on forms furnished and filed with the depart-

Identification programs aim at reducing crime by engraving an identifying number on objects likely to be stolen in a burglary. Engraving equipment is furnished by police departments sponsoring such programs.

ment. Stickers or decals are given to participating citizens to be placed in windows to warn would-be burglars that property in the home has been marked for identification purposes. Not only is return of recovered property facilitated by such programs, but the known difficulty of disposing of marked property discourages the professional burglar from entering. One city using this program reported that 5,000 homes participating experienced only twenty-five burglaries in an eight-year span while the 6,000 homes not participating experienced over 1,000 burglaries in a three-year time period. Not many agencies are able to report such dramatic results, but programs of this type are becoming more widespread as the need for prevention of burglary becomes more acute.

Community relations programs are very common in police agencies today as a means of improving effectiveness in their new role and as the critical need for community support becomes increasingly apparent. Not many programs go to the extent of the Police Community Relations Unit in San Francisco which provides a broad range of services for young people in the community including recreational opportunities, job placement, and even counselling on how to deal with police when the "client" feels he has a complaint to file. Much more common are the organizational changes police departments are making in cities all around the country to emphasize community relations in patrol and other functions.

ORGANIZATIONAL AND DEPLOYMENT DEVELOPMENTS

Team Policing

Probably more attention and interest today center on one particular aspect of police organizational development than any other. Called by various names in the many departments experimenting with it, *team policing* in theory offers a potential solution to a traditional dilemma of police administration. The dilemma arises from the duality of requirements generated by the need for *visibility* of police presence in emergency situations such as riots and to attack problems in high crime areas, and the *invisibility* of authority in handling the service functions. The one need suggests a paramilitary organization and the other a "community helper" approach. While team policing, which amounts basically to decentralization of police authority into the various designated areas of a jurisdiction, may not be the ultimate answer to the whole dilemma, it represents a step which may be combined with other strategies (such as tactical squads, which will be discussed shortly) to effectively deploy police in the community.

Team policing details are as varied as the names: *Community Sector Patrol* in Cincinnati, *Beat Commander Project* in Detroit, *Basic Car Plan* in Los Angeles, *Crime Control Team* in Syracuse, and so on. Many other names and plans exist and the exact details of their operation are not as important as the similarity of concepts involved. In each case, the total area to be patrolled is divided and a team of officers is assigned the primary (if not total) responsibility of exercising police authority in that area on an around-the-clock basis. A senior officer or supervisor is placed in charge of the team and he in effect becomes the chief for that little city within the city. In its ultimate form the officer responsible for the sector even has authority to request or forbid entry of other police units, such as special squads or details, into his sector to assist in handling a special situation. In essence this aspect of team policing is the very embodiment of a cherished police concept, area responsibility. This concept was held to be at its peak with the foot patrolman, who seldom if ever left his beat and thus became intimately aware of its problems. This system has declined since the advent of motorized patrol which effectively eliminated routine contact between officers and their constituency. While patrol is still basically motorized in team policing, some plans provide for officers to leave their cars and patrol on foot if they deem it appropriate. In any event, the relative geographic stability of team policing is a move away from the crisis-to-crisis nature of responding to calls without much regard to the area in which they occur.

Commanders of each team policing area or sector are urged to develop their own liaison with the community and arrange for such activities as they feel are necessary for good police–community relations. Typically, meetings are held with business and social groups, athletic leagues are formed in which teams from the various sectors compete, and so on. Communication between team members is vital, since the three teams constitute the police force for the area. This is also the responsibility of the team commander, as is communication *between* teams.

An obvious problem in such decentralization is the means of providing for specialized services such as detectives. The team assigned to the sector usually consists of just enough patrol officers to provide that function on a 24-hour basis (although some programs do also assign detective teams). In the absence of an assigned detective it becomes imperative that the patrol officer's role become more generalized in nature and his investigative duties are considerably expanded. Officers may or may not work in uniform as they perform investigations and, when the investigation reaches a certain level of complexity or time demand, centralized investigative officers take over.

The expanded role of the officer and the close identification of the team with a given geographical area theoretically increases both the job satisfaction of the officer and the responsiveness of police service to community needs. In addition to these features, team policing claims to provide benefits in uniformity of command styles since with a single commander for the team area, police policies on the street should be the same no matter the time of day. This is beneficial both to officers and citizens in many instances. Greater flexibility in policy setting is also theoretically possible with the decentralized approach. With this goes increased responsibility at lower organizational levels since that is where the policy is being set.

While team policing is and has been tried in a great many areas, the approach and management of the individual programs has been different enough to make evaluation of results most difficult. It will surely be tried more widely in the next few years and as results become more predictable and allow for a meaningful evaluation.

Tactical Squads

Tactical squads are another means of attacking crime problems more effectively through innovative deployment of police forces. In every agency there are frequent occasions when normal deployment of the patrol force lacks sufficient concentration of manpower to effectively deal with a specific crime problem. A high incidence of burglaries, for example, may be beyond the ability of a single patrol officer to deal with and to bring other officers from surrounding areas to bear on the problem would cause undesirable neglect of their own districts. Tactical squads are composed of officers from within the agency who are assigned to the unit and specifically trained for the job. They have no fixed assignment but are capable of attacking any critical problem that arises. Successive assignments might include uniformed presence at selected intersections to reduce accidents and then a plainclothes stakeout in a burglary-plagued area. On shifts where no specific problem is to be attacked, members of the unit may function as extra patrol units or do follow-up investigations to assist detectives until their presence as a tactical squad is needed. When that happens (to help in a search for a dangerous suspect, for example) they can be quickly assembled and brought to bear as an integrated unit without disrupting normal police protection in the rest of the city. Flexibility is one of the main advantages of tactical squads since the concentrated force can be deployed in any way needed. If the situation demands concentrated police presence, without the increased visibility which can aggravate some situations, tactical squads can work in plainclothes whereas the normal patrol force couldn't, even if their responsibilities in their own districts could be temporarily put aside. The importance of specialized training is very important and must be broad since assignments will run the whole gamut of police responsibility from juvenile through narcotics and vice to motorcycle duty. Most major cities now have some form of tactical unit, and an increasing number of smaller cities are finding them useful even if they don't have a particular, high-incidence crime problem. The flexibility of approach offered to combat emerging problems before they become major is a valuable asset to any police department. In cities experimenting with team policing programs, tactical units are a valuable supplemental force that can be called upon in time of need without sacrificing the basic integrity of local command.

Ten-hour Shifts

Ten-hour shifts are being used in many cities to provide concentrated police service during periods of greatest need. Studies are made of experienced demand for police service by hour of day and, since there must be an overlapping period with three ten-hour shifts in a twenty-four-hour day, the overlapping shifts are arranged to coincide with the period of greatest need for police service. While the approach is relatively new and some problems do occur (such as a shortage of patrol vehicles during overlap periods), most cities trying it report that the benefits far outweigh the problems and expect the trend to continue until all agencies are on the ten-hour day. An interesting sidelight of such plans is the morale factor: officers quickly come to cherish the extra day off they gain each week by putting in forty hours in four days instead of five. Other changes noted in many departments using "Ten Plans," as they are generically called, include increased traffic citation issuance, fewer traffic accidents, higher clearance rates, more field interviews conducted, and a decrease in certain crimes, notably burglaries. Response times typically decrease for both routine and emergency calls on all shifts, especially during overlap periods.

Combined Police Service

This service is being used in many forms in different parts of the country by smaller cities that can't afford the cost of the type of police service they want and need. Alternative plans adopted range from contracting with another agency for police service (a county sheriff, for example) to combining total forces with nearby cities. The Los Angeles County Sheriffs Office provides police service for cities within its boundaries on an annual contract basis and similar services are provided in Oregon and Massachusetts. In Kansas City, Missouri, the Metro Squad represents a different approach to combining services. Here various agencies in surrounding communities assign personnel to a joint tactical squad that may be called upon by and act in any of the participating cities, even crossing state boundaries in the process. This arrangement is particularly beneficial in large multi-jurisdictional area. In Kentucky police operations in five police departments in four separate counties have been merged into the Southern Kentucky Regional police agency. Still another type of merger is represented by the joint provision of training, planning and research, records and information, photoservices and identification functions of Jefferson County and the city of Louisville in Kentucky. These and many more examples are indicative of a trend to attempted upgrading of police service by combining resources in a joint effort.

Mutual Aid Agreement

This program, in which neighboring cities' police departments agree to come to the aid of each other in large emergencies, offers another common way of meeting at least one aspect of the problem addressed by combined services—the need for more manpower than a small agency can afford. In cases where one larger city is the hub of several smaller agencies, agreements for use of specialized services are also reached. Jail, crime laboratory, radio transmission and training are typical examples of such services. An important extension of these agreements is hoped for in the programs being developed to increase communication and coordination between adjoining police jurisdictions. There is a recognized need for exchange of information on broad issues such as crime trends and specific cases such as identified modi operandi in multiple crime occurrences between neighboring agencies. While law enforcement too often stops at a community boundary, criminals don't and this provides an advantage that can be considerably overcome by coordinated effort between agencies. Typical areas of operation which are amenable to this approach include intelligence, vice, burglary prevention, armed robbery, bunco, bad checks, and traffic (in fact, any police problem where criminals tend to work an area or where there is a normal flow of activity across a political boundary). Intelligence operations are the area where most accomplishments have taken place. Several states now have effective state and regional intelligence systems. In some counties, participating local agencies contribute personnel and money to a security intelligence agency which members benefit from jointly. These agencies are extremely jealous of the information they gather, as they should be, for a leak could be damaging to an individual or beneficial to criminal operations; membership is limited to carefully qualified law enforcement agencies and those not accepted are unable to gain access to information collected.

Reevaluation of Basic Concepts

This activity is perhaps the most important new development in law enforcement. Police are noted for conservatism but now even the most cherished institutions are being reexamined. The most outstanding example is that of preventive, or repressive, patrol. Long held to be an essential means of reducing some crimes, mere presence of the police in easily identifiable units is now being seriously challenged as to effectiveness. It has been realized for many years that not all types of crime are responsive to preventive patrol, but it was felt that at least it made the citizens feel safe and had an inhibiting effect on such crimes as auto theft, burglary, auto larceny, robbery, and vandalism; now even this value is challenged. Early studies by the Los Angeles Police Department indicated that their Basic Car Plan was going to be more effective overall than simply increasing motorized preventive patrol. Studies made in Kansas City during 1972 and 1973 were even more assertive of the failure of routine patrol to deter crime. Three matched areas of Kansas City were provided, respectively, with *no* routine patrol, *normal* patrol, and *extra* patrol for over a year. The result was no noticeable effect on the crime rates. This is not to say that there is no value to having officers patrol streets because thousands of arrests are made as the direct result of an officer's observations on patrol. But it does mean that the mystique of patrol for patrol's sake, with no hard evidence of its crime preventive value, may no longer be valid. Support is given thereby to the increased need for research, development validation, and acceptance of new and improved methods.

MANPOWER UTILIZATION

Generalization of the Patrol Officer's Function

One of the, if not the single, most important tests of management skill is the utilization of assets. In police work, as in any service business, the only real asset that amounts to anything is the manpower. In recent years increasing realization of this fact has contributed to the design of many innovative projects.

The expansion of the patrol officer's role, for example, is considered by many to be nearly as important a benefit of team policing as the decentralization of police authority. In fact many projects are generalist-oriented, rather than team-oriented even though some of the terminology is the same. The principal difference between the two types of programs has to be that team policing has *geographical decentralization* of police authority as its main thrust with the generalist effect resulting only from necessity. Generalist programs have decentralization of authority to the individual officers as their goal and give no special consideration to geographical areas. There's always a limit to the amount of generalization that can take place, of course, and the fact that detective units are maintained even in generalist-oriented agencies attests to that fact. It would be totally impractical to let the patrol officer follow-up completely on each case he investigates in the field because such investigations could take him away from his assigned area for hours or days at a time. But the expansion of the patrol officer's preliminary investigation role not only provides for more effective fact gathering at a critical time, but also enriches his job. Patrol work is the part of police work most officers really prefer, but under normal organizational practices it does have its limiting aspects in terms of seeing a conclusion to the work being done. Generalization of the role increases, but doesn't assure, the likelihood of seeing a beginning and an end to an incident.

Special Positions

Police agent positions are another means of achieving both a job enlargement opportunity and an organizational change that benefits the total enforcement effort. Police agents are essentially patrolman–technicians who have received special training in crime scene investigation and evidence collection. Agents are deployed on each shift, either in a regular beat when not performing their special function or, more commonly in smaller cities at least, on a city-wide basis until needed in a particular beat. Their pay is usually a step higher than patrolmen and they often have some distinctive marking on their uniform, such as corporal's stripes, to indicate their status. The advantages to the agency of such a position are many: quicker availability of an evidence technician than if one had to be dispatched from headquarters; full-service capability of an extra police officer at the crime scene; an extra patrol unit in the city when an investigation is not being made; general enhancement of the police image in the community as uniformed officers are seen to be making technical analyses of evidence; and, more trained evidence technicians than might otherwise be possible in a small agency. For the officer, the position offers a chance to stay in patrol work with more money and extra status.

Community Service Officers

These officers are quasi-police functionaries who, as paid civilians, perform many duties normally handled by sworn police officers. Uniforms are a different color from regular police and guns are not carried, but their duties include such normal police functions as issuance of parking citations, impounding of cars, traffic control, report taking and, of course, community relations. CSOs often work at counselling centers for unemployed and disadvantaged persons, advising on welfare services, jobs, and interaction with governmental agencies, including police. Participants are generally recruited from among young people in minority populations and limited to ages 18 to 21. The training and exposure to police work often lead to eventual employment as police officers. For the agency the advantages include a release of trained officers from duties that don't fully utilize their ability and a bridge between the department and the community that may be better filled by someone who is not seen as authorized to exert full police power.

Civilianization

Use of civilians in traditional police roles is not limited to community service officers and traffic duties. Civilians are used in specialized fields such as personnel, training, administrative services, budget and finance, data processing, management analysis, and even investigative support positions such as polygraph operator, evidence technician, photo lab technician, fingerprint technician, and criminalist. Civilians with professional expertise in the behavioral sciences, medicine, and law are also used by some departments, but their role is not really as significant in terms of innovation in police organization as the civilianization of roles that have, since the beginning, been filled by sworn officers. The reluctance to civilianize these roles for so many years was not solely due to resistance to innovation

Community service officers relieve regular sworn personnel of duties such as covering the complaint desk, allowing the officers to be deployed in the field.

or conservatism; there are practical aspects as well. Much information held by police is sensitive in nature, for example, and casual access by civilians not carefully selected could be dangerous. Considerable restructuring of an organization may be required for even seemingly easy changes.

Reserve Officer Contingents

Reserve contingents have mixed support among law enforcement administrators. Many are apprehensive of inadequately-trained, less-than-fully-committed personnel visible to the public but not easily discernible from regular officers and resist their use. Certainly history contains enough examples of political favoritism, loose selection and training practices and blatant substandard performance of such units to give anyone pause if he has responsibility for providing professional police service to the community. Assuming, however, that rigid selection and training standards can be enforced, the economic feasibility of reserve units can hardly be challenged. Reserve officers generally serve without pay and, as sworn personnel, have full police authority when on duty. They are required to spend a specified number of hours each month in service. Assignments are generally as second officers in partnership with a regular officer, although some agencies assign two reserve officers to a single car which often has limited assignment potential. Use of reserve cars for report taking only is one example of such limitation, but it is also possible to use such a partnership as an observation unit. There are many problems in utilization of reserve officers such as added liability to city insurance programs, but the potential usefulness of a flexible-sized force, at virtually no cost beyond training expense, makes it a potentially useful tool. The overriding concerns must be selection and training to ensure a performance potential acceptable to the community and the officers of the regular force.

TECHNOLOGICAL DEVELOPMENTS

Some of the technological requirements for innovation in the criminal justice system involve development of new systems and procedures; others consist of new hardware to be applied in old or new systems and still others simply involve adaptation of standard equipment to new procedures.

Patrol Improvements

All three categories of technology are utilized in patrol improvements. Decentralized deployment, as in team policing, is an example of a systems-only innovation. Use of conventional, fixed-wing aircraft is an example of a standard product put to new use. Because of their relative speed and freedom from restrictions on roadways and traffic congestion, they can effectively patrol large areas as part of a team with ground units in speed enforcement, surveillance, and search operations. If slow speeds are required, as in most urban patrol situations, the hovering ability of helicopters may be adapted as a supplement to normal patrol. Helicopters have limitations, however, such as limited air time because of their high fuel consumption rate and the need for extra gear for police duty. This, plus the need for a higher top speed than is available in many choppers, led to a modification to the basic airframe design and the Short Takeoff and Landing (STOL) aircraft. Cheaper to operate and maintain than helicopters, and with a generally higher top speed and longer range, the ability to be airborne and land in relatively short spaces makes the STOL attractive to agencies that don't need the hovering capability enough to pay the difference.

Other conventional equipment adapted to patrol use in

specialized situations includes such standard recreational vehicles as bicycles and watercraft. The quiet mobility of bicycles has special application in concentrated efforts against such crimes as burglary and purse snatching. Many cities have waterways within their jurisdiction and the special capabilities of power boats, either owned by the agency or available upon need from private citizens who are sometimes even organized into auxiliaries or reserve components, offer a mobility available no other way.

Communications Advances

Advanced communications capabilities include both new hardware and systems. Use of a universal telephone number, such as "911," to call for any emergency service has been mandated in some states and is typical of the system type of advance. Digital communication, which allows an officer to send standard messages with a single action of a button on his radio console, requires both system and equipment innovation. With further system development the officer will be able to directly reach computerized data banks without having to go through a human intermediary in the control center. Hardcopy printout units are already installed in many patrol cars to print permanent, readable copies of such important information as warrants, descriptions of wanted persons, and the like. Similarly, cathode ray tubes (little television screens) are installed in many cars to give instant messages directly from computerized data banks containing files on wanted persons and stolen vehicles, among other things. Another feature found on such exotic equipment installations is a signalling device that lets the communications center know exactly where the patrol unit is at any given time. The time saved in emergency situations can be lifesaving.

Communications Networks

These systems developments usually require only minor equipment modification for implementation. California's CLEMARS (California Law Enforcement Mutual Aid Radio System), for example, was designed to allow agencies responding to a mutual emergency to communicate via their car radios which would normally operate on different frequencies. With the common ability to tune in the special CLEMARS frequency, units from different agencies can also communicate during

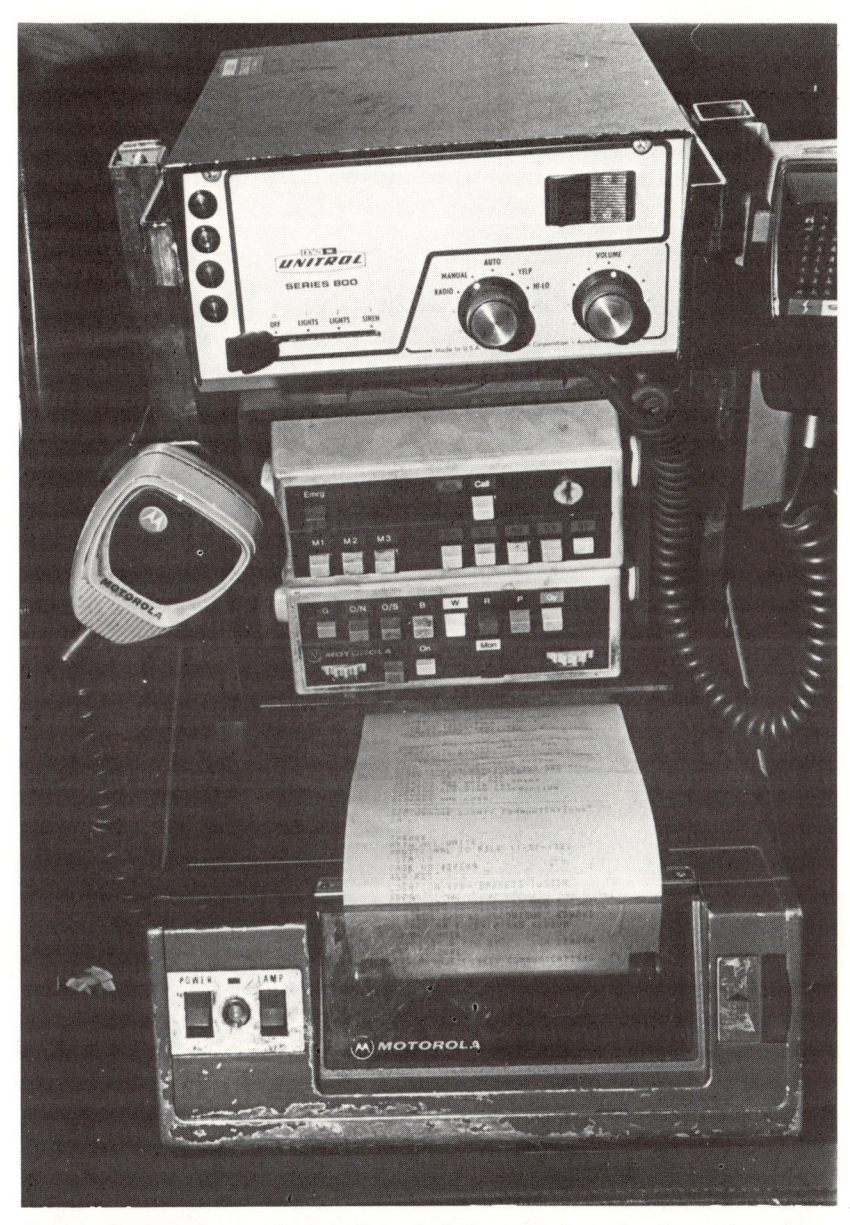

Communication advances for patrol cars include multi-channel radios with pushbutton message transmission (center unit) and hard copy printout capability (lower unit).

joint pursuits and, in areas where radio traffic permits, even use the frequency within an agency as a tactical frequency for communication between units. Perhaps one of the most interesting networks is the Facsimile Identification Network which adapts the capabilities of the old wirephoto system. With FIN fingerprints, photographs, documentary evidence and the like can be sent over long distances and reproduced at the other end in hardcopy form, resulting in several days' time saving with document security and accuracy of communication.

Information Systems

These systems are constantly being developed to the benefit of the entire criminal justice system. Computerized data banks with instant access are typified by such systems as Los Angeles' AWWS (Automated Wants and Warrants System) which provides field officers with knowledge of the wanted status of suspect persons or vehicles. Similar systems are operative in Michigan (LEIN—Law Enforcement Identification Network) and Washington, D.C. (WALES—Washington Area Law Enforcement System), with multiple agencies using the data on a cooperative basis. Regional and even national interfaces are available on many systems. The FBI's NCIC file is accessible to thousands of agencies around the country. California's CLETS (California Law Enforcement Telecommunications System) interfaces with systems in the western region containing information ranging from their Stolen Vehicle System (formerly called AUTOSTATIS and containing constantly updated stolen car data to the exclusion of the need for "hot sheets" in cooperating agencies) to a similar system for stolen bicycles. In Kansas City their ALERT system provides instant tactical information to agencies in two states (this system even includes dangerous locations, as well as dangerous persons or wanted vehicles).

In addition to the tactical information systems, criminal history dossier systems, such as SEARCH (System for Electronic Analysis and Retrieval of Criminal Histories) can verify identity and past criminal involvement, if any, in seconds. The value to prosecutors and courts of such information is at least as great as to police. Similar systems are being developed for automated search of fingerprint files which, when available, will save countless hours each year for enforcement personnel and improve both the speed and quality of the entire criminal justice process. As with any data compilation system, the retrieval system is as important as the data bank itself, for the best information is useless without a rapid, efficient means of access to it. The networks and equipment described above give evidence of the availability of such access throughout the system.

Warrant Systems

Systems for issuing warrants, badly needed in some consolidated form to provide the criminal justice system with some way of coping with the geographical mobility of the criminal, are developing. Identification information is being upgraded and with the coordination of national and regional systems such as AWWS, NCIC, LEIN and ALERT, it's no longer as easy as it once was for a wanted person to simply flee jurisdictions where he is known.

Telephonic search warrants, initiated in California (1970) and Arizona (1971) represent a cooperative innovation involving the courts and police under enabling legislative authority. A police officer in the field with a timely need for a search warrant used to face the choice of waiting around a day to get one or trying to qualify his need under one of the few specific exceptions to the requirement of a court-issued warrant. Now, in states which have passed the necessary legislation, he can swear an affidavit over a telephone and into a recorder, for subsequent transcription into a hardcopy warrant. The saving of time can be critical to the successful investigation, and the involvement of the court in the action improves the likelihood of a successful prosecution.

Recording Devices

The use of recording devices in investigation, prosecution and even report writing, is an example of a standard product adapted through technological improvement to the criminal justice system. Anyone who watches television knows that interviews are both overtly and covertly tape recorded to be used as evidence at trial. Similarly, field sobriety examinations and booking interviews are sometimes videotape-recorded to aid in prosecution. Less glamorous, but just as useful to the operation of a law enforcement agency, are such applications as field dictation of reports for subsequent transcriptions which normally take up so much of an officer's time. Sometimes the recorder is taken into the field or it can be connected to a special telephone in the station, allowing officers to telephone reports in without leaving the field. Many agencies also use voice-actuated tape recorders on a 24-hour basis to record all incoming telephone calls and radio traffic both ways. The resultant tapes have unquestioned evidentiary value in terms of exact time and sequence of events, plus offering an opportunity for precise reexamination of phraseology. Both audio and video recorders are also used extensively in training at all levels of the criminal justice system covering subjects from correctional procedures to citation issuance and court decisions.

Detection Systems

Improvements in detection systems have been adapted for police use from standard civilian designs. Banks are widely protected now with surveillance cameras using both film and, increasingly, videotape to provide visual evidence of robberies including identification of the perpetrators. Alarm systems, while not free yet of the old, easily-activated "ringers," now largely consist of centrally-connected systems which aim at apprehension, rather than warning, of criminals. Some silent systems go directly to police agencies and others connect to the alarm company which in turn notifies police. There are home systems which, upon detecting an intruder, silently dial the telephone, contacting the police and delivering a recorded message to report the incident. It would seem that this last device, while hardly the answer to the needs of the beleaguered criminal justice system, may be the final intolerable insult delivered by machines in their seemingly unstoppable conquest of man. While the best human minds are searching for ways to *increase* citizen involvement with law enforcement activities, the machines have found a way to obviate the need for *any* involvement. Presumably, with this device, one's home could be burgled, the criminal apprehended in the living room and carted off to jail without the victim even being awakened from his sleep!

SUMMARY

Increased *citizen involvement* at all levels of the criminal justice system is universally recognized as a critical need. Programs being developed to promote citizen interaction with judicial, correctional, and police agencies are being coordinated under the Office of National Priority Programs, a function of the Law Enforcement Assistance Administration.

Criminal Justice Coordinating Councils consist of representatives of citizen groups and governmental agencies meeting jointly to promote control and prevention of crime through increased coordination and cooperation among agencies of the criminal justice system.

The federal government, beginning with the *1968 Om-*

nibus Crime Control and Safe Streets Act, has funded billions of dollars worth of research and developmental projects seeking innovative approaches to crime prevention and control. Funds are disbursed by LEAA through state planning agencies to the various state and local agencies developing the programs.

Court projects are currently aimed at reduction of the amount of time required by the process; development of information systems; better relations with the community and other criminal justice agencies; improved diversionary programs and possible decriminalization of some acts; more equitable bail practices; and improvements in the jury system and sentencing practices.

Prosecutor projects include information system improvement; investigation of white-collar crime; expanded services to citizens who are victims or witnesses; restitution programs providing compensation to victims by offenders; improvement in plea-bargaining procedures; and development of higher standards and training programs for professional personnel.

Juvenile programs are now being coordinated by a special Juvenile Justice Division of LEAA and include improvements in diversionary systems used by local agencies to divert young offenders from the criminal justice system and programs designed to reach young people before they become drug users.

Corrections programs are primarily aimed at reducing the rate of recidivism among inmates released via parole or completion of their sentence. Efforts are being made to match different types of programs to different types of inmates; provide different and separate programs for first-time offenders during the period when they are nonsentenced misdemeanants; isolate narcotics addicts from nonaddicted inmates and provide special programs for them; increase training in rehabilitation procedures for custodial personnel; coordinate parole and probational services; and provide counselling programs for inmates.

The *police role* is recognized as being more service than law enforcement, and programs to increase the ability of officers to handle the service aspect, such as family crisis intervention training, now receive high national priority. Crime prevention programs are generally neighborhood security or identification programs.

Organizational and deployment developments in the police function include *team policing,* which decentralizes police authority into smaller geographical areas within the jurisdiction; *generalization,* which broadens the activity of the patrol officer in the preliminary investigation; use of *tactical squads* to provide concentrated police effort on special crime problems; *ten-hour shifts* overlapping to provide more officers in the field during times of greater need for police service; *combined police services* to offer a level of service beyond that which might be available from smaller agency; *mutual aid agreements* and *greater coordination* of efforts and information between neighboring law enforcement agencies; and *reevaluation of basic concepts,* such as the effectiveness of preventive patrol as a crime deterrent.

Technological changes in patrol derive from use of *fixed wing aircraft* (both conventional and STOL) and *helicopters.* Specialized use is also made of *bicycles* and *watercraft.*

Communications developments include *digital* communication systems, *universal telephone numbers* for reporting emergencies, and *networks* for more efficient communication between separate agencies of the criminal justice system. A *facsimile identification network* makes it possible to instantly transmit hard copy duplicates of documents over long distances.

Information systems provide computerized data banks on stolen property, persons and vehicles wanted in connection with crimes, dangerous locations, and criminal history of individuals.

Warrant systems are available to make identification and status of wanted individuals known on regional and national bases. *Telephonic search warrants* may be obtained by officers without leaving the field.

Recording devices are used to obtain evidence for prosecution, record incoming conversations and two-way radio traffic, dictate reports and train personnel in justice agencies.

Detection systems include *surveillance cameras* and *alarm systems* which now tend toward centralized silent alarms for both commercial and residential application.

REVIEW QUESTIONS

Answers to these questions appear on page 387.

1. Which of the following innovations are examples of programs aimed at increased citizen involvement in the criminal justice system? (Circle as many as are correct.)
   a. Criminal Justice Coordinating Councils
   b. Team policing

c. Integrated Information Systems
   d. Diversionary Systems
   e. Tactical Squads
2. What is the name of the top governmental agency (below cabinet level) instrumental in the development of innovative projects in the criminal justice system? _____
3. Which of the *court* projects discussed in this chapter will be of the most direct and immediate benefit to citizens who have been arrested for a crime? _____
4. Which of the *prosecutor* projects discussed in this chapter will be of the most direct and immediate benefit to victims of crimes? _____
5. Which of the *juvenile* projects discussed in this chapter will be of the most direct and immediate benefit to juveniles who have been taken into custody by police? _____
6. Of the *corrections* programs discussed in this chapter, which will most directly benefit first-time offenders who have been taken into custody? _____
7. Which style change (*team policing* or *generalization*) will be most noticed by the general public? _____
8. Which community involvement program (*neighborhood security* or *identification*) more directly relates to the concept of site-hardening? _____
9. Which manpower concentration approach (*Ten Plan* or *tactical squads*):
   a. directly involves more of the department's officers? _____
   b. requires more training for implementation? _____
   c. relates more directly to specific crime occurrences? _____
   d. may require more capital outlay for equipment? _____
10. Which interagency plan (*mutual aid* or *coordination*) more directly affects everyday operation of the department? _____
11. Which job enlargement technique (*generalization* or *special position* creation):
    a. more visibly provides status recognition? _____
    b. affects the larger number of personnel? _____

12. Which use of civilians (*community service officer* or *reserves*):
    a. provides more added personnel with powers of arrest? _____
    b. has a greater potential for bridging the police-citizen cultural gap? _____
13. Of the supplemental patrol methods mentioned in this chapter which has the capability range most compatible with traffic control? _____
14. What change in communications technology seems to offer the greatest potential for reducing time and errors in exchanging information between patrol cars and communications centers? _____
15. Which of the technological developments described has the most far reaching applicability for all levels of the criminal justice system? _____

GLOSSARY

Academy training Formal training provided members of the administration of justice system, at an academy or other educational institution, after their acceptance as employees of some member agency.
Acquittal A finding at trial of innocence on the part of the defendant.
Adjective That aspect of law which defines who shall enforce the law. *See also* Substantive.
Adjudicated delinquent A juvenile who has passed through the justice system and been found delinquent.
Adjudicatory hearing In a juvenile proceeding, the equivalent to the trial for an adult proceeding.
Adversary system The system at trial in which the people of the state, represented by the public prosecutor, attempt to prove the guilt of a defendant, represented by defense counsel, charged with commission of a crime.
Affirmative Action Program A type of program, required by government funding agencies of participating law enforcement agencies, giving evidence that systems and procedures have been implemented to achieve specified goals.
Appeal The removal of a cause from a lower court to one of superior jurisdiction for the purpose of obtaining a review and retrial.

Appellate court A court in which appeals from trial court decisions are heard.

Apprehension That activity of law enforcement aimed at taking into custody those who have committed a crime.

Arraignment, initial The appearance in court of an arrested person for the purpose of advising the arrestee of the nature of the charge against him and his constitutional rights.

Arraignment, juvenile An appearance for purposes of hearing the charges against the juvenile, an interview by the judge, and giving the juvenile his first opportunity to admit to the allegation.

Arraignment, superior court The appearance in court of the accused person for the purpose of reading to him the indictment, and demanding of him whether he is guilty or not guilty, and if appropriate, determining whether he desires a court trial or jury trial.

Arrest Taking a person into custody for the purpose of holding or detaining him to answer to a criminal charge.

Bail Money posted with the court to obtain release of an arrested person until his case comes to trial.

Bail bondsman A person who, for a fee, advances an arrested person the securities required for bail to obtain his release from custody until trial.

Bailiff In early England, a law enforcement officer who patrolled the city by night. In modern American usage, an officer of the court responsible for maintainance of order within the court.

Bertillon system of identification A means of identifying persons by specified body measurements and identifying marks (now largely in disuse in most countries).

Booking The process by which an administrative record is made of a person's arrest.

"Born criminal" theory An early theory of criminal behavior holding that persons liable to commit crimes had recognizable physical characteristics by which they could be identified.

Called-for services Any police activity generated by a citizen's request for assistance or report of an incident.

Case law Precedent established by a particular ruling of a court in applying a statute under specific circumstances; used by attorneys and courts in subsequent application of the same statute under similar circumstances.

Casual criminal A person who infrequently commits criminal acts. *See also* Petty criminal.

Citation An official notice or summons to appear in court.

Civil code Code of laws affecting only individual rights or private wrongs, as opposed to criminal codes which relate to public wrongs.
Classical theory An early theory of criminal behavior holding that people try to avoid pain and seek pleasure and that violation of known rules is based on exercise of free will.
Color of authority A legal term defining the influence exerted by the expressed or implied authority of someone known to be a representative of the law.
Community service officer In some agencies, a non-sworn functionary with duties which relieve sworn officers of some service functions and provide the CSO with experience at law enforcement.
Compensating factor In relation to entrance requirements for employment in a law enforcement agency, an ability which may be substituted, in part, for satisfaction of a requirement not totally met on its own terms (for example, education or special skill may compensate for a minor deficiency in height or weight in an employment application).
Complaint A statement of charge against a person arrested for a crime.
Complaint desk The position in a law enforcement operation which receives complaints or requests for assistance from citizens.
"Contempt-of-cop" arrest An arrest which, though technically correct, probably would not have been made if the arrestee had not antagonized the officer by his behavior toward him.
"Consent" search An examination or inspection, with authority of law, of premises or person with the expressed and voluntary consent of the person to be searched or, in the case of a premise, by the person who has control or joint authority.
Contraband Property or material illegally possessed by person from whom it is taken.
Cooperative training centers Training facilities maintained jointly by several administration of justice agencies for the purpose of providing academy training to its members.
Coroner A public office charged with responsibility for investigating the case of any death occurring from other than natural cause.
Coroner's jury A panel of citizens hearing evidence at an inquest relative to a death being investigated by a coroner.
Corrections That portion of the criminal justice system which deals with persons convicted by the courts.
Correctional institution A jail or prison (jails normally perform

custodial rather than correctional duties) in which a person is kept in custody and given rehabilitative treatments.
Court clerk The administrative, non-judicial position in a court responsible for all clerical duties supportive to the judicial function.
Court reporter Staff member of a court with responsibility for maintaining verbatim records of the proceedings at trial.
Court trial A trial without jury in which a judge decides the verdict.
Counselling and release In juvenile proceedings, the step in which the offender is counselled and, instead of being petitioned into the court system, is released into the custody of an adult.
Crime An act committed or omitted in violation of a penal code provision forbidding or commanding it.
"Crime commission" The President's Commission on Law Enforcement and the Administration of Justice, established to make recommendations for improvements in the administration of justice system.
Crime of passion A crime committed without premeditation, but under the influence of "sudden passion," any emotion such as rage, hatred, resentment, or terror rendering the mind incapable of rational reflection.
Crime prevention Activity of law enforcement agencies aimed at reducing the intent to commit a wrongful act rather than the opportunity to commit it.
Crime repression Activity of law enforcement aimed at reducing the opportunity to commit a crime, rather than the intent to commit it.
Criminalist One who, as a technician, investigates crimes through analysis of data and evidence.
Criminal justice coordinating council A committee or council consisting of representatives of the justice system and the general community formed to improve the effectiveness of the system and its responsiveness to community needs.
Criminologist One who studies the causes and effects of crime as a social phenomenon.
Custodial interrogation Questioning by law enforcement officers of a suspect who has been taken into custody (arrested or deprived in any way of his freedom of action).
Decentralization A style of police organization which provides greater localized authority by assigning a team of officers with full responsibilities within a designated subdivision of the jurisdiction.

Defense counsel The attorney, either private or public, who represents the defendant in a matter at trial.
Derivative evidence rule A doctrine of American law which holds that evidence obtained illegally cannot be used against a person in the trial at hand or any subsequent trial.
Detention Interruption of a person's freedom of movement for purposes of interrogation, or, if convicted of a crime, for purposes of serving a sentence imposed by a court.
Detention center The initial correctional institution for a juvenile.
Diagnostic center *See* Reception center.
Differential association theory One of a group of theories of criminal behavior holding that behavior is influenced by peer group associations and other social factors which interact to lead a person into or away from criminal acts.
Digital communication A communications system which allows the patrol officer to transmit prearranged messages from his car by simply pressing special keys on his radio console.
District attorney A public officer, hired or elected to represent the people in proceedings against individuals who have violated the law.
District court of appeals The first appellate court beyond the superior court level.
Disposition hearing In a juvenile proceeding, the stage at which the judge decides the exact nature of the program the juvenile must follow.
Diversion An alternative program providing for treatment of an arrested person rather than a jail sentence.
Draconian code Early Greek code of laws providing harsh penalties, usually death, for most offenses.
English Common Law British code of laws which established a common set of societal rules for all British citizens; the basis for present law in all states except Louisiana.
Evidence technician *See* Criminalist.
Exclusionary rule A doctrine of American law which holds that evidence illegally obtained is inadmissible in a court of law.
Felony A wrongful act, in violation of the penal code, of a serious nature punishable by fine and/or imprisonment in a state prison and forfeiture of specified rights as a citizen.
Field training Following the formal or academy training of new law enforcement officers, supervised practice at applying principles and techniques acquired in class.
Forensic Scientific activity related specifically to developing arguments suitable for use in courts of law.

"Fruit of the Poisoned Tree" concept *See* Derivative Evidence Rule.

Generalization A style of police organization which broadens the role of patrol officers to include delivery of some services, principally investigative, normally provided by specialized units, such as detectives.

Grand jury A select panel of community members convened for a specified period of time to examine accusations against persons to determine if there is sufficient cause to bring them to trial in a court of law.

Habeus corpus, Writ of Official notification by the court demanding that a person be presented before a magistrate.

Hammurabi, Code of Early Babylonian code of law providing universal application of sanctions to all members of governed society without regard to geopolitical affiliation.

Index crimes The seven major crimes used as an index of criminal occurrence by the FBI in their Uniform Crime Report: murder and non-negligent manslaughter, forcible rape, robbery, aggravated assault, burglary, larceny, and auto theft.

Information A public record, filed by the prosecutor, stating the complaint of the people of the state against the accused person.

Infraction A wrongful act, in violation of penal or other codes of law, less serious than a misdemeanor and not punishable by imprisonment.

Inquest An investigation, most commonly held by the office of coroner to determine the cause of death in suspicious circumstances and called a *coroner's inquest.*

Inservice training Training provided on a continuing basis to law enforcement officers after completion of their preservice, academy, and field training.

Inspectional services Visual inspection of property or premises as a routine procedure.

Intake interview In the juvenile justice system, the initial interview at which the facts relative to the juvenile being held in custody are examined by a representative of the court to decide which path through the system is appropriate.

Intelligence Knowledge gained from the collective consideration of all known information relative to a given subject; specifically, the application of that knowledge to a particular problem. Also, the police function charged with the gathering and evaluation of such information and knowledge.

Internal affairs A branch of law enforcement agencies which investigates possible misconduct within the organization itself.

Internships Cross-training programs where employees of one agency are temporarily exchanged with another to instill mutual understanding of the other agency's problems and needs.

Interrogation Questioning in an accusatory mode (as opposed to the exploratory mode of an interview).

Jail A local or county custodial institution for incarceration of convicted misdemeanants and all arrested persons prior to trial.

Jurisdiction The limits of territory within which authority may be exercised.

Justice court A basic level court, presided over by a justice of the peace rather than a judge. *See also* Municipal Court.

Justinian code Greek code of laws derived from Draconian Code to modernize it. Formed basis for most modern European law.

Juvenile hearing The court process, equivalent to the trial for adults, for a juvenile.

Lateral entry Entry of a person into an organization based on his ability to handle the specific job rather than at the lowest level in that organization.

Law Enforcement Assistance Administration (LEAA) Federal agency, under the Justice Department, responsible for assisting development and implementation of innovative projects in the administration of justice system.

Law Enforcement Educational Program (LEEP) A federally funded program to aid persons in the administration of justice system in achieving advanced formal education.

Lex talionis Principle of law (literally, *law of retaliation*) holding that punishment should be the same in kind as the crime (the eye for an eye principle).

Line beat A method of deployment of police forces (specifically, traffic officers) along one or more heavily travelled thoroughfares to control traffic violations or accidents.

Loansharking Lending activity in which the borrower, who is usually unable to obtain funds through normal channels, is subjected to extremely high interest rates and threatened personal violence for slow payment.

Magistrate Judge.

Malum in prohibitum An act not inherently evil, but which is designated as criminal and legally prohibited by society or its legislative bodies (for example, gambling).

Malum in se A criminal act held to be evil by its very nature (for example, rape, murder).

Marshal, county The enforcement arm of the court responsible for servicing court orders and, if necessary, enforcing compliance.

Miscellaneous services Those police activities demanded by citizens or other governmental agencies, not related to prevention, repression, property recovery, or regulation of noncriminal activity (for example, advising citizens and provision of first aid).

Misdemeanor A wrongful act, in violation of the penal code, but less serious than a felony and punishable by fine and/or sentence to jail rather than prison.

Multiple cause theory A theory of criminal behavior holding that such behavior is brought on by the combination and interplay of physical and emotional aspects of a person as he develops his life style.

Municipal court A basic level court presided over by a judge who hears misdemeanors and preliminary felony hearings.

Mutual aid agreements Pacts between law enforcement agencies to provide help to each other in the event of unusual occurrences requiring action beyond their individual capabilities.

Narcotics-connected crime A crime committed to support a narcotic addiction or under the influence of narcotics (usually the former).

National Crime Information Center (NCIC) The FBI center which maintains a computerized data bank of information on persons and property connected with criminal occurrences.

O-R Release Release of an arrested person on his own recognizance, without posting bail, and promise to appear in court.

Parole Conditional release from prison of a person who has not yet served the full term of his sentence.

Parole officer A functionary of the correctional system responsible for supervision of persons released from prison on parole.

Part I Crimes *See* Index Crimes.

Penal code Code of law covering wrongful acts held to be crimes against the state.

Peremptory challenge Action in which an attorney, defense or prosecution, challenges the right of a prospective juror to be empaneled without having to cite any particular cause.

Petition, juvenile An action seeking to take a juvenile into the court system for processing rather than referring him for counselling.

Petty criminal A person who commits minor criminal acts, often infrequently but in a continuing manner. *See* Casual criminal.

Plea bargaining The negotiation process between prosecutor and defense counsel whereby a person accused of a crime agrees to plead guilty to a reduced charge and gives up his rights to trial.

Police Law enforcement agents employed by municipalities or private parties.

Police agent In some agencies, a position which gives the designee responsibility for conducting scientific evidence gathering and analysis operations at crime scenes.

Political crime A criminal act, usually violent, committed for political purposes against either person or property.

Polygraph An electro-mechanical sensing device which, when affixed to a person's body, measures changes in bodily functions such as heart rate, blood pressure, and moisture at the surface of the skin.

Preliminary hearing The stage of a criminal proceeding at which the evidence against the accused person is first tested and the court decides whether to bind him over for trial, reduce the charge, dismiss it, or divert him into a probationary program.

Preservice training Training or education given to members of the criminal justice system prior to their entry into the system.

Pretrial hearing A hearing conducted by a judge to examine the validity of evidence, the procedure by which it was obtained, or the acceptability of motions by defense counsel.

Prison A state correctional institution for incarceration of convicted felons.

Prisoner control The process or system for placing arrested persons in custodial care with a law enforcement agency.

Probable cause A determinant of legality of a search, detention, or arrest (a state of facts that would lead a man of ordinary care and prudence to believe and conscientiously entertain an honest and strong suspicion that a person is guilty of a crime). *See* Reasonable cause.

Probation A conditional freedom from incarceration granted to persons convicted of a crime.

Probation officer A functionary of the court responsible for investigation of circumstances surrounding commission of a crime to determine if probation is in order and for supervision of persons granted probation by the court.

Probation subsidy A correctional program under which the state releases a person to the custody of a probation agency, rather than keep him in prison, and compensates that agency for his supervision.

Professional criminal A person whose principal activity is crime (for example, car thief who steals cars on order).

Prosecutor The office responsible for representing the state in legal actions against individual citizens.

Psychological criminal A person who commits a crime, often premeditated, because of a psychological imbalance in his nature.

Radio-telephone A communication system or device designed to transmit messages by voice over long distances using radio waves.

Reasonable cause A determinant in establishing when a law enforcement officer may exercise his right to arrest (when the evidence known to him indicates that a public offense has been committed in his presence). *See* Probable cause.

Reception center A correctional institution into which adjudicated delinquents are placed preparatory to beginning their rehabilitative program.

Reference group theory One of a group of theories of criminal behavior holding that behavior is influenced by peer group associations and other social factors which interact to lead a person into or away from criminal acts.

Regulation of noncriminal activity Activities of law enforcement aimed at governing behavior which, while not criminal in nature, violates the best interests of society.

Roll-call training Training activity conducted at the briefing session preceding (or, less often, following) the daily tour of duty for a group of law enforcement officers.

Sanction The penalty, or lack of reward, provided by custom or law for not following the specified pattern of behavior.

School resource officer A law enforcement officer assigned to duty at a school to function as a continuing source of student information on the law enforcement community and, secondarily, to enforce laws on the campus.

Scotland Yard Headquarters of London's Metropolitan Police, loosely used to identify that force.

Search Exploratory investigation; looking for or seeking out in some hidden place that which is concealed.

Search, emergency A search conducted by a law enforcement officer in the belief that it is necessary to preserve the immediate safety and well being of another person.

Search incidental to arrest A search conducted by a law enforcement officer to determine if an arrested person is armed or in possession of evidence pertinent to the crime for which he has been arrested.

Seizure Forcible dispossession of someone's property.

Selective enforcement Police activity directed at reduction of a specific type of undesired citizen activity (such as traffic violations or accidents) by concentration of police presence at times and locations known statistically to be most likely for such occurrences.

Sentencing council A council of several judges formed to review sentencing alternatives in cases pending before the members (aimed at promoting more uniform sentencing practices).

Sex criminal, neurotic A person who commits covert sex offenses, such as Peeping Tom trespasses.

Sex criminal, psycopathic A person who commits aggressive sex crimes, such as rape.

Shelter *See* Detention center.

Sheriff Top law enforcement officer in a county.

Shire-reeve In early England, the head of the sociopolitical unit, equivalent to the sheriff in our county.

Short Take Off and Landing (S.T.O.L.) Slowspeed capability of fixed-wing aircraft able to land or take off in a short distance.

Site hardening The act of making an area or premises less susceptible to successful perpetration of a criminal act.

Star Chamber Early English form of trial held in secret sessions during which torture was commonly used to extract confessions.

State police Any of fifty law enforcement agencies which, though different in specific operation and responsibility, operate at a state rather than county or municipal level.

Statute law Law enacted by a legislative body to define acceptable behavior.

Storefront operation Community relations programs of law enforcement agencies in which officers serve as community advisors located in commercial buildings, making them more accessible to the general public than they would be at a headquarters location.

Strongarm robbery Robbery involving threatened or actual force without the use of a weapon.

Student worker program An employment program allowing students to hold part time jobs in law enforcement agencies during the period they are acquiring their formal education in preparation for a career position in that or some related agency.

Subpoena A court order for a person to appear under penalty for failure.

Substantive That aspect of law which defines behavior as acceptable or unacceptable. *See also* Adjective.

Summary probation A term of probation granted summarily by a judge without benefit of a probation report and which may or may not require supervision by the probation department.

Summons A court order commanding a person to appear in court on a specified day to answer a complaint.

Superior court A county-level court in which felony cases are tried.

Supreme Court, State The highest appellate court in the court structure of a given state; the ultimate appellate court for a matter at trial involving violation of state law. *See* Supreme Court, U.S.

Supreme Court, U.S. The highest court in the nation; the ultimate appellate court for any matter at trial whether it involves a violation of federal or state law. *See* Supreme Court, State.

Tactical squad A special force of police organized and trained to handle specific crime problems in a jurisdication by concentrating all their efforts on those problems.

Team policing An organizational program which decentralizes police forces into subunits responsible for policing relatively small subdivisions of the agency jurisdiction.

Telephonic search warrant system A system which allows officers to obtain needed search warrants without leaving the field by using a telephone in conjunction with electronic recording devices.

Tort A wrongful act in violation of a provision of the civil code.

Training officer The experienced officer to whom a new officer is assigned for guidance during the first few months of duty, or an officer in charge of training for an agency.

Trial assignment A method of evaluating an employee's potential for promotion by letting him work temporarily at the higher position (usually well in advance of his possible promotion).

Trial by ordeal Early English system of adjudication providing primitive tests of innocence such as fire walking or immersion in water.

True bill An indictment; the verdict of a grand jury holding that there is sufficient cause to bring the accused person to trial in court.

U.S. Court of Appeals The first appellate court in the federal court system.

U.S. District Court The basic level court in the federal court system, at which both felony and misdemeanor violations of federal law are tried.

Victimless crimes Acts which, though against the law, allegedly

do no harm to anyone other than the perpetrator (for example, narcotics usage).
Warrant An official court document directing a specified action.
Watch A chronological division of responsibility for providing a service (specifically, a shift in police work).
Watch commander The officer in charge of the patrol function during a specific watch or shift during the day.
White-collar criminal A person who maintains a normal job or business but steals from others (e.g. his employer, customers, etc.).
Writ An order issued by a court to demand performance, or nonperformance, of a specific act.

BIBLIOGRAPHY

Adams, Thomas F. *Law Enforcement, An Introduction to the Police Role in the Community.* Englewood Cliffs: Prentice Hall, Inc., 1968.

American Bar Association. *Standards Relating to the Urban Police Function.* Chicago, 1974.

Anti-defamation League of B'nai Brith and International Association of Chiefs of Police. *. . . with justice for all.* New York, 1963.

Bayley, David H. and Mendelsohn, Harold. *Minorities and the Police: Confrontation in America.* New York: The Free Press, 1968.

Bloch, Peter; Anderson, Deborah; and Gervais, Pamela. *Policewomen on Patrol (Major Findings: First Report)* Volume I. Washington, D.C.: Police Foundation, 1973.

Commission on Peace Officers Standards and Training. *The "Ten Plan" in California Law Enforcement Agencies.* Sacramento, 1973.

Crites, Laura. *Women in Law Enforcement.* Washington, D.C.: International City Management Association, Vol. 5, No. 9, September, 1973.

Eldefonso, Edward; Coffey, Alan; and Grace, Richard C. *Principles of Law Enforcement.* New York: John Wiley & Sons, Inc., 1968.

Federal Bureau of Investigation. *Uniform Crime Reports.* Washington, D.C.: U.S. Government Printing Office, issued annually.

Germann, A. C. "The Police: A Mission and Role," *The Police Chief* (Jan. 1970).

Howard, J. Woodford, Jr. "Law Enforcement in an Urban Society," *The American Psychologist* (April 1974).

Kirkham, George L. "A Professor's 'Street Lessons,'" *FBI Law Enforcement Journal* (March 1974).

Kreins, Edward S. "The Behavioral Scientist in Law Enforcement," *The Police Chief* (Feb. 1974).

Los Angeles Regional Criminal Justice Planning Board. *Comprehensive Criminal Justice System Plan.* Los Angeles, 1972.

Milton, Catherine. *Women in Policing.* Washington, D.C.: Police Foundation, 1972.

National Advisory Commission on Criminal Justice Standards and Goals. *Police.* Washington, D.C.: U.S. Government Printing Office, 1973.

National Criminal Justice Information and Statistics Service. *Children in Custody.* Washington, D.C.: U.S. Government Printing Office, 1973.

President's Commission on Law Enforcement and Administration of Justice. *The Challenge of Crime in a Free Society.* Washington, D.C.: U.S. Government Printing Office, 1967.

―――. *Task Force Report: The Police.* Washington, D.C.: U.S. Government Printing Office, 1967.

Radelet, Louis A. *The Police and the Community.* Beverly Hills: Glencoe Press, 1973.

Reiser, Martin. *Practical Psychology for Police Officers.* Springfield: Charles C. Thomas, Publisher, 1973.

Reiser, Martin and Steinberg, J. Leonard. *To Protect and to Serve.* Los Angeles: Los Angeles Police Commission, 1972.

Saunders, Jr., Charles. B. *Upgrading the American Police.* Washington, D.C.: The Brookings Institution, 1970.

Schlossberg, Harvey and Freeman, Lucy. *Psychologist with a Gun.* New York: Coward, McCann & Geoghegon, Inc., 1974.

Sherman, Lawrence W.; Milton, Catherine H.; and Kelly, Thomas V. *Team Policing: Seven Case Studies.* Washington, D.C.: Police Foundation, 1973.

Starnes, Richard. "Crime, The Unwon War," *North American Newspaper Alliance* (August 1974).

Steadman, Robert F., ed. *The Police and the Community.* Baltimore: The Johns Hopkins University Press, 1972.

Sullivan, John L. *Introduction to Police Science,* 2nd Edition, New York: McGraw Hill Book Co., 1966.

Weston, Paul B. and Wells, Kenneth M. *The Administration of Justice.* Englewood Cliffs: Prentice Hall, 1967.

Whisenand, Paul M. and Ferguson, R. Fred. *The Managing of Police Organizations.* Englewood Cliffs: Prentice Hall, 1973.

Wilson, James Q. *Varieties of Police Behavior.* New York: Atheneum, 1973.

ANSWERS

CHAPTER 1

1. punishment
2. it must be *representative of* and have its *authority derived from* the community
3. justice
4. dismemberment
5. True
6. statute
7. yes
8. *malum in se* (it is evil in itself)
9. Sir Robert Peel
10. trial by ordeal
11. *Vere Dictums*
12. Magna Carta
13. Habeas corpus
14. Bertillon
15. repression
16. prevention

CHAPTER 2

1. a (to satisfy his needs, even though he may be caught)
2. a. social

382 ANSWERS

      b. physiological
      c. psychological
3. Beccaria
4. heredity and environment
5. False (it often lessens the strength of the family unit)
6. c
7. True
8. psychopathic
9. Uniform Crime Report
10. Index Crimes (or Part I crimes)
11. property
12. organized crime
13. a (15-16)
14. b (complexity of the causative factors)

CHAPTER 3

1. a. court
   b. police
   c. corrections
   d. court
   e. court
   f. court
   g. police
2. False (he is obliged to see that *justice is done* rather than strictly convict)
3. False (it indicates there is enough evidence to *accuse* him)
4. indictment
5. a. trial
   b. trial
   c. grand
   d. trial
   e. grand
6. due process
7. coroner's office
8. bailiff
9. reporter
10. clerk
11. a. superior
    b. municipal
    c. justice
    d. superior
12. probation
13. parole

14. prison
15. a. adult
    b. both
    c. adult
    d. both
    e. juvenile
    f. both

CHAPTER 4

1. True
2. booking
3. False (it is usually prepared by the police)
4. initial appearance
5. municipal (or justice)
6. he will bind him over and set a date for arraignment
7. arraignment
8. pretrial hearing
9. c
10. plea bargaining
11. citation in lieu of booking
12. diversion
13. probation subsidy
14. intake interview
15. a. arraignment
    b. petition
    c. adjudication hearing
    d. disposition hearing
16. probation
17. counselling and release to parents
18. a. training school
    b. group centers (halfway houses)
    c. rural facilities (ranches, farms, forestry camps)

CHAPTER 5

1. municipal police or sheriff's office
2. a. Corrections
   b. State Police
   c. State Department of Justice
   d. Alcoholic Beverage Control
   e. Highway Patrol
   f. Fish and Game
3. a. Sheriff

      b. Marshal
      c. District Attorney (Investigation Bureau)
4. a. Drug Enforcement Administration
   b. Immigration and Naturalization (Border Patrol)
   c. FBI
   d. Customs
   e. U.S. Marshal
   f. Secret Service
   g. IRS Intelligence Division
   h. Secret Service
   i. Alcohol, Tobacco and Firearms
   j. FBI
   k. Alcohol, Tobacco and Firearms
5. a. industrial security
   b. guard (or watchman)
   c. private investigator
   d. patrol

CHAPTER 6

1. False
2. watch commander
3. a. lieutenant
   b. sergeant
4. investigator
5. patrol
6. by type of crime
7. juvenile officers
8. True
9. Traffic officers and accident investigation
10. a. vice, narcotic, intelligence (any order)
    b. narcotics
    c. intelligence

CHAPTER 7

1. a. radio-telephone communications
   b. property
   c. personnel and training
   d. records
   e. equipment maintenance
   f. prisoner control
   g. internal affairs
   h. community relations

i. research and planning
   j. statistical analysis

CHAPTER 8

1. a. 14th
   b. 5th
   c. 6th
   d. 4th
2. exclusionary rule
3. derivative evidence
4. *People* v. *Cahan*
5. search and seizure
6. *Gideon* v. *Wainright*
7. *Gitlow* v. *New York*
8. *Escobedo* v. *Illinois*
9. *Chimel* v. *California*
10. *Miranda* v. *Arizona*
11. warrant, incidental to an arrest, consent, emergency (any order)
12. confessions

CHAPTER 9

1. True
2. enforcement
3. symptoms
4. effective
5. affluent; apathy exists when crime is low
6. not enough enforcement
7. lack of support
8. a. comminication
   b. communication
   c. service
   d. communication

CHAPTER 10

1. a. positive
   b. positive
   c. negative
   d. negative
   e. positive
   f. positive

386 ANSWERS

2. law enforcement (or crime fighting)
3. peace keeping and community service (any order)
4. False (intelligence, yes; introspecting, no)
5. patrol
6. decisiveness
7. overrating an offense
8. underrating an offense
9. a. gratuities
   b. special privileges
10. b and d

CHAPTER 11

1. a. psychological screening
   b. testing
   c. background investigation
2. student worker program
3. recruiters feel vested interest in success
4. 400
5. a. career development
   b. field
   c. inservice
   d. academy
6. a. criminal justice
   b. cooperative
7. internship means exchange of duties between officers of equal rank; trial assignment is to a higher rank

CHAPTER 12

1. court-designed programs (which specify numbers and dates to be complied with)
2. a, c, and d
3. women
4. True
5. a and e
6. Equal Rights Amendment and 14th Amendment
7. *Sail'er Inn* v. *Kirby,* 1971 Calif.
8. Title VII
9. peer group disapproval
10. lack of physical strength (all groups conceded this point)
11. a new approach to handling potentially violent situations

CHAPTER 13

1. a and b
2. Law Enforcement Assistance Administration (LEAA)
3. reduced time through the process; diversionary programs; bail practices
4. expanded services; restitution
5. diversionary
6. special programs for unsentenced misdemeanants; isolation of narcotics addicts
7. team policing
8. neighborhood security
9. a. Ten Plan
   b. Tactical Squad
   c. Tactical Squad
   d. Ten Plan
10. coordination
11. a. special position
    b. generalization
12. a. Reserve
    b. Community Service Officer
13. STOL aircraft
14. digital communications
15. information systems

INDEX

Academy training, 286–291
Accident investigation, 169–170
Adjudicated delinquent, 113
Adjudication hearing, 112–113
Adversary process, 64–66
Advisory councils, 240–241
Alarm systems, 360
Alcohol, Tobacco and Firearms, Bureau of, 148–149
Alcoholic Beverage Control Agency, 134–138
ALERT system, 358–359
Allen v. *Mobile*, 305
Anarchism, 4
Anglo-Saxon era, 13–14, 16–17
Appeals, 98, 102
Appearance, initial, 98
Appellate court, 77–78
Appellate review, 337–338
Apprehension, as a police responsibility, 25
Apprenticeship in police work, 250
Arraignment
   adult, 98, 99
   juvenile, 111–112
   without booking, 104

Arrest, 95
Authority of police, 233–234
AUTOSTATIS system, 358

Background investigation, 278–280
Bail, 17–18, 75–77
Bailiff, 14, 77
Basic Car Plan, 242–243
Beccaria, Cesare, 36
Behavioral model, absence of as crime factor, 41
Behavioral objectives of police training, 289
Bertillon system of identification, 23–24
Bias, management or personal, 259
Block clubs, 193
Booking, 95–97
"Born Criminal" theory, 36–37
Bow Street Runners, 14–15
Brandeis, Louis, 215
Brotherhood of the badge, 265
Brown v. *Mississippi*, 209–210
Bureau of Investigation, district attorney, 140–141

389

390   INDEX

Called-for services, 162
Captain, 158
Career development programs, 189, 295–298
Carter v. *Gallagher*, 305
Case law, 10
Casual crime, 45
Centralized training of police, 290–291
Certified plea, 99
Chain of command, 158–159
Charles I, 18
Chief of police, 158
Chimel v. *California*, 219–220
Citation in lieu of booking, 103–104
Citizen involvement programs, 330–331
Citizens' Inititative program, 330
Civil Rights Act of 1964, 317–318
Civilianization of the police function, 186–193, 353–354
Classical theory of criminal behavior, 36
CLETS system, 358
Climate as a crime factor, 55
Code of ethics, 251, 261–267
Codes of law, 8–11
College programs, 296
College recruiting, 283–284
Colonial period, 19–20
Color of authority, 221
Combined police service, 349–350
Comes stabuli, 14
Communications, 22, 180–183, 356–358
Communications Operator, 183
Community Patrol Corps, 344
Community relations, 191–193, 345–346
Community Sector program, 242–243
Community Service Officer, 353
Community surveys, 241
Compensating factors in police selection, 282, 306
Complaint, 68–69, 97–98
Confessions, 222–224
Constitution, U.S., 202–206
Contempt-of-cop arrests, 264–265
Contraband, 185–186
Contract service for police function, 122

Coordination programs, interagency, 349–351
Coroner's office, 74–75
Correctional institutions, 80–82
Corrections, 103, 113–114, 133–134, 340–341
Court
  clerk, 77
  policies as a crime factor, 56
  reporter, 77
  trial, 65–66, 100
Courts, 75–80, 333–338
Crime
  classifications of, 11–12
  data, use of, 54–56
  economic impact of, 50–54
  factors, FBI, 54–56
  prevention of, 24
  reporting of, 48–56
  victimless, 8
Crime Specific program, 25
Criminal behavior
  categories of, 44–48
  early theories of, 36–37
Criminal justice coordinating councils, 331–332
Criminal justice system, aims of, 64–66
Criminal rationale, 34–35
Crisis intervention, 342–343
Cross examination, 100
Customs Agency Service, 147–148

Data banks, computerized, 184
Decentralization of police authority, 27
Declaration, 140
Defense counsel, 65, 73–74
Department of Justice, state, 138–139
Deputy Chief of police, 158
Derivative evidence rule, 208, 220–221
Detection systems, 360
Detention center, 113–114
Detention hearing, 111
Diagnostic center, 113–114
Differential association theory, 38
Direct examination, in a trial, 100
Discipline, lack of as a crime factor, 40
Discovery motion, 100

Discretion, in police actions, 66–68, 96, 249
Dismissal of charges, 108
Disposition, juvenile case, 112–113
District attorney, 68–69
District Court of Appeals, 78
Diversion, 106–107, 114
Draconian Code, 9
Drug Enforcement Administration, 145–146
Due process of law, 73

Education, as a crime factor, 55
Educational standards in law enforcement, 128–129, 275
Education and training of police, 285–298
English Common Law, 9–10
Entrance requirements, reevaluation of, 306
Environmental theory of criminal behavior, 39–44
Equal Rights Amendment, 316
Escobedo v. *Illinois*, 216–218
Evidence collection and analysis, 175–177
Evidence Technician, 175–177
Exclusionary rule, 207, 220–221

Facsimile Identification Network (FIN), 357–358
Family Crisis Intervention Unit, 342–343
Federal Bureau of Investigation, 24, 142–143
Federal court system, 78–79
Federal Firearms Act, 148–149
Federal government, role in innovation, 332–333
Felonies, 11–12, 17
Ferri, Enrico, 37
Fielding, Henry, 14
Field problems, in training, 293–294
Field training of police, 291–294
Fingerprints, early development, 23–24
Fire marshal, 139
Fish and Game, 138
Fixed wing aircraft, in patrol, 355
Foster care agencies, 114
Fruit of the poisoned tree concept, 208

Galton, Sir Francis, 24
Generalization of police duties, 27, 351–352
Geographical theory of criminal behavior, 37
Ghetto, policing in, 236–239
Gideon v. *Wainright*, 216
Gitlow v. *New York*, 208–209
"G-men," 142
Government, forms of, 4–7
Grand jury, 69–72, 97
Gratuities, 259–260, 267
Guards, private, 150
Gun Control Act of 1968, 148–149

Habeas corpus, writ of, 18–19, 103
Habeas Corpus Act of 1679, 19
Halfway house, 107, 114
Hammurabi, code of, 8–9
Haskell, M. R., 38
Helicopters, in patrol, 355
Henry, Edward Richard, 24
Heredity, as a crime factor, 38–39
Highway Patrol, 131–133
Hue and cry, 13

Identification technician, 175–177
Image, police, as affected by women, 311–313
Immigration and Naturalization Service, 143–144
Index crimes, 49
Indictment, 70, 97, 99
Industrial Security, 151–152
Information (complaint), 68–69, 97, 99
Information systems, 358
Infractions, 12
In-service training of police, 294–295
Inspectional services, 162
Intake interview, 111
Integrated information system, 85–86, 95
Integrity training of police, 260
Intelligence function, 173–175
Internal Affairs function, 193–195
Internal Revenue Service, Intelligence Division, 149–150
International City Managers Association, 24
Internship programs, 137, 296
Investigation, 22–24, 163–166

INDEX

Investigator, horse racing, 139

Jail, types of, 80
Jury trial, 100
Justice courts, 75
Justice Department, U.S., 141–142, 145
Justinian Code, 9
Juvenile crime, 48
Juvenile function in police work, 166–167
Juvenile justice process, 109–115
Juvenile justice system, 82–85
Juvenile programs, 242, 339–340

Kennedy, Robert F., 230
Kirkham, George, 123–127

Lateral entry into police agencies, 297
Law, aspects of, 7–8
Law enforcement, responsibility of, 12
Law Enforcement Assistance Administration (LEAA), 49, 317, 332–333
Law Enforcement Education Program (LEEP), 288–289
Lawyer-client relationship, 73
Lex talionis, 9
Lieutenant, 159
Link operator, 182
Lombroso, Cesare, 36

Mafia, 47
Magistrate, 65
Magna Carta, 17
Maintenance, of equipment, 184–185
Malum in prohibitum, 11
Malum in se, 11
Manpower utilization, 351–355
Mapp v. *Ohio*, 213–216
Marshal
 county, 77, 139–140
 U.S., 144–145
McNabb v. *U.S.*, 210–212
Merchant patrols, 14
Metropolitan Police, London, 15
MILE, training program, 190, 288
Minorities in police, 302–309
Minority programs in the community, 242

Miranda v. *Arizona*, 218–219
Miscellaneous services, in police work, 26
Misdemeanor, 11–12, 17
 procedures for, 108–109
Morris, Albert, 37
Motor vehicle inspector, 139
Municipal court, 75–77
Mutual aid agreements among agencies, 350–351

Napoleonic Code, 9
Narcotics function, 171–173
Narcotics-related crimes, 46
Nardonne v. *U.S.*, 208
National Crime Information Center (NCIC), 50, 358–359
National Firearms Act, 148–149
Neighborhood meetings, 240
Neighborhood security programs, 344
Noncriminal activity, regulation of, 25–26
Norman era, 14, 17

Olmstead v. *U.S.*, 215
Organized crime, 46–47, 51–52
Overcrowding of courts, 78
Overrating offenses, 257–258
Own-recognizance release (OR), 104–105

Pain-avoidance theory of criminal behavior, 36
Parole, 66
Parole officer, 82, 133–134
Patrol function, 161–163, 242–243, 351–352
Peace officer, 122
Peace Officer Standards and Training Commission (POST), 278–280
Peel, Sir Robert, 15
People v. *Cahan*, 212–213
Peremptory challenge, 72
Performance evaluation of female officers, 323–324
Personality, police, 255–256
Personnel and training function, 187–190
Petition (juvenile), 111
Petty crime, 45
Plea bargaining, 68, 105–106

INDEX 393

Police
    characteristics of, as a crime factor, 55–56
    civilian control of, 21
    role of, changes in, 341–346
    role of in system, 66–68
Police agent, 352–353
Police Community Relations Unit, San Francisco, 244, 345
Polygraph examination of police applicants, 280
Population characteristics, as crime factors, 54–55
Posse comitatus, 13–14
Poverty as crime factor, 39–40
Preliminary hearing, 98–99
Pretrial hearing, 99–100
Preventive patrol, 162
Prisoner control function, 186–187
Prisons, types of, 80–82
Private law enforcement agencies, 150–152
Probation, 66
    summary, 79
Probation officer, 79–80
Probation subsidy, 108
Professional crime, 46–47
Professionalism in police work, 247–253
Professor's street lessons, 123–128
Promotional opportunities in law enforcement, 128
Property, police function, 185–186
Property identification programs, 193, 344–345
Proportionate need, principle of, 191
Prosecutor, 68–69, 338–339
Prostitution, 48
Psychological crimes, 46
Psychological evaluation of police applicants, 277–280
Public Defender, 73–74
Public Prosecutor, 68–69

Rattle watch, 19
Reception center, juvenile, 113
Recidivism, 48
Recording devices, 359–360
Records function, 183–184
Recovery of stolen property, 25
Recruiting, 280–285
Reed v. *Reed*, 316–317

Reevaluation of basic concepts, 351
Reference group theory of behavior, 38
Refiling of complaints, 98
Regional training centers, 290
Religion, as a crime factor, 41–42
Repression of criminal activity, 25
Repressive patrol, 161
Research and Planning, 190–191
Reserve programs, police, 354–355
Response time, 161–162
Robinson v. *York*, 316
RTO (Radio Telephone Operator), 182

Sail 'er Inn v. *Kirby*, 316–317
Sanctions, 5
School programs, 241
School Resource Officer, 241–242
Schout, 19
Scotland Yard, 15–16
Screening, preemployment, 276–278
Search and seizure, 220–222
SEARCH system, 358
Secret Service, 146–147
Selection of police, 274–280
Selective enforcement, 168
Selectmen, 17
Sentence bargaining, 106
Sentencing 102
Sentencing councils, 337
Sequestering of jurors, 101
Sex crimes, 47–48
Shaftesbury, Earl of, 19
Shaw, Clifford, 37
Shelter, juvenile, 113
Shire-reeve, 13
Short Takeoff and Landing aircraft (STOL), 355
Silverthorne v. *U.S.*, 207–208
Social frustration, as a crime factor, 43
Social mobility, as a crime factor, 43–44
Specialized operational units, 160–177
Special privileges for police, 260
Standards, reevaluation of, 315
Star Chamber, 18
State law enforcement agencies, miscellaneous, 138–139

State police, 130–131
Statistical Analysis, 191
Statute Law, 10
Stolen vehicle system, 358
Storefront operations, 243–244
Student assistant programs, 137
Subpoena, 139–140
Summary trial, 98
Summons, 140
Superior courts, 77
Sutherland, E. H., 37–38

Tactical Squads, 348–349
Team policing, 346–348
Telephone alert system, in courts, 337
Telephonic search warrants, 359
Television and movies, as a crime factor, 41–42
Ten Plan (Ten-hour shifts for police), 349
Testing, preemployment for police, 276–278
Title VII, 317–318
Tort, 11
Traffic function, 167–169
Training centers, criminal justice, 290
Training schools, juvenile, 114
Treasury Department, U.S., 141, 145, 146
Trial, 100
Trial assignment as a training method, 296–297
Trial by ordeal, 16–17

Trial jury, 72–73

Underrating offenses, 258
Uniform Crime Report, FBI, 49
Uniforms for police, 21
Urban group centers, juvenile, 114
Urban Squad, 331

Vere dictums, 17
Vicecomes, 17
Vice function, 171
Videotape
   in police training, 188–189
   in prosecution, 359–360
   in trials, 336
Violence in the media, 41–42
Vucetich, Juan, 24

Warrant, 140
Warrant systems, 359
Warren, Earl, 216, 219
Watch (shift), 159
Watch and ward, 14
Watch and ward societies, 19–20
Watch commander, 159
Watchman, 150
Weeks v. *U.S.*, 206–207
West, Will, 23–24
Westminster period, 17
White collar crime, 45
White House Detail, Secret Service, 146–147
"With cause" dismissal of a juror, 72
Wolf v. *Colorado*, 215
Women in police, 309–325

PICTURE CREDITS

Cover: Left, New York City Police Department (NYPD). Top center, National Council on Crime and Delinquency, Hackensack, N.J. (NCCD). Lower center Department of Correction, City of New York. Right, *Spring 3100*, New York City Police Department.

Page 1 (clockwise from left), Downey, California Police Department; New York Public Library (NYPL); NCCD; NYPL; NYPL; NCCD. Pages 15, 20, NYPL. Pages 43, 51, J. Norman Swaton. Page 52, Downey, California Police Department. Page 61 (clockwise from left), NCCD; NYPL; NYPL; J. Norman Swaton; NCCD; NYPL. Page 65, J. Norman Swaton. Pages 81, 83, NYPL. Page 112, NCCD. Page 119 (clockwise from left), NYPL; J. Norman Swaton; J. Norman Swaton; NCCD; J. Norman Swaton; *Spring 3100*, NYPD. Pages 135, 150, 168, 170, 172, 176, 181, 188, J. Norman Swaton. Page 185, Downey, California Police Department. Page 199 (clockwise from left), NYPL; NYPL; *Spring 3100*, NYPD; NYPD; *Spring 3100*, NYPD; Downey, California Police Department. Page 202, NYPL. Page 214, Supreme Court of the United States. Pages 234, 243, 254, J. Norman Swaton. Page 271 (clockwise from left), J. Norman Swaton; J. Norman Swaton; *Spring 3100*, NYPD; *Spring 3100*, NYPD; J. Norman Swaton; J. Norman Swaton. Pages 279, 286, 288, 345, 354, 357, J. Norman Swaton; Pages 303, 319, *Spring 3100*, NYPD.